MW01172349

This book is available on Amazon.com

Contact the author at: Saiph3141@gmail.com.

Forward

This book is a collection of decisions within the New York Courts (largely the Appellate Division for the Second Department) considering claims seeking orders of special findings that would allow the children involved in these proceedings to seek Special Immigrant Juvenile [SIJ] status pursuant to 8 U.S.C. 1101(a)(27)(J) with the United States Citizenship and Immigration Service [CIS].

Over the past 10 to 15 years there has been an explosion of litigation in this area. This book is an effort to place in one resource a good number of the decisions concerning SIJ claims. However, inevitably, some decisions have been left out. Hopefully, a practitioner will find this to be a handy desk reference to caselaw that can serve as a starting point for any research into the issues that occasionally arise when handling such cases.

Just about all SIJ cases are unopposed. The Respondent-parent almost always fails to appear in family court. In most cases, the Respondent-parent does not even live in the United States. Frequently the absent parent signs a consent form agreeing that the Petitioner should receive guardianship. Often, the consent form states that the absent parent acknowledges he or she does not support the child and has no plans to do so. Nonetheless, under such circumstances, in nearly every case, testimony is required by the Judge or Referee, and there have been some Judges who rarely found the unopposed testimony to be credible, despite the provision of SCPA 509, which states that in an unopposed petition, the factual allegations within the petition must be taken as true. However, that was only a small number of Judges.

The Second Department has come to the rescue in such cases, and as can plainly be seen in the following, routinely reverses decisions. Additionally, everyday in Family Courts in southern New York, many SIJ guardianship cases are approved, but those cases don't result in published decisions. In this regard, the collection of cases published in this volume is not an accurate reflection of routine work of the Family Courts within the Second Department because the decisions presented here represent the small percentage of all the SIJ cases that are denied.

The author is an attorney admitted to practice in the states of New York and New Jersey and various federal courts.

Table of Cases

Table of Topics

11. Court finds abandonment even though there was significant physical mistreatment of the children …….. 59

12. Aging Out………. 59

> Custody Proceedings: A motion for special findings can be granted after the Subject turns 18 in a custody case if the custody order was granted before he or she turned 18.
>
> Matter of Dunia, 170 A.D. 3d 868 (2d Dep't Mar 13, 2019)

13. Jurisdiction………. 62

> A family court has jurisdiction to entertain a guardianship petition where the Subject has never set foot in New York but owns some limited personal property in New York such as a backpack, clothing, purse, wallet and medicines.
>
> Matter of Christian J.C.U., 60 Misc. 3d 706 (Fam Ct Kings County May 17, 2018)

14. Representation……… 68

> The same lawyer can represent the Petitioner and Subject.
>
> Matter of Serrano Sosa, 130 A.D.3d 636 (2d Dep't July 1, 2015)

15. The best interests of the child standard governs SIJ proceedings……. 71

> Matter of Denys O.H., 108 A.D.3d 711 (2d Dep't July 24, 2013)

16.   Service of motions…….. 72

> A motion for special findings may served by regular mail to the Respondent-parent's last known address, as per CPLR 2103[b](2)(c)
>
> Matter of Villatoro, 136 A.D.3d 666 (2d Dep't Feb 3, 2016)

Harmless errors in the papers should be disregarded, as per CPLR 2001.

Matter of Villatoro Ramirez, 136 A.D.3d 666 (2d Dep't Feb 3, 2016)

Matter of Gomez v Sanchez, 133 A.D.3d 658 (2d Dep't Nov 12, 2015)

Matter of Paca Secaira, 159 A.D. 3d 826 (2d Dep't Mar 14, 2018)

Matter of Sanchez, 133 A.D.3d 658 (2d Dep't Nov 12, 2015)

Matter of Alma D.G.L, 152 A.D. 3d 516 (2d Dep't July 5, 2017)

Matter of Gabriela Y.U.M., 119 A.D. 3d 581 (2d Dep't July 2, 2014)

Matter of Dennis X.G.D.V, 153 A.D.3d 628 (2d Dep't August 9, 2017), recalled and vacated at 158 A.D. 3d 721 (2d Dep't Feb 14, 2018).

Matter of Nelson A.G.—L, 157 A.D. 3d 789 (2d Dep't Jan 17, 2018).

Matter of Marisol N.H., 115 A.D. 3d 185 (2d Dep't Feb 5, 2014).

Matter of Maria E.S.G., 114 A.D. 3d 677 (2d Dep't Feb 5, 2014)

Matter of Maura, 114 A.D. 3d 687 (2d Dep't Feb 5, 2014)

Matter of Juana A.C.S., 114 A.D. 3d 689 (2d Dep't Feb 5, 2014)

Matter of Maria G.G.U., 114 A.D. 3d 691 (2d Dep't Feb 5, 2014)

45. Abandonment can be established when the abandonment occurs after the minor turns 18 years of age….. 188

    Matter of Goran S., 152 A.D. 3d 698 (2d Dep't July 19, 2017)

    Matter of Akramul I Khan, 184 A.D. 3d 506 (1st Dep't June 18, 2020)

46. A child's occasional contact with his parents, without more, does not preclude a finding of abandonment…. 191

    Matter of Akramul I Khan, 184 A.D. 3d 506 (1st Dep't June 18, 2020)

47. A natural mother may petition for the custody of her child where the father is deceased….. 198

    Matter of Castellanos, 142 A.D. 3d 552 (2d Dep't August 10, 2016)

48. A mother may petition for the custody of her child without establishing paternity…. 198

    Matter of Galeano, 144 A.D. 3d 1036 (2d Dep't Nov 23, 2016)

49 Neglect and abuse can be found where the father hits the mother and child, even though the child hit back….. 200

    Matter of Ena S.Y., 140 A.D. 3d 778 (2d Dep't June 1, 2016).

50. It is error to dismiss a guardianship petition without a hearing before a Judge.. 203

    Matter of Francisco M-G., 100 A.D.3d 900 (2d Dep't Nov 21, 2012)

51. Inappropriate remarks by a Judge indicating he is predisposed to deny SIJ motions should result in the case being transferred to another Judge… 203

    Matter of Francisco M-G., 100 A.D.3d 900 (2d Dep't Nov 21, 2012)

52.   Guardianship can be granted to an uncle even though the child visits regularly with his mother who is financially unable to support him and does not function as a caretaker.... 203

Matter of Francisco M-G., 100 A.D.3d 900 (2d Dep't Nov 21, 2012)

53. A guardianship petitioner is an aggrieved party where an order of special findings does not contain all the language requested in the proposed special findings order..... 206

Matter of Claudio D.A.I. Segundo, 225 A.D. 3d 868 (2d Dep't Mar. 13, 2024)

54. An AFC is supposed to advocate for the child's desired position.... 206

Matter of Claudio D.A.I. Segundo, 225 A.D. 3d 868 (2d Dep't Mar. 13, 2024)

55. A child is not aggrieved for the purposes of an appeal where the special findings order contains the language he or she requested.... 209

Matter of Josue M.A.P., 143 A.D.3d 827 (2d Dep't Oct 12, 2016)

56.   A Petitioner has an obligation to introduce evidence to establish that reunification with a parent is not viable.... 210

Matter of Marvin E.M, 121 A.D. 3d 892 (2d Dep't Oct 15, 2014)

57.   A finding of neglect by the mother should support a finding that reunification with her is not viable... 213

Matter of Eddy A.P.C, 226 A.D. 3d 1005 (2d Dep't April 24, 2024)

58.   Parental neglect includes the infliction of excessive corporal punishment and requiring the child to begin working at a young age
instead of attending school on a regular basis..... 216

Matter of Palwinder K., 148 A.D. 3d 1149 (2d Dep't Mar 29, 2017)

Matter of Gurwinder S., 155 A.D. 3d 959 (2d Dep't Nov 22, 2017)

Matter of Kamaljit S., 114 A.D. 3d 949 (2d Dep't Feb 26, 2024)

Matter of Varinder S., 147 A.D. 3d 854 (2d Dep't Feb 8, 2017)

Matter of Briceyda M.A.X., 190 A.D.3d 752 (2d Dep't Jan 13, 2021)

Matter of Maria P.E.A., 111 A.D.3d 619 (2d Dep't Nov 6, 2013).

Matter of Rosa M.M.G., 194 A.D. 3d 813 (2d Dep't May 12, 2021)

Matter of Rosa M.M.G., 194 A.D. 3d 813 (2d Dep't May 12, 2021)

65. It is appropriate to make a finding that it is not in the child's best interests to return to Nicaragua where (1) his mother resides with him in the United States; (2) the child's mother consistently cared for and supported him; (3) in Nicaragua, there was no one who could care for him or support him; (4) the child's grandparents in Nicaragua were elderly and began to struggle to care for him; (5) the child was kidnapped by gangs for 8 days in Nicaragua and they threatened him. … 232

Matter of Rosa M.M.G., 194 A.D. 3d 813 (2d Dep't May 12, 2021)

66. Family Court's focus on circumstances concering the Subject's overstaying his visa in the United States was unwarranted as having no bearing on the SIJ motion. …. 236

Matter of Mohamed B., 83 A.D.3d 829 (2d Dep't April 12, 2011).

67. Where the minor's father beat him regularly, and neither parent provided him with emotional and financial support, it is appropriate to find he was neglected and abandoned. … 236

Matter of Mohamed B., 83 A.D.3d 829 (2d Dep't April 12, 2011).

68. Paternity need not be established in a guardianship petition brought by the child's mother…. 239

Matter of Mardin, 187 A.D. 3d 913 (2d Dep't Oct 14, 2020)

69. It is appropriate to issue an order of special findings where the child's father abandoned her since birth and her mother inflicted excessive corporal punishment and failed to supply her with adequate food and supervision… 243

Matter of Trudy-Ann, 73 A.D. 3d 793 (2d Dep't May 4, 2010)

70. It is appropriate to find that it is not in the child's best interests to return to Jamaica where she would have no place to live and no means of supporting herself…. 243

Matter of Trudy-Ann, 73 A.D. 3d 793 (2d Dep't May 4, 2010)

78. An appeal will be dismissed where the order of guardianship and special findings were granted by the Family Court and the purpose of the appeal is to merely change some language in the orders.... 265

Matter of Lourdes B.V.I., 147 A.D. 3d 948 (2d Dep't Feb 15, 2017)

79. There must be evidence to support a conclusion that the child's reunification with one parent is not viable due to one of the statutory grounds.... 266

Matter of Del Cid Martinez, 144 A.D. 3d 905 (2d Dep't Nov 16, 2016)

80. Where the mother received financial assistance for the child's benefit but failed to provide for him, the record established that the child's "physical, mental, or emotional condition. . . had been impaired or was in imminent danger of becoming impaired" under Family Court Act 1012[f][i][A] to support a motion for special findings.... 268

Matter of Wilson A.T.Z., 147 A.D.3d 962 (2d Dep't Feb 15, 2017)

81. It is possible for the "nonparty child" to file an appeal with the Second Department.... 268

Matter of Wilson A.T.Z., 147 A.D.3d 962 (2d Dep't Feb 15, 2017)

82. It was appropriate to make a finding of neglect under Family Court Act 1012[f][i][A] where the mother received money for the child's benefit and failed to support him.... 269

Matter of Wilson A.T.Z., 147 A.D.3d 962 (2d Dep't Feb 15, 2017)

83. A parent may sign a waiver to waive the issuance of process.... 272

Matter of Paca Secaira, 159 A.D. 3d 826 (2d Dep't Mar 14, 2018)

84. It is possible to file a motion seeking to amend a prior special findings order... 274

Matter of Santos D. Interiano Argueta, 166 A.D. 3d 608 (2d Dep't Nov 7, 2018)

85.   Where the minor seeks to appeal a Family Court Judge's refusal to amend an order of special findings, it is wise to have the guardian file the appeal (as well as the minor).... 274

Matter of Santos D. Interiano Argueta, 166 A.D. 3d 608 (2d Dep't Nov 7, 2018)

86. It is appropriate to find that it is not in the child's best interests to return to El Salvador where the mother is unable to protect the child from harm by gang members who made threats against him.... 274

Matter of Santos D. Interiano Argueta, 166 A.D. 3d 608 (2d Dep't Nov 7, 2018)

87.   Adjudication as a juvenile delinquent does not establish dependency upon the Family Court for SIJ purposes.... 276

Matter of Keanu S., 167 A.D. 3d 27 (2d Dep't Oct 17, 2018), aff'g 56 Misc 3d 938.

[Comment: There does not appear to be any obstacle to prevent filing a subsequent guardianship petition seeking special findings for such a minor]

But see: In re K.O.—T, 2017 Md. App. LEXIS 1206 (Court of Special Appeals, Md, 2016).

88.   If a motion for special findings is denied by the Family Court, it is possible to file a motion to renew (albeit within the statutorily permitted time period)... 277

Matter of Keanu S., 167 A.D. 3d 27 (2d Dep't Oct 17, 2018), aff'g 56 Misc 3d 938.

89.   A motion for leave to renew pursuant to CPLR 2221 can be filed with a Family Court Judge and must assert, among various possibilities, that the child's relationship with her parents has changed since the time of her first Family Court hearing... 296

Matter of Leslie J.D., 167 A.D. 3d 1004 (2d Dep't Dec. 26, 2018)

[Comment: Leslie eventually turned 18 and filed a new guardianship petition and motion for special findings that were eventually granted]

90.   Appeal of a denial of a motion for leave to renew a prior denied SIJ motion was denied where the facts offered in the renewal motion before the Family Court would not change the prior determination… 298

Matter of Leslie J.D., 136 A.D. 3d 902 (2d Dep't Feb. 17, 2016)

91. "The law does not require a finding that reunification with neither of the parents is viable."… 301

Matter of Leslie J.D., 136 A.D. 3d 902 (2d Dep't Feb. 17, 2016)

92. It is error for the Famly Court to make a decision without an "assessment of the credibility of witnesses " and without examining "the facts of the case within the context of the required best interests analysis". … 303

See Matter of Grechel, below

93.   Parental neglect is established where "the father inflicted excessive corporal punishment on the child" where "the father often struck her with his belt 'with all his force,' leaving her with 'really painful red marks'" and "the father kicked the mother, in the presence of the child, 'so hard that [the mother] was left with a limp and a bunch of bruises'"… 303

See Matter of Grechel, below

94.   The "child's physical, mental, or emotional condition was impaired or in imminent danger of becoming impaired as the result of the father's misuse of alcoholic beverages" where "the father regularly drank alcoholic beverages to the point that he became 'very angry and aggressive,' that the father beat her and the

mother when he returned to the house drunk, and that when the father drank she and her siblings 'tried to hide from him because we were so scared'" as per Family Court Act 1012[f][i][B].... 304

See Matter of Grechel, below

95.   It would not be in the child's best interests to return to Nicaragua where the child "was harassed by gang members in Nicaragua who threatened to hurt her and" told her to watch herself, "that she was afraid to go to the police 'because the gang members had friends in the police,' that she told her mother about the gang members, but her mother ws unable to protect her, and that she was afraid that, if returned to Nicaragua, the gang members ' will carry out the threats they made to me'"..... 304

Matter of Grechel, 167 A.D. 3d 1011 (2d Dep't Dec. 26, 2018)

96. It was error to fail to find a presumption of neglect where the child's father, when living with the child in the United States, "would 'drink every day'" causing him "to become 'aggressive,' '[h]e hit doors, walls, and started to yell at all times of the night,' and that the child became 'scared of [the father]'" and that the "father '[drank] to the point that he could not walk,'" and where the child believed she could not live with him in El Salvador "due to his excessive drinking."... 308

See Matter of Agustin E., below.

97. It was error for the Family Court Judge not to decide that it was not in the child's best interests to return to El Salvador "where gang members had threatened the father in the presence of the child, made the father 'complete tasks and favors for them,' and murdered the child's cousin."... 308

Matter of Agustin, 168 A.D. 3d 840 (2d Dep't Jan 16, 2019)

98. The appellate court is free to make its own credibility determination where the Family Court's determination is not supported by the record.... 311

See Matter of Lucas, below.

99.   A finding of neglect by the father is appropriate where the father physically mistreated the mother "in the presence of the child by hitting her with objects such as a book or shoes" causing bruises and, "when the child attempted to defend the mother the father would hit the child", and the father yelled at and punched the child, and the "mother indicated that she had to send the child to live" with a grandparent in El Salvador "because she was afraid of what the father would do to the child," and the father "provided no financial support for the child since she was ten years old."… 311

See Matter of Lucas, below.

100. The Family Court erred in failing to find it was not in the minor's best interests to return to El Salvador where, following the minor's refusal to join a gang, they threatened and assaulted him "multiple times" and hurt him badly, leaving him on the street "and would have killed him on one occasion if not for a police patrol 'coming by that moment'" and "that he was afraid to go outside after the incident when he was almost killed" and the child testified "'if I go back [to El Salvador] they will kill me"…. 312

Matter of Lucas F.V., 169 A.D. 3d 802 (2d Dep't Feb 13, 2019)

101. In a custody proceeding, "Where the father listed the mother's address as 'unknown' on the petition and testified at a hearing that he had no information about the mother's whereaouts. Since the parties had separated 13 or 14 years earlier, the process server's three attempts to serve process at an address in Honduras, without attesting to any efforts to verify that this was the mother's address, did not constitute due diligence."… 315

Matter of Gutierrez Ferrera, 189 A.D. 3d 1230 (2d Dep't Dec. 16, 2020)

102. Under the Uniform Child Custody Jurisdiction and Enforcement Act (D.R.L sec 75 et seq), a child needs 6 months in New York before filing custody petition… 318

Matter of Aida T.M 197 A.D. 3d 596 (2d Dep't Aug 17, 2021)

103.   If a child is married, the New York Family Court will dismiss an SIJ guardianship petition…. 320

Matter of Elena G.R, 212 A.D.3d 628 (2d Dep't Jan 11, 2023)

104.   Although a child was born in Canada, it may be possible to show that his country of nationality is Peru…. 322

Matter of Fernandez v Otero, 228 A.D.3d 756 (2d Dep't Jun 12, 2024)

105.   The Petitioner must submit enough evidence to establish abandonment… 322

Matter of Fernandez v Otero, 228 A.D.3d 756 (2d Dep't Jun 12, 2024)

106.   It can be established that reunification with the child's parents is not viable where neither parent contributed to the financial support of the child since the child arrived in the United States…. 324

See Matter of Eriseldo, below

107.   It can be established that it is not in his best interests to return to Albania where he had "been the target of several assaults because of his family's political affiliation, and the parents were unable to protect him" and he was "doing well" in the Petitioner's care…. 324

Matter of Eriseldo v Dashmir, 217 A.D. 3d 512 (2d Dep't June 13, 2013)

108.   The Family court can vacate an SIJ guardianship order following the Subject's 21st birthday…. 327

Matter of Rosa M.G.G, 217 A.D. 3d 863 (2d Dep't June 21, 2023)

109. Where mother sent child to live with father in the USA, who "quickly abandoned" her, leaving her with her aunt, and the record contains a statement from the mother stating she was unable to give the child the "love and attention she

needs", the record "clearly established" that it was in the child's best interests to remain living with her aunt.... 329

See Matter of Antowa McD, below

110.   The "Family Court's appointment of a guardian constitutes the necessary declaration of dependency on a juvenile court" for SIJ purposes.... 329

Matter of Antowa McD, 50 A.D. 3d 507 (2d Dep't April 24, 2008)

111. It is apropriate to find abandonment and neglect where the child's parents lived in Bangladesh, "his parents inflicted excessive corporal punishment and failed to provide him with adequate supervision" and failed to communicate with him for more than seven years.... 330

See Matter of Alamgir, below.

112.   It is not impermissible forum shopping for a minor, who moved from Florida to New York and resided in New York more than 6 months, to see guardianship in the New York Courts.... 330

See Matter of Alamgir, below.

113.   A petitioner in an SIJ guardianship proceeding need not show "extraordinary circumstances" to obtain guardianship.... 330

See Matter of Alamgir, below.

114   It is not in a minor's best interest to return to Bangladesh where he "would have no where to live, and no means of supporting himself.".. 331

Matter of Alamgir A., 81 A.D. 3d 937 (2d Dep't Feb 22, 2011)

115. Once the Family Court appoints a guardian, the minor is dependent on a juvenile court. … 335

Matter of Jisun L.,75 A.D. 3d 510 (2d Dep't July 6, 2010)

116. An order of adoption satisfies the requirement of dependency on the Family Court which can then decide a motion for special findings.… 337

Matter of Emma M, 74 A.D. 3d 968 (2d Dep't June 8, 2010)

117. "The law does not require a finding that reunification with one or both" parents is viable, but the contrary.… 340

Matter of Haide L.G.M.,130 A.D. 3d 734 (2d Dep't July 8, 2015)

118. A record must contain sufficient evidence to establish that the minor's reunification with one or both parents is not viable based upon the statutorily enumerated grounds.… 342

Matter of Nieto Mira,118 A.D. 3d 1008 (2d Dep't June 25, 2014)

119. It is only necessary to show that reunification with one parent is not viable for purposes of an SIJ motion.… 344

Matter of Karen C.,111 A.D. 3d 622 (2d Dep't Nov 6, 2013)

120. The fact that the minor has an aunt and other family in Honduras does not mean it is not in her best interests to remain with her mother, who was granted custody, and who lived in New York.… 347

Matter of Mayra P. Diaz, 118 A.D. 3d 989 (2d Dep't June 25, 2014)

121. Children become dependent upon the family court in a family offense proceeding and thus can move for an order of special findings where the family offense proceeding determines the children were neglected by their father based upon his physical, mental, and verbal abuse.　　… 350

　　Matter of Eliverta Fifo, 127 A.D. 748 (2d Dep't April 1, 2015)

122. A child support order does not satisfy the requirement for SIJ status "that a child be 'dependent on a juvenile court'". See Family Court Act sec 413… 355

　　Matter of Hei Ting C.,109 A.D. 100 (2d Dep't July 17, 2013)

123. A natural parent may petition for custody of her own children.… 364

　　See Matter of Pineda Sanchez, below.

124.　Mother and children were entitled to a hearing on their custody petition and motion of special findings.… 364

　　Matter of Pineda Sanchez 115 A.D. 3d 868 (2d Dep't March 19, 2014)

125. An appellate court can render an independent factual review of the record.… 366

　　Matter of Tommy E.H., 134 A.D. 3d 840 (2d Dep't. Dec. 19, 2015)

126.　A mother may be appointed guardian of her own children.…368

　　See Matter of Maria G.G.U below

127.　The Petitioner and Subject in an SIJ guardianship petition have the right to a hearing before a Family Court Judge.… 369

　　Matter of Maria G.G.U.,114 A.D.3d 691 (2d Dep't Feb 5, 2014)

128. The record must contain enough evidence to prove the required elements of an SIJ claim – in this case, either neglect or abandonment and that it is not in the child's best interests to return to her home country…. 370

See Matter of Tzu Y.W. below

129. The fact that a child enters the United States with an F-1 visa to attend school may indicate the child has not been abandoned…. 371

Matter of Tzu Y.W, 228 A.D. 3d 875 (2d Dep't June 20, 2024)

130. Neither the Petitioner nor the child were aggrieved in an appeal of an order granting SIJ status…. 373

Matter of Saul E.B.M., 145 A.D. 3d 1009 (2d Dep't Dec. 28, 2016)

Cases

1. The Second Department can do cases quickly, but does not accept orders to show cause.

> ☐ **In the Matter of Jose E.S.G. Felix Mejia, Appellant; Maria Estela Salguero et al., Respondents.**

193 A.D.3d 856 (2d Dep't 2021). Decided April 14, 2021

Bruno J. Bembi, Hempstead, NY, for appellant.

In a guardianship proceeding pursuant to Family Court Act article 6, the petitioner appeals from an order of the Family Court, Nassau County (Lisa A. Cairo, J.), dated March 23, 2021. The order, after a hearing, dismissed the guardianship petition and denied the petitioner's motion for the issuance of an order, inter alia, making specific findings so as to enable the subject child to petition the United States Citizen and Immigration Services for special immigrant juvenile status pursuant to 8 USC § 1101 (a) (27) (J).

Ordered that the order is reversed, on the facts, without costs or disbursements, the petition to appoint the petitioner as the guardian of the subject child is reinstated and granted, the petitioner is appointed as the guardian of the subject child, an order of the same court dated March 24, 2021, is vacated, the petitioner's motion for the issuance of an order, inter alia, making specific findings so as to enable the subject child to petition the United States Citizen and Immigration Services for special immigrant juvenile status pursuant to 8 USC § 1101 (a) (27) (J) is granted, it is declared that the subject child is dependent on a juvenile court, and it is found that the subject child is unmarried and under 21 years of age, that reunification with his father is not viable due to parental abandonment, and that it would not be in the subject child's best interests to return to El Salvador, his previous country of nationality and last habitual residence.

In 2019, the petitioner commenced this proceeding pursuant to Family Court Act article 6 to be appointed the guardian of Jose E.S.G. (hereinafter the subject child). Thereafter, the petitioner moved for the issuance of an order declaring that the subject child is dependent on the Family Court and making specific findings that the subject child is unmarried and under 21 years of age, that reunification with one or both of his parents is not viable due to parental neglect or abandonment, and that it would not be in his best interests to be returned to El Salvador, his previous country of nationality and last habitual residence, so as to enable him to petition the United States Citizenship and Immigration Services for special immigrant juvenile status (hereinafter SIJS) pursuant to 8 USC § 1101 (a) (27) (J). In an order dated March 23, 2021, the Family Court denied the motion and dismissed the guardianship petition.

"[W]hen considering guardianship appointments, the infant's best interests is paramount" (*Matter of Alamgir A.*, 81 AD3d 937, 938 [2011]; *see* SCPA 1707 [1]; *Matter of Grechel L.J.*, 167 AD3d 1011, 1012 [2018]; *Matter of Axel S.D.C. v Elena A.C.*, 139 AD3d 1050, 1051 [2016]; *Matter of Trudy-Ann W. v Joan W.*, 73 AD3d 793, 794 [2010]). Upon our independent factual review of the record, we find that the subject child's best interests would be served by the appointment of the petitioner as his guardian (*see Matter of Grechel L.J.*, 167 AD3d at 1012; *Matter of Axel S.D.C. v Elena A.C.*, 139 AD3d at 1051; *Matter of Alamgir A.*, 81 AD3d at 938).

Further, the Family Court should have granted the petitioner's motion for the issuance of an order making the requisite specific findings so as to enable the subject child to petition for SIJS. "Pursuant to 8 USC § 1101 (a) (27) (J) (as amended by the William Wilberforce Trafficking Victims Protection Reauthorization Act of 2008, Pub L 110-457, 122 US Stat 5044) and 8 CFR 204.11, a 'special immigrant' is a resident alien who is, inter alia, under 21 years of age, unmarried, and dependent upon a juvenile court or legally committed to an individual appointed by a state or juvenile court" (*Matter of Trudy-Ann W. v Joan W.*, 73 AD3d at 795). "Additionally, for a juvenile to qualify for special immigrant juvenile status, a court must find that reunification of the juvenile with one or both of the juvenile's parents is not viable due to parental abuse, neglect, abandonment, or a similar basis found under State law, and that it would not be in the juvenile's best interests to be returned to his or her native country or country of last habitual residence" (*Matter of Maria P.E.A. v Sergio A.G.G.*, 111 AD3d 619, 620 [2013] [citations omitted]; *see* 8 USC § 1101 [a] [27] [J]; 8 CFR 204.11 [c] [6]).

Here, the subject child is under the age of 21 and unmarried, and since we have appointed the petitioner as the subject child's guardian, the subject child is dependent on a juvenile court within the meaning of 8 USC § 1101 (a) (27) (J) (i) (*see Matter of Grechel L.J.*, 167 AD3d at 1013; *Matter of Axel S.D.C. v Elena A.C.*, 139 AD3d at 1052; *Matter of Maura A.R.-R. [Santos F.R.—Fidel R.]*, 114 AD3d 687, 689 [2014]; *Matter of Trudy-Ann W. v Joan W.*, 73 AD3d at 796). Further, based upon our independent factual review, the record supports a finding that reunification of the subject child with his father is not a viable option due to parental abandonment (*see Matter of Briceyda M.A.X. [Hugo R.A.O.]*, 190 AD3d 752 [2021]; *Matter of Mardin A.M.-I. [Reyna E.M.-I.—Mardin H.]*, 187 AD3d 913 [2020]; *Matter of Rina M.G.C. [Oscar L.G.—Ana M.C.H.]*, 169 AD3d 1031, 1033 [2019]). Lastly, the record reflects that it would not be in the subject child's best interests to be returned to El Salvador, his previous country of nationality or country of last habitual residence (*see Matter of Palwinder K. v Kuldeep K.*, 148 AD3d 1149, 1151 [2017]; *Matter of*

Mohamed B., 83 AD3d 829, 832 [2011]; *Matter of Alamgir A.*, 81 AD3d at 940; *Matter of Trudy-Ann W. v Joan W.*, 73 AD3d at 796).

Accordingly, the Family Court should have granted the guardianship petition and the motion for the issuance of an order, inter alia, making the requisite declaration and specific findings so as to enable the subject child to petition for SIJS. Chambers, J.P., Austin, Brathwaite Nelson and Iannacci, JJ., concur.

Comments: Note that the Court indicates the family court guardianship petition was filed in 2019. Two years later, in 2021, very close to the Subject's 21st birthday, the guardianship petition and motion for special findings were denied.

Upon appeal, the Second Department can apply an independent factual review of the record. In Matter of Jose E.S.G. (Mejia – Salguero), the Family Court Judge entered a decision dated March 24, 2021. The Second Department reversed in an order dated April 14, 2021, allowing the Subject to obtain an order of guardianship and special findings. The Subject was about to age out and turn 21 years of age, and the Court rendered a prompt decsion as soon as the Appellant's brief and transcripts were submitted while allowing time for the absent Respondent to file a response, which was not filed. The Clerks of the Court made clear that the Second Department does not entertain orders to show cause, but will respond promptly when circumstances warrant. Additionally, note that often times the Second Department does not go into detail with the facts of the case, nor in describing legal principles involved in the case].

2. Service: An unopposed foreign affidavit of service in which the server attests he or she knows the Respondent personally and effected personal service satisfies the service requirement for a custody petition.

☐ **In the Matter of Daniela Leticia Reyes, Appellant,** **v** **Jose Oqueli Reyes Munoz, Respondent.**

199 A.D.3d 813 (2d Dep't, Nov 10, 2021).

Bruno J. Bembi, Hempstead, NY, for appellant.

Laurette D. Mulry, Central Islip, NY (John B. Belmonte of counsel), attorney for the child.

In a proceeding pursuant to Family Court Act article 6, the mother appeals from an order of the Family Court, Suffolk County (James W. Malone, J.), dated March 19, 2021. The order dismissed the mother's petition for custody on the ground that the court lacked jurisdiction.

Ordered that the order is reversed, on the law, without costs or disbursements, the petition is reinstated, and the matter is remitted to the Family Court, Suffolk County, for further proceedings consistent herewith.

The parties are the parents of the subject child, who was born in December 2009. In October 2019, the mother filed a petition seeking custody of the child. In an order dated March 19, 2021, the Family Court dismissed the petition for lack of jurisdiction over the father. The mother appeals.

Service without New York State may be made in the same manner as service is made within the state (*see* Domestic Relations Law § 75-g [1] [a]; CPLR 313; *Matter of Romero v Ramirez, 100 AD3d 909*, 910 [2012]). "Proof of service outside the state shall be by affidavit of the individual who made the service" (Domestic Relations Law § 75-g [2]). "Generally, a process server's affidavit of service establishes a prima facie case as to the method of service and, therefore, gives rise to a presumption of proper service" (*Matter of Romero v Ramirez*, 100 AD3d at 910 [internal quotation marks omitted]; *see Matter of Nwabueze v Okafor*, 166 AD3d 780, 780-781 [2018]).

Here, the mother submitted an affidavit from a process server, accompanied by an affidavit of translation, attesting that the process server recognized the father personally, and on the process server's third attempt, delivered the custody petition, motion for special findings, and notice of next court date to the father in Honduras. The affidavit of service of the mother's process server constituted prima facie evidence of proper service of the custody petition on the father (*see Matter of Nwabueze v Okafor*, 166 AD3d at 781). The record does not contain a sworn denial by the father of receipt of service with specific facts to rebut the statements in the process server's affidavit. Therefore, no hearing on the validity of process of service was necessary (*see id.* at 781-782; *Matter of Romero v Ramirez*, 100 AD3d at 910), and the Family Court should not have dismissed the petition.

Accordingly, we reverse the order, reinstate the petition, and remit the matter to the Family Court, Suffolk County, for further proceedings consistent herewith. Mastro, J.P., Austin, Duffy and Connolly, JJ., concur.

[A foreign language affidavit from a process server in Honduras "attesting that the process server recognized the father personally, and on the process server's third attempt, delivered the custody petition, motion for special findings, and notice of next court date to the father in Honduras. . . . constituted prima facie evidence of proper service of the custody petition on the father" and since the record was devoid of a sworn denial by the father "of receipt of service with specific facts to rebut the statements in the process server's affidavit. . . . no hearing on the validity of process of service was necessary . . .."]

3. There is no express requirement to submit certified copies of birth certficates or death certificates in guardianship or custody proceedings

In the Matter of Anuar S.A.O. Yari C.B.M., Appellant; Lizeth O.M., Respondent.

217 A.D. 3d 869 (2d Dep't June 21, 2023)

Bruno J. Bembi, Hempstead, NY, for appellant.

In a guardianship proceeding pursuant to Family Court Act article 6, the petitioner appeals from two orders of the Family Court, Nassau County (Sharon N. Clarke, Ct. Atty. Ref.), both dated December 21, 2022. The first order dismissed, without a hearing, the petition to appoint the petitioner as the guardian of the subject child. The second order denied the petitioner's motion for the issuance of an order, inter alia, making specific findings so as to enable the subject child to petition the United States Citizenship and Immigration Services for special immigrant juvenile status pursuant to 8 USC § 1101 (a) (27) (J).

Ordered that the orders are reversed, on the law, without costs or disbursements, the petition to appoint the petitioner as the guardian of the subject child is reinstated, and the matter is remitted to the Family Court, Nassau County, for an expedited hearing and a new determination thereafter of the petition and the petitioner's motion for the issuance of an order, inter alia, making specific findings so as to enable the subject child to petition the United States Citizenship and Immigration Services for special immigrant juvenile status pursuant to 8 USC § 1101 (a) (27) (J).

In 2022, the petitioner, an alleged friend of the subject child's family, commenced this proceeding pursuant to Family Court Act article 6 to be appointed as the guardian of the child. Thereafter, the petitioner moved for the issuance of an order, inter alia, making specific findings so as to enable the child to petition the United States Citizenship and Immigration Services for special immigrant juvenile status (hereinafter SIJS) pursuant to 8 USC § 1101 (a) (27) (J). In two orders, both dated December 21, 2022, the Family Court dismissed the petition and denied the petitioner's motion. The petitioner appeals.

Contrary to the Family Court's determination, there is no express requirement to submit certified copies of birth certificates or death certificates in a proceeding such as this pursuant to Family Court Act § 661 (a) (*see Matter of Jose S.S.G. [Elmer W.G.G.—Norma C.G.C.]*, 217 AD3d 864 [2023] [decided herewith]; *Matter of Joel A.A.R. [Sara I.R.T.—Eddy A.A.G.]*, 216 AD3d 1167 [2d Dept 2023]; *see also Matter of Rosa Amanda L.R. v Carlos Arnoldo O.R.*, 189 AD3d 1250 [2020]). Accordingly, since the court dismissed the petition without conducting a hearing or considering the child's best interests, we remit the matter to the Family Court, Nassau County, for an expedited hearing and a new determination thereafter of the petition and the petitioner's motion for the issuance of an order, inter alia, making specific findings so as to enable the child to petition for SIJS pursuant to 8 USC § 1101 (a) (27) (J) (*see Matter of Linares-Mendez v Cazanga-Payes*, 183 AD3d 738 [2020]; *Matter of Olga L.G.M. [Santos T.F.]*, 164 AD3d 1341, 1342 [2018]).

The petitioner's remaining contentions are improperly raised for the first time on appeal. Connolly, J.P., Brathwaite Nelson, Chambers and Voutsinas, JJ., concur.

> ☐ In the Matter of Jose S.S.G. Elmer W.G.G., Appellant; Norma C.G.C., Respondent. (Proceeding No. 1.) In the Matter of Kevin F.S.G. Elmer W.G.G., Appellant; Norma C.G.C., Respondent. (Proceeding No. 2.)

217 A.D. 3d 864 (2d Dep't Jun 21, 2023)

Bruno J. Bembi, Hempstead, NY, for appellant.

In related guardianship proceedings pursuant to Family Court Act article 6, the petitioner appeals from four orders of the Family Court, Nassau County (Sharon N. Clarke, Ct. Atty. Ref.), all dated October 24, 2022. The first order, after a hearing, dismissed the petition to appoint the petitioner as the guardian of the child Kevin F.S.G. The second order denied the petitioner's motion for the issuance of an order, inter alia, making specific findings so as to enable the child Kevin F.S.G. to petition the United States Citizenship and Immigration Services for special immigrant juvenile status pursuant to 8 USC § 1101 (a) (27) (J). The third order, after a hearing, dismissed the petition to appoint the petitioner as the guardian of the child Jose S.S.G. The fourth order denied the petitioner's motion for the issuance of an order, inter alia, making specific findings so as to enable the child Jose S.S.G. to petition the United States Citizenship and Immigration Services for special immigrant juvenile status pursuant to 8 USC § 1101 (a) (27) (J).

Ordered that the orders are reversed, on the law and the facts, without costs or disbursements, the petitions to appoint the petitioner as guardian of the subject children are reinstated and granted, the petitioner is appointed as the guardian of the subject children, the petitioner's motions for the issuance of orders, inter alia, making specific findings so as to enable the subject children to petition the United States Citizen and Immigration Services for special immigrant juvenile status pursuant to 8 USC § 1101 (a) (27) (J) are granted, it is declared that the subject children are dependent on a juvenile court, and it is found that the subject children are unmarried and under 21 years of age, that reunification with their father is not viable due to parental abuse, neglect, abandonment, or a similar basis found under state law, and that it would not be in their best interests to be returned to El Salvador, their previous country of nationality and last habitual residence.

In 2022, the petitioner commenced these proceedings pursuant to Family Court Act article 6 to be appointed the guardian of his two nephews, the child Kevin F.S.G., who allegedly was born in 2003 in El Salvador, and the child Jose S.S.G., who allegedly was born in 2005 in El Salvador. Thereafter, the petitioner moved for the issuance of orders, inter alia, making specific findings so as to enable the children to petition the United States Citizenship and Immigration Services for special immigrant juvenile status (hereinafter SIJS) pursuant to 8 USC § 1101 (a) (27) (J). Following a hearing, in four orders dated October 24, 2022, the Family Court dismissed the guardianship petitions and denied the motions. The petitioner appeals.

"[W]hen considering guardianship appointments, the infant's best interest is paramount" (*Matter of Alamgir A.*, 81 AD3d 937, 938 [2011]; *see* SCPA 1707 [1]; *Matter of Jose E.S.G. [Mejia—Salguero]*, 193 AD3d 856, 856 [2021]). Contrary to the Family Court's determination, there is no express requirement to submit certified copies of birth certificates in a proceeding such as this pursuant to Family Court Act § 661 (a) (*see Matter of Joel A.A.R. [Sara I.R.T.—Eddy A.A.G.]*, 216 AD3d 1167 [2d Dept 2023]). Likewise, there is no express requirement to submit certified copies of death certificates in a proceeding pursuant to Family Court Act § 661 (a) (*cf. id.* § 661 [b]; SCPA 1704 [8] [b]).

Here, for purposes of this proceeding pursuant to Family Court Act § 661 (a), the record supports a finding that the children are under the age of 21 (*see Matter of Joel A.A.R. [Sara I.R.T.—Eddy A.A.G.]*, 216 AD3d 1167 [2d Dept 2023]; *Matter of Rosa Amanda L.R. v Carlos Arnoldo O.R.*, 189 AD3d 1250 [2020]). Further, based upon our independent factual review, we find that the children's best interests would be served by the appointment of the petitioner as their guardian (*see* SCPA 1707 [1]; *Matter of Jose E.S.G. [Mejia—Salguero]*, 193 AD3d at 856; *Matter of Mardin A.M.-I. [Reyna E.M.-I.—Mardin H.]*, 187 AD3d 913, 913 [2020]; *Matter of Silvia N.P.L. v Estate of Jorge M.N.P.*, 141

AD3d 654, 655 [2016]; *Matter of Maura A.R.-R. [Santos F.R.—Fidel R.]*, 114 AD3d 687, 689 [2014]).

Further, the Family Court should have granted the petitioner's motions for the issuance of orders, inter alia, making the requisite specific findings so as to enable the children to petition for SIJS. "Pursuant to 8 USC § 1101 (a) (27) (J) (as amended by the William Wilberforce Trafficking Victims Protection Reauthorization Act of 2008, Pub L 110-457, 122 US Stat 5044) and 8 CFR 204.11, a 'special immigrant' is a resident alien who is, inter alia, under 21 years of age, unmarried, and dependent upon a juvenile court or legally committed to an individual appointed by a state or juvenile court" (*Matter of Trudy-Ann W. v Joan W.*, 73 AD3d 793, 795 [2010]; *see Matter of Jose E.S.G. [Mejia—Salguero]*, 193 AD3d at 857-858). Additionally, for a juvenile to qualify for SIJS, a court must find that reunification of the juvenile with one or both of the juvenile's parents is not viable due to parental abuse, neglect, abandonment, or a similar basis found under state law (*see* 8 USC § 1101 [a] [27] [J] [i]; *Matter of Elena G.R. v Oscar D.V.H.*, 212 AD3d 628, 628 [2023]; *Matter of Trudy-Ann W. v Joan W.*, 73 AD3d at 795), and that it would not be in the juvenile's best interests to be returned to his or her previous country of nationality or country of last habitual residence (*see* 8 USC § 1101 [a] [27] [J] [ii]; *Matter of Trudy-Ann W. v Joan W.*, 73 AD3d at 795).

Here, the record supports a finding that the children are under the age of 21 and unmarried, and, since we have appointed the petitioner as the children's guardian, the children are dependent on a juvenile court within the meaning of 8 USC § 1101 (a) (27) (J) (i) (*see Matter of Jose E.S.G. [Mejia—Salguero]*, 193 AD3d at 858; *Matter of Mardin A.M.-I. [Reyna E.M.-I.—Mardin H.]*, 187 AD3d at 913; *Matter of Maura A.R.-R. [Santos F.R.—Fidel R.]*, 114 AD3d at 688-689; *Matter of Trudy-Ann W. v Joan W.*, 73 AD3d at 795-796). Further, based upon our independent factual review, the record supports a finding that the children's father is deceased, and therefore, reunification is not possible (*see Matter of Luis R. v Maria Elena G.*, 120 AD3d 581, 582 [2014]). Lastly, the record supports a finding that it would not be in the best interests of the children to return to El Salvador, their previous country of nationality or country of last habitual residence (*see Matter of Mardin A.M.-I. [Reyna E.M.-I.—Mardin H.]*, 187 AD3d at 913; *Matter of Varinder S. v Satwinder S.*, 147 AD3d 854, 856 [2017]; *Matter of Axel S.D.C. v Elena A.C.*, 139 AD3d 1050, 1052 [2016]; *Matter of Luis R. v Maria Elena G.*, 120 AD3d at 583).

We need not reach the petitioner's remaining contentions in light of our determination.

Accordingly, the Family Court should have granted the guardianship petitions and the petitioner's motions for the issuance of orders making the requisite declaration and specific findings so as to enable the children to petition for SIJS. Connolly, J.P., Brathwaite Nelson, Chambers and Voutsinas, JJ., concur.

Same: Matter of Joel A.A.R. 216 A.D. 3d 1167 (2d Dep't 2023)(copy below).

4. Where an attorney certifies a copy of a birth certificate in conformance with CPLR 2105, it is error to dismiss the case for failure to submit a certified birth certificate:

☐ **In the Matter of Rosa Amanda L.R., Appellant,**

v

Carlos Arnoldo O.R., Respondent.

189 A.D.3d 1250 (2d Dep't Dec 16, 2020)

Bruno Joseph Bembi, Hempstead, NY, for appellant.

In a guardianship proceeding pursuant to Family Court Act article 6, the mother appeals from three orders of the Family Court, Nassau County (Catherine Rizzo, J.), all dated January 31, 2020. The first order, without a hearing, dismissed the petition to appoint the mother as guardian of the subject child. The second order denied the mother's motion to dispense with service on the father. The third order denied the mother's motion for the issuance of an order, inter alia, making specific findings so as to enable the child to petition the United States Citizenship and Immigration Services for special immigrant juvenile status pursuant to 8 USC § 1101 (a) (27) (J).

Ordered that the orders are reversed, on the law, without costs or disbursements, the petition to appoint the mother as guardian of the subject child is reinstated, and the matter is remitted to the Family Court, Nassau County, for an expedited hearing and a new determination thereafter of the petition and the two motions.

In May 2019, the mother filed a petition pursuant to Family Court Act article 6 to be appointed the guardian of the subject child for the purpose of obtaining an order, inter alia, making specific findings so as to enable the child to petition the United States Citizenship and Immigration Services for special immigrant juvenile status (hereinafter SIJS) pursuant to 8 USC § 1101 (a) (27) (J). In an order dated January 31, 2020, the Family Court dismissed the mother's petition, without a hearing, on the ground that the mother's counsel failed to properly certify the copy of the child's birth certificate submitted in support of the petition. The court also denied the mother's motions (1) to dispense with service on the father, and (2) for the issuance of an order making the requisite declarations and specific findings so as to enable the child to petition for SIJS, on the basis that it had dismissed the guardianship petition. The mother appeals.

We disagree with the Family Court's determination to dismiss the petition on the ground that counsel's identification of the child's birth certificate in his attorney certification was inadequate. Counsel's identification in the attorney certification he submitted with a copy of the child's birth certificate was sufficient to satisfy the requirements of CPLR 2105.

Accordingly, since the Family Court dismissed the guardianship petition without conducting a hearing or considering the child's best interests, we remit the matter to the Family Court, Nassau County, for an expedited hearing and a new determination thereafter of the guardianship petition (*see Matter of Linares-Mendez v Cazanga-Payes*, 183 AD3d 738[2020]; *Matter of Olga L.G.M. [Santos T.F.]*, 164 AD3d 1341, 1342 [2018]), the motion to dispense with service on the father, and, if warranted, an order, inter alia, making specific findings so as to enable the child to petition for SIJS pursuant to 8 USC § 1101 (a) (27) (J) (*see Matter of Olga L.G.M. [Santos T.F.]*, 164 AD3d 1341, 1342 [2018]).

The mother's remaining contentions either need not be reached in light of our determination or are not properly before this Court because the contention was not raised before the Family Court. Rivera, J.P., Hinds-Radix, Duffy and Brathwaite Nelson, JJ., concur.

5. It is possible to grant a motion to dispense with service

☐ In the Matter of Joel A.A.R. Sara I.R.T., Appellant; Eddy A.A.G., Respondent.

216 A.D. 3d 1167 (2d Dep't May 31, 2023)

Bruno J. Bembi, Hempstead, NY, for appellant.

In a guardianship proceeding pursuant to Family Court Act article 6, the mother appeals from three orders of the Family Court, Nassau County (Sharon N. Clarke, Ct. Atty. Ref.), all dated October 24, 2022. The first order dismissed, without a hearing, the petition to appoint the mother as guardian of the subject child. The second order denied the mother's motion to dispense with service on the father. The third order denied the mother's motion for the issuance of an order, inter alia, making specific findings so as to enable the subject child to petition the United States Citizenship and Immigration Services for special immigrant juvenile status pursuant to 8 USC § 1101 (a) (27) (J).

Ordered that the orders are reversed, on the law, on the facts, and in the exercise of discretion, without costs or disbursements, the petition to appoint the mother as guardian of the subject child is reinstated and granted, the mother is appointed as the guardian of the subject child, the mother's motion to dispense with service on the father is granted, the mother's motion for the issuance of an order, inter alia, making specific findings so as to enable the subject child to petition the United States Citizen and Immigration Services for special immigrant juvenile status pursuant to 8 USC § 1101 (a) (27) (J) is granted, it is declared that the subject child is dependent on a juvenile court, and it is found that the subject child is unmarried and under 21 years of age, that reunification with his father is not viable due to parental abandonment, and that it would not be in his best interests to be returned to Honduras, his previous country of nationality and last habitual residence.

In 2022, the mother commenced this proceeding pursuant to Family Court Act article 6 to be appointed as the guardian of the subject child, who allegedly was born in 2003 in Honduras. Thereafter, the mother moved to dispense with service upon the father, who allegedly was in Honduras. She also moved for the issuance of an order declaring that the child was dependent on the Family Court and making specific findings that the child is unmarried and under 21 years of age, that reunification with one or both of his parents is not viable, and that it would not be in his best interests to be returned to Honduras, his previous country of nationality and his last habitual residence, so as to enable him to petition the United States Citizenship and Immigration Services (hereinafter USCIS) for special immigration juvenile status (hereinafter SIJS) pursuant to 8 USC § 1101 (a) (27) (J). In three orders, all dated October 24, 2022, the court dismissed the petition and denied the mother's motions. The mother appeals.

Pursuant to 8 USC § 1101 (a) (27) (J) (as amended by the William Wilberforce Trafficking Victims Protection Reauthorization Act of 2008, Pub L 110-457, 122 US Stat 5044) and 8 CFR 204.11, a special immigrant juvenile is a resident alien who, among other things, is under 21 years of age, unmarried, and dependent upon a juvenile court or legally committed to an individual appointed by a state or juvenile court (*see Matter of Trudy-Ann W. v Joan W.*, 73 AD3d 793, 795 [2010]). Additionally, for a juvenile to qualify for SIJS, a court must find that reunification of the juvenile with one or both of the juvenile's parents is not viable due to parental abuse, neglect, abandonment, or a similar basis found under state law (*see* 8 USC § 1101 [a] [27] [J] [i]; *Matter of Elena G.R. v Oscar D.V.H.*, 212 AD3d 628, 628 [2023]; *Matter of Trudy-Ann W. v Joan W.*, 73 AD3d at 795), and that it would not be in the juvenile's best interests to be returned to his or her previous country of nationality or country of last habitual residence (*see* 8 USC § 1101 [a] [27] [J] [ii]; *Matter of Trudy-Ann W. v Joan W.*, 73 AD3d at 795).

Family Court Act § 661 (a) permits the Family Court to appoint a guardian for a youth between the ages of 18 and 21 in order to establish that the youth is "dependent on a juvenile court" (8 USC § 1101 [a] [27] [J] [i]) for purposes of an application for SIJS (*see Matter of Sing W.C. [Sing Y.C.—Wai M.C.]*, 83 AD3d 84, 87 [2011]). The provisions of the Surrogate's Court Procedure Act (hereinafter SCPA) apply to the extent they are applicable to guardianship of the person of a minor or infant and do not conflict with the provisions of the Family Court Act (*see* Family Ct Act § 661 [a]; *Matter of Alonso R.L.V. [Berlin J.V.Y.—Misael L.V.]*, 147 AD3d 1070, 1071 [2017]). "[W]hen considering guardianship appointments, the infant's best interests is paramount" (*Matter of Alamgir A.*, 81 AD3d 937, 938 [2011]; *see* SCPA 1707 [1]; *Matter of Jose E.S.G. [Mejia—Salguero]*, 193 AD3d 856, 857 [2021]).

Nevertheless, "significantly, the findings by the state juvenile court do not bestow any immigration status on SIJS applicants" (*Matter of Marcelina M.-G. v Israel S.*, 112 AD3d 100, 113 [2013] [internal quotation marks omitted]). Ultimately, the Secretary of the Department of Homeland Security determines whether the applicant meets the requirements for SIJS under federal law, and the decision whether to grant SIJS is discretionary (*see* 8 USC § 1101 [a] [27] [J] [iii]; *Matter of Marisol N.H.*, 115 AD3d 185, 189 [2014]; *Matter of Marcelina M.-G. v Israel S.*, 112 AD3d at 114). Thus, by making the preliminary factual findings, the juvenile court is not rendering an immigration determination (*see Matter of Marcelina M.-G. v Israel S.*, 112 AD3d at 109).

Contrary to the Family Court's determination, there is no express requirement to submit certified copies of birth certificates in a proceeding such as this pursuant to Family Court Act § 661 (a) (*but see Matter of Zaim R.*, 13 Misc 3d 180, 184 [Fam Ct, Orange County 2006], *appeal dismissed* 43 AD3d 824 [2007]; *see generally Matter of Rosa Amanda L.R. v Carlos Arnoldo O.R.*, 189 AD3d 1250 [2020]). Although an application to USCIS for SIJS must be supported by "[d]ocumentary evidence of the [applicant's] age, in the form of a valid birth certificate, official government-issued identification, or other document that in USCIS' discretion establishes the [applicant's] age" (8 CFR 204.11 [d] [2]), in proceedings pursuant to Family Court Act § 661 (a), the Family Court is only required to ascertain the juvenile's age, and there is no statutory requirement that a petitioner submit any particular evidence to establish the juvenile's age (*see id.*; SCPA 1706 [1]). Here, for purposes of this proceeding pursuant to Family Court Act § 661 (a), the record supports a finding that the child is under the age of 21 (*see Matter of Rosa Amanda L.R. v Carlos Arnoldo O.R.*, 189 AD3d 1250 [2020]). Further, based upon our independent factual review, we find that the child's best interests would be served by the appointment of the mother as his guardian (*see* SCPA 1707 [1]; *see Matter of Jose E.S.G. [Mejia—Salguero]*, 193 AD3d at 857; *Matter of Mardin A.M.-I. [Reyna E.M.-I.—Mardin H.]*, 187 AD3d 913, 913 [2020]; *Matter of Silvia N.P.L. v Estate of Jorge M.N.P.*, 141 AD3d 654, 655 [2016]; *Matter of Maura A.R.-R. [Santos F.R.—Fidel R.]*, 114 AD3d 687, 689 [2014]).

Pursuant to SCPA 1705 (1) (a), "[u]pon presentation of the petition process shall issue . □□ [t]o the . □□ parents . □□ if such persons are within the state and their residences therein are known." Nevertheless, even where, as here, a parent is not within the state and service upon that parent is not required pursuant to SCPA 1705 (1) (a), the Family Court possesses discretion to issue [*3]process to any relative "domiciled in its county or elsewhere" (*id.* § 1705 [3]; *see Matter of Alonso R.L.V. [Berlin J.V.Y.—Misael L.V.]*, 147 AD3d at 1071). However, in this case, we find that the record supports dispensing with service on the father.

Further, as the record supports that the child is under the age of 21 and unmarried, and that the mother should have been appointed as the child's guardian, we find that the child is dependent on a juvenile court within the meaning of 8 USC § 1101 (a) (27) (J) (i) (*see Matter of Mardin A.M.-I. [Reyna E.M.-I.—Mardin H.]*, 187 AD3d at 913; *Matter of Maura A.R.-R. [Santos F.R.—Fidel R.]*, 114 AD3d at 688-689; *Matter of Trudy-Ann W. v Joan W.*, 73 AD3d at 795-796). Additionally, based upon our independent factual review, the record supports a finding that reunification of the child with his father is not a viable option due to parental abandonment (*see Matter of Rina M.G.C. [Oscar L.G.—Ana M.C.H.]*, 169 AD3d 1031, 1033 [2019]; *Matter of Enis A.C.M.*

[Blanca E.M.—Carlos V.C.P.], 152 AD3d 690, 692 [2017]). Lastly, the record supports a finding that it would not be in the best interests of the child to return to Honduras, his previous country of nationality and last habitual residence (*see Matter of Axel S.D.C. v Elena A.C.*, 139 AD3d 1050, 1052 [2016]).

We need not reach the mother's remaining contentions in light of our determination.

Accordingly, the Family Court should have granted the guardianship petition and the mother's motions to dispense with service on the father and for the issuance of an order making the requisite declaration and specific findings so as to enable the child to petition for SIJS. Connolly, J.P., Brathwaite Nelson, Chambers and Voutsinas, JJ., concur.

6. It is possible to grant a motion for special findings where the guardian and subject do not live together

☐ In the Matter of Rina M.G.C. Oscar L.G., Appellant; Ana M.C.H., Respondent.

169 A.D. 3d 1031 (2d Dep't Feb 27, 2019)

Bruno J. Bembi, Hempstead, NY, for appellant.

In a proceeding pursuant to Family Court Act article 6, the father appeals from an order of the Family Court, Nassau County (Christopher Pizzolo, Ct. Atty. Ref.), dated June 29, 2018. The order, insofar as appealed from, denied the father's motion for the issuance of an order, inter alia, making specific findings so as to enable the subject child to petition the United States Citizenship and Immigration Services for special immigrant juvenile status pursuant to 8 USC § 1101 (a) (27) (J).

Ordered that the order is reversed insofar as appealed from, on the law and the facts, without costs or disbursements, the father's motion for the issuance of an order, inter alia, making specific findings so as to enable the subject child to petition the United States Citizenship and Immigration Services for special immigrant juvenile status pursuant to 8 USC § 1101 (a) (27) (J) is granted, and it is found that reunification of the child with her mother is not viable due to parental abandonment, and that it would not be in the child's best interests to return to El Salvador, her previous country of nationality and last habitual residence.

In November 2014, the father filed a petition pursuant to Family Court Act article 6 to be appointed as guardian of Rina M.G.C. (hereinafter the child), for the purpose of obtaining an order declaring that the child is dependent on the Family Court and making specific findings that she is unmarried and under 21 years of age, that reunification of the child with the mother is not viable due to parental abandonment, and that it would not be in the best interests of the child to be returned to El Salvador, her previous country of nationality and last habitual residence, so as to enable the child to petition the United States Citizenship and Immigration Services for special immigrant juvenile status (hereinafter SIJS) pursuant to 8 USC § 1101 (a) (27) (J). Thereafter, the father moved for the issuance of an order making the requisite declaration and specific findings so as to enable the child to petition for SIJS.

In an order dated March 13, 2015, the Family Court granted the guardianship petition. However, in an order dated March 15, 2016, the court denied the father's motion for the issuance of an order, inter alia, making specific findings so as to enable the child to petition for SIJS, on the ground that the child "no longer lives with either parent." Thereafter, the father again moved for the issuance of an order making the requisite declaration and specific findings so as to enable the child to petition for SIJS. In an order dated June 29,

2018, the court, among other things, denied the father's second motion for the issuance of an order, inter alia, making specific findings so as to enable the child to petition for SIJS, based upon the doctrine of the law of the case. The father appeals from the order dated June 29, 2018.

Pursuant to 8 USC § 1101 (a) (27) (J) (as amended by the William Wilberforce Trafficking Victims Protection Reauthorization Act of 2008, Pub L 110-457, 122 US Stat 5044) and 8 CFR 204.11, a special immigrant juvenile is a resident alien who, inter alia, is under 21 years of age, unmarried, and dependent upon a juvenile court or legally committed to an individual appointed by a state or juvenile court. Additionally, for a child to qualify for SIJS, a court must find that reunification of the child with one or both parents is not viable due to parental abuse, neglect, abandonment, or a similar basis found under state law (*see* 8 USC § 1101 [a] [27] [J] [i]; *Matter of Maria P.E.A. v Sergio A.G.G.*, 111 AD3d 619, 620 [2013]; *Matter of Trudy-Ann W. v Joan W.*, 73 AD3d 793, 795 [2010]), and that it would not be in the child's best interests to be returned to his or her previous country of nationality or country of last habitual residence (*see* 8 USC § 1101 [a] [27] [J] [ii]; 8 CFR 204.11 [c] [6]; *Matter of Maria P.E.A. v Sergio A.G.G.*, 111 AD3d at 620; *Matter of Trudy-Ann W. v Joan W.*, 73 AD3d at 795).

Here, although the father had previously unsuccessfully moved for the issuance of an order, inter alia, making specific findings so as to enable the child to petition for SIJS in a prior motion, "[t]he doctrine of the law of the case does not bind appellate courts, and thus, this Court is not bound by the law of the case established by the prior determination" (*Lee v Allen*, 165 AD3d 907, 908 [2018] [internal quotation marks omitted]). Further, contrary to the Family Court's determination, the issuance of an order making the requisite declaration and specific findings to enable a child to petition for SIJS is not dependent on the child living with either parent.

This Court's power to review the evidence is as broad as that of the hearing court, and where, as here, the record is sufficiently complete to make our own factual determinations, we may do so (*see Matter of Denia M.E.C. v Carlos R.M.O.*, 161 AD3d 853, 855 [2018]). Based upon our independent factual review, we find that the record establishes that the child met the age and marital status requirements for special immigrant status (*see Matter of Enis A.C.M. [Blanca E.M.—Carlos V.C.P.]*, 152 AD3d 690, 692-693 [2017]), and the dependency requirement has been satisfied by the granting of the father's guardianship petition prior to the child's 21st birthday (*see Matter of Miguel A.G.G. [Milton N.G.G.]*, 127 AD3d 858 [2015]; *Matter of Trudy-Ann W. v Joan W.*, 73 AD3d at 795). Further, we find that reunification of the child with her mother is not a viable option due to parental abandonment (*see Matter of Enis A.C.M. [Blanca E.M.—Carlos V.C.P.]*, 152 AD3d 690 [2017]; *Matter of Marlene G.H. [Maria G.G.U.—Pedro H.P.]*, 138 AD3d 843 [2016]; *Matter of Fatima J.A.J. [Ana A.J.S.—Carlos E.A.F.]*, 137 AD3d 912 [2016]; *see also Matter of Dallas Keith M.*, 55 AD3d 612 [2008]). The record reflects that after the child came to the United States in February 2014, she did not live with the mother because the "mother did not want to support her," and that the child lived in close proximity to the mother, but the mother only visited the child once, in March 2014, and did not visit or even contact the child from that time through the time the father made the subject motion in April 2018. We also find that the record supports a finding that it would not be in the best interests of the child to return to El Salvador, her previous country of nationality or country of last habitual residence. The record reflects that the child was threatened by gang members in El Salvador while walking home from school, that the gang members "wanted to recruit [the child] and have her sell drugs" and told her that "she had to join them or they would murder her and her family," that the gang members started texting her to "extort money from her," that the child was sent to live with a family friend, but the threats continued, and that the child left El

Salvador to escape from the gangs (*see Matter of Argueta v Santos*, 166 AD3d 608[2018]; *Matter of A.M.G. v Gladis A.G.*, 162 AD3d 768 [2018]).

Accordingly, the father's motion for the issuance of an order making the requisite declaration and specific findings so as to enable the child to petition for SIJS is granted. Since the record is sufficient for this Court to make its own findings of fact and conclusions of law, we find that the child is eligible to petition for SIJS status, that reunification of the child with her mother is not viable due to parental abandonment, and that it would not be in the best interests of the child to return to El Salvador. Dillon, J.P., Cohen, Duffy and Christopher, JJ., concur.

7. The doctrine of the law of the case does not bind the appellate courts.

See: Matter of Rina M.G.C (Oscar L.G. – Ana M.C.H), 169 A.D. 3d 1032 (2d Dept 2019)(above).   Therefore, if a motion for special findings is filed and denied by the family court, and then a second such motion is filed and denied based upon the doctrine of the law of the case, there can still be appellate review of the denial of the second motion.

8. It is appropriate to grant guardianship and a motion for special findings based upon abandonment even where the subject minor lived in close proximity to the mother and where the father was the petitioner.

See: Matter of Rina M.G.C (Oscar L.G. – Ana M.C.H), 169 A.D. 3d 1032 (2d Dept 2019)(above).   In Rina, the minor visited with the mother once in 2014 after arriving to the United States, but there were visits or contacts for 4 years thereafter and the mother did not want to support her child.

9. It is not in a subject minor's best interests to return to a country such as El Salvador where the child was threatenedd by gang members who wanted to

recruit her, threatened her, wanted her to sell drugs, and who threatened to murder her and her whole family.

See: Matter of Rina M.G.C (Oscar L.G. – Ana M.C.H), 169 A.D. 3d 1032 (2d Dept 2019)(above).

10. A Family Court's credibility determination that is not supported by the record permits the Appellate Division to make its own credibility assessments.

☐ **In the Matter of Norma U., Appellant,**
v
Herman T.R.F. et al., Respondents.

---

169 A.D. 3d 1055 (2d Dep't Feb 27, 2019)

Bruno J. Bembi, Hempstead, NY, for appellant.

In related guardianship proceedings pursuant to Family Court Act article 6, the petitioner appeals from two orders of the Family Court, Nassau County (Eileen Daly-Sapraicone, J.) (one as to each child), both dated June 22, 2018. The first order, after a hearing, denied the petitioner's motion for the issuance of an order, inter alia, making specific findings so as to enable the child Ana M.R.U. to petition the United States Citizen and Immigration Services for special immigrant juvenile status pursuant to 8 USC § 1101 (a) (27) (J). The second order, after a hearing, denied the petitioner's motion for the issuance of an order, inter alia, making specific findings so as to enable the child Francis M.R.U. to petition the United States Citizen and Immigration Services for special immigrant juvenile status pursuant to 8 USC § 1101 (a) (27) (J).

Ordered that the orders are reversed, on the facts, without costs or disbursements, the petitioner's motions for the issuance of orders, inter alia, making specific findings so as to enable the subject children to petition the United States Citizen and Immigration Services for special immigrant juvenile status pursuant to 8 USC § 1101 (a) (27) (J) are granted, and it is found that reunification of the children with their mother is not viable due to parental abandonment and that it would not be in the best interests of the children to return to Honduras, their previous country of nationality and last habitual residence.

In June 2017, Norma Urbina (hereinafter the petitioner) filed two related petitions pursuant to Family Court Act article 6 to be appointed as guardian of Ana M.R.U. and Francis M.R.U. (hereinafter together the children), for the purpose of obtaining orders declaring that the children are dependent on the Family Court and making specific findings so as to enable them to petition the United States Citizenship and Immigration Services for special immigrant juvenile status (hereinafter SIJS) pursuant to 8 USC § 1101 (a) (27) (J). Thereafter, the petitioner moved for the issuance of orders, inter alia, making the requisite declaration and specific findings so as to enable the children to petition for SIJS. In two orders, both dated May 24, 2018 (one as to each child), the Family Court granted the guardianship petitions. In two orders, both dated June 22, 2018 (one as to each child), the court denied the motions, finding that although the children were under 21 years of age, unmarried, and dependent on the Family Court, the evidence did not establish that reunification of the children with one or both of their parents was not viable due to parental abandonment, neglect, or abuse. The petitioner appeals.

Pursuant to 8 USC § 1101 (a) (27) (J) (as amended by the William Wilberforce Trafficking Victims Protection Reauthorization Act of 2008, Pub L 110-457, 122 US Stat 5044) and 8 CFR 204.11, a special immigrant is a resident alien who, inter alia, is under 21 years of age, unmarried, and dependent upon a juvenile court or legally committed to an individual appointed by a state or juvenile court. Additionally, for a child to qualify for SIJS, a court must find that reunification of the child with one or both parents is not viable due to parental abuse, neglect, abandonment, or a similar basis found under state law (*see* 8 USC § 1101 [a] [27] [J] [i]; *Matter of Maria P.E.A. v Sergio A.G.G.*, 111 AD3d 619, 620 [2013]; *Matter of Trudy-Ann W. v Joan W.*, 73 AD3d 793, 795 [2010]), and that it would not be in the child's best interests to be returned to his or her previous country of nationality or country of last habitual residence (*see* 8 USC § 1101 [a] [27] [J] [ii]; 8 CFR 204.11 [c] [6]; *Matter of Maria P.E.A. v Sergio A.G.G.*, 111 AD3d at 620; *Matter of Trudy-Ann W. v Joan W.*, 73 AD3d at 795).

"While the credibility assessment of a hearing court is accorded considerable deference on appeal, where, as here, the Family Court's credibility determination is not supported by the record, this Court is free to make its own credibility assessments and overturn the determination of the hearing court" (*Matter of Dennis X.G.D.V.*, 158 AD3d 712, 714 [2018] [citations omitted]). Here, based upon our independent factual review, the record supports a finding that reunification of the children with their mother is not viable due to parental abandonment (*see Matter of Alejandro V.P. v Floyland V.D.*, 150 AD3d 741, 743 [2017]). The children testified that the mother left when they were both only three years old, and that they have not seen or spoken to the mother since that time. Thus, the record establishes that the mother has had no involvement with the children for the majority of their lives (*see Matter of Alan S.M.C.*, 160 AD3d 721, 724 [2018]; *Matter of Alejandro V.P. v Floyland V.D.*, 150 AD3d at 743; *Matter of Varinder S. v Satwinder S.*, 147 AD3d 854, 856 [2017]).

Further, the record supports a finding that it would not be in the best interests of the children to return to Honduras, their previous country of nationality or country of last habitual residence (*see Matter of Maura A.R.-R. [Santos F.R.—Fidel R.]*, 114 AD3d 687, 689 [2014]). Francis testified that when the children lived with their paternal aunt in Honduras, they were "mistreat[ed] .□□ emotionally and physically." The children testified that when they then went to live with their father and stepmother in Honduras, the stepmother beat them and "wouldn't give us food" when the father was not around, and that the stepmother was "verbally abusive," telling the children, among other things, that they were "good for nothing." The record reflects that the children had no one else to take care of them if they returned to Honduras. Consequently, the record demonstrates that it would not be in the best interests of the children to return to Honduras (see Matter of Marcelina M.-G. v Israel S., 112 AD3d 100, 114-115 [2013]).

Accordingly, the Family Court should have granted the petitioner's motions for the issuance of orders making the requisite declaration and specific findings so as to enable the children to petition for SIJS. Since the record is sufficient for this Court to make its own findings of fact and conclusions of law, we find that reunification of the children with their mother is not viable due to parental abandonment, and that it would not be in the best interests of the children to return to Honduras, their previous country of nationality and last habitual residence. Rivera, J.P., Chambers, Cohen and Iannacci, JJ., concur.

11. Court finds abandonment even though there was significant physical mistreatement of the children

See Matter of Norma U. v Herman T.R.F, 169 A.D. 3d 1055 (2d Dep't 2019)(above).

12. There is no jurisdictional impediment to prevent the issuance of an order of special findings filed after the minor turned 18 years old where a custody order was granted before the minor's 18th birthday.

| In the Matter of Dunia Y. Ochoa Vasquez, Appellant,
v
Carlos A. Cruz Mejia, Respondent. |

170 A.D. 3d 868 (2d Dep't March 13, 2019)

Bruno J. Bembi, Hempstead, NY, for appellant.

Michael Kaszubski, Westbury, NY, attorney for the child.

In a proceeding pursuant to Family Court Act article 6, the mother appeals from an order of the Family Court, Nassau County (Sharon N. Clarke, Ct. Atty. Ref.), dated July 6, 2018. The order, without a hearing, denied the mother's motion for the issuance of an order, inter alia, making specific findings so as to enable the subject child to petition the United States Citizenship and Immigration Services for special immigrant juvenile status pursuant to 8 USC § 1101 (a) (27) (J).

Ordered that the order is reversed, on the law, without costs or disbursements, and the matter is remitted to the Family Court, Nassau County, for a hearing and a new determination thereafter of the mother's motion for the issuance of an order, inter alia, making specific findings so as to enable the subject child to petition the United States Citizenship and Immigration Services for special immigrant juvenile status pursuant to 8 USC § 1101 (a) (27) (J).

In January 2018, the mother filed a petition pursuant to Family Court Act article 6 for custody of Fernando A.C.O. (hereinafter the child), for the purpose of obtaining an order declaring that the child is dependent on the Family Court and making specific findings that he is unmarried and under 21 years of age, that reunification with his father is not viable due to parental neglect or abandonment, and that it would not be in the child's best interests to be returned to Honduras, his previous country of nationality and last habitual residence, so as to enable the child to petition the United States Citizenship and Immigration Services (hereinafter USCIS) for special immigrant juvenile status (hereinafter SIJS) pursuant to 8 USC § 1101 (a) (27) (J). In an order dated April 4, 2018, the Family Court granted the custody petition. In May 2018, the mother moved for an order making the requisite declaration and specific findings to enable the child to petition for SIJS. In an order dated July 6, 2018, the court denied the mother's motion on the ground of lack of jurisdiction due to the child having reached the age of 18. The mother appeals.

While the Family Court lacks jurisdiction to determine a petition for custody once the subject child reaches the age of 18 (*see Matter of Batista v Gaton*, 126 AD3d 895 [2015]), "there is no jurisdictional impediment to the issuance of an order making the requisite declaration and specific findings to enable the child to petition for SIJS" where the petition was granted before the court was divested of jurisdiction (*Matter of Juan R.E.M. [Juan R.E.]*, 154 AD3d 725, 727 [2017]). Here, since the custody petition was granted on April 4, 2018, prior to the child's 18th birthday on May 6, 2018, the court should not have denied the mother's motion on the ground of lack of jurisdiction.

Pursuant to 8 USC § 1101 (a) (27) (J) (as amended by the William Wilberforce Trafficking Victims Protection Reauthorization Act of 2008, Pub L 110-457, 122 US Stat 5044) and 8 CFR 204.11, a special immigrant is a resident alien who, inter alia, is under 21 years of age, unmarried, and has been legally committed to, or placed under the custody of, an individual appointed by a state or juvenile court. Additionally, for a child to qualify for SIJS, a court must find that reunification of the child with one or both parents is not viable due to parental abuse, neglect, abandonment, or a similar basis found under state law (*see* 8 USC § 1101 [a] [27] [J] [i]; *Matter of Maria P.E.A. v Sergio A.G.G.*, 111

AD3d 619, 620 [2013]; *Matter of Trudy-Ann W. v Joan W.*, 73 AD3d 793, 795 [2010]), and that it would not be in the child's best interests to be returned to his or her previous country of nationality or country of last habitual residence (*see* 8 USC § 1101 [a] [27] [J] [ii]; 8 CFR 204.11 [c] [6]; *Matter of Maria P.E.A. v Sergio A.G.G.*, 111 AD3d at 620; *Matter of Trudy-Ann W. v Joan W.*, 73 AD3d at 795).

Here, based upon our independent factual review (*see Matter of Gomez v Sibrian*, 133 AD3d 658 [2015]), we find that the record establishes that the child meets the age and marital status requirements for special immigrant status, and that the child has been legally committed to, or placed under the custody of, an individual appointed by a state or juvenile court (*see Matter of Pineda v Diaz*, 127 AD3d 1203, 1203-1204 [2015]). However, the record is insufficient to determine whether reunification of the child with the father is not viable due to parental neglect or abandonment, and whether it would not be in the best interests of the child to return to Honduras (*see Matter of A.M.G. v Gladis A.G.*, 162 AD3d 768, 770 [2018]; *Matter of Alma D.G.-L. v Juan C.-P.*, 152 AD3d 516, 517 [2017]).

Accordingly, we reverse the order, and remit the matter to the Family Court, Nassau County, for a hearing and a new determination thereafter of the mother's motion for the issuance of an order, inter alia, making specific findings so as to enable the child to petition for SIJS (*see Matter of A.M.G. v Gladis A.G.*, 162 AD3d at 770; *Matter of Alma D.G.-L. v Juan C.-P.*, 152 AD3d at 517). Chambers, J.P., Roman, Barros and Christopher, JJ., concur.

13. A Family Court has jurisdiction where the child was never in New York State but owns property within the state

Matter of Christian J.C.U. (Jorge R.C.), 60 Misc. 3d 706

Family Court of New York, Kings County

May 17, 2018, Decided

G-10061-2018

Catholic Migration Services, Brooklyn (*Hector R. Rojas* of counsel), Attorney for the Child.

Alisha W., respondent pro se.

Javier E. Vargas, **J.**

The motion by petitioner Christian J. C.U., also known as Monica C. U., for the appointment of a guardian and the issuance of an order making special immigrant juvenile status (SIJS) findings, is granted and SIJS findings made in accordance with the following decision.

The following facts are undisputed. Monica was born biologically as male in Honduras to respondents Maria N. U.P. (mother) and Jorge A. C.M. (father). From an early age, however, Monica's gender identity has been female. Because of a family tragedy blamed on her, the parents disliked and abandoned Monica in a Honduran orphanage when she was three years old, but she was rescued by her paternal grandmother, who took her in, nurtured her and provided for her schooling throughout her childhood. Despite this, the parents continued to abuse and mistreat Monica with brutal beatings, which once resulted in broken ribs requiring medical attention, as well as by inflicting cigarette burns and scars. She was also victimized at the hands of one of her older brother s, Jorge C., who repeatedly raped and sexually abused her during her infancy. Although Monica told the grandmother about the rapes, her brother continued the sexual abuse after only a short reprieve.

On one occasion, Monica's father saw her dressed in a manner consistent with her gender identity, and he beat her up to the point that she was taken to the hospital and the Honduran child protective authorities were called and investigated, yet nothing was done civilly or criminally against the father to subvert the abuse. To the contrary, the father resumed his physical abuse against Monica, threatening that if she continued to dress as a woman or be a "fa . . . t" that he was going to beat her until she became a man, make her disappear or institutionalize her. Everything came to a head upon the passing of her grandmother in 2013, when Monica was 16 years of age and left all her little property to her. In 2014, Monica fled her native Honduras escaping her nightmarish parents and brother's abuse, threats and harassment because of her gender identity, and searched for a new life and peace in the United States. She crossed the U.S. border illegally and was returned to Honduras.

Upon reentering in 2017, Monica was captured by the U.S. Immigration and Customs Enforcement and detained at the transgendered section of the Cibola County Detention Center located in Milan, New Mexico, where she is currently detained. Catholic Migration Services took over Monica's defense and the totality of her personal property in Brooklyn, consisting of her backpack with clothing, a purse, a wallet, medication and other items. By petition dated April 17, 2018, just days before her 21st birthday, Monica commenced the instant Family Court Act article 6 proceeding against her parents in the Kings County Family Court, seeking the appointment of her friend and mentor, respondent Alisha W., as her guardian for the purpose of obtaining SIJS findings in order to petition to the United States Citizenship and Immigration Services (USCIS) for special immigrant juvenile status pursuant to 8 USC § 1101 (a) (27) (J). Thereafter, by order to show cause dated April 18, 2018, Monica moved for an order making the requisite declaration and specific findings so as to enable her to petition for SIJS, alleging that she is unmarried, under 21 years of age, that reunification with one or both of her parents is not viable due to abuse, neglect and abandonment, and that it would not be in her best interests to be returned to Honduras.

Given her dire circumstances and the proximity of Monica's 21st birthday, this court expedited the guardianship petition and afforded counsel time to locate and serve the parents with the petition by order to show cause. Following counsel's unsuccessful search for their whereabouts, the court waived service upon the parents on the return date pursuant to Surrogate's Court Procedure Act ("SCPA") § 1705 (2) based on their abandonment of Monica. On April 20, 2018, the Family Court (Vargas, J.) conducted a hearing on the guardianship petition finding that the court has jurisdiction over the person of Monica based on the location of her property in Brooklyn, New York, pursuant to SCPA 1702 (1) (b), and crediting Ms. W.'s hopeful testimony and plans she has in assuming the guardianship and care of Monica once she is released from USCIS detention in New Mexico and travels to Brooklyn. A final order of guardianship was issued appointing Ms. W. as Monica's guardian until she turned 21. The court heard additional testimony and accepted into evidence Monica's affidavit retelling her harrowing life story in Honduras, thereby granting Monica's SIJS motion and issuing an SIJS order dated April 20, 2018, finding that she is eligible to petition for SIJS status, that reunification with both of her parents is not viable due to their neglect and abandonment, and that it would not be in her best interests to be returned to Honduras. However, the court reserved the opportunity to write an opinion on the novel jurisdictional issues presented and expound on the rulings made.

Preliminarily, the novel, threshold jurisdictional issue presented is whether SCPA 1702 confers the Family Court with jurisdiction over Monica's guardianship petition based not on her physical presence in New York, but on the location of her "property" here. The Family Court "is a court of limited jurisdiction, constrained to exercise only those powers granted to it by the State Constitution or by statute" (*Matter of H.M. v E.T.*, 14 NY3d 521, 526, 930 NE2d 206, 904 NYS2d 285 [2010], quoting *Matter of Johna M.S. v Russell E.S.*, 10 NY3d 364, 366, 889 NE2d 471, 859 NYS2d 594 [2008]). However, pursuant to Family Court Act § 661 and SCPA 103 (27), the Family Court, concurrently with the Surrogate's Court, has jurisdiction to make judicial determinations regarding the care, control, guardianship and custody of minors, which include within its definition juveniles up to the age of 21 years old (SCPA 1706; *see Matter of Marisol N.H.*, 115 AD3d 185, 979 NYS2d 643 [2d Dept 2014]). Where a minor has no guardian, the Family Court

"may appoint a guardian of his person or property, or of both, in the following cases:

"(a) Where the infant is domiciled in that county or has sojourned therein immediately preceding the application[, or]

"(b) *Where the infant is a non-domiciliary of the state but has property situate[d] in that county*" (SCPA 1702 [1] [emphasis supplied]).

Courts have long recognized a Surrogate's jurisdiction to appoint a guardian of a minor who resides outside the state, but has property in the county in question (*see Matter of Thorne*, 240 NY 444, 450, 148 NE 630 [1925]; *Matter of Klineman*, 105 Misc 2d 896, 898, 430 NYS2d 24 [Sur Ct, NY County 1980] [infant's "property" consisted of securities and cash, valued at approximately $120,000, on bank deposit]).

Applying these legal principles to the matter at bar, the court finds that the Family Court has the same jurisdiction over Monica's guardianship proceeding as the

Surrogate's Court would. It is undisputed that Monica is currently detained by USCIS in New Mexico and, as such, is a "non-domiciliary of the state" (SCPA 1702 [1] [b]). But, as the statute provides, Monica "has property situate[d] in [the] county" (*id.*), consisting of her personal property located in Kings County. It does not consist of real estate property, substantial assets or any significant monetary property, but merely Monica's own personal property items, including her backpack, clothing, purse, wallet and medicines. Nevertheless, those items are Monica's only "property" in the world! Unlike the Civil and Supreme Court which have monetary minimums for their jurisdiction, the Family Court is the real "People's Court" which welcomes all parties with open arms regardless of their gender, sexual orientation, gender identity, race, national origin, financial or citizenship status. That Monica's property is de minimis should not stymie her jurisdictional right to pursue her guardianship proceeding here. "When considering guardianship appointments, the infant's best interests are paramount" (*Matter of Axel S.D.C. v Elena A.C.*, 139 AD3d 1050, 1051, 32 NYS3d 295 [2d Dept 2016]; *see Matter of Alamgir A.*, 81 AD3d 937, 938, 917 NYS2d 309 [2d Dept 2011]; SCPA 1707 [1]). As such, this court rules that it has subject matter jurisdiction over the person of Monica to rule on her guardianship petition and hereby appoints Ms. W. as Monica's guardian until she turns 21.

Once subject matter jurisdiction has been established, the court may proceed with its SIJS findings. Pursuant to the Immigration and Nationality Act (8 USC § 1101 [a] [27] [J] [as amended by the William Wilberforce Trafficking Victims Protection Reauthorization Act of 2008, Pub L 110-457, 122 US Stat 5044]; 8 CFR 204.11), Congress provided a pathway for abused, neglected or abandoned noncitizen children to obtain lawful permanent residence in the U.S. through SIJS, if they are, inter alia, under 21 years of age, unmarried, and dependent upon a juvenile court or legally committed to an individual appointed by a state or juvenile court. It must also be established that reunification with one or both parents is not viable due to their prior misconduct (*see* 8 USC § 1101 [a] [27] [J] [i]; *Matter of Denia M.E.C. v Carlos R.M.O.*, 161 AD3d 853, 77 NYS3d 104, 2018 NY Slip Op 03355 [2d Dept 2018]; *Matter of Trudy-Ann W. v Joan W.*, 73 AD3d 793, 795, 901 NYS2d 296 [2d Dept 2010]), and that it would not be in the child's best interests to be returned to his or her previous country of nationality or country of last habitual residence (*see* 8 USC §1101 [a] [27] [J] [ii]; 8 CFR 204.11 [c] [6]; *Matter of Trudy-Ann W.*, 73 AD3d at 795). "Ultimately, the determination of whether to grant SIJS to a particular juvenile rests with USCIS and its parent agency, the Department of Homeland Security. Thus, when making the requisite SIJS findings, the state or juvenile court is not actually 'rendering an immigration determination' " (*Matter of Enis A.C.M. [Blanca E.M.—Carlos V.C.P.]*, 152 AD3d 690, 692, 59

NYS3d 396 [2d Dept 2017], quoting *Matter of Marcelina M.-G. v Israel S.*, 112 AD3d 100, 109, 973 NYS2d 714 [2d Dept 2013]).

Here, this court found that Monica is fully entitled to SIJS findings. The record establishes that Monica meets the age and marital status requirements for special immigrant status, and the dependency requirement has been satisfied by the Family Court granting her guardianship to Ms. W. (*see Matter of Silvia N.P.L. v Estate of Jorge M.N.P.*, 141 AD3d 654, 655, 37 NYS3d 270 [2d Dept 2016]; *Matter of Trudy-Ann W.*, 73 AD3d at 795; SCPA 1706). Moreover, Monica's parents have violently rejected her, physically abused her and refused to accept her gender identity issues since very early in her short life. Her father neglected her by burning her with cigarettes and using excessive corporal punishment, as defined by Family Court Act § 1012 (f) (i) (B), that impaired Monica's [**839] emotional and physical condition (*see Matter of Padmine M. [Sandra M.]*, 84 AD3d 806, 922 NYS2d 527 [2d Dept 2011]; *Matter of Justyce M. [Shavon E.]*, 77 AD3d 1407, 908 NYS2d 783 [4th Dept 2010]). Nor have they shown any inclination to support her financially, emotionally, educationally or medically in any way since 2014. Therefore, reunification with either of her parents is not viable, even impossible (*see Matter of Luis R. v Maria Elena G.*, 120 AD3d 581, 582-583, 990 NYS2d 851 [2d Dept 2014]; *Matter of Cristal M.R.M.*, 118 AD3d 889, 891, 987 NYS2d 614 [2d Dept 2014]). This court further finds that it would certainly not be in Monica's best interests to be returned to Honduras—her previous country of nationality and last habitual residence—given the evidence establishing that there is no one there who loves or is able to care for her, and that she was threatened with violence or worse if she were to return (*see Matter of Keilyn GG. [Marlene HH.]*, 159 AD3d 1295, 1298, 74 NYS3d 378 [3d Dept 2018]).

Monica's harrowing life cries for her to be permitted to remain, restart and enjoy her new life on these shores of New York City. As the words of Emma Lazarus's famous 1883 sonnet "The New Colossus," emblazoned on our Statue of Liberty, exhorts:

"Give me your tired, your poor,

"Your huddled masses yearning to breathe free,

"The wretched refuse of your teeming shore.

"Send these, the homeless, tempest-tost to me,

"I lift my lamp beside the golden door!"

In accordance with the foregoing, the court grants Monica's guardianship petition, and her motion for SIJS findings in her favor, as per the order (<u>Vargas</u>, J.) dated April 20, 2018.

14.   The   same   attorney   can   represent   both   the   Petitioner   and   Subject

> ☐ **In the Matter of Noemy Serrano Sosa, Appellant,**
> **v**
> **Alexander Serrano, Respondent.**

130 A.D. 3d 636 (2d Dep't July 1, 2015)

Bruno Joseph Bembi, Hempstead, N.Y., for appellant.

Toba Beth Stutz, Jamaica, N.Y., attorney for the child.

Appeal from an order of the Family Court, Queens County (Juanita E. Wing, Ct. Atty. Ref.), dated December 10, 2014. The order, sua sponte, relieved Bruno Joseph Bembi as the mother's attorney and, in effect, directed that Bruno Joseph Bembi be prohibited from representing the subject child in this proceeding.

Ordered that, on the Court's own motion, the notice of appeal is deemed an application for leave to appeal, and leave to appeal is granted (*see* Family Ct Act § 1112 [a]); and it is further,

Ordered that the order is reversed, on the facts and in the exercise of discretion, without costs or disbursements.

In this custody proceeding, the mother, who was awarded custody of the subject child, moved for the issuance of an order making the requisite declaration and specific findings so as to enable the child to petition the United States Citizenship and Immigration Services for special immigrant juvenile status pursuant to 8 USC § 1101 (a) (27) (J). While that motion was pending, the Family Court issued an order which, sua sponte, relieved Bruno Joseph Bembi as the mother's attorney and, in effect, directed that Bembi be prohibited from representing the subject child in this proceeding.

The Family Court improvidently exercised its discretion in, sua sponte, relieving Bembi as the mother's attorney and, in effect, directing that Bembi be prohibited from representing the subject child in this proceeding. Although the disqualification of an attorney is a matter which rests within the discretion of the court (*see Matter of Madris v Oliviera, 97 AD3d 823*, 825 [2012]), " '[a] party's entitlement to be represented in ongoing litigation by counsel of his or her own choosing is a valued right which should not be abridged absent a clear showing that disqualification is warranted' " (*id.* at 824, quoting *Gulino v Gulino, 35 AD3d 812*, 812 [2006]). Further, Family Court Act § 241 provides that children "should be represented by counsel of their own choosing or by assigned counsel." Here, there is nothing in the record to support the Family Court's determination that Bembi must be disqualified from representing the mother or the child in this proceeding (*see Bentz v Bentz, 37 AD3d 386* [2007]; *Rose v Thrifty Rent-A-Car Sys.*, 305 AD2d 484 [2003]), and the court's conclusory assertions and speculation as to the existence of a conflict of interest based on, among other things, the fact that Bembi represented both the mother and the child in a proceeding in federal court, were insufficient to warrant disqualification (*see Dominguez v Community Health Plan of Suffolk*, 284 AD2d 294 [2001]).

The mother's remaining contentions either are without merit or need not be reached in light of our determination. Chambers, J.P., Hall, Cohen and Maltese, JJ., concur.

[Editor's Note: Mother's have a right to raise their children without ever setting foot in Family Court. Think of this set of rights as encompassed in what the New

York Court of Appeals referred to in <u>In Re Thorne,</u> 240 N.Y. 444, 448 (NY 1925) as the *matria potestas,* just as the father's rights are bundled up in concept of *patria potestas.* Neither parent relinquishes these inherent rights by filing a petition for guardianship or custody with the Family Court, although quite often that is not how it seems. In fact, procedures exist to terminate these inherent rights, such as adversarial hearings in an Article 10 proceeding which puts the Government to its proof to show that either the mother or father has committed such acts as renders that parent unfit to raise his or her child. Notably, this loss of rights occurs after an evidentiary hearing and record is made, with the Judge then making a decision by applying the law. The loss of rights does not occur before the proceedings begin. Among the rights that a mother or father possesses without ever setting foot in Family Court, is the right to name his or her child, the right to decide where that child will live, and with whom, the right to choose the child's doctor and lawyer. In fact, Family Court Act section 249 codifies the mother or father's right to choose an attorney for the child where it states that for certain proceedings in the Family Court "the court shall not permit the respondent [ie, the minor] to waive the right to be represented by counsel chosen by the respondent, respondent's parent . . .." There is generally little likelihood of the existence of a conflict of interest where the mother choses the same attorney to represent herself as will represent her child. <u>See, In re Abrams,</u> 62 N.Y.2d 183 (1984), where the New York Court of Appeals held that there is not a conflict until there is an actual articulable conflict, and even then, very often, that conflict can be waived. So where the Government has made no accusations of any wrong-doing by the petitioning parent, and that parent wishes to have the same attorney represent herself and her child, her decision must be respected. However, the reality is many judges feel uncomfortable with this situation and a positive report from the Attorney for the Child does a great deal to relieve the courtroom anxiety.]

15. The best interest of the child standard is applicable

In the Matter of Denys O.H., Appellant,
v
Vilma A.G., Respondent.

---

108 A.D.3d 711 (2d Dep't July 24, 2013)

Bruno Joseph Bembi, Hempstead, N.Y., for appellant.

Ngozi Rosaline Asonye, Freeport, N.Y., attorney for the child.

In a proceeding pursuant to Family Court Act article 6 for the appointment of the petitioner, Denys O.H., as the guardian of Luis A.G., a person under 21 years of age, the petitioner appeals from an order of the Family Court, Nassau County (Aaron, J.), dated August 7, 2012, which, after a hearing, in effect, denied the petition and dismissed the proceeding.

Ordered that the order is reversed, on the law, without costs or disbursements, the petition is reinstated, and the matter is remitted to the Family Court, Nassau County, for further proceedings, including a new determination of the petition.

Luis A.G. was born in El Salvador in 1995. In March 2012, he entered this country illegally, and was apprehended by the United States Citizen and Immigration Services. He was subsequently released to the care of his maternal uncle, Denys O.H. In May 2012, Denys O.H. commenced the instant proceeding, seeking to be appointed Luis's guardian. The Family Court, in effect, denied the petition and dismissed the proceeding.

When considering guardianship appointments, the infant's best interests are paramount (*see* SCPA 1707 [1]; *Matter of Stuart*, 280 NY 245, 250

[1939]; _Matter of Melissa B. v Dean S._, 89 AD3d 1018, 1019 [2011]; _Matter of Alexander N._, 5 AD3d 776 [2004]; _Matter of Amrhein v Signorelli_, 153 AD2d 28, 31 [1989]). The order appealed from, however, is devoid of any references to Luis's best interests. Accordingly, we remit the matter to the Family Court, Nassau County, for further proceedings, including a new determination of the petition. Mastro, J.P., Hall, Lott and Sgroi, JJ., concur.

16. Service of the SIJ motion

See Villatoro Ramirez, below.

A motion for special findings may be served by regular mail to the Respondent-parent's last known address. CPLR 2103[b](2)(c).

17. Mistakes in the paperwork

Harmless errors in the papers should be disregarded, CPLR 2001, even where the SIJ motion incorrectly states it was made on the "Court's own motion."

☐ **In the Matter of Elida Edith Villatoro Ramirez, Appellant,**
v
Raul Antonio Palacios, Respondent.

---

136 A.D. 3d 666 (2d Dep't Feb 3, 2016)

Bruno Joseph Bembi, Hempstead, NY, for appellant.

Gail Jacobs, Great Neck, NY, attorney for the child.

Appeal from an order of the Family Court, Nassau County (Christopher Pizzolo, Ct. Atty. Ref.), dated March 31, 2015. The order, without a hearing, in effect, denied the mother's motion for the issuance of an order, inter alia, making special findings so as to enable the subject child, Milagro G.P.R., to petition the United States Citizenship and Immigration Services for special immigrant juvenile status pursuant to 8 USC § 1101 (a) (27) (J).

Ordered that the order is reversed, on the law and the facts, without costs or disbursements, the mother's motion for the issuance of an order, inter alia, making special findings so as to enable the subject child, Milagro G.P.R., to petition the United States Citizenship and Immigration Services for special immigrant juvenile status pursuant to 8 USC § 1101 (a) (27) (J) is granted, it is declared that Milagro G.P.R. has been legally committed to, or placed under the custody of, an individual appointed by a State or juvenile court, and it is found that Milagro G.P.R. is unmarried and under 21 years of age, that reunification with one of her parents is not viable due to parental abandonment, and that it would not be in her best interests to return to El Salvador, her previous country of nationality or last habitual residence.

In November 2013, the mother commenced this proceeding for custody of the subject child, Milagro G.P.R., who was born in El Salvador. In June 2014, the mother moved for the issuance of an order, inter alia, making special findings so as to enable the child to petition the United States Citizenship and Immigration Services for special immigrant juvenile status (hereinafter SIJS) pursuant to 8 USC § 1101 (a) (27) (J). In an order dated August 18, 2014, the mother was awarded sole custody of the child. In an order dated March 31, 2015, the Family Court, in effect, denied the mother's motion on the grounds that the mother failed to personally serve the father with the motion papers and that the notice of motion was "defective" because it erroneously stated that it was made on the "Court's own motion."

Under the circumstances of this case, the mother was not required to personally serve the father with the motion papers. Rather, the mother appropriately served the motion papers by mailing them to the father's last known address (see CPLR 2103 [b] [2]; [c]). Further, since no substantial right of any party was prejudiced by the mistake in the mother's notice of motion, the Family Court should have disregarded the mistake and determined the motion on the merits (*see* CPLR 2001; *Matter of Gomez v Sibrian*, 133 AD3d 658 [2015]).

Pursuant to 8 USC § 1101 (a) (27) (J) (as amended by the William Wilberforce Trafficking Victims Protection Reauthorization Act of 2008, Pub L 110-457, 122 US Stat 5044) and 8 CFR 204.11, a "special immigrant" is a resident alien who, inter alia, is under 21 years of age, is unmarried, and has been legally committed to, or placed under the custody of, an individual appointed by a State or juvenile court. Additionally, for a juvenile to qualify for SIJS, a court must find that reunification of the juvenile with one or both of the juvenile's parents is not viable due to parental abuse, neglect, abandonment, or a similar basis found under State law (*see* 8 USC § 1101 [a] [27] [J] [i]; *Matter of Marcelina M.-G. v Israel* S., 112 AD3d 100 [2013]; *Matter of Trudy-Ann W. v Joan W.*, 73 AD3d 793, 795 [2010]), and that it would not be in the juvenile's best interests to be returned to his or her native country or country of last habitual residence (*see* 8 USC § 1101 [a] [27] [J] [ii]; 8 CFR 204.11 [c] [6]; *Matter of Trudy-Ann W. v Joan W.*, 73 AD3d at 795).

Here, the child is under the age of 21 and unmarried, and has been "legally committed to, or placed under the custody of . □□ an individual . □□ appointed by a State or juvenile court" within the meaning of 8 USC § 1101 (a) (27) (J) (i) (*see Matter of Pineda v Diaz*, 127 AD3d 1203, 1204 [2015]). Furthermore, based upon our independent factual review, we find that the record fully supports a finding that reunification of the child with the father is not a viable option due to abandonment (*see Matter of Diaz v Munoz*, 118 AD3d 989, 991 [2014]), and that it would not be in the best interests of the child to be returned to El Salvador (*see Matter of Marcelina M.-G. v Israel S.*, 112 AD3d at 114-115). Accordingly, the Family Court should have granted the mother's motion for an order making the requisite special findings so as to enable the child to apply for SIJS. Inasmuch as the record is sufficient for this Court to make its own findings of fact and conclusions of law, we grant the mother's motion, declare that the child has been legally committed to, or placed under the custody of, an individual appointed by a State or juvenile court, and find that the child is unmarried and under 21 years of age, that reunification with one of her parents is not viable due to parental abandonment, and that it would not be in her best interests to return to El Salvador (*see Matter of Diaz v Munoz*, 118 AD3d at 991; *Matter of Marcelina M.-G. v Israel S.*, 112 AD3d at 115; *Matter of Trudy-Ann W. v Joan W.*, 73 AD3d at 795). Dickerson, J.P., Hall, Roman and Sgroi, JJ., concur.

18.   A parent can waive service of process.

> ☐ **In the Matter of Carminda Sanchez Gomez, Appellant,**
> **v**
> **Fredy Garcia Sibrian, Respondent.**

133 A.D 3d 658 (2nd Dep't November 12, 2015)

Bruno Joseph Bembi, Hempstead, N.Y., for appellant.

Lisa Siano, Merrick, N.Y., attorney for the child.

Appeal from an order of the Family Court, Nassau County (Christopher Pizzolo, Ct. Atty. Ref.), dated March 31, 2015. The order, without a hearing, in effect, denied the mother's motions for the issuance of an order, inter alia, making special findings so as to enable the subject child, Jose Fredy Garcia Sibrian, to petition the United States Citizenship and Immigration Services for special immigrant juvenile status pursuant to 8 USC § 1101 (a) (27) (J).

Ordered that the order is reversed, on the law and the facts, without costs or disbursements, the mother's motions for the issuance of an order, inter alia, making special findings so as to enable the subject child, Jose Fredy Garcia

Sibrian, to petition the United States Citizenship and Immigration Services for special immigrant juvenile status pursuant to 8 USC § 1101 (a) (27) (J) are granted, it is declared that Jose Fredy Garcia Sibrian has been legally committed to, or placed under the custody of, an individual appointed by a State or juvenile court, and it is found that Jose Fredy Garcia Sibrian is unmarried and under 21 years of age, that reunification with one of his parents is not viable due to parental abandonment, and that it would not be in his best interests to return to Honduras, his previous country of nationality or last habitual residence.

In January 2014, the mother commenced this proceeding for custody of the subject child, Jose Fredy Garcia Sibrian, who was born in Honduras. In March 2014, the father, who also lived in Honduras, executed a document consenting, inter alia, to an award of custody of the child to the mother, to "waive[ ] the issuance of service of process in this matter," and to "waive[ ] the right to notice of any future hearings on this matter in the Family Court of Nassau County." In May 2014, the mother moved for the issuance of an order, inter alia, making special findings so as to enable the child to petition the United States Citizenship and Immigration Services (hereinafter USCIS) for special immigrant juvenile status (hereinafter SIJS) pursuant to 8 USC § 1101 (a) (27) (J). In an order dated August 20, 2014, the mother was awarded sole custody of the child upon the father's consent. Thereafter, the mother, prior to a determination on her earlier motion, again moved for the issuance of an order, among other things, making special findings so as to enable the child to petition for SIJS. In an order dated March 31, 2015, the Family Court, in effect, denied the mother's motions on the grounds that the mother failed to personally serve the father with the motion papers and that the motions were "defective" because they erroneously stated that they were made on the "Court's own motion."

Under the circumstances of this case, the mother was not required to personally serve the father with the motion papers. The father consented to "waive[ ] the issuance of service of process in this matter," and to "waive[ ] the right to notice of any future hearings on this matter in the Family Court of Nassau County," which would include a hearing on the subject motions. Further, since no substantial right of any party was prejudiced by the mistake in the mother's notices of motion, the court should have disregarded the mistake and determined the motions on the merits (*see* CPLR 2001).

Pursuant to 8 USC § 1101 (a) (27) (J) (as amended by the William Wilberforce Trafficking Victims Protection Reauthorization Act of 2008, Pub L 110-457, 122 US Stat 5044) and 8 CFR 204.11, a "special immigrant" is a resident alien who, inter alia, is under 21 years of age, is unmarried, and has been legally committed to, or placed under the custody of, an individual appointed by a State or juvenile court. Additionally, for a juvenile to qualify for SIJS, a court must find that reunification of the juvenile with one or both of the juvenile's parents is not viable due to parental abuse, neglect, abandonment, or a similar basis found under State law (*see* 8 USC § 1101 [a] [27] [J] [i]; *Matter of Marcelina M.-G. v Israel S.*, 112 AD3d 100 [2013]; *Matter of Trudy-Ann W. v Joan W.*, 73 AD3d 793, 795 [2010]), and that it would not be in the juvenile's best interests to be returned to his or her native country or country of last habitual residence (*see* 8 USC § 1101 [a] [27] [J] [ii]; 8 CFR 204.11 [c] [6]; *Matter of Trudy-Ann W. v Joan W.*, 73 AD3d at 795).

Here, the child is under the age of 21 and unmarried, and has been "legally committed to, or placed under the custody of . □□ an individual appointed by a State or juvenile court" within the meaning of 8 USC § 1101 (a) (27) (J) (I) (*see Matter of Pineda v Diaz*, 127 AD3d 1203, 1204 [2015]). Furthermore, based upon our independent factual review, we find that the record fully supports a finding that reunification of the child with the father is not a viable option due to abandonment (*see Matter of Pineda v Diaz*, 127 AD3d at 1204; *Matter of Marcelina M.-G. v Israel S.*, 112 AD3d at 104), and that it would not be in the best interests of the child to be returned to Honduras (*see Matter of Gabriela Y.U.M. [Palacios]*, 119 AD3d 581, 583-584 [2014]; *Matter of Trudy-Ann W. v Joan W.*, 73 AD3d at 796). Accordingly, the Family Court should have granted the mother's motions for an order making the requisite special findings so as to enable the child to apply for SIJS. Inasmuch as the record is sufficient for this Court to make its own findings of fact and conclusions of law, the mother's motions are granted, we declare that the child has been legally committed to, or placed under the custody of, an individual appointed by a State or juvenile court, and we find that the child is unmarried and under 21 years of age, that reunification with one of his parents is not viable due to parental abandonment, and that it would not be in his best interests to return to Honduras (*see Matter of Diaz v Munoz*, 118 AD3d 989, 991 [2014]; *Matter of Marcelina M.-G. v Israel S.*, 112 AD3d at 115; *Matter of Trudy-Ann W. v Joan W.*, 73 AD3d at 795).

In light of our determination, we need not reach the mother's remaining contentions. Hall, J.P., Roman, Sgroi and Hinds-Radix, JJ., concur.

19. A motion for special findings should not be dismissed without a hearing.

☐ In the Matter of Alma D.G.-L., Appellant,

v

Juan C.-P., Respondent.

---

152 A.D 3d 516 (2nd Dep't July 5, 2017)

Bruno J. Bembi, Hempstead, NY, for appellant.

Appeal by the mother from an order of the Family Court, Dutchess County (Denise M. Watson, J.), entered December 16, 2016. The order, without a hearing, in effect, denied the mother's motion for the issuance of an order, inter alia, making specific findings so as to enable the subject child to petition the

United States Citizenship and Immigration Services for special immigrant juvenile status pursuant to 8 USC § 1101 (a) (27) (J).

Ordered that the order is reversed, on the law, without costs or disbursements, and the matter is remitted to the Family Court, Dutchess County, for a hearing and a determination thereafter of the mother's motion.

The parties have a child in common. On September 1, 2015, the mother filed a petition pursuant to Family Court Act article 6 for sole custody of the child. In a corrected order dated October 22, 2015, the Family Court awarded the mother sole legal and residential custody of the child.

On August 1, 2016, the mother moved for an order declaring that the child is dependent on the Family Court and making specific findings that the child is unmarried and under 21 years of age, that reunification with the father is not viable due to abandonment, and that it would not be in the child's best interests to be returned to Mexico, her previous country of nationality and last habitual residence, so as to enable the child to petition the United States Citizenship and Immigration Services for special immigrant juvenile status (hereinafter SIJS) pursuant to 8 USC § 1101 (a) (27) (J). In an order entered December 16, 2016, the court determined the mother's motion by stating that "the petition is dismissed due to failure to state cause of action." The mother appeals.

The Family Court erred in denying the mother's motion—which the court mistakenly denominated a "petition"—without a hearing. In her affidavit in support of the motion, the mother averred that the child was under 21 and unmarried; that the Family Court had awarded the mother sole custody of the child; that the father had abandoned the child after her birth, never provided support, and never had a relationship with the child; and that it was not in the child's best interests to return to Mexico. The record is insufficient to provide a basis for a determination of the mother's motion as to whether reunification with the father is not viable due to abandonment. Accordingly, we reverse the order and remit the matter to the Family Court, Dutchess County, for a hearing and a determination thereafter of the motion (*see* 8 USC § 1101 [a] [27] [J] [ii]; 8 CFR 204.11 [c] [6]; *Matter of Jimenez v Perez*, 144 AD3d 1036, 1037 [2016]). Balkin, J.P., Chambers, Barros and Brathwaite Nelson, JJ., concur.

20. A finding of neglect is appropriate where the father fails to support the child who must live with other relatives because the step-mother does not get along with her and the other relatives to whom the child is sent to live abuse her.

1☐ In the Matter of Gabriela Y.U.M. Joselino Umana Palacios, Appellant.

---

119 A.D 3d 581 (2nd Dep't July 2, 2014)

Bruno Joseph Bembi, Hempstead, N.Y., for appellant.

James E. Flood, Jr., Massapequa, N.Y., attorney for the child.

In a guardianship proceeding pursuant to Family Court Act article 6, the petitioner appeals from an order of the Family Court, Nassau County (Stack, J.H.O.), dated October 9, 2013, which, upon the granting of that branch of the guardianship petition which was for the appointment of the petitioner as the guardian of the subject child, Gabriela Y.U.M., in an order of the same court dated August 19, 2013, and after a hearing, in effect, denied that branch of the petition which was for the appointment of the petitioner as the guardian of Gabriela Y.U.M. until she reaches the age of 21 and denied his motion for the issuance of an order making special findings so as to enable Gabriela Y.U.M. to petition the United States Citizenship and Immigration Services for special immigrant juvenile status pursuant to 8 USC § 1101 (A) (27) (J).

Ordered that the order is reversed, on the law and the facts, without costs or disbursements, that branch of the petition which was for the appointment of the petitioner as the guardian of Gabriela Y.U.M. until Gabriela Y.U.M. reaches the age of 21 is granted, the motion for special findings is granted, it is declared that Gabriela Y.U.M. is dependent on the Family Court, and it is found that she is unmarried and under 21 years of age, that reunification with one or both of her parents is not viable due to parental neglect, and that it would not be in the best interests of Gabriela Y.U.M. to return to El Salvador, her previous country of nationality and last habitual residence.

The subject child, Gabriela Y.U.M., is a native of El Salvador, 18 years old, unmarried, and has lived with the petitioner, her uncle, in Nassau County since she surrendered to immigration authorities in 2012. Gabriela's mother died when she was six years old. From the age of 12, Gabriela was not financially supported by her father, and lived with various relatives in El Salvador because the father's wife had problems living with the father's children. After moving in with her grandmother, whose husband sexually abused her, Gabriela moved in with an aunt, whose husband also abused her. Gabriela then moved in with her sister, where she was living at the time her father arranged for her to leave El Salvador with a smuggler and her sister's boyfriend.

After an arduous trip through Guatemala and Mexico, Gabriela and another juvenile were left in the desert with little food and water. Gabriela surrendered to immigration authorities, who eventually released her to the custody of the petitioner and his wife.

The petitioner commenced this proceeding to become Gabriela's guardian until she reaches the age of 21, to which Gabriela and her father consented. The Family Court granted that branch of the petition which was for the appointment of the petitioner as Gabriela's guardian by order dated August 19, 2013 (hereinafter the guardianship order), which stated that the appointment was to last until Gabriela's 18th birthday, "unless the Court approves an application for an extension of the appointment until the age of 21 upon the consent of the subject if the subject is over 18."

The petitioner moved for an order making special findings that would allow Gabriela to apply to the United States Citizenship and Immigration Services for special immigrant juvenile status (hereinafter SIJS), as provided in 8 USC § 1101 (a) (27) (J). In an order dated October 9, 2013, the Family Court, inter alia, denied the motion. The court held, in relevant part, that Gabriela was not eligible for SIJS because reunification with one of her parents was viable, as her father did not abuse, neglect, or abandon her. Although the court further found that "nothing prevents unification with her father," it noted that "[i]t is uncertain that her father would welcome her back, given her history with the father's wife." The court also found that "[t]he best interests of any immigrant child living in the United States would be to remain here" and noted that Gabriela would have more safety, comfort, and security in the United States than she would find in El Salvador. In addition, at a hearing on the motion for special findings on September 26, 2013, when the attorney for the petitioner stated that it was "our request to extend the guardianship to the age of 21," and that the petitioner would testify, the Family Court responded, "I don't really need any testimony as to that since the state has made that a very simple matter." Nevertheless, the Family Court , in effect, denied that branch of the petition which was for the appointment of the petitioner as the guardian of Gabriela until Gabriela reaches the age of 21. Accordingly, the guardianship order expired by its terms on Gabriela's 18th birthday, on September 5, 2013.

Pursuant to 8 USC § 1101 (a) (27) (J) (as amended by the William Wilberforce Trafficking Victims Protection Reauthorization Act of 2008, Pub L 110-457, 122 US Stat 5044) and 8 CFR 204.11, a juvenile "special immigrant" is a resident alien who is, inter alia, under 21 years of age, unmarried, and "declared dependent on a juvenile court located in the United States or whom such a court has legally committed to, or placed under the custody of, an agency or department of a State, or an individual or entity appointed by a State or juvenile court located in the United States" (8 USC § 1101 [a] [27] [J] [i]). For a juvenile to qualify for SIJS, it must be shown that reunification of the juvenile with one or both of his or her parents is not viable due to parental abuse, neglect, abandonment, or a similar basis found under state law (*see* 8 USC § 1101 [a] [27] [J] [i]; *Matter of Marcelina M.-G. v Israel S.*, 112 AD3d 100, 108 [2013]; *Matter of Karen C.*, 111 AD3d 622, 623 [2013]; *Matter of Mohamed B.*, 83 AD3d 829, 831 [2011]; *Matter of Trudy-Ann W. v Joan W.*, 73 AD3d 793, 795 [2010]), and that it would not be in the juvenile's best interests to be returned to his or her native country or country of last habitual residence (*see* 8 USC § 1101 [a] [27] [J] [ii]; 8 CFR 204.11 [c] [6]; *Matter of Marcelina M.-G. v Israel S.*, 112 AD3d at 109; *Matter of Karen C.*, 111 AD3d at 623; *Matter of Mohamed B.*, 83 AD3d at 831; *Matter of Trudy-Ann W. v Joan W.*, 73 AD3d at 795).

As a threshold matter, the Family Court should have granted that branch of the petition which was for the appointment of the petitioner as Gabriela's guardian until Gabriela reaches the age of 21, which is in her best interests, the paramount concern in a guardianship proceeding (*see* SCPA 1707 [1]; *Matter of Maura A.R.-R. [Santos F.R.—Fidel R.]*, 114 AD3d 687, 688 [2014]; *Matter of Denys O.H. v Vilma A.G.*, 108 AD3d 711, 712 [2013]) and establishes Gabriela's dependency on the Family Court within the meaning of 8 USC § 1101 (a) (27) (J) (i) (*see Matter of Trudy-Ann W. v Joan W.*, 73 AD3d at 795).

Based upon our independent factual review, we find that the record fully supports the conclusion that, because her father neglected her, Gabriela's reunification with her one surviving parent is not a viable option (*see Matter of Mohamed B.*, 83 AD3d at 832; *Matter of Alamgir A.*, 81 AD3d 937, 939-940 [2011]; *Matter of Trudy-Ann W. v Joan W.*, 73 AD3d at 796). The record also reflects that it would not be in Gabriela's best interests to be returned to El Salvador, where she has nowhere to live and no means of financial support (*see Matter of Kamaljit S.*, 114 AD3d 949 [2014]; *Matter of Jisun L. v Young Sun P.*, 75 AD3d 510, 512 [2010]; *Matter of Trudy-Ann W. v Joan W.*, 73 AD3d at 796). Accordingly, the Family Court should have granted the motion for the issuance of an order making specific findings so as to enable Gabriela to petition for SIJS. Rivera, J.P., Balkin, Leventhal and Roman, JJ., concur.

21. A parent's failure to take steps within her means to protect the child from criminal gangs can serve as a basis for a finding of neglect.

See Matter of Dennis X.G.D.V., 158 A.D.3d 721 (2d Dep't Feb 14, 2018), below.

22.   It is possible to file an appeal of a denial of a motion to renew and reargue.

See Matter of Dennis X.G.D.V., 158 A.D.3d 721 (2d Dep't Feb 14, 2018), below.

23.   An appellate court can make its own credibility determination where such determination by the Family Court is not supported by the record.

☐ In the Matter of Dennis X.G.D.V., Appellant.

153 A.D 3d 628 (2nd Dep't August 9, 2017)

[Recalled and vacated, see 158 AD3d 712.]

Fried, Frank, Harris, Shriver & Jacobson, LLP, New York, NY (Jennifer L. Colyer and Michael P. Sternheim of counsel), for appellant.

Appeal by the child from an order of the Family Court, Queens County (Nicolette M. Pach, J.H.O.), dated August 22, 2016. The order, insofar as appealed from, upon renewal and reargument, adhered to the original determination in a prior order of that court dated March 29, 2016, in effect, denying that branch of the child's motion which was for a specific finding that reunification of the child with one or both of his parents is not viable due to parental neglect.

Ordered that the order dated August 22, 2016, is reversed insofar as appealed from, on the facts, without costs or disbursements, upon renewal and reargument, the determination in the order dated March 29, 2016, in effect, denying that branch of the child's motion which was for a specific finding that reunification of the child with one or both of his parents is not viable due to parental neglect is vacated, that branch of the motion is granted, and it is found that reunification of the child with one or both of his parents is not viable due to parental neglect.

In April 2015, Dennis X.G.D.V. (hereinafter the child) filed a petition pursuant to Family Court Act article 6 for the father to be appointed as his guardian. The child subsequently moved for the issuance of an order making the requisite declaration and specific findings so as to enable him to petition the United States Citizenship and Immigration Services for special immigrant juvenile status (hereinafter SIJS) pursuant to 8 USC § 1101 (a) (27) (J). In an order dated March 29, 2016, made after a hearing, the Family Court found that the child was under 21 years of age, unmarried, and dependent on the court, and that it would not be in his best interests to be returned to El Salvador, his previous country of nationality and last habitual residence. However, the court, in effect, denied that branch of the child's motion which was for a specific finding that reunification of the child with one or both of his parents is not viable on the ground of parental neglect. Thereafter, the child moved for leave to renew and reargue that branch of his prior motion. In an order dated August 22, 2016, the court, upon renewal and reargument, adhered to the original determination in the order dated March 29, 2016.

Pursuant to 8 USC § 1101 (a) (27) (J) (as amended by the William Wilberforce Trafficking Victims Protection Reauthorization Act of 2008, Pub L 110-457, 122 US Stat 5044) and 8 CFR 204.11, a "special immigrant" is a resident alien who, inter alia, is under 21 years of age, is unmarried, and has been legally committed to, or placed under the custody of, an individual appointed by a state or juvenile court. Additionally, for a juvenile to qualify for SIJS, a court must find that reunification of the juvenile with one or both of the juvenile's parents is not viable due to parental abuse, neglect, abandonment, or a similar basis found under state law (*see* 8 USC § 1101 [a] [27] [J] [i]; *Matter of Marvin E.M. de P. [Milagro C.C.—Mario Enrique M.G.]*, 121 AD3d 892, 893 [2014]; *Matter of Maria P.E.A. v Sergio A.G.G.*, 111 AD3d 619, 620 [2013]; *Matter of Trudy-Ann W. v Joan W.*, 73 AD3d 793, 795 [2010]), and that it would not be in the juvenile's best interests to be returned to his or her native country or country of last habitual residence (*see* 8 USC § 1101 [a] [27] [J] [ii]; 8 CFR 204.11 [c] [6]; *Matter of Marvin E.M. de P. [Milagro C.C.—Mario Enrique M.G.]*, 121 AD3d at 893; *Matter of Maria P.E.A. v Sergio A.G.G.*, 111 AD3d at 620; *Matter of Trudy-Ann W. v Joan W.*, 73 AD3d at 795).

While the credibility assessment of a hearing court is accorded considerable deference on appeal (*see Matter of Arthur G. [Tiffany M.]*, 112 AD3d 925, 926 [2013]; *Matter of Marte v Biondo*, 104 AD3d 947 [2013]; *Matter of Aranova v Aranov*, 77 AD3d 740, 741 [2010]), where, as here, the Family Court's credibility determination is not supported by the record, this Court is free to make its own credibility assessments and overturn the determination of the hearing court (*see Matter of Jasmine W. [Michael J.]*, 132 AD3d 774, 775 [2015]; *Matter of Arthur G. [Tiffany M.]*, 112 AD3d at 926; *Matter of Serenity S. [Tyesha A.]*, 89 AD3d 737, 739 [2011]). Based upon our independent factual review, we conclude that the record supports a finding that reunification of the child with his mother is not a viable option based upon parental neglect. The record reflects that the mother failed to meet the educational needs of the child (*see Matter of Wilson A.T.Z. [Jose M.T.G.—Manuela Z.M.]*, 147 AD3d 962, 963 [2017]). The child testified that, although he was prevented from attending school by gang members who beat him while walking to school, the mother did not arrange for transportation, which was within her financial means, but instead, told him to stay home. Additionally, the child was expelled from one school due to excessive tardiness, and he failed the seventh grade (*see id.*; *see also Matter of Kiamal E. [Kim R.]*, 139 AD3d 1062, 1063 [2016]; *Matter of Justin R. [Gilbert R.]*, 127 AD3d 758, 759 [2015]). Further, the mother did not provide adequate supervision, often leaving the then eight-year-old child home alone at night in the neighborhood where he had encountered the gang violence (*see Matter of Alan B.*, 267 AD2d 306, 307 [1999]).

The child's remaining contentions either are without merit or need not be addressed in light of our determination.

Accordingly, the Family Court should have, upon renewal and reargument, granted that branch of the child's motion which was for a specific finding that reunification with one or both of his parents is not viable on the ground of parental neglect. Since the record is sufficient for this Court to make its own findings of fact and conclusions of law, we find that reunification of the child with one or both of his parents is not viable due to parental neglect (*see Matter of Varinder S. v Satwinder S.*, 147 AD3d 854, 856 [2017]). Roman, Hinds-Radix and LaSalle, JJ., concur.

Balkin, J.P., dissents, and votes to affirm the order insofar as appealed from, with the following memorandum: Under 8 USC § 1101 (a) (27) (J), as amended, a "special immigrant" is a resident alien who is, inter alia, under 21 years of age, unmarried, and dependent upon a juvenile court or legally committed to an individual appointed by a state or juvenile court (*see Matter of Trudy-Ann W. v Joan W.*, 73 AD3d 793, 795 [2010]). For juveniles to qualify for special immigrant juvenile status, courts must find that their reunification with one or both parents is not viable due to, among other things, parental abuse, neglect, or abandonment, and that it would not be in their best interests to be returned to their native country (*see Matter of Marvin E.M. de P. [Milagro C.C.—Mario Enrique M.G.], 121 AD3d 892,* 893 [2014]; *Matter of Trudy-Ann W. v Joan W.,* 73 AD3d at 795; 8 USC § 1101 [a] [27] [J]; 8 CFR 204.11 [c] [6]).

Here, the Family Court, upon renewal and reargument, declined to find that the mother abandoned, neglected, or abused the child. The court's finding rested, in large part, on its determination that the child was not credible. Although we have the power to conduct our own "independent factual review," we generally accord deference to the Family Court's credibility determinations and are reluctant to disturb them unless they are clearly unsupported by the record (*see Matter of Porter v Moore, 149 AD3d 1082,* 1083 [2017]; *Matter of Andrew R. [Andrew R.], 146 AD3d 709,* 710 [2017]; *Matter of Brandon V., 133 AD3d 769,* 769-770 [2015]). I find no basis on this record to reject the court's credibility determinations, which the court explained in detail, both in its original determination of March 29, 2016, and in its order upon renewal and reargument dated August 22, 2016. Moreover, even aside from the court's credibility determinations as to the child, I agree with the court's well-founded conclusion that the mother has always been, and continues to be, a resource for her son.

Accordingly, I would affirm that part of the Family Court's order as declined to find that reunification of the child with his mother is not viable on the basis of neglect, abandonment, or abuse (*see Matter of Christian P.S.-A. [Humberto R.S.-B.—Laura S.A.-C.], 148 AD3d 1032,* 1034 [2017]).

☐ **In the Matter of Dennis X.G.D.V., Appellant.**

158 A.D.3d 712 (2d Dep't Feb 14, 2018)

Fried, Frank, Harris, Shriver & Jacobson, LLP, New York, NY (Jennifer L. Colyer and Michael P. Sternheim of counsel), for appellant.

Motion by the appellant, inter alia, for leave to reargue an appeal from an order of the Family Court, Queens County, dated August 22, 2016, which was determined by decision and order of this Court dated August 9, 2017.

Upon the papers filed in support of the motion and no papers having been filed in opposition or in relation thereto, it is

Ordered that the motion is granted to the extent that leave to reargue is granted, and upon reargument, the decision and order of this Court dated August 9, 2017, is recalled and vacated, the following decision and order is substituted therefor, nunc pro tunc to August 9, 2017 (153 AD3d 628), and the motion is otherwise denied:

Appeal by the child from an order of the Family Court, Queens County (Nicolette M. Pach, J.H.O.), dated August 22, 2016. The order, insofar as appealed from, upon renewal and reargument, adhered to the original determination in a prior order of that court dated March 29, 2016, in effect, denying that branch of the child's motion which was for a specific finding that reunification of the child with one or both of his parents is not viable due to parental neglect.

Ordered that the order dated August 22, 2016, is reversed insofar as appealed from, on the facts, without costs or disbursements, upon renewal and reargument, the determination in the order dated March 29, 2016, in effect, denying that branch of the child's motion which was for a specific finding that reunification of the child with one or both of his parents is not viable due to parental neglect is vacated, that branch of the motion is granted, it is found that reunification of the child with one or both of his parents is not viable due to parental neglect, and the matter is remitted to the Family Court, Queens County, for the entry of an order making the requisite declaration and specific findings so as to enable the child to petition the United States Citizenship and Immigration Services for special immigrant juvenile status, which includes the finding that reunification of the child with one or both of his parents is not viable on the ground of parental neglect.

In April 2015, Dennis X.G.D.V. (hereinafter the child) filed a petition pursuant to Family Court Act article 6 for the father to be appointed as his guardian. The child subsequently moved for the issuance of an order making the requisite declaration and specific findings so as to enable him to petition the United States Citizenship and Immigration Services for special immigrant juvenile status (hereinafter SIJS) pursuant to 8 USC § 1101 (a) (27) (J). In an order dated March 29, 2016, made after a hearing, the Family Court found that the child was under 21 years of age, unmarried, and dependent on the court, and that it would not be in his best interests to be returned to El Salvador, his previous country of nationality and last habitual residence. However, the court, in effect, denied that branch of the child's motion which was for a specific finding that reunification of the child with one or both of his parents is not viable on the ground of parental neglect. Thereafter, the child moved for leave to renew and reargue that branch of his prior motion. In an order dated August 22, 2016, the court, upon renewal and reargument, adhered to the original determination in the order dated March 29, 2016.

Pursuant to 8 USC § 1101 (a) (27) (J) (as amended by the William Wilberforce Trafficking Victims Protection Reauthorization Act of 2008, Pub L 110-457, 122 US Stat 5044) and 8 CFR 204.11, a "special immigrant" is a resident alien who, inter alia, is under 21 years of age, is unmarried, and has been legally committed to, or placed under the custody of, an individual appointed by a state or juvenile court. Additionally, for a juvenile to qualify for SIJS, a court must find that reunification of the juvenile with one or both of the juvenile's parents is not viable due to parental abuse, neglect, abandonment, or a similar basis found under state law (*see* 8 USC § 1101 [a] [27] [J] [i]; *Matter of Marvin E.M. de P. [Milagro C.C.—Mario Enrique M.G.]*, 121 AD3d 892, 893 [2014]; *Matter of Maria P.E.A. v Sergio A.G.G.*, 111 AD3d 619, 620 [2013]; *Matter of Trudy-Ann W. v Joan W.*, 73 AD3d 793, 795 [2010]), and that it would not be in the juvenile's best interests to be returned to his or her native country or country of last habitual residence (*see* 8 USC § 1101 [a] [27] [J] [ii]; 8 CFR 204.11 [c] [6]; *Matter of Marvin E.M. de P. [Milagro C.C.—Mario Enrique M.G.]*, 121 AD3d at 893; *Matter of Maria P.E.A. v Sergio A.G.G.*, 111 AD3d at 620; *Matter of Trudy-Ann W. v Joan W.*, 73 AD3d at 795).

While the credibility assessment of a hearing court is accorded considerable deference on appeal (*see Matter of Arthur G. [Tiffany M.]*, 112 AD3d 925, 926 [2013]; *Matter of Marte v Biondo*, 104 AD3d 947 [2013]; *Matter of Aranova v Aranov*, 77 AD3d 740, 741 [2010]), where, as here, the Family Court's credibility determination is not supported by the record, this Court is free to make its own credibility assessments and overturn the determination of the hearing court (*see Matter of Jasmine W. [Michael J.]*, 132 AD3d 774, 775 [2015]; *Matter of Arthur G. [Tiffany M.]*, 112 AD3d at 926; *Matter of Serenity S. [Tyesha A.]*, 89 AD3d 737, 739 [2011]). Based upon our independent factual review, we conclude that the record supports a finding that reunification of the child with his mother is not a viable option based upon parental neglect. The record reflects that the mother failed to meet the educational needs of the child (*see Matter of Wilson A.T.Z. [Jose M.T.G.—Manuela Z.M.]*, 147 AD3d 962, 963 [2017]). The child testified that, although he was prevented from attending school by gang members who beat him while walking to school, the mother did not arrange for transportation, which was within her financial means, but instead, told him to stay home. Additionally, the child was expelled from one school due to excessive tardiness, and he failed the seventh grade (*see id.*; *see also Matter of Kiamal E. [Kim R.]*, 139 AD3d 1062, 1063 [2016]; *Matter of Justin R. [Gilbert R.]*, 127 AD3d 758, 759 [2015]). Further, the mother did not provide adequate supervision, often leaving the then eight-year-old child home alone at night in the neighborhood where he had encountered the gang violence (*see Matter of Alan B.*, 267 AD2d 306, 307 [1999]).

The child's remaining contentions either are without merit or need not be addressed in light of our determination.

Accordingly, the Family Court should have, upon renewal and reargument, granted that branch of the child's motion which was for a specific finding that reunification with one or both of his parents is not viable on the ground of parental neglect. Since the record is sufficient for this Court to make its own findings of fact and conclusions of law, we find that reunification of the child with one or both of his parents is not viable due to parental neglect (*see Matter of Varinder S. v Satwinder S.*, 147 AD3d 854, 856 [2017]). Roman, Hinds-Radix and LaSalle, JJ., concur.

Balkin, J.P., dissents, and votes to affirm the order insofar as appealed from, with the following memorandaum: Under 8 USC § 1101 (a) (27) (J), as amended, a "special immigrant" is a resident alien who is, inter alia, under 21 years of age, unmarried, and dependent upon a juvenile court or legally committed to an individual appointed by a state or juvenile court (*see Matter of Trudy-Ann W. v Joan W.*, 73 AD3d 793, 795 [2010]). For juveniles to qualify for special immigrant juvenile status, courts must find that their reunification with one or both parents is not viable due to, among other things, parental abuse, neglect, or abandonment, and that it would not be in their best interests to be returned to their native country (*see Matter of Marvin E.M. de P. [Milagro C.C.—Mario Enrique M.G.]*, 121 AD3d 892, 893 [2014]; *Matter of Trudy-Ann*

W. v Joan W., 73 AD3d at 795; 8 USC § 1101 [a] [27] [J]; 8 CFR 204.11 [c] [6]).

Here, the Family Court, upon renewal and reargument, declined to find that the mother abandoned, neglected, or abused the child. The court's finding rested, in large part, on its determination that the child was not credible. Although we have the power to conduct our own "independent factual review," we generally accord deference to the Family Court's credibility determinations and are reluctant to disturb them unless they are clearly unsupported by the record (*see Matter of Porter v Moore*, 149 AD3d 1082, 1083 [2017]; *Matter of Andrew R. [Andrew R.]*, 146 AD3d 709, 710 [2017]; *Matter of Brandon V.*, 133 AD3d 769, 769-770 [2015]). I find no basis on this record to reject the court's credibility determinations, which the court explained in detail, both in its original determination of March 29, 2016, and in its order upon renewal and reargument dated August 22, 2016. Moreover, even aside from the court's credibility determinations as to the child, I agree with the court's well-founded conclusion that the mother has always been, and continues to be, a resource for her son.

Accordingly, I would affirm that part of the Family Court's order as declined to find that reunification of the child with his mother is not viable on the basis of neglect, abandonment, or abuse (*see Matter of Christian P.S.-A. [Humberto R.S.-B.—Laura S.A.-C.]*, 148 AD3d 1032, 1034 [2017]).

☐ In the Matter of Nelson A.G.-L. Maria Y.G.S., Appellant.

---

157 A.D 3d 789 (2nd Dep't January 17, 2018)

Immigration Legal Services of Long Island, Inc., Water Mill, NY (Carlos Piovanetti and Patricia Weiss of counsel), for appellant.

Laurette Mulry, Central Islip, NY (John B. Belmonte of counsel), attorney for the child.

Appeal from an order of the Family Court, Suffolk County (George F. Harkin, J.), dated July 31, 2017. The order, insofar as appealed from, after a hearing, denied the petitioner's motion for the issuance of an order, inter alia, making specific findings so as to enable the subject child to petition the United States Citizenship and Immigration Services for special immigrant juvenile status pursuant to 8 USC § 1101 (a) (27) (J).

Ordered that the order is reversed insofar as appealed from, on the facts, without costs or disbursements, the petitioner's motion for the issuance of an order, inter alia, making specific findings so as to enable the subject child to petition the United States Citizenship and Immigration Services for special immigrant juvenile status pursuant to 8 USC § 1101 (a) (27) (J) is granted, and it is found that reunification of the subject child with his parents is not viable due to parental neglect and abandonment.

In December 2016, Maria Y.G.S. (hereinafter the petitioner) filed a petition pursuant to Family Court Act article 6 to be appointed as guardian of Nelson A.G.-L. (hereinafter the child), a native of El Salvador, for the purpose of obtaining an order declaring that the child was dependent on the Family Court and making specific findings that he was unmarried and under 21 years of age, that reunification with one or both of his parents is not viable due to parental neglect and abandonment, and that it would not be in his best interests to be returned to his previous country of nationality and last habitual residence, so as to enable the child to petition the United States Citizenship and Immigration Services (hereinafter USCIS) for special immigrant juvenile status (hereinafter SIJS) pursuant to 8 USC § 1101 (a) (27) (J). Thereafter, the petitioner moved for the issuance of an order making the requisite declaration and specific findings so as to enable the child to petition for SIJS. In an order dated July 31, 2017, made after a hearing, the court, inter alia, denied the petitioner's motion on the basis that, although the child was under 21, unmarried, and dependent on the Family Court, and that it was not in his best interests to be returned to El Salvador, the evidence did not establish that reunification of the child with one or both of his parents was not viable due to parental neglect and abandonment. The petitioner appeals.

"Pursuant to 8 USC § 1101 (a) (27) (J) (as amended by the William Wilberforce Trafficking Victims Protection Reauthorization Act of 2008, Pub L 110-457, 122 US Stat 5044) and 8 CFR 204.11, a special immigrant is a resident alien who is, inter alia, under 21 years of age, unmarried, and dependent upon a juvenile court or legally committed to an individual appointed by a state or juvenile court" (*Matter of Trudy-Ann W. v Joan W.*, 73 AD3d 793, 795 [2010] [internal quotation marks omitted]; *see Matter of Gurwinder S.*, 155 AD3d 959 [2017]; *Matter of Maria P.E.A. v Sergio A.G.G.*, 111 AD3d 619, 620 [2013]). "Additionally, for a juvenile to qualify for special immigrant juvenile status, a court must find that reunification of the juvenile with one or both of the juvenile's parents is not viable due to parental abuse, neglect, abandonment, or similar parental conduct defined under State law, and that it would not be in the juvenile's best interest to be returned to his or her native country or country of last habitual residence" (*Matter of Marvin E.M. de P. [Milagro C.C.—Mario Enrique M.G.]*, 121 AD3d 892, 893 [2014]; *see Matter of Maria P.E.A. v Sergio A.G.G.*, 111 AD3d at 620; *Matter of Trudy-Ann W. v Joan W.*, 73 AD3d at 795).

"Only once a state juvenile court has issued this factual predicate order may the child, or someone acting on his or her behalf, petition the [USCIS] for SIJS" (*Matter of Marisol N.H.*, 115 AD3d 185, 188-189 [2014]). "Ultimately, the determination of whether to grant SIJS to a particular juvenile rests with USCIS and its parent agency, the Department of Homeland Security" (*Matter of Enis A.C.M. [Blanca E.M.—Carlos V.C.P.]*, 152 AD3d 690, 692 [2017]).

Consequently, the state or juvenile court is not making an immigration determination when it makes the requisite SIJS findings (*see id.* at 692).

Based upon our independent factual review, we conclude that the record supports a finding that reunification of the child with one or both of his parents is not viable due to parental neglect and abandonment (*see Matter of Dennis X.G.D.V.*, 153 AD3d 628, 630 [2017]; *Matter of Enis A.C.M. [Blanca E.M.—Carlos V.C.P.]*, 152 AD3d at 692; *Matter of Oscar J.L.J. [Segundo R.L.T.]*, 151 AD3d 969 [2017]). The child testified that, while in El Salvador, although he was approached by gang members to join their gang during his walk to school, his parents did not make any arrangements for his transportation to and from school to ensure his safety or do anything to deter such recruitment activities although aware of such activities and the fact that a neighborhood boy, who resisted the gang's efforts, was killed while traveling to another village (*see Matter of Dennis X.G.D.V.*, 153 AD3d at 630). Moreover, the child testified that his parents strongly encouraged him to leave the family home in El Salvador but did not provide alternate living arrangements and have not supported him since his arrival in New York.

Accordingly, the Family Court should have granted the petitioner's motion for the issuance of an order, inter alia, making specific findings so as to enable the child to petition for SIJS. Since the record is sufficient for this Court to make its own findings of fact and conclusions of law, we find that reunification of the child with one or both of his parents is not viable due to parental neglect and abandonment. Austin, J.P., Sgroi, Hinds-Radix and Iannacci, JJ., concur.

24. In guardianship proceedings, service upon an out-of-state parent is not statutorily required.

☐ **In the Matter of Alonso R.L.V. Berlin J.V.Y., Appellant; Misael L.V.,**

Respondent.

147 A.D. 3d 1070 (2nd Dep't February 22, 2017)

Bruno J. Bembi, Hempstead, NY, for petitioner-appellant.

Appeal by the mother from an order of the Family Court, Queens County (Craig Ramseur, Ct. Atty. Ref.), dated September 29, 2016. The order denied the mother's motion to dispense with service of the petition on the father.

Ordered that on the Court's own motion, the notice of appeal is deemed to be an application for leave to appeal, and leave to appeal is granted (see Family Ct Act § 1112 [a]); and it is further,

Ordered that the order is affirmed, without costs or disbursements.

In February 2016, the mother commenced this proceeding pursuant to Family Court Act article 6 to be appointed as guardian for Alonso R.L.V. (hereinafter the child), for the purpose of obtaining an order making the requisite declaration and specific findings to enable the child to petition the United States Citizenship and Immigration Services for special immigrant juvenile status pursuant to 8 USC § 1101 (a) (27) (J). Thereafter, the mother moved to dispense with service of the petition on the father. In an order dated September 29, 2016, the Family Court denied the motion.

Contrary to the mother's contention, the Family Court providently exercised its discretion in denying her motion to dispense with service of the petition on the father. Family Court Act § 661 (a) provides that "[w]hen making a determination regarding the guardianship of the person of a minor or infant, the provisions of the surrogate's court procedure act [hereinafter SCPA] shall apply to the extent they are applicable to guardianship of the person of a minor or infant and do not conflict with the specific provisions of this act." Pursuant to

SCPA 1705, "[u]pon presentation of the petition process shall issue .□□ [t]o the parents .□□ if such persons are within the state and their residences therein are known" (SCPA 1705 [1]). Since the father lives outside the state, service of the petition on him is not statutorily required. Nevertheless, the Family Court possesses discretion to issue process to any relative "domiciled in its county *or elsewhere*" (SCPA 1705 [3] [emphasis added]). The mother's remaining contentions are without merit. Under the circumstances presented, the Family Court appropriately exercised its discretion in denying the mother's motion to dispense with service of the petition on the father. Chambers, J.P., Roman, LaSalle and Barros, JJ., concur.

25. It must only be shown that reunification with one parent is not possible in order for the family court to approve a motion for special findings.

In the Matter of Marcelina M.-G., Appellant,

v

Israel S. et al., Respondents. Susy M.-G., Nonparty Appellant.

---

112 A.D. 3d 100 (2nd Dep't October 23, 2013)

Second Department, October 23, 2013

APPEARANCES OF COUNSEL

Helene Migdon Greenberg, Elmsford, for petitioner-appellant.

Paul Hastings LLP, New York City (*Kevin Broughel* and *Shafiq R. Perry* of counsel), for nonparty appellant.

Stephen Kolnik, Yonkers, for respondent Francisco G.

OPINION OF THE COURT

Roman, J.

Introduction

In 1990, Congress enacted the special immigrant juvenile provisions of the Immigration and Nationality Act (*see* 8 USC § 1101 [a] [27] [J], as added by Pub L 101-649, § 153, 104 US Stat 4978 [101st Cong, 2d Sess, Nov. 29, 1990]), which provide a gateway for undocumented children who have been abused, neglected, or abandoned to obtain lawful permanent residency in the United States. Prior to petitioning the relevant federal agency for special immigrant juvenile status, an immigrant juvenile must obtain an order from a state juvenile court making findings that the juvenile satisfies certain criteria. Among those findings is a determination that reunification with "1 or both" of the juvenile's parents "is not viable due to abuse, neglect, abandonment, or a similar basis found under State law" (8 USC § 1101 [a] [27] [J] [i]). The principal issue presented on this appeal is whether a juvenile may satisfy this statutory reunification requirement when the juvenile court determines that reunification is not viable with just one, as opposed to both, of the juvenile's parents. For the reasons that follow, we conclude that the "1 or both" language requires only a finding that reunification is not viable with one parent.

Factual and Procedural Background

Susy M.-G. was born in November 1994, in Honduras. As recounted in Susy's affidavit in support of her motion, she lived alone with her mother, Marcelina M.-G., until she was about six years old. At that time, the mother's boyfriend "Tony" began living with them part-time. Susy indicated that Tony was "mean and violent" toward her. Her mother "threw [Tony] out of [the] house" prior to the birth of Susy's half-brother Jason in November 2001.

When Susy was about 10 years old, her mother left Honduras to work in the United States. The mother had told Susy that "[s]he was leaving in three days," and that Susy and Jason would be going to live with their aunt "Estella." Susy asserted that "[l]ife at Estella's was miserable." According to Susy, "Estella was physically violent and verbally abusive" toward her, as were Susy's cousins. "Estella would smack [Susy] with whatever she could find, for no good reason at all," and called her names, including telling Susy that she was a "whore." Estella also used the money that Susy's mother sent for Susy for Estella's own family.

Susy averred that she had never lived with her father, Israel, whose last name she did not know. According to Susy, her mother said that the father was an alcoholic and violent toward the mother, and that they were "better off without him." Susy indicated that she did not think that her father had ever supported her or her mother financially, and that her father "never was present in [her] life." Although Susy indicated that she talked to her father "on the phone sometimes," she stated that they were "not close."

In 2008, Susy arranged for herself and her younger brother to travel to the United States with the help of "coyotes" (smugglers), because "[l]ife with Estella was unbearable." When Susy told her mother about this plan, her mother was initially "not happy at all with us coming to the United States," but eventually "relented and asked her boyfriend to help pay for the trip." Susy indicated that during the "very long trip," they "traveled with different people and smugglers by bus and car," and that they "had to sleep in strange places on the way." She explained that when they arrived at the United States-Mexico border, they tried crossing, but the coyotes saw border patrol and ordered them to run away back toward Mexico. They crossed the border into the United States on their next attempt, but were pursued by the border patrol. "Everyone started running" in different directions, and Susy lost sight of Jason. When Susy heard that Jason had been picked up, she back-tracked so that he would not be alone, and she was detained by border patrol.

Susy and Jason were taken to a group home where they remained for about three days, and were then transferred to a foster home in Texas. After approximately 80 days, Susy's uncle, Francisco G., arrived, and took Susy and her brother to New York to stay with Francisco and his family. Francisco enrolled Susy and Jason in school. With respect to her living situation, Susy explained as follows:

"At first it was hard adjusting to a new place and a new language but I now feel a lot more comfortable in the United States and I have friends. It is the first time I feel safe and taken care of as a child—it is a wonderful feeling to be provided for and be part of a loving family. I see my mother who lives close by with her boyfriend and their baby daughter but my caretaker and head of family is Francisco. I am happy living with him and his family."

The Guardianship Petition and Motion for Special Findings

On or about December 17, 2009, Francisco, who resided in Westchester County, filed a petition seeking his appointment as Susy's guardian. The petition alleged, among other things, that Susy's birth parents, although living, should not be appointed guardian of the person of the child, since the father had never been a part of her life and had never provided for her, and the mother had abandoned Susy in Honduras along with her younger brother Jason. Susy submitted a form indicating that she was more than 14 years of age and expressing a preference for the appointment of her uncle Francisco as her guardian.

In December 2009, Francisco also filed a petition to be appointed guardian of Susy's younger brother, Jason.

On or about December 23, 2009, Susy moved for the issuance of an order making the requisite declaration and specific findings that would allow her to apply to the United States Citizenship and Immigration Services for special immigrant juvenile status pursuant to 8 USC § 1101 (a) (27) (J). In support of the motion, Susy alleged that she was under 21 years of age, unmarried, and dependent upon the Family Court in that the court had accepted jurisdiction over the matter of her guardianship, and her parents had effectively relinquished control over her. Additionally, Susy maintained that reunification with one or both of her parents was not viable due to neglect and abandonment. Specifically, Susy alleged that her father had abandoned her and had not provided any financial support or parental guidance. In addition, Susy asserted that her mother had neglected her by failing to provide her with adequate food, clothing, shelter, and education in Honduras, and by allowing her to travel unaccompanied to the United States. Lastly, she alleged that her mother had abandoned her by failing to provide her with any substantial financial assistance or provisions since she arrived in the United States.

In support of her motion, Susy submitted her affidavit and birth certificate, as well as her brother's affidavit. In addition, Susy submitted an affidavit from her mother. In her affidavit, the mother averred that Susy's father, Israel, "never was responsible—he drank, used drugs, and was violent towards [the mother], even breaking [her] nose once." The mother asserted that the father had "never been involved in [Susy's] life," and had also "never shown an interest in being involved in [the child's] life, or offered to pay for her expenses in any way." The mother also indicated that her former boyfriend, Jason's father, had "beat[en]" the child.

The mother stated that when she lived in Honduras, she had relied on her sister Estella to take care of her children while she worked. She was aware that Estella had hit Susy, and that Estella would deprive the child of meals as a punishment. The mother indicated that she "continued to have Estella take care of [Susy] because [she] had no other choice."

The mother acknowledged having left her children in the care of Estella when she left Honduras and immigrated to the United States in 2004. The mother stated that after she left Honduras, "Susy related on several occasions that Estella beat her frequently and permitted her daughters to hit her as well. She also told [the mother] that Estella would frequently not feed [Susy and Jason], and only provided them with one meal a day on average." The mother indicated that she sent money to Estella to pay for room and board for the children, and to cover expenses such as medical bills for Jason and school clothes.

According to the mother, in 2008, Susy informed her that she had contacted a "coyote" about transporting her and Jason to the United States. "Although [the mother] did not want them to come to the United States," she "was afraid [Susy] otherwise would run away from home," so she "agreed to speak to the coyote and pay him to bring Jason and Susy to the United States." The mother ultimately learned from immigration authorities that the children had been arrested. The mother noted that her brother-in-law, Francisco, agreed to pick up the children in Texas and bring them back to live with him and his family. The mother asserted that she currently lived with her youngest daughter in a small apartment in the same town as Francisco, and that she did not have the resources to support Susy or Jason. She indicated that the children were "very happy" living with Francisco and his family, and that she wanted them "to stay with their Aunt and Uncle," noting that "it [was] much better for them than to be with [her]."

In further support of her motion for an order of special findings, Susy submitted a letter from a licensed clinical social worker, Maribel Rivera, dated December 9, 2009. Rivera stated that Susy was attending individual psychotherapy sessions, and had been diagnosed with post-traumatic stress disorder and "depressed mood due to multiple changes in her life." Susy also submitted a "Record of Deportable/Inadmissible Alien" document issued by the United States Department of Homeland Security, which reflected, inter alia, that Susy was apprehended on August 19, 2008, at or near Rio Grande City, Texas.

The Mother's Custody Petition

Although the mother had initially supported Francisco's application for guardianship of Susy, in May 2011, the mother filed a petition for custody of Susy. The mother indicated that she resided in Westchester County, and that it would be in Susy's best interests to have custody awarded to her because the father was not involved in the child's life, and the child "want[ed] to live with [the] mother." The mother also submitted a memorandum of law in support of Susy's motion for special findings.

The Family Court's Determination

At a court appearance on June 21, 2011, the Family Court, inter alia, granted the mother's petition for sole custody of Susy and, as a result, dismissed Francisco's petition for guardianship of the child. In addition, the court denied Susy's motion for a special findings order. Counsel for the mother argued that because Susy had been neglected by her father, she was eligible for special findings under "the new law" even though the mother obtained custody. The court responded, "I think that is a strained reading of a statute. I think that it is a bending over more than backwards in order to create an artificial citizenship, frankly, and I will not make a special finding." The court indicated that Susy was "with her natural parent," and that she "doesn't need them both."

On September 13, 2011, the Family Court issued an order granting the mother's petition for custody, denying Susy's motion for a special findings order, and reciting that Francisco withdrew his guardianship petition.

Special Immigrant Juvenile Status

On appeal, Susy and the mother contend that the Family Court erred in denying Susy's motion for an order of special findings on the basis that custody was awarded to the mother. They argue that the court's determination was contrary to the plain language of the special immigrant juvenile status (hereinafter SIJS) statute, which permits SIJS eligibility where, as here, reunification is not viable with one of the child's parents. Additionally, Susy and her mother contend that Susy satisfied the other eligibility requirements for SIJS and, therefore, Susy's motion should have been granted.

The SIJS provisions of the Immigration and Nationality Act were enacted by Congress in 1990 (*see* 8 USC § 1101 [a] [27] [J], as added by Pub L 101-649, § 153, 104 US Stat 4978; *Matter of Hei Ting C.*, 109 AD3d 100 [2013]; *see also Yeboah v United States Dept. of Justice*, 345 F3d 216, 221 [3d Cir 2003]; *Perez-Olano v Gonzalez*, 248 FRD 248, 252 [CD Cal 2008]). Under the statute, immigrant juveniles, or any person acting on their behalf (*see* 8 CFR 204.11 [b]), may petition the United States Citizenship and Immigration Services (hereinafter USCIS)[FN1] for SIJS (*see Matter of Hei Ting C.*, 109 AD3d at 102-103; *see also Perez-Olano v Gonzalez*, 248 FRD at 253). To be eligible for SIJS, an immigrant juvenile must obtain an order from a state juvenile court making findings that the juvenile satisfies certain criteria (*see* 8 CFR 204.11 [d]; *Perez-Olano v Gonzalez*, 248 FRD at 253). Once the state court makes an SIJS predicate order, a juvenile may apply to the USCIS for SIJS using an I-360 petition, and if the juvenile is granted SIJS, he or she may be considered for adjustment to lawful permanent resident status (*see Perez-*

Olano v Gonzalez, 248 FRD at 253; *In re Y.M.*, 207 Cal App 4th 892, 910, 144 Cal Rptr 3d 54, 67-68 [2012]; *see also* 8 CFR 204.11 [c] [7]).

At the time of the enactment of the statute in 1990, a state court's SIJS predicate order was required to find that (1) the juvenile was dependent on a juvenile court located in the United States and had been deemed eligible for long-term foster care, and (2) it would not be in the juvenile's best interest to be returned to the juvenile's or parent's home country (*see*Pub L 101-649, § 153, 104 US Stat 4978, 5005-5006; *Gao v Jenifer*, 185 F3d 548 [6th Cir 1999]; *Perez-Olano v Gonzalez*, 248 FRD at 265; *Matter of Hei Ting C.*, 109 AD3d at 102-103; *Matter of Mario S.*, 38 Misc 3d 444, 449 [Fam Ct, Queens County 2012]). In 1997, Congress amended the law out of concern that juveniles entering the United States as visiting students were abusing the SIJS process (*see Yeboah v United States Dept. of Justice*, 345 F3d at 221; *Perez-Olano v Gonzalez*, 248 FRD at 265 n 10; My Xuan T. Mai, *Children under the Radar: The Unique Plight of Special Immigrant Juveniles*, 12 Barry L Rev 241, 246 [spring 2009]). The amendments modified the SIJS definition to include an immigrant whom a juvenile court had "legally committed to, or placed under the custody of, an agency or department of a State," and added the requirement that the finding of eligibility for long-term foster care be "due to abuse, neglect, or abandonment" (Pub L 105-119, § 113, 111 US Stat 2440, 2460 [105th Cong, 1st Sess, Nov. 26, 1997]; *see Matter of Hei Ting C.*, 109 AD3d at 103; 3-35 Immigration Law and Procedure § 35.09 [1] [Matthew Bender 2013]). Congress also added consent provisions, requiring the express consent of the United States Attorney General to the dependency order, and providing that no juvenile court had jurisdiction to determine the custody status or placement of a juvenile in the actual or constructive custody of the Attorney General unless the Attorney General specifically consented to such jurisdiction (*see* Pub L 105-119, § 113, 111 US Stat 2440, 2460; *M.B. v Quarantillo*, 301 F3d 109, 114 [3d Cir 2002]; *F.L. v Thompson*, 293 F Supp 2d at 90). According to the House

Conference Report, the modifications in the statute were made "in order to limit the beneficiaries of this provision to those juveniles for whom it was created, namely abandoned, neglected, or abused children" (HR Rep 105-405, 105th Cong, 1st Sess at 130, reprinted in 1997 US Code Cong & Admin News at 2941, 2954; *see Yeboah v United States Dept. of Justice*, 345 F3d at 222; *Matter of Hei Ting C.*, 109 AD3d at 103).

In 2008, the requirements for SIJS were again amended, this time by the William Wilberforce Trafficking Victims Protection Reauthorization Act of 2008 (*see* Pub L 110-457, 122 US Stat 5044 [110th Cong, 2d Sess, Dec. 23, 2008]). The 2008 amendments expanded eligibility to include those immigrant children who had been placed in the custody of an individual or entity appointed by a state or juvenile court (*see* Pub L 110-457, 122 US Stat 5044, 5079; *Matter of Hei Ting C.*, 109 AD3d at 103-104). Congress also removed the requirement that the immigrant child had to be deemed eligible for long-term foster care due to abuse, neglect, or abandonment, and replaced it with a requirement that the juvenile court find that "reunification with 1 or both of the immigrant's parents is not viable due to abuse, neglect, abandonment, or a similar basis found under State law" (Pub L 110-457, 122 US Stat 5044, 5079; *see Matter of Hei Ting C.*, 109 AD3d at 104; *Matter of Mario S.*, 38 Misc 3d at 449). The amendments also modified the consent requirement by deleting the language requiring the Attorney General to "expressly consent[ ] to the dependency order," and replacing it with, "the Secretary of Homeland Security consents to the grant of special immigrant juvenile status" (Pub L 110-457, 122 US Stat 5044, 5079).[FN2]

Thus, under the current law, a "special immigrant" is a resident alien who is under 21 years of age, unmarried, and dependent on a juvenile court located in the United States or "legally committed to, or placed under the custody of, an agency or department of a State, or an individual or entity appointed by a State or juvenile court located in the United States" (8 USC § 1101 [a] [27] [J] [i]; *see* 8 CFR 204.11;[FN3] *Matter of Hei Ting C.*, 109 AD3d at 103-104; *Matter of Mario S.*, 38 Misc 3d at 450-451; *see also In re J.J.X.C.*, 318 Ga App 420, 424, 734 SE2d 120, 123 [2012]). Additionally, the court must find that "reunification with 1 or both of the immigrant's parents is not viable due to abuse, neglect, abandonment, or a similar basis found under State law," and "that it would not be in the alien's best interest to be returned to the alien's or parent's previous country of nationality or country of last habitual residence" (8 USC § 1101 [a] [27] [J] [i], [ii]; *see Matter of Hei Ting C.*, 109 AD3d at 104; *Matter of Nirmal S. v Rajinder K.*, 101 AD3d 1130, 1131 [2012]; *Matter of Mohamed B.*, 83 AD3d 829, 831 [2011]; *Matter of Trudy-Ann W. v Joan W.*, 73 AD3d 793, 795 [2010]).

By making these preliminary factual findings, the juvenile court is not rendering an immigration determination (*see In re Welfare of D.A.M.*, 2012 WL 6097225, *2, 2012 Minn App Unpub LEXIS 1158, *5 [2012]; *In re J.J.X.C.*, 318 Ga App at 424-425, 734 SE2d at 123; 3-35 Immigration Law and Procedure § 35.09 [3] [a] [Matthew Bender 2013]). Rather, "the final decision regarding [SIJS] rests with the federal government, and, as shown, the child must apply to that authority" (*In re J.J.X.C.*, 318 Ga App at 424-425, 734 SE2d at 123; *see* 8 USC § 1101 [a] [27] [J] [iii]).

Analysis

In the present case, we find that the Family Court erred in denying Susy's motion for the issuance of an order making a declaration and specific findings that would allow her to apply to the USCIS for SIJS. The record establishes that Susy is under 21 years of age and unmarried (*see* 8 CFR 204.11 [c] [1], [2]). Additionally, since the Family Court placed Susy in the custody of her mother, she has been "legally committed to, or placed under the custody of . . . an individual . . . appointed by a State or juvenile court located in the United

States[FN4]" (8 USC § 1101 [a] [27] [J] [i]; *see Matter of Ashley W. [Verdele F.]*, 85 AD3d 807, 809 [2011]; *Matter of Jisun L. v Young Sun P.*, 75 AD3d 510, 512 [2010]; *cf. Matter of Hei Ting C.*, 109 AD3d at 103-104).

With respect to the nonviability of reunification with one or both parents, the record reveals that Susy was abandoned by her father. Susy averred in her affidavit that she never lived with her father, and that she did not think he ever provided financial support. Although Susy indicated that she talked to her father "on the phone sometimes," she asserted that he had never been present in her life. Susy's mother confirmed in her affidavit that the father was never involved in Susy's life. According to the mother, the father "never was responsible—he drank, used drugs, and was violent towards [her]," and "had never shown an interest in being involved in Susy's life, or offered to pay for her expenses in any way." Thus, Susy established that reunification with her father was not viable due to abandonment (*see* 8 USC § 1101 [a] [27] [J] [i]; *Matter of Mohamed B.*, 83 AD3d at 832). The Family Court, as evidenced by its comments at the hearing, denied Susy's application for a special findings order on the ground that the viability of reunification with Susy's mother rendered Susy ineligible for SIJS. However, we disagree with the Family Court's interpretation of the reunification component of the statute.

"To interpret a statute, we first look to its plain language, as that represents the most compelling evidence of the Legislature's intent" (*Matter of Tompkins County Support Collection Unit v Chamberlin*, 99 NY2d 328, 335 [2003]; *see Brown v Maple3, LLC*, 88 AD3d 224, 231 [2011]; *Matter of Richardson v Richardson*, 80 AD3d 32, 37 [2010]). Under the plain language of the statute, to be eligible for SIJS, a court must find that "reunification with *1 or both* of the immigrant's parents is not viable due to abuse, neglect, abandonment, or a similar basis found under State law" (8 USC § 1101 [a] [27] [J] [i] [emphasis added]). We interpret the "1 or both" language to provide SIJS eligibility where reunification with just one parent is not viable as a result of abuse, neglect, abandonment, or a similar state law basis (*see In re Welfare of D.A.M.*, 2012 WL 6097225, *3, 2012 Minn App Unpub LEXIS 1158, *8-9 [2012] ["A possibility of reunification with one parent does not bar SIJS eligibility. Rather, even when reunification with one parent is viable, courts must determine the viability of reunification with the other parent"]; Angie Junck, *Special Immigrant Juvenile Status: Relief for Neglected, Abused, and Abandoned Undocumented Children*, 63 Juv & Fam Ct J 48, 56 [winter 2012] ["The 'one or both parents' language . . . signifies that the child need not be separated from both parents to be eligible for SIJS," and permits SIJS eligibility "even while the child remains in the care of the other parent or while the court is actively trying to reunite the child with the other parent"]; 3-35 Immigration Law and Procedure § 35.09 [3] [a] [Matthew Bender 2013]). Thus, contrary to the Family Court's determination, the fact that the mother was available as a custodial resource for Susy does not, by itself, preclude the issuance of special findings under the SIJS statute (*see Matter of Mario S.*, 38 Misc 3d at 454 ["Although respondent was able to be returned to the custody of his mother upon his discharge from agency custody and the jurisdiction of the Family Court, he was both dependent upon the Family Court and abandoned by his biological father at the time of the motion. The fact that respondent was returned to the care of his mother should not be determinative of his application for SIJ findings"]; *see also Matter of E.G.*, 24 Misc 3d 1238[A], 2009 NY Slip Op 51797[U], *3 [Fam Ct, Nassau County 2009] ["in light of the recent amendment to 8 USC § 1101 (a) (27) (J), a child may petition for SIJS even if there is a fit parent living abroad, so long as the minor has been abused, neglected or abandoned by *one* parent"]).

The legislative history of the SIJS statute supports this interpretation of the reunification requirement (*see Matter of Tompkins County Support Collection Unit v Chamberlin*, 99 NY2d at 335 ["the legislative history of an enactment may also be relevant and is not to be ignored, even if words be clear" (internal quotation marks omitted)]). As set forth above, prior to the 2008 amendments, the statute required a determination that the child was eligible for long-term foster care (*see* Pub L 105-119, § 113, 111 US Stat 2440, 2460). The phrase "[e]ligible for long-term foster care" meant a determination "by the juvenile court that family reunification is no longer a viable option" (8 CFR 204.11 [a]). Thus, under the former version of the statute, "SIJS was only available when reunification with *both* parents was not possible" (*In re Welfare of D.A.M.*, 2012 WL 6097225, *3, 2012 Minn App Unpub LEXIS 1158, *9 [2012]). "[B]y eliminating the long-term foster-care requirement and instead requiring only a finding that 'reunification with 1 or both' parents is not viable," the statute, as amended in 2008, "requires only a finding that reunification is not viable with one of the child's parents" (2012 WL 6097225, *4, 2012 Minn App Unpub LEXIS 1158, *10 [emphasis omitted], quoting Pub L 110-457, 122 US Stat 5044).

The expansion in the definition of SIJS to allow a juvenile court to consider the nonviability of family reunification with just one parent, rather than both, permits "more vulnerable and mistreated children to qualify for this form of legal relief" (Deborah Lee et al., *Practice Advisory, Update on Legal Relief Options for Unaccompanied Alien Children Following the Enactment of the William Wilberforce Trafficking Victims Protection Reauthorization Act of 2008* at 4 [Feb. 19, 2009], available at http://www.ilrc.org/files/235_tvpra_practice_advisory.infonet.pdf). Notably, despite the expansion in SIJS eligibility under the 2008 amendments, the number of immigrant youths who have obtained lawful permanent residency through SIJS has remained relatively low when compared to the total number of immigrants under age 21 who have obtained lawful permanent residency since 2008 (*see* Department of Homeland Security, Yearbooks of Immigration Statistics, 2009-2012 [Tables 7-8], available at http://www.dhs.gov/yearbook-immigration-statistics; *see also* Angie Junck, *Special Immigrant Juvenile Status: Relief for Neglected, Abused, and Abandoned Undocumented Children*, 63 Juv & Fam Ct J at 52 ["SIJS was created over 20 years ago, but it is still an underused form of immigration relief"]; Kristen Jackson, *Special Status Seekers: Through the Underused SIJS Process, Immigrant Juveniles May Obtain Legal Status*, 34 Los Angeles Lawyer 20, 22 [Feb. 2012], available at http://www.lacba.org/Files/LAL/Vol34No11/2893.pdf [stating, with respect to the 2010 statistics, that "(r)ather than a flood anticipated by some SIJS detractors, the number of SIJS grantees has been only a trickle"]). In 2012, of the 258,554 immigrants under age 21 who obtained lawful permanent residency, only 2,280, or less than one percent, did so through SIJS (*see* Department of Homeland Security, Yearbook of Immigration Statistics: 2012 Legal Permanent Residents [Tables 7-8], available at http://www.dhs.gov/yearbook-immigration-statistics-2012-legal-permanent-residents).

We note while we find a literal reading of the phrase "1 or both" to be supported by the plain language of the statute, the Supreme Court of Nebraska has declined to adopt a literal reading of the phrase (*see In re Erick M.*, 284 Neb 340, 352, 820 NW2d 639, 648 [2012]). In *Erick M.*, the court found the phrase "1 or both" to be ambiguous because it can reasonably be interpreted "to mean that a juvenile court must find, depending on the circumstances, that *either* reunification with one parent is not feasible *or* reunification with both parents is not feasible" (*In re Erick M.*, 284 Neb at 345, 820 NW2d at 644). After holding that courts "should generally consider whether reunification with either parent is feasible," the *Erick M.* court determined that the petitioner therein was not eligible for SIJS predicate findings because reunification with his mother was feasible (248 Neb at 341, 352, 820 NW2d at 642, 648).

Initially, to the extent the language of the statute can indeed be viewed as ambiguous, it has been held that "ambiguities in immigration statutes must be read in favor of the immigrant" (*Yu v Brown*, 92 F Supp 2d 1236, 1248 [D NM 2000], citing *INS v Cardoza-Fonseca*, 480 US 421, 449 [1987] [noting "the longstanding principle of construing any lingering ambiguities in deportation statutes in favor of the alien"]). In any event, for the reasons discussed, we decline to adopt the Nebraska Supreme Court's interpretation of the statute. Absent a grant of special findings in this case, Susy might face deportation to Honduras where her father has abandoned her and there appear to be no other fit relatives to care for her, essentially rendering the fact that the child has a fit parent in the United States immaterial. We believe this would be contrary to the purpose of the SIJS statute. "Indeed, the very reason for the existence of special immigrant juvenile status is to protect the applicant from further abuse or maltreatment by preventing him or her from being returned to a place where he or she is likely to suffer further abuse or neglect" (*Matter of Sing W.C. [Sing Y.C.—Wai M.C.]*, 83 AD3d 84, 91 [2011] [internal quotation marks omitted]).

Moreover, and indeed significantly, the findings by the state juvenile court "do not bestow any immigration status on SIJS applicants" (*In re Welfare of D.A.M.*, 2012 WL 6097225, *2, 2012 Minn App Unpub LEXIS 1158, *5 [2012]), but, instead, are prerequisites to applying for SIJS classification with the USCIS (*see id.*; *In re J.J.X.C.*, 318 Ga App at 424-425, 734 SE2d at 123-124; 3-35 Immigration Law and Procedure § 35.09 [3] [a] [Matthew Bender 2013] [noting that "in refusing to make SIJ findings where one parent was present, the Nebraska court blurred the federal and state roles under the SIJ statute," and that "(t)he decision has the troubling effect of precluding the USCIS from applying its interpretation of the federal statute to determine whether a youth would qualify in a particular case"]). As discussed above, the Secretary of Homeland Security ultimately must consent to the grant of SIJS (*see* 8 USC § 1101 [a] [27] [J] [iii]).

"The consent determination by the Secretary, through the USCIS District Director, is an acknowledgement that the request for SIJ classification is bona fide. This means that the SIJ benefit was not 'sought primarily for the purpose of obtaining the status of an alien lawfully admitted for permanent residence, rather than for the purpose of obtaining relief from abuse or neglect or abandonment' " (Mem of Donald Neufeld, USCIS Acting Associate Director, Domestic Operations, to Field Leadership, *Trafficking Victims Protection Reauthorization Act of 2008: Special Immigrant Juvenile Status Provisions* at 3 [Mar. 24, 2009], quoting HR Rep 105-405, 105th Cong, 1st Sess at 130 [1997], available at http://www.uscis.gov/sites/default/files/USCIS/Laws/Memoranda/Static_Files_Me moranda/2009/TVPRA_SIJ.pdf).

Thus, the USCIS ultimately "determines whether the applicant meets the requirements for SIJS under federal law," and "[i]ts decision whether to grant SIJS is discretionary" (*In re Welfare of D.A.M.*, 2012 WL 6097225, *2, 2012 Minn App Unpub LEXIS 1158, *5 [2012]; *see Matter of Mario S.*, 38 Misc 3d at 456 ["Whether or not a juvenile's application constitutes a potential abuse or misuse of the SIJ provisions of the immigration law is an issue to be determined by the USCIS"]). Indeed, the USCIS has approved SIJS applications where reunification with one parent was viable (*see* 3-35 Immigration Law and Procedure § 35.09 [3] [a] [Matthew Bender 2013]; Angie Junck, *Special Immigrant Juvenile Status*: *Relief for Neglected, Abused, and Abandoned Undocumented Children*, 63 Juv & Fam Ct J at 56). In sum, we find that Susy has satisfied the statute's reunification requirement by demonstrating that reunification with her father was not viable.

Turning to the best interests component, as discussed, the record shows that the father, who apparently continues to live in Honduras, abandoned Susy.

Additionally, Susy's aunt, Estella, with whom she previously lived in Honduras, was neglectful and abusive toward her. The mother stated that she had left Susy with Estella because she had no other alternative, which indicates that there are no other relatives available to care for Susy in Honduras. The record also reveals that the child has suffered psychological distress. By contrast, the record demonstrates that in the United States, Susy is attending school, has made friends, and has family members to care for her, including her mother, as well as her uncle and aunt. Under these circumstances, the record demonstrates that it would not be in the best interests of the child to return to Honduras (*see Matter of Alamgir A.*, 81 AD3d 937, 940 [2011] [finding that it was in the best interests of the child to continue living in the United States where the record reflected that in the child's native country of Bangladesh, he "would have nowhere to live, and no means of supporting himself"]; *Matter of Trudy-Ann W. v Joan W.*, 73 AD3d at 796).

Finally, it is not necessary to remit the matter for a hearing on Susy's application. "[W]here, as here, the record is sufficiently complete for us to make our own factual determinations, we may do so" (*Matter of Trudy-Ann W. v Joan W.*, 73 AD3d at 795 [internal quotation marks and citation omitted]; *see Matter of Alamgir A.*, 81 AD3d at 938-939; *Matter of Jisun L. v Young Sun P.*, 75 AD3d at 511-512). Therefore, based on the foregoing, we find that the Family Court erred in denying Susy's motion for the issuance of an order making a declaration and specific findings that would allow her to apply to the USCIS for SIJS.

Accordingly, the order is reversed insofar as appealed from, on the law and the facts, the motion is granted, it is declared that Susy is dependent on the Family Court, and it is found that she is unmarried and under 21 years of age, that reunification with one or both of her parents is not viable due to parental abuse, neglect, and abandonment, and that it would not be in Susy's best interests to return to Honduras, her previous country of nationality and last habitual residence.

Rivera, J.P., Dickerson and Leventhal, JJ., concur.

Ordered that the order is reversed insofar as appealed from, on the law and the facts, without costs or disbursements, the motion is granted, it is declared that Susy M.-G. is dependent on the Family Court, and it is found that Susy M.-G. is unmarried and under 21 years of age, that reunification with one or both of her parents is not viable due to parental abuse, neglect, and abandonment, and that it would not be in the best interests of Susy M.-G. to return to Honduras, her previous country of nationality and last habitual residence.

Footnotes

Footnote 1: The Homeland Security Act of 2002 (6 USC § 101 *et seq.*, as added by Pub L 107-296, 116 US Stat 2153), abolished the Immigration and Naturalization Service, and created the Department of Homeland Security (hereinafter the DHS). The USCIS, an agency within the DHS, assumed responsibility for the administration of SIJS benefit applications (*see Perez-Olano v Gonzalez*, 248 FRD at 253 n 2; *F.L. v Thompson*, 293 F Supp 2d 86, 91 [D DC 2003]).

Footnote 2: With respect to those juveniles in federal custody, the statute, as amended, provides that "no juvenile court has jurisdiction to determine the custody status or placement of an alien in the custody of the Secretary of Health and Human Services unless the Secretary of Health and Human Services specifically consents to such jurisdiction" (8 USC § 1101 [a] [27] [J] [iii] [I]).

Footnote 3: The federal regulations have not been updated to reflect the 2008 amendments to the SIJS statute (*see* 76 Fed Reg 54978 [2011], to be codified at 8

CFR parts 204, 205, 245; *In re Welfare of D.A.M.*, 2012 WL 6097225, *3 n 1, 2012 Minn App Unpub LEXIS 1158, *9-10 n 1 [Ct App, Dec. 10, 2012, No. A12-0427]).

Footnote 4: We note that this Court's recent decision in *Matter of Hei Ting C. (109 AD3d 100* [2013]), does not address the issue raised here. In *Matter of Hei Ting C.*, this Court held that a child support order does not satisfy the requirement in the SIJS statute that a child be " 'dependent on a juvenile court' " (*id.* at 102, quoting 8 USC § 1101 [a] [27] [J] [i]). By contrast, the present case, which involves a custody order, primarily concerns the interpretation of the statutory term "1 or both" (8 USC § 1101 [a] [27] [J] [i]).

26. The Third Department followed Matter of Marcelina M.—G.

Matter of Keilyn GG (Marlene HH)

159 A.D. 3d 1295 (3d Dep't March 29, 2018)

Calendar Date: March 27, 2018
Before: Egan Jr., J.P., Lynch, Devine, Clark and Mulvey, JJ.

―――――――――

Theo Liebmann, Hofstra Law Clinic, Hempstead, for appellant.

―――――――――

Clark, J.

Appeal from an order of the Family Court of Sullivan County (McGuire, J.), entered March 8, 2017, which, in a proceeding pursuant to Family Ct Act article 6, among other things, denied petitioner's motion for a special findings order pursuant to 8 USC § 1101 (a) (27) (J).

In January 2017, petitioner (hereinafter the mother) filed a petition seeking to be appointed guardian of her daughter, Keilyn[1] GG. (hereinafter the child). In support of the guardianship petition, the mother's attorney submitted an

[1
Family Court mispelled the child's name as Kellyn in the decision and order from which the child appeals.]

affirmation requesting that Family Court make specific findings in the order of guardianship that would allow the child to apply to the United States Citizenship and Immigration Services (hereinafter USCIS) for special immigrant juvenile status (hereinafter SIJS). Family Court granted the mother permanent letters of guardianship, but denied the request for an order making special findings for the purpose of filing an SIJS application. The child now appeals.

Before a child may seek SIJS from USCIS, a state court with jurisdiction over the juvenile must first issue a special findings order determining that (1) the child is under the age of 21, (2) the child is unmarried, (3) the child is dependent upon a juvenile court or legally committed to an individual appointed by that court, (4) reunification with one or both parents is not viable due to abuse, neglect, abandonment or a similar basis under state law and (5) it would not be in the child's best interests to return to his or her native country (see 8 USC § 1101 [a] [27] [J] [i], [ii]; Matter of Jose YY., 158 AD3d 200, 201 [2018]; Matter of Marlene G.H. [Maria G.G.U.–Pedro H.P.], 138

AD3d 843, 845 [2016]). By issuing a special findings order, Family Court is not rendering an immigration determination (see Matter of Jose YY., 158 AD3d at 201; Matter of Marisol N.H., 115 AD3d 185, 189 [2014]; Matter of Marcelina M.-G. v Israel S., 112 AD3d 100, 109 [2013]); such order is merely a step in the process to assist USCIS and its parent agency, the Department of Homeland Security, in making the ultimate immigration determination (see Matter of Enis A.C.M. [Blanca E.M.–Carlos V.C.P.], 152 AD3d 690, 692 [2017]; Matter of Marcelina M.-G. v Israel S., 112 AD3d at 109).

There is no dispute that the first two criteria are met here. Indeed, the child is under the age of 21, as she was born on March 31, 2000, and she is unmarried. However, as in Matter of Jose YY. (supra), Family Court denied the application for a special findings order after erroneously determining that the third, fourth and fifth criteria were not met. With respect to the third criterion, Family Court's appointment of the mother as the child's permanent guardian constitutes the necessary declaration of dependency on a juvenile court (see Matter of Enis A.C.M. [Blanca E.M.–Carlos V.C.P.], 152 AD3d at 691; Matter of Fatima J.A.J. [Ana A.J.S.–Carlos E.A.F.], 137 AD3d 912, 913-914 [2016]; Matter of Antowa McD., 50 AD3d 507, 507 [2008]).[2]

Turning to the fourth criterion, which requires that "reunification with 1 or both . . . parents . . . not [be] viable due to abuse, neglect, abandonment, or a similar basis found under [s]tate law" (8 USC § 1101 [a] [27] [J] [i]), Family Court mistakenly interpreted this statutory language to mean that reunification with both parents must be impossible. Based on a plain reading of the statute, we, like the Second Department, "interpret the '1 or both' language to provide SIJS eligibility where reunification with just one parent is not viable as a result of abuse, neglect, abandonment, or a similar state law basis" (Matter of Marcelina M.-G. v Israel S., 112 AD3d at 110 [emphasis added], quoting 8 USC § 1101 [a] [27] [J] [i]; see Matter of Marisol N.H., 115 AD3d at 190-191). "[T]he fact that the mother was available as a custodial resource for [the child] does not, by itself, preclude the issuance of special findings under the SIJS statute" (Matter of Marcelina M.-G. v Israel S., 112 AD3d at 111; see Matter of Fifo v Fifo, 127 AD3d 748, 751 [2015]; Matter of Karen C., 111 AD3d 622, 623 [2013]).

Notwithstanding Family Court's mistaken application of the fourth criterion, this Court's authority to review the evidence is as broad as that of Family Court, and we may make our own factual determinations if the record is sufficiently complete (see Matter of Marlene G.H. [Maria G.G.U.–Pedro H.P.], 138 AD3d at 845; Matter of Haide L.G.M. v Santo D.S.M., 130 AD3d 734, 736 [2015]). Based upon our independent factual review of the record, which includes the affidavits of the mother, the child and the child's maternal grandmother, as well as limited testimony, we find that reunification with the child's father is not a viable option. In her affidavit, the mother sets forth [2 Inasmuch as Family Court's order – and the letters of guardianship issued upon that order – did not specifically state that the guardianship shall extend until the age of 21, as the mother requested in her guardianship petition, we hereby modify the order and direct that the guardianship shall extend until the child reaches the age of 21.]

specific instances in which the father perpetrated severe domestic violence against her in the presence of the child, and stated that she fled Honduras – where the father resides – to escape his abuse. The grandmother confirmed the mother's account of severe domestic abuse perpetrated by the father. The mother left the child in the care of the maternal grandparents until the child was brought to the United States in 2007. The affidavits of the mother, the grandmother and the child all establish that, after the mother fled Honduras, the father never provided for the child emotionally, physically or financially. In the child's words, after the mother left Honduras, the father "was never a part of [her] life at all." Together, this record evidence fully supports the conclusion that the child was abandoned by her father and, thus, that reunification with him is not a viable option (see Matter of Cristal M.R.M., 118 AD3d 889, 891 [2014]; Matter of Marcelina M.-G. v. Israel S., 112 AD3d at 110; Matter of Karen C., 111 AD3d at 623).

As to the fifth and final criterion, our independent review of the testimony and affidavits establishes that the child's best interests are served by remaining in the United States. In determining whether it would be in the child's "best interest to be returned to [his or her or the] parent's previous country of nationality or country of last habitual residence" (8 USC § 1101 [a] [27] [J] [ii]), Family Court must balance a number of factors, including the child's safety and well-being in each country (see Matter of Jose YY., 158 AD3d at 202; Matter of Juan R.E.M. [Juan R.E.], 154 AD3d 725, 727 [2017]; Matter of Diaz v Munoz, 118 AD3d 989, 990 [2014]; Matter of Marcelina M.-G. v Israel S., 112 AD3d at 114-115), the availability of a place to live and someone to care for the child were the child returned to his or her native country or place of last habitual residence (see Matter of Jose YY., 158 AD3d at 202; Matter of Gabriela Y.U.M. [Palacios], 119 AD3d 581, 583-584 [2014]; Matter of Alamgir A., 81 AD3d 937, 940 [2011]; Matter of Trudy-Ann W. v Joan W., 73 AD3d 793, 796 [2010]) and the relative educational and employment opportunities available to the child (see Matter of Jose YY., 158 AD3d at 202; Matter of Marcelina M.–G. v Israel S., 112 AD3d at 115).

The record reflects that, if the child were returned to Honduras, she would have no one to care for her and no prospect of obtaining an education or securing employment (see Matter of Gabriela Y.U.M. [Palacios], 119 AD3d at 583-584; Matter of Alamgir A., 81 AD3d at 940; Matter of Trudy-Ann W. v Joan W., 73 AD3d at 796). The affidavits of the mother, the grandmother and the child further establish that, were the child to return to Honduras, she would be exposed to violence and live in constant fear of gangs (see Matter of Juan R.E.M. [Juan R.E.], 154 AD3d at 727; Matter of Diaz v Munoz, 118 AD3d at 990). In contrast, it was established that, in the United States, the child lives with her emotionally supportive mother, stepfather and half siblings in a safe home environment, where she has the opportunity to obtain a college degree. At the time of the hearing, the child was a high school student, employed at a fast food restaurant and involved in school athletics, her church and other extracurricular activities. The child stated that she dreamed of becoming a Spanish or early childhood education teacher. Considering the foregoing, we find that it would not be in the child's best interests to be returned to Honduras (see Matter of Jose YY., 158 AD3d at 202; Matter of Juan R.E.M. [Juan R.E.], 154 AD3d at 727; Matter of Gabriela Y.U.M. [Palacios], 119 AD3d at 583-584). Based upon all of the criteria having been established, Family Court should have granted the request for a special findings order.

Egan Jr., J.P., Lynch, Devine and Mulvey, JJ., concur. ORDERED that the order is modified, on the law, without costs, motion granted, it is declared, in accordance with 8 USC § 1101 (a) (27) (J), that: (1) the child is under 21 years of age; (2) the child is unmarried; (3) the child is dependent upon Family Court due to the March 2017 guardianship order issued pursuant to Family Ct Act § 661; (4) reunification of the child with her father is impossible due to the father's abandonment of the child; and (5) it is not in the child's best interests to be returned to Honduras, and petitioner's appointment as guardian of the child shall extend until the child reaches the age of 21; and, as so modified, affirmed.

ENTER:

> Robert D. Mayberger
>
> Clerk of the Court

27. A mother may petition for the guardianship of her own child.

In the Matter of Marisol N.H., Appellant. (Proceeding No. 1.)
In the Matter of Samuel D.H., Appellant. (Proceeding No. 2.)
In the Matter of Silvia J.H., Appellant. (Proceeding No. 3.)

115 A.D. 3d 185 (2nd Dep't February 5, 2014)

Second Department, February 5, 2014

APPEARANCES OF COUNSEL

Theo Liebmann, Hempstead, for appellants.

OPINION OF THE COURT

Chambers, J.

On this appeal, we conclude that the subject children, facing the possibility of being separated from their only parent and returned to their native country where gang members have threatened their lives, may seek to have their natural mother appointed as their guardian as a first step toward obtaining legal residency in the United States.

The subject children, Samuel D.H., Marisol N.H., and Silvia J.H., ages 19, 18, and 16, respectively, were born in El Salvador to Miriam A.G. (hereinafter the mother) and Leonidas H. (hereinafter the father). According to the allegations made in support of the petitions, the father drank often, and he verbally and physically abused the mother. When Samuel was just four years old, the mother left the father, taking the children with her to her mother's home. The father never again had meaningful contact with the children; he did not provide them with any financial support, give them any birthday or Christmas presents, or show any interest in them.

It is further alleged that in El Salvador, in the small neighborhood where the mother and the subject children settled, now abandoned by their father, they lived under the constant threat of violence from gangs. Members of a certain gang threatened to kill Samuel, as they did with many other children, if he refused to join their ranks, and they tried to extort money from his grandmother in exchange for sparing his life. Samuel knew nine children, one a close friend, who had refused to join that gang and were later killed. One gang member told the mother he would kill her, if she did not have sexual relations with him. The perilous situation led the mother to leave El Salvador for the United States so that she could establish a safe home for the children. She found work and lived with family and friends, saving money so that she could bring the children to her. Meanwhile, though, Samuel had stopped attending school because gang members had continued to threaten to kill him if he did not join them. Fearing for Samuel's life, the mother arranged for him to travel to the United States. Marisol and Silvia stayed behind with their grandmother. Subsequently, while the children's grandmother was walking home from work, she was killed by members of that gang. Three gang members were arrested for the murder, but the threats did not abate; other gang members threatened the lives of all the members of the mother's family. Marisol and Silvia stopped attending school, and would only leave their house if an unrelated adult male accompanied them. The mother then brought Marisol and Silvia to the United States.

Now, the children live with their mother in Nassau County, along with their teenaged uncle, Javier, who was left orphaned by the death of the children's grandmother. The mother, who is Javier's legal guardian, works 60 hours per week in order to support him and the children.

The children petitioned the Family Court for the appointment of the mother as their guardian so that they could pursue special immigrant juvenile status (hereinafter SIJS) as a means to obtaining lawful residency status in the United States, and be freed from the fear of being returned to El Salvador, where they would have no parent to support and protect them.

At a conference on the matter, the Family Court concluded that a best interests hearing was not warranted, inter alia, because the children had the "mother to protect them." There was "no reason," even if it was just "strictly for immigration purposes," to award the mother guardianship "of her own children." The Family Court issued an order dismissing the petitions without prejudice for failure to state a cause of action. We reverse.

SIJS is a form of immigration relief that affords undocumented children a pathway to lawful permanent residency and citizenship (*see Matter of Marcelina M.-G. v Israel S.*, 112 AD3d 100, 106-107 [2013]; *E.C.D. v P.D.R.D.*, 114 So 3d 33, 35 [Ala Ct Civ App 2012]; Angie Junck, *Special Immigrant Juvenile Status: Relief for Neglected, Abused, and Abandoned Undocumented Children*, 63 Juv & Fam Ct J 48 [winter 2012]). The Immigration and Nationality Act, which established SIJS (*see* 8 USC § 1101 [a] [27] [J], added by Pub L 101-649, § 153, 104 US Stat 4978 [101st Cong, 2d Sess, Nov 29, 1990]), employs "a unique hybrid procedure that directs the collaboration of state and federal systems" (*Matter of Hei Ting C.*, 109 AD3d 100, 104 [2013]). The child, or someone acting on his or her behalf, must first petition a state juvenile court to issue an order making special findings of fact that the child is dependent upon a juvenile court or legally committed to an individual appointed by a state or juvenile court. Further, a state juvenile court must find that reunification with one or both parents is not viable due to parental abuse, neglect, abandonment, or a similar basis, and that it is not in the child's best interests to be returned to his or her home country (*see* 8 USC § 1101 [a] [27] [J] [iii]; 8 CFR 204.11 [c]; *Matter of Marcelina M.-G. v Israel S.*, 112 AD3d at 107). Only once a state juvenile court has issued this factual predicate order may the child, or someone acting on his or her behalf, petition the United States Citizenship and Immigration Services (hereinafter USCIS) for SIJS (*see* 8 CFR 204.11 [d]; *Matter of Hei Ting C.*, 109 AD3d at 104). In addition, to be eligible for SIJS, the child must be unmarried and under 21 years of age (*see* 8 CFR 204.11 [c] [1], [2]). Ultimately, the Secretary of the Department of Homeland Security must consent to the grant of SIJS (*see* 8 USC § 1101 [a] [27] [J] [iii]; *Matter of Marcelina M.-G. v Israel S.*, 112 AD3d at 114). The Secretary's consent ensures that the child is seeking SIJS for the purpose of obtaining relief from abuse, neglect, or abandonment, and not primarily for the purpose of obtaining lawful permanent residency status (*see* Mem of Donald Neufeld, USCIS Acting Associate Director, Domestic Operations, to Field Leadership, *Trafficking Victims Protection Reauthorization Act of 2008: Special Immigrant Juvenile Status Provisions* at 3 [Mar. 24, 2009], quoting HR Rep 105-405, 105th Cong, 1st Sess at 130, reprinted in 1997 US Code Cong & Admin News at 2941, 2981). Since ultimately the Secretary must give consent, the Family Court "is not rendering an immigration determination" (*Matter of Marcelina M.-G. v Israel S.*, 112 AD3d at 109; *see Matter of Hei Ting C.*, 109 AD3d at 104).

In this instance, in order to satisfy the requirement that the subject children be legally committed to an individual appointed by a state or juvenile court, they are requesting that their natural mother be appointed as their guardian. We begin our analysis by considering the threshold issue of whether the Family Court has the statutory authority to appoint a natural parent to be the guardian of his or her children. Family Court Act § 661 provides that "the provisions of the surrogate's court procedure act shall apply to the extent they are applicable to guardianship of the person of a minor or infant and do not conflict with the specific provisions of this act" (Family Ct Act § 661 [a]). Under the Surrogate's Court Procedure Act, "any person" (SCPA 1703) may petition to be named as guardian of an infant, and a guardian is "[a]ny person to whom letters of guardianship have been issued by a court of this state, pursuant to this act, the family court act or article 81 of the mental hygiene law" (SCPA 103 [24]).[FN*] Since these statutes are without limitation, they must include even the appointment of a natural parent as guardian.

Indeed, it is well established that in a contest for guardianship between a natural parent and a relative or nonrelative of the child, the natural parent may be named as the guardian or coguardian of the child. For example, in *Matter of Revis v Marzan* (100 AD3d 1004 [2012]), in a proceeding where the maternal aunt and maternal uncle were seeking guardianship of their niece, this Court affirmed an order awarding custody of the child to her natural mother. In *Matter of Justina S.* (180 AD2d 641 [1992]), over the natural father's objection, the natural mother and her new husband were awarded coguardianship of her natural child.

The only distinction between those cases and the present case is that there is no contest for guardianship of the children. No one is opposing the appointment of the mother as guardian of the children. This distinction, however, does not make a difference. Unopposed petitions for custody brought by a natural parent have been granted (*see Matter of Maria P.E.A. v Sergio A.G.G.*, 111 AD3d 619 [2013] [Family Court granted mother's unopposed petition for custody of her own child]). There is no basis for treating an unopposed guardianship petition more restrictively than an unopposed custody petition (*see Matter of Karen C.*, 111 AD3d 622 [2013]). The distinctions between guardianship and custody are elusive, as both forms of legal responsibility to a child have very similar attributes (*see* Merril Sobie, Supp Practice Commentaries, McKinney's Cons Laws of NY, Book 29A, Family Ct Act § 661, 2014 Pocket Part at 97-98). Yet, at least for Samuel, since he is over 18, he cannot be subjected to a custody order (*see e.g. Matter of Julian B. v Williams*, 97 AD3d 670[2012]). Accordingly, we conclude that the Family Court has the statutory authority to grant a natural parent's petition for guardianship of his or her child, regardless of whether the petition is opposed.

Further, the Family Court erred in refusing to conduct a hearing to determine whether granting the guardianship petition would be in the best interests of the children. "When considering guardianship appointments, the infant's best interests are paramount" (*Matter of Denys O.H. v Vilma A.G.*, 108 AD3d 711, 712 [2013]). The Family Court's comments indicate that it found it unnecessary to hold a hearing because the children's mother was available to protect them. However, as we explained in *Matter of Marcelina M.-G. v Israel S.*(112 AD3d at 111), the fact that a child has one fit parent available to care for him or her "does not, by itself, preclude the issuance of special findings under the SIJS statute." Rather, a child may be eligible for SIJS findings "where reunification with just one parent is not viable as a result of abuse, neglect, abandonment, or a similar state law basis" (*id.* at 110). Moreover, in determining whether it is in the best interests of a child to grant a guardianship petition, it is entirely consistent with the legislative aim of the SIJS statute to consider the plight the child would face if returned to his or her native country and placed in the care of a parent who had previously abused, neglected, or abandoned him or her.

In the case before us, there are sufficient allegations in the guardianship petitions and supporting papers to suggest that naming the mother as guardian of the subject children would be in their best interests (*see Matter of Deven Meza*

F. [Maria F.—Oneyda M.], 108 AD3d 701 [2013]; *see also Matter of Baby K.*, 188 Misc 2d 228 [2001] [grandparents were awarded temporary guardianship of their daughter's unborn baby, with both parents' consent, so that the child would be covered under the grandfather's health insurance policy]). The father has abandoned the children (*see Matter of Marcelina M.-G. v Israel S.*, 112 AD3d at 110, 114). If the children are returned to their native country, they may be separated from their only other parent, who first left El Salvador because she was threatened with sexual assault and wanted to earn enough money to bring the children to the United States. The children will not have the protection of their grandmother who became their temporary, de facto guardian in El Salvador once the mother immigrated to the United States, as members of a gang murdered her. Alone, without either parent or their maternal grandmother, the children would face the prospect of having to protect themselves from violent gang members, which, cruelly, may be possible only by joining them (*see Yeboah v United States Dept. of Justice*, 345 F3d 216, 221 [3d Cir 2003] [noting that SIJS is designed to prevent a child from being deported to a parent who has abandoned him or her]). Naming the mother as guardian of the children may potentially enable the children to pursue legal status in the United States. If legal status is granted, the children may avoid being separated from their mother and instead keep their family intact and safe, away from the perils present in El Salvador (*see Matter of Maria P.E.A. v Sergio A.G.G.*, 111 AD3d at 620-621). In sum, assuming the truth of the allegations, we disagree with the Family Court's conclusion that there is "no reason" to appoint the mother as guardian of the children.

Therefore, the order is reversed, on the law, the guardianship petitions are reinstated, and the matters are remitted to the Family Court, Nassau County, for a hearing and a new determination of the guardianship petitions thereafter (*see Matter of Francisco M.-G. v Marcelina M.-G.*, 100 AD3d 900, 901 [2012]; *Matter of Ashley W. [Verdele F.]*, 85 AD3d 807, 809 [2011]).

Mastro, J.P., Rivera and Leventhal, JJ., concur.

Ordered that the order is reversed, on the law, without costs or disbursements, the guardianship petitions are reinstated, and the matters are remitted to the Family Court, Nassau County, for a hearing and new determination of the guardianship petitions thereafter.

Footnotes

Footnote *: An infant now includes a person less than 21 years of age who consents to the appointment of a guardian (*see* Family Ct Act § 661 [a]). In 2008, the legislature amended Family Court Act § 661 (a) in response to the federal law permitting persons under the age of 21 to seek SIJS (*see Matter of Sing W.C. [Sing Y.C.—Wai M.C.]*, 83 AD3d 84, 87 [2011]).

In the Matter of Maria E.S.G., Appellant,
v
Jose C.G.L., Respondent.

---

114 A.D. 3d 677 (2nd Dep't February 5, 2014)

— Bruno Joseph Bembi, Hempstead, N.Y., for appellant.

In a guardianship proceeding pursuant to Family Court Act article 6, the petitioner appeals from an order of the Family Court, Nassau County (Eisman, J.), dated December 13, 2012, which, without a hearing, dismissed the guardianship petition.

Ordered that the order is reversed, on the law, without costs or disbursements, the guardianship petition is reinstated, and the matter is remitted to the Family Court, Nassau County, for an expedited hearing and determination of the petition thereafter.

The Family Court erred in dismissing the petition in which Maria E.S.G. sought to be appointed as guardian of her natural child. A natural parent may be appointed as guardian of his or her own child (*see Matter of Marisol N.H.*, 115 AD3d 185 [2014] [decided herewith] SCPA 1703). Here, the petitioner has alleged that appointing her as guardian would be in the best interests of the child since it would enable the child to apply for special immigrant juvenile status (hereinafter SIJS) (*see Matter of Marisol N.H.*, 115 AD3d 185 [2014] [decided herewith]). According to the petitioner's submissions, the child's father has abandoned the child, and, without SIJS, the child may be returned to El Salvador where gang members have threatened her and no one is there to support or protect her.

Accordingly, since the Family Court dismissed the subject petition without conducting a hearing or considering the best interests of the child, the matter must be remitted to the Family Court, Nassau County, for an expedited hearing and determination of the guardianship petition thereafter (*see Matter of Francisco M.-G. v Marcelina M.-G.*, 100 AD3d 900, 901 [2012] *Matter of Ashley W. [Verdele F.]*, 85 AD3d 807, 809 [2011]). Mastro, J.P., Rivera, Leventhal and Chambers, JJ., concur.

In the Matter of Maura A.R.-R. Santos F.R., Appellant; Fidel R., Respondent.

114 A.D. 3d 687 (2nd Dep't February 5, 2014)

— Bruno Joseph Bembi, Hempstead, N.Y., for appellant.

Donna M. McCabe, East Atlantic Beach, N.Y., attorney for the child (no brief filed).

In a guardianship proceeding pursuant to Family Court Act article 6, the mother appeals from an order of the Family Court, Nassau County (Singer, J.), dated July 2, 2013, which, after a hearing, in effect, denied her motion for the issuance of an order declaring that the subject child, Maura A.R.-R., is dependent on the Family Court and making specific findings that she is unmarried and under 21 years of age, that reunification with one or both of her parents is not viable due to parental abuse, neglect, or abandonment, and that it would not be in her best interests to be returned to her previous country of nationality or last habitual residence, so as to enable her to petition the United States Citizenship and Immigration Services for special immigrant juvenile status pursuant to 8 USC § 1101 (a) (27) (J), and dismissed the guardianship petition.

Ordered that the order is reversed, on the law and the facts, without costs or disbursements, the petition is reinstated and granted, the mother is appointed as the guardian of Maura A.R.-R., the motion is granted, it is declared that Maura A.R.-R. is dependent on a juvenile court, and it is found that Maura A.R.-R. is unmarried and under 21 years of age, that reunification with one or both of her parents is not viable due to parental abuse, neglect, and abandonment, and that it would not be in the best interests of Maura A.R.-R. to return to El Salvador, her previous country of nationality and last habitual residence.

In September 2012, Santos F.R. (hereinafter the mother) filed a petition pursuant to Family Court Act article 6 to be appointed guardian of her daughter, Maura A.R.-R. (hereinafter the child), for the purpose of obtaining an order declaring that the child is dependent on the Family Court and making specific findings that she is unmarried and under 21 years of age, that reunification with her father is not viable due to abandonment, and that it would not be in her best interests to be returned to El Salvador, her previous country of nationality and last habitual residence, so as to enable her to petition the United States Citizenship and Immigration Services for special immigrant juvenile status (hereinafter SIJS) pursuant to 8 USC § 1101 (a) (27) (J). In May 2013, the mother moved for the issuance of an order making the requisite declaration and special findings to enable the child to petition for SIJS. In an order dated July 2, 2013, made after a hearing, the Family Court, in effect, denied the motion and dismissed the proceeding on the grounds that there was "no proof [*2]or need shown for an order of guardianship," and there was no showing that the child "cannot return to El Salvador." The mother appeals, and we reverse.

The Surrogate's Court Procedure Act (hereinafter SCPA), which is applicable to determinations regarding the guardianship of the person of a minor or infant to the extent it does not conflict with the Family Court Act (*see* Family Ct Act § 661 [a]), broadly defines a "guardian" as "[*a*]*ny person* to whom letters of guardianship have been issued by a court of this state" (SCPA 103 [24] [emphasis added]), and permits "any person" to file a guardianship petition on the infant's behalf (SCPA 1703). Further, there is no restriction as to who may qualify as a guardian under the Family Court Act, which permits the appointment of a guardian for "a person who is less than twenty-one years old who consents to the appointment or continuation of a guardian after the age of eighteen" (Family Ct Act § 661 [a]). Thus, the fact that the petitioner was the child's mother was not an automatic bar to the granting of her petition (*see* *Matter of Marisol N.H.*, 115 AD3d 185 [2014] [decided herewith] *Matter of Maria E.S.G. v Jose C.G.L.*, 114 AD3d 677 [2014] [decided herewith] *Matter of Juana A.C.S. v Dagoberto D.*, 114 AD3d 689 [2014] [decided herewith] *Matter of Maria G.G.U. v Pedro H.P.*, 114 AD3d 691— [2014] [decided herewith]).

"When considering guardianship appointments, the infant's best interests are paramount" (*Matter of Denys O.H. v Vilma A.G., 108 AD3d 711*, 712 [2013]).

"The 'appointment of a guardian constitutes the necessary declaration of dependency on a juvenile court' for special immigrant juvenile status purposes," which would enable the child to obtain lawful permanent residency in the United States (*Matter of Trudy-Ann W. v Joan W.*, 73 AD3d 793, 795 [2010], quoting *Matter of Antowa McD.*, 50 AD3d 507, 507 [2008]). "Additionally, for a juvenile to qualify for special immigrant juvenile status, a court must find that reunification of the juvenile with one or both of the juvenile's parents is not viable due to parental abuse, neglect, abandonment, or similar parental conduct defined under State law (*see* 8 USC § 1101 [a] [27] [J] [i]), and that it would not be in the juvenile's best interest to be returned to his or her native country or country of last habitual residence (*see* 8 USC § 1101 [a] [27] [J] [ii] 8 CFR 204.11 [c] [6])" (*Matter of Trudy-Ann W. v Joan W.*, 73 AD3d at 795 [citation omitted]).

Based upon our independent factual review, we find that the child's best interests would be served by the appointment of the mother as her guardian (*see Matter of Stuart*, 280 NY 245, 250 [1939] *Matter of Francisco M.-G. v Marcelina M.-G.*, 100 AD3d 900, 901 [2012] *Matter of Alamgir A.*, 81 AD3d 937, 939 [2011]). As such, the child is dependent on the Family Court. We further find that the record fully supports the mother's contention that, because the child's father abandoned her, reunification with her father is not a viable option (*see Matter of Maria P.E.A. v Sergio A.G.G.*, 111 AD3d 619 [2013] *Matter of Karen C.*, 111 AD3d 622 [2013] *Matter of Mohamed B.*, 83 AD3d 829, 832 [2011]). Lastly, the record, which includes affidavits from the child, reflects that it would not be in the child's best interests to be returned to El Salvador.

Thus, the Family Court erred by, in effect, denying the mother's motion for the issuance of an order making the requisite declaration and special findings so as to enable the child to petition for SIJS and dismissing the guardianship petition. Since the record is sufficient for this Court to make its own findings of fact and conclusions of law, we now grant the guardianship petition and declare that the child is dependent on a juvenile court, and we find that the child is unmarried and under 21 years of age, that reunification of the child with one or both of her parents is not viable due to parental abuse, neglect, and abandonment, and that it would not be in the best interests of the child to return to El Salvador.

In light of our determination, we need not reach the mother's remaining contentions. Skelos, J.P., Chambers, Hall and Miller, JJ., concur.

> **In the Matter of Juana A.C.S. et al., Appellants,**
> **v**
> **Dagoberto D., Respondent.**

114 A.D. 3d 689 (2nd Dep't February 5, 2014)

— Bruno Joseph Bembi, Hempstead, N.Y., for appellants.

Gail Jacobs, Great Neck, N.Y., attorney for the child.

In a guardianship proceeding pursuant to Family Court Act article 6, the petitioners, Juana A.C.S. and Marlon F.G., appeal from an order of the Family Court, Nassau County (Aaron, J.), dated January 16, 2013, which, without a hearing, denied the motion of Marlon F.G. for the issuance of an order declaring that the subject child, Fernando J.C.S., is dependent on the Family Court and making special findings that he is unmarried and under 21 years of age, that reunification with one or both of his parents is not viable due to parental abuse, neglect, or abandonment, and that it would not be in his best interests to be returned to his previous country of nationality or last habitual residence, so as to enable him to petition the United States Citizenship and Immigration Services for special immigrant juvenile status pursuant to 8 USC § 1101 (a) (27) (J), and dismissed the guardianship petition.

Ordered that the order is reversed, on the law, without costs or disbursements, the guardianship petition is reinstated, and the matter is remitted to the Family Court, Nassau County, for a hearing and new determination of the guardianship petition, and, thereafter, if warranted, a hearing and a new determination of the motion for the issuance of an order making the requisite declaration and special findings.

The Family Court erred in dismissing the petition of Juana A.C.S. (hereinafter the mother) and her companion, Marlon F.G., seeking to be appointed as coguardians of the mother's natural child. A natural parent may be appointed as guardian of his or her own child (*see Matter of Marisol N.H.*, 115 AD3d 185 [2014] [decided herewith] SCPA 1703). Here, the mother has alleged that appointing her as guardian would be in the best interests of the child, since it would enable the child to apply for special immigrant juvenile status (hereinafter SIJS) (*see Matter of Marisol N.H.*, 115 AD3d 185 [2014] [decided herewith]). According to the mother's submissions, the father has abandoned the child, and, without SIJS, the child may be returned to Honduras where there is no one to support him.

Accordingly, since the Family Court dismissed the guardianship petition without conducting a hearing or considering the child's best interests, the matter must be remitted to the Family Court, Nassau County, for a hearing and new determination of the guardianship petition thereafter (*see Matter of Francisco M.-G. v Marcelina M.-G.*, 100 AD3d 900, 901 [2012] *Matter of Ashley W. [Verdele F.]*, 85 AD3d 807, 809 [2011]). A hearing on the motion for an order making the requisite declaration and special findings, as required by federal law in support of an application for SIJS, should be held thereafter, if warranted (*see* 8 USC § 1101 [a] [27] [J] [i] *Matter of Francisco M.-G. v Marcelina M.-G.*, 100 AD3d at 901). Mastro, J.P., Rivera, Leventhal and Chambers, JJ., concur.

> **In the Matter of Maria G.G.U., Appellant,**
> **v**
> **Pedro H.P., Respondent.**

114 A.D. 3d 691 (2nd Dep't February 5, 2014)

— Bruno Joseph Bembi, Hempstead, N.Y., for appellant.

In three related guardianship proceedings pursuant to Family Court Act article 6, the petitioner appeals from an order of the Family Court, Nassau County (Stack, J.H.O.), dated January 9, 2013, which, without a hearing, denied her applications for the issuance of an order declaring that the subject children, Anibal H., Jose P.H., and Marlene G.H., are dependent on the Family Court and making specific findings that they are unmarried and under 21 years of age, that reunification with one or both of their parents is not viable due to parental abuse, neglect, or abandonment, and that it would not be in their best interests to be returned to their previous country of nationality or last habitual residence, so as to enable them to petition the United States Citizenship and Immigration Services for special immigrant juvenile status pursuant to 8 USC § 1101 (a) (27) (J), and dismissed the guardianship petitions.

Ordered that the order is reversed, on the law, without costs or disbursements, the guardianship petitions are reinstated, and the matters are remitted to the Family Court, Nassau County, for a hearing and new determination of the petitions, and, thereafter, if warranted, a hearing and a new determination of the applications for the issuance of an order making the requisite declaration and special findings.

The Family Court erred in dismissing the petitions in which Maria G.G.U. sought to be appointed as guardian of her natural children. Contrary to the Family Court's determination, the fact that the petitioner is the natural parent of the children does not preclude the court from appointing the petitioner as guardian of the children (*see Matter of Marisol N.H.*, 115 AD3d 185 [2014] [decided herewith] SCPA 1703). Here, the petitioner has alleged that appointing her as guardian would be in the best interests of the children, since it would enable the children to apply for special immigrant juvenile status (hereinafter SIJS) (*see Matter of Marisol N.H.*, 115 AD3d 185 [2014] [decided herewith]). According to the petitioner, the children's father has abandoned the children, and, without SIJS, the children may be returned to El Salvador where gang members have threatened and extorted them and there is no one to support or protect them.

Accordingly, since the Family Court dismissed the guardianship petitions without conducting a hearing or considering the children's best interests, the matter must be remitted to the Family Court, Nassau County, for a hearing and new determination of the guardianship petitions thereafter (*see Matter of Francisco M.-G. v Marcelina M.-G.*, 100 AD3d 900, 901 [2012] *Matter of Ashley W. [Verdele F.]*, 85 AD3d 807, 809 [2011]). A hearing on the applications for an order making the requisite declaration and findings, as required by federal law in support of an application for SIJS, should be held thereafter, if warranted (*see* 8 USC § 1101 [a] [27] [J] [i] *Matter of Francisco M.-G. v Marcelina M.-G.*, 100 AD3d at 901). Mastro, J.P., Rivera, Leventhal and Chambers, JJ., concur.

28. It is possible to do an SIJ case where the father's name does not appear on the child's birth certificate.

In a guardianship case seeking an order of special findings, it is possible to obtain relief even though paternity has not been established. This is also the case concerning custody petitions.

☐ In the Matter of Olga L.G.M., Appellant,

v

Santos T.F., Respondent.

---

116 A.D. 3d 960 (2d Dep't April 23, 2014)

Bruno Joseph Bembi, Hempstead, NY, for appellant.

In a guardianship proceeding pursuant to Family Court Act article 6, the mother appeals from an order of the Family Court, Nassau County (Christopher Pizzolo, Ct. Atty. Ref.), dated April 9, 2018. The order, without a hearing, dismissed the petition.

Ordered that the order is reversed, on the law, without costs or disbursements, the guardianship petition is reinstated, and the matter is remitted to the Family Court, Nassau County, for an expedited hearing and a new determination thereafter of the guardianship petition.

In November 2017, the mother filed a petition pursuant to Family Court Act article 6 to be appointed the guardian of the subject child for the purpose of obtaining an order, inter alia, so as to enable the child to petition the United States Citizenship and Immigration Services for special immigrant juvenile status (hereinafter SIJS) pursuant to 8 USC § 1101 (a) (27) (J). In an order dated April 9, 2018, the Family Court dismissed the petition, without a hearing, on the ground that it failed to state a cause of action because the putative father's paternity had not been established. The mother appeals.

We disagree with the Family Court's determination to dismiss the petition, in which the mother sought to be appointed guardian of her child. A natural parent may be appointed guardian of his or her child (*see* Family Ct Act § 661 [a]; *Matter of Cecilia M.P.S. v Santos H.B.*, 116 AD3d 960, 961 [2014]; *Matter of Marisol N.H.*, 115 AD3d 185, 190 [2014]), and the mere fact that paternity has not been established for the putative father does not preclude the mother's guardianship petition (*see Matter of Jimenez v Perez*, 144 AD3d 1036, 1037 [2016]; *Matter of Marisol N.H.*, 115 AD3d at 190).

Accordingly, since the Family Court dismissed the guardianship petition without conducting a hearing or considering the child's best interests, the matter must be remitted to the Family Court, Nassau County, for an expedited hearing and a new determination thereafter of the guardianship petition (*see Matter of Cecilia M.P.S. v Santos H.B.*, 116 AD3d at 961;*Matter of Marisol N.H.*, 115 AD3d at 191-192) and, if warranted, an order, inter alia, making specific findings so as to enable the child to petition for SIJS pursuant to 8 USC § 1101 (a) (27) (J) (*see Matter of Jimenez v Perez*, 144 AD3d at 1037; *Matter of Juana A.C.S. v Dagoberto D.*, 114 AD3d 689, 690-691 [2014]). Dillon, J.P., Roman, Miller and Duffy, JJ., concur.

29. Motions to resettle

Where USCIS decides that the findings contained within an order of special findings are deficient, a Family Court Judge should entertain a motion to amend (ie motion to resettle) an earlier order. See Matter of Jose S.J., below.

30. A child's alleged involvement with MS-13, a criminal gang, does no preclude a finding that it is not in the child's best interests to return to El Salvador.

☐ In the Matter of Jose S.J. Veronica E.J., Appellant.

168 A.D. 3d 844 (2nd Dep't January 16, 2019)

Karen F. La Grega, Jr., Bay Shore, NY, for appellant.

Laurette D. Mulry, Central Islip, NY (John B. Belmonte of counsel), attorney for the child.

In a proceeding pursuant to Family Court Act article 6, the mother appeals from an order of the Family Court, Suffolk County (Frank A. Tantone, J.), dated April 6, 2018. The order, in effect, denied the mother's motion, inter alia, to amend a prior specific findings order of the same court dated June 30, 2017.

Ordered that the order dated April 6, 2018, is reversed, on the law, without costs or disbursements, and the matter is remitted to the Family Court, Suffolk County, for a hearing in accordance herewith, and for a new determination thereafter of the mother's motion, inter alia, to amend the specific findings order dated June 30, 2017.

In January 2017, the mother filed a petition pursuant to Family Court Act article 6 to be appointed guardian of Jose S. J. (hereinafter the child), for the purpose of obtaining an order declaring that the child is dependent on the Family Court and making specific findings that he is unmarried and under 21 years of age, that reunification with his father is not viable due to parental abandonment, and that it would not be in the child's best interests to be returned to El Salvador, his previous country of nationality and last habitual residence, so as to enable the child to petition the United States Citizenship and Immigration Services (hereinafter USCIS) for special immigrant juvenile status (hereinafter SIJS) pursuant to 8 USC § 1101 (a) (27) (J). In June 2017, the mother moved for an order making the requisite declaration and specific findings so as to enable the child to petition for SIJS. In an order dated June 30, 2017, the Family Court granted the guardianship petition. In a separate order, also dated June 30, 2017 (hereinafter the specific findings order), the Family Court granted the mother's motion.

Thereafter, the child submitted an I-360 petition for SIJS to USCIS, and USCIS notified the child that the petition would be denied due to several deficiencies in the specific findings order. USCIS indicated, inter alia, that the Family Court failed to consider the child's alleged involvement with the MS-13 gang, and thus, the court did not make an "informed decision" that it would not be in the child's best interests to be returned to El Salvador. The mother moved, among other things, to amend the specific findings order to address the deficiencies identified by USCIS. In an order dated April 6, 2018, the court, in effect, denied the mother's motion, without specifically addressing any of the amendments to the specific findings order requested by the mother. The mother appeals from that order.

The Family Court improperly, in effect, denied the subject motion on the basis that the mother failed to state a sufficient reason to amend the specific findings order in light of the fact that the USCIS found the specific findings order to be deficient (*see e.g. Matter of Argueta v Santos*, 166 AD3d 608 [2018]; *Matter of Juan R.E.M. [Juan R.E.]*, 154 AD3d 725, 727 [2017]). Given USCIS's determination, the Family Court, having granted the mother's guardianship petition in the first instance, should have considered the merits of the subject motion as to whether an amendment of the specific findings order was appropriate, and, if so, amended the specific findings order. Although "[t]his Court's power to review the evidence is as broad as that of the hearing court, and where . □□ the record is sufficiently complete to make our own factual determinations, we may do so" (*Matter of Luis R. v Maria Elena G.*, 120 AD3d 581, 582 [2014]), here, the record is insufficient to determine whether the Family Court considered the child's alleged involvement with the MS-13 gang, which would not necessarily preclude a finding that it is not in the child's best interests to be returned to El Salvador. Consequently, the matter must be remitted to the Family Court, Suffolk County, for a hearing on that issue and a new determination thereafter of the mother's motion, inter alia, to amend the specific findings order (*see Matter of A.M.G. v Gladis A.G.*, 162 AD3d 768, 770 [2018]; *Matter of Pineda v Diaz*, 127 AD3d 1203, 1204 [2015]).

Upon remittal, the Family Court should also render a determination as to each of the proposed amendments to the specific findings order requested by the mother. Leventhal, J.P., Austin, Duffy and Iannacci, JJ., concur.

31. If a guardianship petition is granted before the minor's 21st birthday, a motion to amend (ie resettle) an order of special findings may be entertained after the child turns 21.

☐ **In the Matter of Juan R.E.M. Juan R.E., Appellant.**

154 A.D. 3d 725 (2nd Dep't October 4, 2017)

Harold A. Solis, New York, NY (Leah Glowacki of counsel), for appellant.

Appeal from an order of the Family Court, Suffolk County (George F. Harkin, J.), dated August 23, 2017. The order denied the father's motion to amend a prior special findings order of that court dated December 7, 2016, in accordance with a "Request for Evidence" received from the United States Citizenship and Immigration Services in connection with the subject child's petition for special immigrant juvenile status.

Ordered that the order dated August 23, 2017, is reversed, on the facts, without costs or disbursements, and the father's motion to amend the special findings order dated December 7, 2016, is granted to the extent of (1) deleting from the third numbered paragraph thereof the words "or has been committed to or placed in the custody of a state agency or department, or an individual or entity appointed by the state or Family Court," and substituting therefor the words "since the Family Court granted the guardianship petition in this proceeding pursuant to Family Court Act § 661 (a) and the child is under 21 years of age, which constitutes the necessary declaration of dependency on a juvenile court (*see Matter of Enis A.C.M. [Blanca E.M.—Carlos V.C.P.]*, 152 AD3d 690, 691 [2017])"; (2) deleting from the fourth numbered paragraph thereof the name "Veronica," and substituting therefor the name "Juan"; (3) adding to the fourth numbered paragraph thereof, after the words "of at least ten years," the words "(*see* Social Services Law § 384-b [5] [a])"; (4) adding to the fifth numbered paragraph thereof, after the words "removed from the United States," the words ", where he has lived for more than 10 years,"; and (5) adding to the fifth numbered paragraph thereof, after the words "of his birth parent or parents," the words "because the mother is unable to protect the child from harm by gang members in El Salvador, who had made specific threats of violence against the child's sister (*see Matter of Carlos A.M. v Maria T.M.*, 141 AD3d 526, 528-529 [2016])," and the motion is otherwise denied.

In April 2016, Juan R.E.M. (hereinafter the child) filed a petition pursuant to Family Court Act article 6 to have his father appointed as his guardian for the purpose of obtaining an order declaring that he is dependent on the Family Court and making specific findings that he is unmarried and under 21 years of age, that reunification with his mother is not viable due to parental abuse, neglect, or abandonment, and that it would not be in his best interests to be returned to El Salvador, his previous country of nationality and last habitual residence, so as to enable him to petition the United States Citizenship and Immigration Services (hereinafter USCIS) for special immigrant juvenile status (hereinafter SIJS) pursuant to 8 USC § 1101 (a) (27) (J). In November 2016, the father moved for the issuance of an order making the requisite declaration and specific findings so as to enable the child to petition for SIJS. In an order dated December 7, 2016, the Family Court granted the guardianship petition. In a separate order, also dated December 7, 2016, the Family Court granted the father's motion (hereinafter the special findings order).

On December 30, 2016, the child submitted an I-360 petition for SIJS to USCIS. Thereafter, USCIS sent the child a document entitled "Request for Evidence," stating that the special findings order was deficient in several respects, and that additional information was needed to process the child's SIJS petition. The father moved to amend the special findings order to address the deficiencies identified by USCIS. In an order dated August 23, 2017, the Family Court denied the father's motion to amend the special findings order on the ground of lack of subject matter jurisdiction since the child, who was born in May of 1996, had turned 21 years old. The father appeals from that order.

Where a child who consented to the appointment of a guardian after his or her 18th birthday turns 21, the court is divested of subject matter jurisdiction in the guardianship proceeding (*see Matter of Lourdes B.V.I. v Jose R.D.L.C.Q.*, 144 AD3d 909, 910 [2016]; *Matter of Maria C.R. v Rafael G.*, 142 AD3d 165, 170 [2016]). However, where the guardianship petition was granted prior to the child's 21st birthday, there is no jurisdictional impediment to the issuance of an order making the requisite declaration and specific findings to enable the child to petition for SIJS (*see Matter of Alejandro V.P. v Floyland V.D.*, 150 AD3d 741 [2017]; *Matter of Maria C.R. v Rafael G.*, 142 AD3d at 174). Here, since the guardianship petition was granted on December 7, 2016, prior to the child's 21st birthday, the Family Court improperly determined that it lacked subject matter jurisdiction to entertain the father's motion to amend the special findings order.

Furthermore, under the circumstances presented, we deem it appropriate to grant the father's motion to amend the special findings order to clarify that the Family Court exercised its jurisdiction to grant the guardianship petition in this proceeding pursuant to Family Court Act § 661 (a) and the child is under 21 years of age, which constitutes the necessary declaration of dependency on a juvenile court (*see Matter of Enis A.C.M. [Blanca E.M.—Carlos V.C.P.]*, 152 AD3d 690, 691 [2017]). We also deem it appropriate to amend the special findings order to specify that it would not be in the best interests of the child to be removed from the United States, where he has lived for more than 10 years, and returned to El Salvador because the mother is unable to protect the child from harm by gang members in El Salvador, who had made specific threats of violence against the child's sister (*see Matter of Carlos A.M. v Maria T.M.*, 141 AD3d 526, 528-529 [2016]). Since the special findings order set forth the basis for its finding that reunification of the child with the mother was not viable on the ground of parental abandonment, stating that "[the] mother evinced her intent to forego parental rights and responsibilities when she failed to emotionally and financially support [the child] for a period of at least ten years," we do not deem it appropriate to amend that finding, except to correct the name of the subject child and to add a citation to Social Services Law § 384-b (5) (a). Balkin, J.P., Maltese, Barros and Connolly, JJ., concur.

32.   An Article 78 may be appropriate to overcome delay in Family Court proceedings.

        See Matter of Maria C.R., below

33.   Fingerprints are not necessary to do a guardianship case.

In the Matter of Maria C.R., Appellant,

v

Rafael G., Respondent.

---

142 A.D. 3d 165 (2nd Dep't July 13, 2016)

Second Department, July 13, 2016

APPEARANCES OF COUNSEL

Bruno Joseph Bembi, Hempstead, for appellant.

Theresa Kloeckener, Lynbrook, Attorney for the Child.

OPINION OF THE COURT

Sgroi, J.

On July 30, 2014, the petitioner filed a petition in the Family Court, Nassau County, pursuant to Family Court Act article 6, to be appointed as guardian of a child who was then 20 years old. The petitioner also sought an order making special findings so as to allow the child to apply for special immigrant juvenile status under federal law. A hearing on the petition was repeatedly adjourned for various reasons, and ultimately scheduled to take place in January 2015. In the interim, however, on October 16, 2014, the child attained the age of 21 years. As a result, the Family Court, Nassau County, issued an order dated November 26, 2014 which, without a hearing, dismissed the guardianship petition "due to lack of jurisdiction." On this appeal, we examine the propriety of that order and whether certain federal statutes may, in effect, extend the Family Court's jurisdiction to entertain a guardianship petition and issue an order of special findings.

Background

We begin with the underlying factual background to this petition and appeal. Maria L.R. (hereinafter the mother) and Rafael G. (hereinafter the father) are the parents of Santos A.G.R. (hereinafter the child), who was born to them in El Salvador in October 1993. According to the child's affidavit, which was made part of the application in this case, the mother died in 2007 or 2008, when the child was about 14 years old, and the father thereafter essentially abandoned the child and his 10 siblings. The child further averred that when the mother was alive, the father "fought with her a great deal" while the child was present, "was usually drunk," and "would grab [the] mother and threaten to beat her," and that after the mother died, the father "drank a great deal and found another woman and left [the children] alone at home" and "did not support [the children]." According to the child, the children were supported in El Salvador by an older brother living in the United States who sent "money to pay for our necessities."

In 2010, the child left El Salvador and came to the United States to live with a brother in Texas. He lived with the brother for about one year, and then came to New York, where he lived with another brother for two years. In or around December 2013, the child moved in with his friend, Maria C.R. (hereinafter the petitioner). According to the child, the petitioner "has been like a mother to me," "helps me a lot," and "gives me food, .□□ clothing, and a place to live."

Also, according to his affidavit, the child has had virtually no contact and no support from the father since coming to the United States. The child stated that the father has "never asked me to return to live with him," "has no plan to live with me in the future," and "has no plans for my future." Finally, the child averred that he was "afraid" to return to El Salvador because "[w]hen I was living in El Salvador there were numerous people killed or robbed by the various criminal gangs in my home town."

The Petition and Motion for an Order of Special Findings

On July 30, 2014, when the child was 20 years old, the petitioner filed a petition in Family Court, Nassau County, pursuant to Family Court Act article 6, to be appointed guardian of the child. The petitioner alleged that "I have taken care of [the child] since I've met him, making sure his needs are met," "I encourage him to continue going to school and better his life," "I feed him and give him all the emotional support he needs," and "I will continue caring for him into adulthood and even after that I will always take care of him." On July

19, 2014, the child consented to the appointment of a guardian until he reached the age of 21.

By notice of motion dated September 1, 2014, the petitioner moved for an order, inter alia, making special findings so as to enable the child to petition the United States Citizenship and Immigration Services (hereinafter USCIS) for special immigrant juvenile status (hereinafter SIJS) pursuant to 8 USC § 1101 (a) (27) (J). This motion was supported by, inter alia, the above-referenced affidavit of the child, and a "Waiver of Process, Renunciation, or Consent to Guardianship" form signed by the father, who consented to the appointment of the petitioner as guardian, and who acknowledged that "I have abandoned my son" and "I have no plans to support him in the future."

Court Proceedings

On September 19, 2014, the Family Court adjourned commencement of a hearing on the petition and the motion until October 3, 2014 so that the petitioner's husband could be fingerprinted, and to await a response from the Office of Children and Family Services (hereinafter OCFS) to the petition and motion. The court also appointed an attorney for the child.

On October 3, 2014, the Family Court further adjourned the hearing date to October 14, 2014 to await processing of the fingerprints, which had been obtained on October 2, 2014, and for "a report from OCFS." At that time, the petitioner's attorney informed the court that the child would be turning 21 years old on October 16, 2014, and requested a "temporary order of guardianship today" and to "take the testimony on the issue of special findings this morning." The court denied those requests.

On November 26, 2014, the Family Court noted that the fingerprints had been furnished and received an assurance from the petitioner that she was willing to assume guardianship over the child. The court then indicated that it would grant the order of guardianship, instructed the petitioner to wait for that order, and scheduled a hearing on the petitioner's motion for January 14, 2015. Following a recess, the court informed the petitioner that after examining "the papers more closely I realized that [the child] is already 21 years old . □□ [and therefore] I am without the jurisdiction to give you an order of guardianship at this time."

In an order dated November 26, 2014, the Family Court issued an "Order on Motion" denying the petitioner's motion for the issuance of an order, inter alia, making special findings so as to enable the child to petition for SIJS. In a separate order, also dated November 26, 2014, the Family Court dismissed the guardianship petition, with prejudice, "due to lack of jurisdiction."

Discussion

The petitioner contends that it was error for the Family Court to twice adjourn the proceeding when the child was about to turn 21 years old, and that there was sufficient evidence in the record to grant the guardianship petition and motion for special findings prior to the child's 21st birthday. The attorney for the child argues that there was no jurisdictional defect to granting the guardianship petition since it was filed prior to the child's 21st birthday, and since the Family Court could grant the guardianship petition nunc pro tunc to the date the petition was filed.

The Family Court is a court of limited subject matter jurisdiction and "cannot exercise powers beyond those granted to it by statute" (*Matter of Johna M.S. v Russell E.S.*, 10 NY3d 364, 366 [2008]; *see Matter of Riedel v Vasquez*, 88 AD3d 725, 726 [2011]). Family Court Act § 661 (a) governs "[g]uardianship of the person of a minor or infant." That statute, which had previously been interpreted as applying only to persons under the age of 18 (*see Matter of*

Vanessa D., 51 AD3d 790 [2008]; *Matter of Luis A.-S.*, 33 AD3d 793, 794 [2006]), was amended by the legislature in 2008 in response to the federal law and regulations creating special immigrant juvenile status and making it available to immigrants under the age of 21 (*see* Merril Sobie, 2010 Practice Commentaries, McKinney's Cons Laws of NY, Book 29A, Family Ct Act § 661, 2016 Pocket Part at 138-139). The statute now provides, in pertinent part, that "[f]or purposes of appointment of a guardian of the person pursuant to this part, the terms infant or minor shall include a person who is less than twenty-one years old who consents to the appointment or continuation of a guardian after the age of eighteen" (Family Ct Act § 661 [a]; *see Matter of Trudy-Ann W. v Joan W.*, 73 AD3d 793 [2010]).

By the clear wording of the statute, the Family Court's subject matter jurisdiction to grant the guardianship petition herein expired on the date of the child's 21st birthday, or October 16, 2014 (*see Matter of Luis A.-S.*, 33 AD3d at 794). While SCPA 1707 (2) provides that the term of appointment of a guardian does not expire when the child turns 18 where the child "consents to the continuation of or appointment of a guardian after his or her eighteenth birthday," that provision states that in such case the term of appointment *"expires on [the child's] twenty-first birthday*, or after such other shorter period as the court establishes upon good cause shown" (emphasis added). Nor is there any authority for the contention by the attorney for the child that "there was no jurisdictional defect" because the Family Court "had full statutory authority to issue Letters of Guardianship nunc pro tunc to the date of the filing of the petition." Indeed, the opposite is true. Where a court is divested of subject matter jurisdiction, it cannot exercise such jurisdiction by virtue of an order nunc pro tunc (*see Davis v State of New York*, 22 AD2d 733, 733 [1964] ["(w)here, as here, the subject matter is jurisdictional, the error cannot be corrected by an order *nunc pro tunc*"]; *see also Stock v Mann*, 255 NY 100, 103 [1930]).

It would, of course, have been better practice for the Family Court to have timely ruled on the guardianship petition. Indeed, while the court twice adjourned this matter to await fingerprint results, there is no statutory fingerprinting requirement in a guardianship proceeding, and it appears to be simply a matter of Family Court protocol that any individual over the age of 18 living in the proposed guardian's home must be fingerprinted prior to the commencement of a hearing (*see Matter of Herson O.A.M. [Ana D.V.—Gloria E.M.L.], 128 AD3d 827* [2015]). Of course, the fingerprinting of members of the household does facilitate criminal background checks to ensure that appointment of the guardian would be in the child's best interests. However, this would serve little purpose where, as here, the child was already living in the proposed guardian's home, and the granting of the guardianship petition would have changed nothing other than to facilitate the issuance of an order making the requisite special findings to enable the child to petition for SIJS. We further observe that the proper course of action in cases where a Family Court Judge is refusing to commence a special findings hearing or is allegedly improperly delaying a proceeding may be to file a mandamus petition to compel the court to promptly conduct the hearing and render a determination on the motion (*see Matter of Levy v Rooney, 129 AD3d 728* [2015]; *Matter of Orok-Edem v Family Ct., Kings County, 17 AD3d 470* [2005]).

Nevertheless, regardless of whether the Family Court improvidently exercised its discretion in adjourning this matter, as explained above, it correctly concluded that once the child had reached the age of 21 years, it lacked the authority to grant a guardianship petition (*see Matter of Hei Ting C., 109 AD3d 100*, 106 [2013]).

Special Findings

We now turn to the issue of whether federal statutory law can be utilized to counter the above conclusion, at least to the extent of extending the Family

Court's jurisdiction to entertain a guardianship petition and related motion for SIJS findings in circumstances such as those at bar where the child attains the age of 21 after the petition has been filed. We begin with a background discussion of the SIJS statute.

In 1990, Congress created SIJS to address the issue of undocumented and unaccompanied children. These children lacked lawful immigration status and were subject to the threat of deportation and vulnerable to exploitation. As originally enacted, the legislation defined an eligible immigrant as being one who "*has been declared dependent on a juvenile court* located in the United States and has been deemed eligible by that court for long-term foster care" (Immigration Act of 1990, Pub L 101-649, tit I, § 153 [a], 104 US Stat 4978, 5005, adding 8 USC § 1101 [a] [27] [J] [i] [emphasis added]). In 2008, Congress amended the SIJS provision. In the "William Wilberforce Trafficking Victims Protection Reauthorization Act of 2008," Congress expanded the definition of who qualified as a "special immigrant juvenile," enabling more children to qualify for that status (Pub L 110-457, 122 US Stat 5044). These amendments, inter alia, broadened eligibility to include, in addition to children declared dependent on a juvenile court, those who had been placed in the custody of "an individual or entity *appointed by a State or juvenile court*" (Pub L 110-457, 122 US Stat 5044, 5079, amending 8 USC § 1101 [a] [27] [J] [i] [emphasis added]). Following the 2008 amendments, the United States Department of Homeland Security (hereinafter the Department of Homeland Security) issued a memorandum explaining that the new language added to the definition of "Special Immigrant Juvenile" meant that "a petition filed by an alien on whose behalf a juvenile court *appointed a guardian* now may be eligible" (Mem of Donald Neufeld, USCIS Acting Associate Director, Domestic Operations, & Pearl Chang, USCIS Acting Chief, Office of Policy & Strategy, *Trafficking Victims Protection Reauthorization Act of 2008: Special Immigrant Juvenile Status Provisions* at 2 [Mar. 24, 2009] [emphasis added]). Thus, as per the 2008 amendments, a "special immigrant" is a resident alien who is under 21 years old, is unmarried, and *has been either declared dependent on a juvenile court or legally committed to the custody of an individual appointed by a state or juvenile court* (*see* 8 USC § 1101 [a] [27] [J] [i]; 8 CFR 204.11).

In New York, a child may request that the Family Court, recognized as a juvenile court under federal regulations (*see* 8 CFR 204.11 [a]), issue an order making special findings and a declaration as part of the process to petition USCIS for SIJS (*see e.g. Matter of Jisun L. v Young Sun P.*, 75 AD3d 510 [2010]). Specifically, the findings of fact must establish that: (1) the child is under 21 years of age; (2) the child is unmarried; (3) the child is dependent upon a juvenile court or legally committed to an individual appointed by a state or juvenile court (*see* 8 USC § 1101 [a] [27] [J] [i]); (4) reunification with one or both parents is not viable due to abuse, neglect, abandonment, or a similar basis (*see* 8 USC § 1101 [a] [27] [J] [i]); and (5) it is not in the child's best interests to be returned to his or her home country (*see* 8 USC § 1101 [a] [27] [J] [ii]; 8 CFR 204.11 [c]). With the declaration and special findings, the eligible child may then seek the consent of the Department of Homeland Security for SIJS (*see* 8 USC § 1101 [a] [27] [J] [iii]). Moreover, pursuant to federal law, a child "may not be denied special immigrant status under [SIJS] after December 23, 2008 based on age if the alien was a child on the date on which the alien applied for such status" (8 USC § 1232 [d] [6]). The term "child" for purposes of this statute "means an unmarried person under twenty-one years of age" (8 USC § 1101 [b] [1]).

Given this background, the question arises as to whether a New York Family Court may still issue an order making special findings and a declaration allowing a child to petition the USCIS for SIJS where, as here, the child has reached 21 years of age but no order of guardianship has yet been obtained. We conclude that, under such circumstances, a special findings order cannot be granted.

As noted, in order for an alien child to petition the USCIS for SIJS, a court must make certain special findings. Included among these are that the child is under 21 years of age; that the child is unmarried; and that the child has been declared dependent upon a juvenile court or legally committed to an individual appointed by a state or juvenile court.

"The requirement that a child be dependent upon the juvenile court or, alternatively, committed to the custody of an individual appointed by a state or juvenile court, ensures that the process is not employed inappropriately by children who have sufficient family support and stability to pursue permanent residency in the United States through other, albeit more protracted, procedures" (*Matter of Hei Ting C.*, 109 AD3d at 106).

In the case at bar, the request to the Family Court for the SIJS declaration was made when the child was under 21, and, as indicated, federal law states that "an alien .□□ may not be denied [SIJS] .□□ based on age if the alien was a child on the date on which the alien applied for such status" (8 USC § 1232 [d] [6]) (i.e, when the child submits Form I-360 "Petition for Amerasian, Widow[er], or Special Immigrant" to the Department of Homeland Security, USCIS). In addition, it appears clear that federal law permits an alien, who is under the age of 21, to apply for SIJS status even though he or she has yet to be declared dependent upon a state juvenile court. Indeed, the application form specifically asks whether the child has been declared a dependent of a juvenile court; and if the answer is "no," the form requests an explanation. Such inquiry indicates that the application may be filed in a situation such as the one at bar where the child was about to turn 21 but had yet to obtain the special findings from Family Court.

However, no such application was filed in this case, nor had the Family Court issued any order before the subject child turned 21 years old. Thus, even though the child filed his Family Court petition before he turned 21, once he attained that age, the Family Court was divested of subject matter jurisdiction to grant the guardianship petition. Consequently, after that point, the Family Court could not have made a special finding, as is necessary to the SIJS declaration, that the "child is dependent upon a juvenile court or legally committed to an individual appointed by a state or juvenile court." Nor does the federal statute alter this fact. The statute only states that SIJS status may not be denied simply because a child "ages out" during the SIJS process. It does not, and indeed cannot, be read to confer subject matter jurisdiction on the Family Court to grant a guardianship petition for a "child" who is already 21 years old. Therefore, even assuming that the child in this case met all of the other requirements for an SIJS declaration, and even if he had filed his application form with the Department of Homeland Security before he turned 21 years old, his ineligibility for a guardianship petition precluded the Family Court from issuing such a declaration. Put differently, guardianship status, which the Family Court can only grant to individuals under 21, is a condition precedent to a declaration allowing a child to seek SIJS.

In sum, once the subject child turned 21 years old, the Family Court no longer possessed authority to determine the guardianship petition. Furthermore, since dependency upon a juvenile court is a prerequisite for the issuance of an order making the declaration and specific findings to enable a child to petition for SIJS, the Family Court also properly denied the petitioner's SIJS motion. Accordingly, the order dated November 26, 2014 is affirmed.

Hall, J.P., Austin and Hinds-Radix, JJ., concur.

Ordered that the order dated November 26, 2014 is affirmed, without costs or disbursements.

33.1 Denial of an Article 78

SUPREME COURT- STATE OF NEW YORK

PRESENT:

> **Honorable James P. McCormack**
> **Justice**

_____X   **TRIAL/IAS, PART 8**
                                                                 NASSAU COUNTY

ALCIDES C. M.
and MARTIN O. M. C.,

                                                      Index No.: 606342/24
                                                      Motion Seq. No.: 001

                        Petitioner(s),

For a Judgement under Article 78 of the
Civil Patrice law and Rules

                                                      Motion Submitted: 6/14/243

-against-

JUDGE EILEEN GOGGIN, NASSAU COUNTY FAMILY COURT,
IN HER OFFICIAL CAPACITY, ANTONIA C., MOTHER,
MARTINEZ M. D., FATHER,

                        Respondent(s).
_____X

The following papers read on this motion:

> Notice of Petition/Supporting Exhibits..................................X
> Verified Answer and Objections in Point of Law...........................X

Petitioners, Alcides C. (M) and Martin O. M.

C. (Martin), bring this proceeding, pursuant to CPLR Article 78, seeking a Judgement from this court directing that the Hon. Judge Eileen Goggin, Nassau County Family, hold and conduct a guardianship hearing. Judge Goggin opposes the petition.

M is Martin's uncle. Martin was born in El Salvador on August XX, 2004. M originally filed a guardianship in December, 2021. The Petition was withdrawn and re-filed in July, 2022. The ultimate intent of the gaurdianship proceeding is for the court to find that Special Findings exist, so that Martin can file an application for Special Immigrant Juvenile Status with the United States Citizenship and Immigration service, pursuant to 8 USC § 1101.

The guardianship petition was adjourned numerous times while the court awaited fingerprints for M and three other members of his household. The court also directed that the Office of Children and Family Services (OCFS) provide a report. The petition was amended January, 2023. The prior proceedings were before the Hon. Lisa A. Cairo, formerly of Nassau County Family Court. In Febraury, 2023, the matter was assigned to Judge Goggin. There would be more adjournments while awaiting for the results of the fingerprinting, and while waiting for OCFS' report. In December, 2023, the court learned that M had an indicated child protective case from 2011. This resulted in further delays. A hearing was scheduled for April 18, 2024, but this petition was filed on April 12, 2024. The hearing on April 18, 2024 would take place, but the fingerprints results indicated that M had a prior DWI. Mdenied that, and his counsel requested he be re-fingerprinted, an application Judge Goggin granted. The hearing was adjourned to June 24, 2024. As of the drafting of this order, the court is unaware what, if anything, occured at the June 24, 2024 court date.

Petitioners now petition this court for an order directing Judge Goggin to hold and conduct the guardianship hearing. Petitioners argue that the fingerprinting and the OCFS reports are not mandatory and are not a reason for holding up the hearing. Further, the hearing must take place prior to Martin turning 21 in August 2025.

The petition will be denied. Mandamus is only available to direct a public official to perform a duty required by law. (New York Civ. Liberties Union v State of New York, 4 NY3d 175 [2005]). Deciding when to conduct a hearing is a matter of discretion. (Matter of Martinez v DiFiore, 188 AD3d 605 [1st Dept 2020]). Therefore, mandamus is not available to Petitioners under these circumstances, and this court lacks to power to grant the relief requested,

Accordingly, it is hereby

ORDERED, that the petition is DENIED in its entirety.

This shall constitute the decision and order of this court.

Date: August 15, 2024
    Mineola, N.Y.

34. It is legal error to dismiss a guardianship petition based upon the failure of household members to be fingerprinted.

> ☐ **In the Matter of Silvia N.P.L., Petitioner,**
>
> **v**
>
> **Estate of Jorge M.N.P., Respondent, and Kimberly I.N.P., Appellant.**

141 A.D 3d 654 (2nd Dep't July 20, 2016)

Merrill J. Clark, New York, NY, for appellant.

Appeal from an order of the Family Court, Orange County (Andrew P. Bivona, J.), dated December 23, 2014. The order, without a hearing, in effect, vacated a prior order of that court dated November 24, 2014, in effect, granting a motion by the subject child for the issuance of an order declaring that she is dependent on the Family Court and making specific findings so as to enable her to petition the United States Citizenship and Immigration Services for special immigrant juvenile status pursuant to 8 USC § 1101 (a) (27) (J), and thereupon dismissed the guardianship petition.

Ordered that the order dated December 23, 2014, is reversed, on the law and the facts, without costs or disbursements, the petition is reinstated and granted, the petitioner is appointed as the guardian of the subject child, and the order dated November 24, 2014, is reinstated.

In September 2014, the petitioner commenced this proceeding to be appointed guardian of her daughter, Kimberly I.N.P. (hereinafter the child). Thereafter, the child moved for the issuance of an order declaring that she is dependent on the Family Court and making specific findings that would allow her to petition the United States Citizenship and Immigration Services for special immigrant juvenile status (hereinafter SIJS) pursuant to 8 USC § 1101 (a) (27) (J). In an order dated November 24, 2014, the Family Court, in effect, granted the child's motion. In an order dated December 23, 2014, the Family Court, in effect, vacated the order dated November 24, 2014, and dismissed the guardianship petition on the ground that the petitioner did not comply with a court directive to obtain fingerprinting for purposes of a criminal background check.

Contrary to the Family Court's determination, there is no express statutory fingerprinting requirement in a proceeding such as this pursuant to Family Court Act § 661 (a) for "[g]uardianship of the person of a minor or infant" (*see* Family Ct Act § 661 [a]; *Matter of Maria C.R. v Rafael G.*, — AD3d &mdash, 2016 NY Slip Op 05503 [2d Dept 2016]; *cf.*Family Ct Act § 661 [b]; SCPA 1704 [8]). Consequently, it was improper for the Family Court to dismiss the petition based solely on the petitioner's failure to comply with a directive to obtain fingerprinting, and to, in effect, vacate the prior order dated November 24, 2014, granting the child's motion for the issuance of an order declaring that she is dependent on the Family Court and making the requisite specific findings so as to enable her to petition for SIJS.

Further, the Family Court should have granted the petition for the appointment of the petitioner as the child's guardian until the child reaches the age of 21, which is in the child's best interests, the paramount concern in a guardianship proceeding (*see* SCPA 1707 [1]; *Matter of Gabriela Y.U.M. [Palacios]*, 119 AD3d 581, 583 [2014]; *Matter of Maura A.R.-R. [Santos F.R.— Fidel R.]*, 114 AD3d 687, 689 [2014]). Thus, the child is dependent on the Family Court, as the Family Court had determined in the order dated November 24, 2014 (*see Matter of Gabriela Y.U.M. [Palacios]*, 119 AD3d at 583; *Matter of Hei Ting C.*, 109 AD3d 100, 106-107 [2013]).

The child's remaining contentions need not be addressed in light of our determination.

Accordingly, the petition is reinstated and granted, the petitioner is appointed as the guardian of the child, and the order dated November 24, 2014, granting the child's motion for the issuance of an order declaring that she is dependent on the Family Court and making the requisite specific findings so as to enable her to petition for SIJS, is reinstated. Rivera, J.P., Leventhal, Miller and Duffy, JJ., concur.

35. There is no express statutory requirement for fingerprints in a guardianship case.

☐ In the Matter of Silvia N.P.L., Petitioner,

v

Estate of Jorge M.N.P., Respondent, and Brandon M.N.P., Appellant.

---

141 A.D. 3d 656 (2nd Dep't July 20, 2016)

Merrill J. Clark, New York, NY, for appellant.

Appeal from an order of the Family Court, Orange County (Andrew P. Bivona, J.), dated December 23, 2014. The order, without a hearing, in effect, vacated a prior order of that court dated November 24, 2014, in effect, granting a motion by the subject child for the issuance of an order declaring that he is dependent on the Family Court and making specific findings so as to enable him to petition the United States Citizenship and Immigration Services for special immigrant juvenile status pursuant to 8 USC § 1101 (a) (27) (J), and thereupon dismissed the guardianship petition.

Ordered that the order dated December 23, 2014, is reversed, on the law and the facts, without costs or disbursements, the petition is reinstated and granted, the petitioner is appointed as the guardian of the subject child, and the order dated November 24, 2014, is reinstated.

In September 2014, the petitioner commenced this proceeding to be appointed guardian of her son, Brandon M.N.P. (hereinafter the child). Thereafter, the child moved for the issuance of an order declaring that he is dependent on the Family Court and making specific findings that would allow him to petition the United States Citizenship and Immigration Services for special immigrant juvenile status (hereinafter SIJS) pursuant to 8 USC § 1101 (a) (27) (J). In an order dated November 24, 2014, the Family Court, in effect, granted the child's motion. In an order dated December 23, 2014, the Family Court, in effect, vacated the order dated November 24, 2014, and dismissed the guardianship petition on the ground that the petitioner did not comply with a court directive to obtain fingerprinting for purposes of a criminal background check.

As stated in the companion case, *Matter of Silvia N.P.L. v Estate of Jorge M.N.P.*, 141 AD3d 654 [2016] [decided herewith]), it was improper for the Family Court to dismiss the guardianship petition based solely on the petitioner's failure to comply with a directive to obtain fingerprinting, and, in effect, to vacate the prior order dated November 24, 2014, granting the child's motion for the issuance of an order declaring that he is dependent on the Family

Court and making the requisite specific findings so as to enable him to petition for SIJS.

Further, the Family Court should have granted the petition for the appointment of the petitioner as the child's guardian until the child reaches the age of 21, which is in the child's best interests, the paramount concern in a guardianship proceeding (*see* SCPA 1707 [1]; *Matter of Gabriela Y.U.M. [Palacios]*, 119 AD3d 581, 583 [2014]; *Matter of Maura A.R.-R. [Santos F.R.— Fidel R.]*, 114 AD3d 687, 689 [2014]). Thus, the child is dependent on the Family Court, as the Family Court had determined in the order dated November 24, 2014 (*see Matter of Gabriela Y.U.M. [Palacios]*, 119 AD3d at 583; *Matter of Hei Ting C.*, 109 AD3d 100, 106-107 [2013]).

The child's remaining contentions need not be addressed in light of our determination.

Accordingly, the petition is reinstated and granted, the petitioner is appointed as the guardian of the child, and the order dated November 24, 2014, granting the child's motion for the issuance of an order declaring that he is dependent on the Family Court and making the requisite specific findings so as to enable him to petition for SIJS, is reinstated. Rivera, J.P., Leventhal, Miller and Duffy, JJ., concur.

36. Failure to be fingerprinted in a guardianship case does not constitute a failure to prosecute.

☐ **In the Matter of Fermina B., Appellant,**
v
Rene P., Respondent.

156 A.D. 3d 879 (2nd Dep't December 27, 2017)

Amoachi & Johnson, PLLC, Bay Shore, NY (Ala Amoachi of counsel), for appellant.

Appeals from two orders of the Family Court, Nassau County (Felice J. Muraca, J.), both dated March 13, 2017. The first order, without a hearing, denied the mother's motion for the issuance of an order, inter alia, making specific findings so as to enable the subject child to petition the United States Citizenship and Immigration Services for special immigrant juvenile status pursuant to 8 USC § 1101 (a) (27) (J). The second order dismissed, without a hearing, the guardianship petition.

Ordered that the orders are reversed, on the law, without costs or disbursements, the petition is reinstated, and the matter is remitted to the Family Court, Nassau County, for a hearing and a new determination of the petition and the mother's motion.

In September 2016, the mother commenced this proceeding to be appointed guardian of the subject child for the purpose of obtaining an order declaring that the child is dependent on the Family Court and making specific findings so as to enable the child to petition the United States Citizenship and Immigration Services for special immigrant juvenile status (hereinafter SIJS) pursuant to 8 USC § 1101 (a) (27) (J). Thereafter, the mother moved for the issuance of an order making the requisite declaration and specific findings so as to enable the child to petition for SIJS. The Family Court denied the motion without a hearing and dismissed the guardianship petition for "failure to prosecute" based on the mother's failure to obtain fingerprinting. The mother appeals.

Since there is no express statutory fingerprinting requirement in a proceeding such as this pursuant to Family Court Act § 661 (a) for "[g]uardianship of the person of a minor or infant" (*Matter of Maria C.R. v Rafael G.*, 142 AD3d 165, 171 [2016]), the Family Court erred in denying the mother's motion based on her failure to comply with the court's directive to obtain fingerprinting (*see Matter of Silvia N.P.L. v Estate of Jorge M.N.P.*, 141 AD3d 654, 655 [2016]). Further, under the circumstances of this case, the court erred in dismissing the petition for "failure to prosecute" based on the mother's failure to obtain fingerprinting (*see* CPLR 3216; *Matter of Francisca M.V.R. v Jose G.H.G.*, 154 AD3d 856 [2017]).

The mother's remaining contention is without merit.

Since the Family Court dismissed the guardianship petition and denied the mother's motion without conducting a hearing or considering the child's best interests, we remit the matter to the Family Court, Nassau County, for a hearing and a new determination of the petition and the motion (*see Matter of Jimenez v Perez*, 144 AD3d 1036, 1037 [2016]). Chambers, J.P., Hall, Duffy and Barros, JJ., concur.

37. It is not fatal to a guardianship petition if the Petitioner or a household member has a criminal conviction.

73 A.D. 3d 793 (2d Dep't May 4, 2010)

> **In the Matter of Ashley W., Appellant. Verdele F., Appellant. (Proceeding No. 1.) In the Matter of Wrenggor W., Appellant. Verdele F., Appellant. (Proceeding No. 2.)**

Theo Liebmann, Hempstead, N.Y., for appellants.

In related guardianship proceedings pursuant to Family Court Act article 6, the subject children, Ashley W. and Wrenggor W., and Verdele F., the paternal aunt of the subject children, appeal from an order of the Family Court, Nassau County (Zimmerman, J.), dated November 5, 2010, which, without a hearing, denied the petitions for the appointment of Verdele F. as the guardian of both of the subject children and, without a hearing, denied the motion of the subject children for the issuance of an order declaring that they are dependent on the Family Court and making specific findings that they are unmarried and under 21 years of age, that reunification with one or both of their parents is not viable due to parental abuse, neglect, abandonment, or a similar basis under state law, and that it would not be in their best interests to be returned to their previous country of nationality or last habitual residence, so as to enable them to petition the United States Citizenship and Immigration Services for special immigrant juvenile status pursuant to 8 USC § 1101 (a) (27) (J).

Ordered that the appeal by Verdele F. is dismissed as abandoned, without costs or disbursements; and it is further,

Ordered that the order is reversed on the appeal by Ashley W. and Wrenggor W., on the law and the facts, without costs or disbursements, and the matter is remitted to the Family Court, Nassau County, for a hearing and new determination thereafter on the petitions for guardianship, and, thereafter, a hearing and new determination on the motion for the issuance of an order making the requisite declaration and specific findings, if warranted.

Brother and sister Wrenggor W. and Ashley W. (hereinafter together the children) are natives of Haiti who are under 21 years of age and unmarried. Their childhood home was destroyed by last year's devastating earthquake, and the children have lived with their paternal aunt (hereinafter the aunt) and her husband (hereinafter the uncle) since March 2010. The children's parents remain in Haiti, where they have no means of support and are homeless.

On April 30, 2010, the aunt filed petitions seeking appointment as guardian of both children. Wrenggor, who had recently turned 18, consented to the proposed appointment (*see* Family Ct Act § 661 [a]), and the aunt maintains that the children's parents have also consented to both proposed appointments. Following a home study, a licensed social worker and licensed family therapist both opined that the aunt's home was a suitable placement for the children.

On August 31, 2010, both children moved for the issuance of an order making the requisite declaration and specific findings, so as to enable them to apply to the United States Citizenship and Immigration Services for special immigrant juvenile status pursuant to 8 USC § 1101 (a) (27) (J). The petitions and motion were unopposed.

A background check directed by the Family Court reflects that the uncle pleaded guilty to endangering the welfare of a child in 1997. The record further reveals that the uncle was sentenced to a one-year conditional discharge, served no jail time, and obtained a certificate of relief from disabilities, excluding the right to be eligible for public office.

Without a hearing, the Family Court denied the guardianship petitions due to the uncle's conviction, and stated that either a different individual could apply to be the children's guardian, or that the aunt could reapply if the uncle no longer resided in her home. In light of its determination regarding the guardianship petitions, the Family Court denied the children's motion for the issuance of the order making the declaration and specific findings, without addressing the merits. The aunt and the children appeal. The aunt has not filed a brief. We reverse the order on the appeal by the children.

The Family Court erred in denying the guardianship petitions without a hearing. When considering guardianship appointments, the infant's best interests is paramount (*see* SCPA 1707 [1]; *Matter of Stuart*, 280 NY 245, 250 [1939]; *Matter of Trudy-Ann W. v Joan W., 73 AD3d 793*, 794 [2010]). The uncle's criminal record is not an automatic bar to the granting of the aunt's petitions (*see Matter of Ronald F. v Lawrence G.,* 181 Misc 2d 760, 766-767

[1999]; *cf. Matter of Michael JJ.*, 200 AD2d 80, 81-83 [1994]; *Matter of Donald U.*, 105 AD2d 875, 875-876 [1984]), and the order appealed from is devoid of any references to the children's best interests.

Accordingly, the matter must be remitted to the Family Court, Nassau County, for a hearing and new determination on the guardianship petitions. A hearing on the children's motion for an order of special findings should be held thereafter, if warranted, as the children may be able to satisfy one of the prerequisites for obtaining such an order based on the new determination regarding guardianship. More specifically, if the guardianship petitions are granted, the children will be able to establish their dependency on a juvenile court (*see* 8 USC § 1101 [a] [27] [J] [i]; *Matter of Jisun L. v Young Sun P.*, 75 AD3d 510, 512 [2010]; *Matter of Trudy-Ann W. v Joan W.*, 73 AD3d at 795; *Matter of Antowa McD.*, 50 AD3d 507[2008]). At the hearing on the guardianship petitions, the parties may supplement the record to include additional documents reflecting the alleged consent of the children's parents to the proposed appointments of a guardian, as only one of four consent forms was included in the record provided to this Court. Prudenti, P.J., Angiolillo, Florio and Cohen, JJ., concur.

38. Death of a parent establishes that reunification with that parent is not possible.

☐ In the Matter of Luis R., Appellant,

v

Maria Elena G., Respondent.

---

120 A.D. 3d 581 (2nd Dep't August 13, 2014)

Miriam Chocron, Hicksville, N.Y., for appellant.

Kellie Stabile, Westbury, N.Y., attorney for the child.

In a guardianship proceeding pursuant to Family Court Act article 6, the petitioner appeals from an order of the Family Court, Nassau County (Singer, J.), dated July 31, 2013, which, upon the granting of the guardianship petition in an order of the same court dated April 16, 2013, and after a hearing, in effect, denied his motion for the issuance of an order declaring that the subject child, Cristian F.M.G., is dependent on the Family Court and making specific findings that he is unmarried and under 21 years of age, that reunification with one or both of his parents is not viable due to parental abuse, neglect, abandonment, or a similar basis found under state law, and that it would not be in his best interests to be returned to his previous country of nationality or last habitual residence, so as to enable him to petition the United States Citizenship and Immigration Services for special immigrant juvenile status pursuant to 8 USC § 1101 (a) (27) (J).

Ordered that the order is reversed, on the law and the facts, without costs or disbursements, the petitioner's motion is granted, it is declared that Cristian F.M.G. is dependent on the Family Court, and it is found that he is unmarried and under 21 years of age, that reunification with one or both of his parents is not viable due to parental abuse, neglect, abandonment, or similar parental conduct defined under state law, and that it would not be in his best interest to return to El Salvador, his previous country of nationality and last habitual residence.

In August 2012, the petitioner filed a petition pursuant to Family Court Act article 6 for custody of his nephew, Cristian F.M.G. (hereinafter the child), for the purpose of obtaining an order declaring that the child is dependent on the Family Court and making specific findings that he is unmarried and under 21 years of age, that reunification with one or both of his parents is not viable due to parental abuse, neglect, abandonment, or similar parental conduct defined under state law, and that it would not be in his best interests to be returned to El Salvador, his previous country of nationality and last habitual residence, so as to enable the child to petition the United States Citizenship and Immigration Services for special immigrant juvenile status (hereinafter SIJS) pursuant to 8 USC § 1101 (a) (27). Thereafter, the petitioner moved for the issuance of an order making the requisite declaration and specific findings so as to enable the child to petition for SIJS. In an order dated April 16, 2013, the Family Court granted the guardianship petition. In an order dated July 31, 2013, made after a hearing, the Family Court, in effect, denied the petitioner's motion.

Pursuant to 8 USC § 1101 (a) (27) (J) (as amended by the William Wilberforce Trafficking Victims Protection Reauthorization Act of 2008 [Pub L 110-457, 122 US Stat 5044]) and 8 CFR 204.11, a "special immigrant" is a resident alien who, inter alia, is under 21 years of age, is unmarried, and has been legally committed to, or placed under the custody of, an individual appointed by a state or juvenile court. Additionally, for a juvenile to qualify for special immigrant juvenile status, a court must find that reunification of the juvenile with one or both of the juvenile's parents is not viable due to parental abuse, neglect, abandonment, or a similar basis found under State law (*see* 8 USC § 1101 [a] [27] [J] [i]; *Matter of Maria P.E.A. v Sergio A.G.G.*, 111 AD3d 619, 620 [2013]; *Matter of Trudy-Ann W. v Joan W.*, 73 AD3d 793, 795 [2010]), and that it would not be in the juvenile's best interests to be returned to his or her native country or country of last habitual residence (*see* 8 USC § 1101 [a] [27] [J] [ii]; 8 CFR 204.11 [c] [6]; *Matter of Maria P.E.A. v Sergio A.G.G.*, 111 AD3d at 620; *Matter of Trudy-Ann W. v Joan W.*, 73 AD3d at 795).

This Court's power to review the evidence is as broad as that of the hearing court, and where, as here, the record is sufficiently complete to make our own factual determinations, we may do so (*see Matter of Gabriel H.M. [Juan B.F.]*, 116 AD3d 855, 857 [2014]; *Matter of Kamaljit S.*, 114 AD3d 949 [2014]).

Based upon our independent factual review, the record establishes that the child's father is deceased, and therefore, reunification is not possible (*see Matter of Cristal M.R.M.*, 118 AD3d 889 [2014]). Since the statutory reunification requirement may be satisfied upon a finding that reunification is not viable with just one parent, we need not address the petitioner's contention that the record supports the conclusion that the child's reunification with his mother was not a viable option (*see Matter of Gabriel H.M. [Juan B.F.]*, 116 AD3d at 857; *Matter of Marcelina M.-G. v Israel S.*, 112 AD3d 100, 110-113 [2013]). We further find that the record reflects that it would not be in the child's best interests to be returned to El Salvador.

Thus, the Family Court erred by, in effect, denying the petitioner's motion for the issuance of an order making the requisite declaration and special findings so as to enable the child to petition for SIJS. Since the record is sufficient for this Court to make its own findings of fact and conclusions of law, we declare that the child is dependent on a juvenile court, and we find that the child is unmarried and under 21 years of age, that reunification of the child with one or both of his parents is not viable due to the death of his father, and that it would not be in the best interests of the child to be returned to El Salvador. Dickerson, J.P., Leventhal, Austin and Hinds-Radix, JJ., concur.

☐ **In the Matter of Carlos A.M., Appellant,**
v
Maria T.M. et al., Respondents.

141 A.D. 3d 526 (2nd Dep't July 6, 2016)

Michael J. Meehan, Hicksville, NY, for appellant.

Dennis G. Monahan, Nesconset, NY, attorney for the child.

Appeal from an order of the Family Court, Nassau County (Conrad D. Singer, J.), dated May 5, 2015. The order, in effect, denied the petitioner's motion for an order making specific findings that reunification of the subject child, Nelsy V.M.M., with her father was not possible due to parental abuse, neglect, abandonment, or a similar basis found under state law, and that it would not be in the child's best interest to be returned to El Salvador.

Ordered that the order is reversed, on the law and the facts, without costs or disbursements, the petitioner's motion is granted, and it is found that reunification of Nelsy V.M.M. with her father is not possible due to parental abuse, neglect, abandonment, or a similar basis found under state law, and that it would not be in her best interest to return to El Salvador, her previous country of nationality and last habitual residence.

In May 2014, Carlos A.M. (hereinafter the petitioner) filed a petition pursuant to Family Court Act article 6 to be appointed guardian of Nelsy V.M.M. (hereinafter the child), for the purpose of obtaining an order declaring that the child is dependent on the Family Court and making specific findings that she is unmarried and under 21 years of age, that reunification with one or both of her parents is not possible due to parental abuse, neglect, abandonment, or a similar basis found under state law, and that it would not be in her best interest to be returned to El Salvador, her previous country of nationality and country of last habitual residence, so as to enable the child to petition the United States Citizenship and Immigration Services (hereinafter USCIS) for special immigrant juvenile status (hereinafter SIJS) pursuant to 8 USC § 1101 (a) (27). In an order dated January 12, 2015, the Family Court granted the guardianship petition. Thereafter, the petitioner moved for the issuance of an order making the requisite declaration and specific findings to enable the child to petition for SIJS. In an order dated February 5, 2015, made after a hearing, the court found that the child was under 21 years of age and unmarried, and, in effect, found that the child was dependent on the court. The court also found that "it is in [the child's] best interest to remain in the United States." However, the order did not make a finding that the child's reunification with one or both of her parents was not possible due to parental abuse, neglect, abandonment, or a similar basis found under state law.

In April 2015, USCIS denied a petition filed by the child for SIJS on the grounds that the order dated February 5, 2015 failed to find that reunification with one or both of her parents was not possible, or that it would not be in the child's best interest to be returned to El Salvador. Thereafter, the petitioner moved in the Family Court for an order making specific findings that reunification of the child with her father was not possible due to parental abuse, neglect, abandonment, or a similar basis found under state law, and that it would not be in the child's best interest to be returned to El Salvador. In an order dated May 5, 2015, the Family Court, in effect, denied the petitioner's motion.

Pursuant to 8 USC § 1101 (a) (27) (J) (as amended by the William Wilberforce Trafficking Victims Protection Reauthorization Act of 2008, Pub L 110-457, 122 US Stat 5044) and 8 CFR 204.11, a special immigrant is a resident alien who, inter alia, is under 21 years of age, unmarried, and dependent upon a juvenile court or legally committed to an individual appointed by a state or juvenile court. Additionally, for a juvenile to qualify for SIJS, a court must find that reunification of the juvenile with one or both of the juvenile's parents is not possible due to parental abuse, neglect, abandonment, or a similar basis found under state law (*see* 8 USC § 1101 [a] [27] [J] [i]; *Matter of Maria P.E.A. v Sergio A.G.G.*, 111 AD3d 619, 620 [2013]; *Matter of Trudy-Ann W. v Joan W.*, 73 AD3d 793, 795 [2010]), and that it would not be in the juvenile's best interest to be returned to his or her previous country of nationality or country of last habitual residence (*see* 8 USC § 1101 [a] [27] [J] [ii]; 8 CFR 204.11 [c]

[6]; *Matter of Maria P.E.A. v Sergio A.G.G.*, 111 AD3d at 620; *Matter of Trudy-Ann W. v Joan W.*, 73 AD3d at 795).

Based upon our independent factual review, the record establishes that the child's father is deceased, and therefore, reunification of the child with the father is not possible (*see Matter of Luis R. v Maria Elena G.*, 120 AD3d 581, 583 [2014]; *Matter of Emma M.*, 74 AD3d 968 [2010]).

Further, the Family Court erred with respect to its recital of the best interest element. The law does not require a finding that "it is in [the child's] best interest to remain in the United States," but that "it would not be in the [child's] best interest to be returned to [his or her] previous country of nationality or country of last habitual residence" (8 USC § 1101 [a] [27] [J] [ii]). Here, the record reflects that it would not be in the child's best interest to be returned to El Salvador, her previous country of nationality and last habitual residence.

Accordingly, the Family Court erred by, in effect, denying the petitioner's motion for an order making specific findings that reunification of the child with her father was not possible due to parental abuse, neglect, abandonment, or a similar basis found under state law, and that it would not be in the child's best interest to be returned to El Salvador. Since the record is sufficient for this Court to make its own findings of fact and conclusions of law, we find that reunification of the child with her father is not possible due to parental abuse, neglect, abandonment, or a similar basis found under state law, and that it would not be in her best interest to be returned to El Salvador, her previous country of nationality and last habitual residence. Balkin, J.P., Roman, Cohen and Connolly, JJ., concur.

39. Death of a parent constitutes a similar basis under state law.

> **In the Matter of the Guardianship of Jose YY., an Infant. Ericza K., Petitioner. Jose YY., Appellant.**

158 A.D.3d 200 (3rd Dep't, Jan 18. 2018)

APPEARANCES OF COUNSEL

Wilson Elser Moskowitz Edelman & Decker LLP, New York City (*Judy C. Selmeci* of counsel), and *James Tourangeau, Safe Passage Project*, New York City, for appellant.

Paul, Weiss, Rifkind, Wharton & Garrison LLP, New York City (*Jacqueline P. Rubin* of counsel), for Kids in Need of Defense, amicus curiae.

OPINION OF THE COURT

Lynch, J.

Appeal from an order of the Family Court of Sullivan County (McGuire, J.), entered November 14, 2016, which, in a proceeding pursuant to Family Ct Act article 6, denied Jose YY.'s motion for a special findings order pursuant to 8 USC § 1101 (a) (27) (J).

In November 2015, Family Court granted the petition of Ericza K. and appointed her as the permanent guardian of her brother, Jose YY., born in 2000 (hereinafter the child). In April 2016, the child moved for a threshold order that would enable him to petition the United States Citizenship and Immigration Services (hereinafter USCIS) for special immigrant juvenile status (hereinafter SIJS) which, in turn, would enable him to obtain lawful permanent residency in the United States (*see* 8 USC §§ 1101 [a] [27] [J]; 1153 [b] [4]; 8 CFR 204.11). A child seeking SIJS from USCIS must first obtain a special findings order from a state court with jurisdiction over the juvenile, which must determine that (1) the child is under 21 years of age, (2) the child is unmarried, (3) the child is dependent upon a juvenile court or legally committed to an individual appointed by that court, (4) reunification with one or both parents is not viable due to abuse, neglect, abandonment or a similar basis under state law, and (5) it would not be in the child's best interests to be returned to his or her native country (*see* 8 USC § 1101 [a] [27] [J] [i], [ii]). Upon such an application, the role of Family Court is to render specific findings as to the above criteria, with the ultimate determination as to whether to grant SIJS to a child to be made by USCIS and its parent agency, the Department of Homeland Security (*see Matter of Castellanos v Recarte*, 142 AD3d 552, 553-554 [2016]). Correspondingly, it is not Family Court's role to render an immigration determination (*see id.*). Following a brief hearing, Family Court denied the child's motion. The child appeals.[FN*]

We reverse. There is no dispute that the child was under the age of 21 and unmarried when he filed the motion at issue. Family Court denied the application upon finding that he failed to meet the third, fourth and fifth factors. The court erred on each count. The third factor of dependency was established by virtue of the court having already appointed a permanent guardian for the child (*see Matter of Fifo v Fifo*, 127 AD3d 748, 749 [2015]; *Matter of Trudy-Ann W. v Joan W.*, 73 AD3d 793, 794-795 [2010]). The record further establishes that both parents are deceased making reunification impossible. This orphan status, effectively leaving the child abandoned and/or a destitute child, falls within the "similar basis" category of factor four (*see* Family Ct Act §§ 1012 [e], [f]; 1092 [a] [1]; *Matter of Carlos A.M. v Maria T.M.*, 141 AD3d 526, 528 [2016]; *Matter of Victor C.-G. v Santos C.-T.*, 140 AD3d 951, 953 [2016]; *Matter of Luis R. v Maria Elena G.*, 120 AD3d 581, 582 [2014]). As for the fifth factor, we conclude, upon our independent review of the record, that returning the child to Honduras would not be in his best interests (*see Matter of Luis R. v Maria Elena G.*, 120 AD3d at 582-583). The child testified that his father died in 2003 and his mother in 2012, and their death certificates are consistent with such testimony. After his mother's death, he lived with an older sister who operated a billiards business, where the child was fearful and exposed to people smoking, drinking and using cocaine in his presence. That sister has since relocated to Virginia, and the child no longer has family residing in Honduras. In sharp contrast, his guardian has provided a stable home for the child where he feels safe and is attending school. Given the above, the child's motion for a special findings order should have been granted.

Egan Jr., J.P., Clark, Mulvey and Rumsey, JJ., concur.

Ordered that the order is reversed, on the law, without costs, motion granted, and it is hereby declared, in accordance with 8 USC § 1101 (a) (27) (J), that: (1) the child is under 21 years of age; (2) the child is unmarried; (3) the child is dependent upon Family Court due to the November 2015 guardianship order issued pursuant to Family Ct Act § 661; (4) reunification of the child with his parents is impossible since both parents are deceased, which, under state law, leaves the child abandoned or in the alternative, makes him a destitute child, a state basis similar to abandonment; and (5) it is not in the child's best interests to be returned to Honduras.

Footnotes

Footnote *:This Court granted permission to Kids in Need of Defense to file an amicus brief.

40. It is necessary to introduce evidence demonstrating why it is not in the child's best interest to return to his or her home country.

☐ **In the Matter of Victor C.-G., Petitioner,**

v

Santos C.-T., Respondent. Arnoldo B.G.-C., Nonparty Appellant.

---

140 A.D. 3d 951 (2nd Dep't June 15, 2016)

Macina & Pietrzak, LLC, New York, NY (Gregory B. Pietrzak of counsel), for nonparty appellant.

Appeal from an order of the Family Court, Queens County (Julie Stanton, Ct. Atty. Ref.), dated May 8, 2015. The order, after a hearing, denied the motion of the subject child, Arnoldo B.G.-C., for the issuance of an order, inter alia, making specific findings so as to enable him to petition the United States Citizenship and Immigration Services for special immigrant juvenile status pursuant to 8 USC § 1101 (a) (27) (J).

Ordered that the order is affirmed, without costs or disbursements.

In May 2014, the petitioner filed a petition pursuant to Family Court Act article 6 to be appointed guardian of his cousin, Arnoldo B.G.-C. (hereinafter the child), for the purpose of obtaining an order declaring that the child is dependent on the Family Court and making specific findings that he is unmarried and under 21 years of age, that reunification with one or both of his parents is not viable due to parental abuse, neglect, abandonment, or a similar basis found under State law, and that it would not be in his best interests to be returned to Guatemala, his native country and country of last habitual residence, so as to enable him to petition the United States Citizenship and Immigration Services for special immigrant juvenile status (hereinafter SIJS) pursuant to 8 USC § 1101 (a) (27) (J). Thereafter, the child moved for the issuance of an order making the requisite declaration and specific findings so as to enable him to petition for SIJS. Following a hearing, the Family Court denied the motion.

Pursuant to 8 USC § 1101 (a) (27) (J) (as amended by the William Wilberforce Trafficking Victims Protection Reauthorization Act of 2008, Pub L 110-457, 122 US Stat 5044) and 8 CFR 204.11, a "special immigrant" is a resident alien who, inter alia, is under 21 years of age, is unmarried, and has been legally committed to, or placed under the custody of, an individual appointed by a state or juvenile court. Additionally, for a juvenile to qualify for SIJS, a court must find that reunification of the juvenile with one or both of the juvenile's parents is not viable due to parental abuse, neglect, abandonment, or a similar basis found under state law (*see* 8 USC § 1101 [a] [27] [J] [i]; *Matter of Maria P.E.A. v Sergio A.G.G.*, 111 AD3d 619, 620 [2013]; *Matter of Trudy-Ann W. v Joan W.*, 73 AD3d 793, 795 [2010]), and that it would not be in the juvenile's best interests to be returned to his or her native country or country of last habitual residence (*see* 8 USC § 1101 [a] [27] [J] [ii]; 8 CFR 204.11 [c] [6]; *Matter of Maria P.E.A. v Sergio A.G.G.*, 111 AD3d at 620; *Matter of Trudy-Ann W. v Joan W.*, 73 AD3d at 795).

Based upon our independent factual review, the record establishes that the child's father is deceased, and therefore, reunification is not possible (*see Matter of Luis R. v Maria Elena G.*, 120 AD3d 581, 582 [2014]). Since the statutory reunification requirement may be satisfied upon a finding that reunification is not viable with just one parent, we need not address the child's contention that the record supports the conclusion that his reunification with his mother was not a viable option (*see id.* at 582). However, the record does not support a finding that it would not be in the child's best interests to be returned to his native country and country of last habitual residence, where his mother lives (*see Matter of Malkeet S.*, 137 AD3d 799 [2016]).

Accordingly, the Family Court properly denied the child's motion for the issuance of an order, inter alia, making specific findings so as to enable him to petition for SIJS. Mastro, J.P., Dickerson, Austin and Roman, JJ., concur.

41. The fact that a minor is wearing a ring on the fourth finger of her left hand is not irrebuttable evidence that she is married.

> ☐ **In the Matter of Enis A.C.M., Nonparty Appellant. Blanca E.M., Appellant; Carlos V.C.P., Respondent.**

152 A.D. 3d 690 (2nd Dep't July 19, 2017)

Bruno J. Bembi, Hempstead, NY, for nonparty-appellant and petitioner-appellant.

Appeals by the mother and the subject child from an order of the Family Court, Suffolk County (Philip Goglas, J.), dated November 3, 2016. The order, after a hearing, denied the mother's motion for the issuance of an order, inter alia, making specific findings so as to enable the child to petition the United States Citizenship and Immigration Services for special immigrant juvenile status pursuant to 8 USC § 1101 (a) (27) (J).

Ordered that the order is reversed, on the law and the facts, without costs or disbursements, the mother's motion for the issuance of an order, inter alia, making specific findings so as to enable the subject child to petition the United States Citizenship and Immigration Services for special immigrant juvenile status pursuant to 8 USC § 1101 (a) (27) (J) is granted, and it is found that reunification of the child with one of her parents is not viable due to parental abandonment, and that it would not be in the child's best interests to return to El Salvador, her previous country of nationality and last habitual residence.

In August 2015, the child filed a petition pursuant to Family Court Act article 6 to have her mother appointed her guardian. Thereafter, the mother moved for the issuance of an order declaring that the child is dependent on the

Family Court and making specific findings that she is unmarried and under 21 years of age, that reunification with the father is not viable due to abandonment, and that it would not be in the child's best interests to be returned to El Salvador, her previous country of nationality and last habitual residence, so as to enable the child to petition the United States Citizenship and Immigration Services (hereinafter USCIS) for special immigrant juvenile status (hereinafter SIJS) pursuant to 8 USC § 1101 (a) (27) (J).

In an order dated October 3, 2016, the Family Court granted the guardianship petition. In an order dated November 3, 2016, made after a hearing, the Family Court denied the mother's motion for an order making the requisite specific findings.

Pursuant to 8 USC § 1101 (a) (27) (J) (as amended by the William Wilberforce Trafficking Victims Protection Reauthorization Act of 2008, Pub L 110-457, 122 US Stat 5044) and 8 CFR 204.11, a "special immigrant" is a resident alien who, inter alia, is under 21 years of age, is unmarried, and has been legally committed to, or placed under the custody of, an individual appointed by a state or juvenile court (*see* 8 USC § 1101 [a] [27] [J] [i]). The appointment of a guardian constitutes the necessary declaration of dependency on a juvenile court (*see Matter of Sing W.C. [Sing Y.C.—Wai M.C.]*, 83 AD3d 84, 86 [2011]; *Matter of Jisun L. v Young Sun P.*, 75 AD3d 510, 512 [2010]). Additionally, for a juvenile to qualify for SIJS, a state juvenile court must find that reunification of the juvenile with one or both of the juvenile's parents is not viable due to parental abuse, neglect, abandonment, or a similar basis found under State law (*see* 8 USC § 1101 [a] [27] [J] [i]; *Matter of Castellanos v Recarte*, 142 AD3d 552, 553 [2016]; *Matter of Marvin E.M. de P. [Milagro C.C.—Mario Enrique M.G.]*, 121 AD3d 892, 893 [2014]; *Matter of Trudy-Ann W. v Joan W.*, 73 AD3d 793, 795 [2010]), and that it would not be in the juvenile's best interests to be returned to his or her native country or country of last habitual residence (*see* 8 USC § 1101 [a] [27] [J] [ii]; 8 CFR 204.11 [c] [6]; *Matter of Maria P.E.A. v Sergio A.G.G.*, 111 AD3d 619, 620 [2013]; *Matter of Trudy-Ann W. v Joan W.*, 73 AD3d at 795). "Only once a state juvenile court has issued this factual predicate order may the child, or someone acting on his or her behalf, petition the [USCIS] for SIJS" (*Matter of Marisol N.H.*, 115 AD3d 185, 188-189 [2014], citing 8 CFR 204.11 [d]; *see Matter of Castellanos v Recarte*, 142 AD3d at 554). Ultimately, the determination of whether to grant SIJS to a particular juvenile rests with USCIS and its parent agency, the Department of Homeland Security. Thus, when making the requisite SIJS findings, the state or juvenile court is not actually "rendering an immigration determination" (*Matter of Marcelina M.-G. v Israel S.*, 112 AD3d 100, 109 [2013]; *see Matter of Castellanos v Recarte*, 142 AD3d at 554; *Matter of Marisol N.H.*, 115 AD3d at 188-189).

Here, when the Family Court issued the order appealed from, the child was under the age of 21 and, contrary to certain observations contained in the order appealed from, the record demonstrates that she was unmarried. Further, she is dependent upon a juvenile court or legally committed to an individual appointed by a state or juvenile court within the meaning of 8 USC § 1101 (a) (27) (J) (i) (*see Matter of Marlene G.H. [Maria G.G.U.—Pedro H.P.]*, 138 AD3d 843, 845 [2016]).

Based upon our independent factual review, we find that reunification of the child with her father is not a viable option due to parental abandonment (*see Matter of Alejandro V.P. v Floyland V.D.*, 150 AD3d 741, 743 [2017]; *Matter of Marlene G.H. [Maria G.G.U.—Pedro H.P.]*, 138 AD3d at 845; *Matter of Anibal H. [Maria G.G.H.]*, 138 AD3d 841, 843 [2016]; *Matter of Fatima J.A.J. [Ana A.J.S.—Carlos E.A.F.]*, 137 AD3d 912, 914 [2016]; *Matter of Saul A.F.H. v Ivan L.M.*, 118 AD3d 878, 879 [2014]; *cf. Matter of Nelson R.N.C. v Maria G.V.P.*, 147 AD3d 824 [2017]), and that it would not be in her best interests to return to El Salvador (*see Matter of Anibal H. [Maria G.G.H.]*, 138 AD3d at 843).

Accordingly, the Family Court should have granted the mother's motion for the issuance of an order making the requisite special findings so as to enable the child to petition for SIJS. Inasmuch as the record is sufficient for this Court to make its own findings of fact and conclusions of law, we grant the mother's motion, declare that the child has been legally committed to, or placed under the custody of, an individual appointed by a state or juvenile court, and find that, when the Family Court issued the order appealed from, the child was unmarried and under 21 years of age, that reunification of the child with one of her parents is not viable due to parental abandonment, and that it would not be in her best interests to return to El Salvador, her previous country of nationality and last habitual residence (*see Matter of Fatima J.A.J. [Ana A.J.S.—Carlos E.A.F.]*, 137 AD3d at 914). Mastro, J.P., Rivera, Sgroi and Maltese, JJ., concur.

42. An OCFS background check is not required for a guardianship case.

> ☐ **In the Matter of Francisca M.V.R., Appellant,**
> **v**
> **Jose G.H.G., Respondent.**

154 A.D. 3d 856 (2nd Dep't October 18, 2017)

Amoachi & Johnson, PLLC, Bay Shore, NY (Ala Amoachi of counsel), for appellant.

Appeal by the mother from an order of the Family Court, Nassau County (Felice J. Muraca, J.), dated December 1, 2016. The order, without a hearing, dismissed the mother's guardianship petition.

Ordered that the order is reversed, on the law, without costs or disbursements, the petition is reinstated, a separate order of that court, also dated December 1, 2016, which, without a hearing, denied the mother's motion for the issuance of an order, inter alia, making specific findings so as to enable the subject child to petition the United States Citizenship and Immigration Services for special immigrant juvenile status pursuant to 8 USC § 1101 (a) (27) (J), is vacated, and the matter is remitted to the Family Court, Nassau County, for a hearing and a new determination thereafter of the petition and the mother's motion.

In June 2016, the mother commenced this proceeding pursuant to Family Court Act article 6 to be appointed guardian of the subject child for the purpose of obtaining an order declaring that the child is dependent on the Family Court and making specific findings so as to enable the child to petition the United States Citizenship and Immigration Services for special immigrant juvenile status (hereinafter SIJS) pursuant to 8 USC § 1101 (a) (27) (J). Thereafter, the mother moved for the issuance of an order making the requisite declaration and specific findings so as to enable the child to petition for SIJS. The Family Court, in two orders, both dated December 1, 2016, denied the motion without a hearing and dismissed the guardianship petition "for failure to produce required documentation" and "for failure to prosecute." The mother appeals from the order dismissing the guardianship petition.

Contrary to the Family Court's determination, there is no express requirement to submit documentation pertaining to the Office of Children and Family Services in a proceeding such as this pursuant to Family Court Act § 661 (a) for "[g]uardianship of the person of a minor or infant" (*cf.* Family Ct Act § 661 [b]; SCPA 1704 [8]). Consequently, it was improper for the court to dismiss the petition based on the mother's "failure to produce required documentation." Further, under the circumstances of this case, it was improper for the court to dismiss the petition "for failure to prosecute" (*see* CPLR 3216; *Matter of Brudasca v Cottone*, 110 AD3d 1067 [2013]).

The mother's remaining contentions are based on matter dehors the record and, thus, are not properly before this Court (*see Matter of Ishakis v Lieberman*, 150 AD3d 1114, 1115-1116 [2017]).

Accordingly, since the Family Court dismissed the guardianship petition and denied the mother's motion without conducting a hearing or considering the child's best interests, the matter must be remitted to the Family Court, Nassau County, for a hearing and a new determination thereafter of the petition and the motion (*see Matter of Jimenez v Perez*, 144 AD3d 1036, 1037 [2016]). Eng, P.J., Roman, Miller and Christopher, JJ., concur.

43. No OCFS report is required for a guardianship petition, and neither is it appropriate to require school records.

See Matter of A v P, below.

44. Additionally, it is appropriate to assign a case to a different Judge where the first Judge makes inappropriate comments.

161 A.D. 3d 1068 (2d Dep't May 23, 2018)

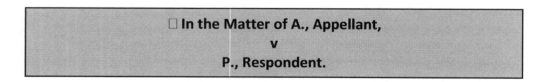

In the Matter of A., Appellant,
v
P., Respondent.

Bruno J. Bembi, Hempstead, NY, for appellant.

In a proceeding pursuant to Family Court Act article 6, the mother appeals from two orders of the Family Court, Nassau County (Merik R. Aaron, J.), both dated November 8, 2017. The first order, without a hearing, denied the mother's motion for the issuance of an order, inter alia, making specific findings so as to enable the subject child to petition the United States Citizenship and Immigration Services for special immigrant juvenile status pursuant to 8 USC § 1101 (a) (27) (J). The second order, without a hearing, dismissed the guardianship petition.

Ordered that the orders are reversed, on the law, without costs or disbursements, the petition is reinstated, and the matter is remitted to the Family Court, Nassau County, for a hearing and a new determination thereafter of the petition and the mother's motion, before a different Judge.

In June 2016, the mother commenced this proceeding pursuant to Family Court Act article 6 to be appointed guardian of the subject child for the purpose of obtaining an order declaring that the child is dependent on the Family Court and making specific findings so as to enable the child to petition the United States Citizenship and Immigration Services for special immigrant juvenile status (hereinafter SIJS) pursuant to 8 USC § 1101 (a) (27) (J). The mother also moved for the issuance of an order making the requisite declaration and specific findings so as to enable the child to petition for SIJS. In the orders appealed from, the Family Court denied the mother's motion without a hearing and dismissed the guardianship petition for "failure to prosecute," respectively.

Contrary to the Family Court's determination, in a proceeding such as this pursuant to Family Court Act § 661 (a) for "[g]uardianship of the person of a minor or infant," there is no express statutory fingerprinting requirement (*see Matter of Fermina B. v Rene P.*, 156 AD3d 879, 880 [2017]; *Matter of Silvia N.P.L. v Estate of Jorge M.N.P.*, 141 AD3d 654, 655 [2016]), or any express requirement to submit documentation pertaining to the Office of Children and Family Services (*see Matter of Francisca M.V.R. v Jose G.H.G.*, 154 AD3d 856, 857 [2017]). Further, under the circumstances of this case, the court erred in dismissing the petition and denying the motion for "failure to prosecute" based upon the mother's failure to submit documentation regarding, inter alia, the child's enrollment in school (*see* CPLR 3216; *Matter of Francisca M.V.R. v Jose G.H.G.*, 154 AD3d at 857).

Since the Family Court dismissed the guardianship petition and denied the mother's motion without conducting a hearing or considering the child's best interests, we remit the matter to the Family Court, Nassau County, for a hearing and a new determination thereafter of the petition and the motion (*see Matter of Jimenez v Perez*, 144 AD3d 1036, 1037 [2016]). In addition, in light of certain remarks made by the Family Court Judge during the course of the proceedings, we deem it appropriate that the matter be heard by a different Judge. The remarks included: that the child "should be speaking English a lot better" after having been in the United States for two years; that the child should "make some friends who speak English"; that if the child only spoke Spanish, "what are you gonna do, you're gonna be hanging around just where you are"; and that the child "[c]an't speak English, doesn't go to school, it's wonderful. It's a great country America." These remarks were inappropriate and cannot be countenanced. Mastro, J.P., Rivera, Austin and LaSalle, JJ., concur.

45. Abandonment can be established where the subject is between 18 and 21 years of age.

☐ In the Matter of Goran S., Appellant.

---

152 A.D. 3d 698 (2nd Dep't July 19, 2017)

Gencian Gjoni, New York, NY, for appellant.

Appeal by the child from an order of the Family Court, Queens County (Nicolette M. Pach, J.H.O.), dated May 17, 2016. The order, insofar as appealed from, upon reargument and renewal, after a hearing, in effect, adhered to so much of an original determination in an order dated April 4, 2016, denying that branch of his motion which was for a specific finding that reunification with one or both biological parents was not viable due to parental abuse, neglect, or abandonment.

Ordered that the order is affirmed insofar as appealed from, without costs or disbursements.

In January 2015, the grandmother of the subject child, Goran S., commenced this proceeding pursuant to Family Court Act article 6 to be appointed the guardian of the child for the purpose of obtaining an order declaring that he is dependent on the Family Court and making specific findings that he is unmarried and under 21 years of age, that reunification with one or both parents is not viable due to parental abuse, neglect, or abandonment, and that it would not be in his best interests to be returned to Serbia, his previous country of nationality and last habitual residence, so as to enable him to petition the United States Citizenship and Immigration Services for special immigrant juvenile status (hereinafter SIJS) pursuant to 8 USC § 1101 (a) (27) (J). Thereafter, the child moved for the issuance of an order making the requisite declaration and specific findings so as to enable him to petition for SIJS. In an order dated April 4, 2016, after a hearing, the Family Court denied the motion for the issuance of an order of specific findings, concluding that the child was under 21, unmarried, dependent on the Family Court, and that it was not in his best interests to be returned to Serbia, but that the evidence did not establish that reunification of the child with one or both parents was not viable due to parental abuse, neglect, or abandonment.

Thereafter, the child moved by order to show cause for leave to renew and reargue that branch of his prior motion which was for a specific finding that reunification with one or both of his biological parents was not viable due to parental abuse, neglect, or abandonment. The Family Court granted leave to renew and reargue. In an order dated May 17, 2016, after a hearing at which both the child and the grandmother testified, the Family Court, inter alia, in effect, adhered to so much of its original determination as denied that branch of the child's motion which was for a specific finding that reunification with one or both parents was not viable due to parental abuse, neglect, or abandonment. The child appeals.

"Pursuant to 8 USC § 1101 (a) (27) (J) (as amended by the William Wilberforce Trafficking Victims Protection Reauthorization Act of 2008, Pub L 110-457, 122 US Stat 5044) and 8 CFR 204.11, a 'special immigrant' is a resident alien who is, inter alia, under 21 years of age, unmarried, and dependent upon a juvenile court or legally committed to an individual appointed by a state or juvenile court" (*Matter of Trudy-Ann W. v Joan W.*, 73 AD3d 793, 795 [2010]). "Additionally, for a juvenile to qualify for special immigrant juvenile status, a court must find that reunification of the juvenile with one or both of the juvenile's parents is not viable due to parental abuse, neglect, abandonment, or similar parental conduct defined under State law, and that it would not be in the juvenile's best interest to be returned to his or her native country or country of last habitual residence" (*Matter of Marvin E.M. de P. [Milagro C.C.—Mario Enrique M.G.]*, 121 AD3d 892, 893 [2014]; *see Matter of Maria P.E.A. v Sergio A.G.G.*, 111 AD3d 619, 620 [2013]).

Here, the record does not support a determination that reunification of the child with one or both of his parents is not viable due to parental abuse neglect, abandonment, or a similar basis found under State law. Although the Family Court should not have refused to consider evidence of circumstances which occurred after the child's 18th birthday (*see Matter of Sing W.C. [Sing Y.C.— Wai M.C.]*, 83 AD3d 84, 90-91 [2011]), even taking such evidence into account, and considering the psychological stress occasioned by his parents' divorce, the child failed to prove that his reunification with one or both parents was not viable due to parental abuse, neglect, or abandonment (*see Matter of Christian P.S.-A. [Humberto R.S.-B.—Laura S.A.-C.]*, 148 AD3d 1032 [2017]; *Matter of Nelson R.N.C. v Maria G.V.P.*, 147 AD3d 824 [2017]; *Matter of Del Cid Martinez v Martinez*, 144 AD3d 905[2016]; *Matter of Jasbir S. [Dayal S.— Gurdev S.]*, 138 AD3d 750 [2016]; *Matter of Miguel A.G.G. [Milton N.G.G.]*, 127 AD3d 858 [2015]). Accordingly, the Family Court properly, in effect, adhered to so much of its original determination as denied that branch of the child's motion which was for a specific finding that reunification with one or both parents was not viable due to parental abuse, neglect, or abandonment. Dillon, J.P., Leventhal, Miller and Brathwaite Nelson, JJ., concur.

46.   A child's occasional contact with his parents, without more, does not preclude a finding of abandonment.

> ☐ **In the Matter of Akramul I. Khan, Appellant,**
> **v**
> **Shahida Z. et al., Respondents.**

184 A.D. 3d 506 (1st Dep't June 18, 2020)

Law Office of Genet Getachew, Brooklyn (Genet Getachew of counsel), for appellant.

Order, Family Court, Bronx County (Jennifer S. Burtt, Referee), entered on or about August 30, 2018, which denied petitioner and the subject child's motion for an order of special findings enabling the child to petition for Special Immigrant Juvenile Status, unanimously reversed, on the law and the facts, without costs, and the motion granted.

The evidence shows that the subject child was unmarried and under the age of 21 at the time of the special findings hearing and order (*see generally* 8 USC § 1101 [a] [27] [J]; 8 CFR 204.11 [c]; *Matter of Marisol N.H.*, 115 AD3d 185, 188-189 [2d Dept 2014]). The Family Court's appointment of a guardian rendered the child dependent on a juvenile court (*see Matter of Antowa McD.*, 50 AD3d 507 [1st Dept 2008]).

The evidence also established that reunification with the child's parents was not viable due to neglect or abandonment. The child testified that, with no prior warning, his father left him in the United States with his uncle (petitioner), and that his parents later told him that they could not support him and did not want him back. The child further stated, and petitioner corroborated, that he had only occasional contact with his parents, and received no gifts or support from them, since coming here. This was sufficient to "evince[ ] an intent to forego .□□ parental rights and obligations" or a failure to exercise a minimum degree of care to supply the child with adequate food, clothing, shelter, education, or supervision (Social Services Law § 384-b [5] [a]; *see* Family Ct Act § 1012 [f] [i], [ii]; *Antowa McD.*, 50 AD3d at 507).

In determining whether reunification was viable, the Family Court should not have refused to consider evidence of circumstances which occurred after the child's 18th, but before his 21st, birthday (*see* Family Ct Act § 661 [a]; 8 CFR 204.11 [c] [1]; *Matter of Goran S.*, 152 AD3d 698, 700 [2d Dept 2017]; *Matter of Sing W.C. [Sing Y.C.—Wai M.C.]*, 83 AD3d 84 [2d Dept 2011]).

The evidence also demonstrated that it is not in the best interests of the child to return to Thailand, where his parents reside, or to be sent to live in Bangladesh, where he has citizenship but has never resided. The child presented evidence that his parents would not accept him if he returned to Thailand, that his Thai visa was on the verge of expiring and he had no way to renew it, and that he had no other place to live or way to support himself in Thailand or

Bangladesh (*see Matter of Alamgir A.*, 81 AD3d 937, 940 [2d Dept 2011]). He also presented evidence that he was doing well in petitioner's care (*see Antowa McD.* at 507; *Matter of Marcelina M.-G. v Israel S.*, 112 AD3d 100, 114-115 [2d Dept 2013]). Concur—Richter, J.P., Kapnick, Webber, Gesmer, Moulton, JJ.

□ **In the Matter of Lavdie H., Appellant,**

v

Saimira V. et al., Respondents.

---

184 A.D.3d 409 (1st Dep't June 4, 2020)

Turturro Law, P.C., Brooklyn (Natraj S. Bhushan of counsel), for appellant.

Karen P. Simmons, The Children's Law Center, Brooklyn (Janet Neustaetter of counsel), attorney for the child.

Order, Family Court, Bronx County (Jennifer Burtt, Ref.), entered on or about September 20, 2016, which denied the subject child's motion for an order of special findings enabling him to petition the United States Citizenship and Immigration Services (CIS) for special immigrant juvenile status, unanimously reversed, on the law and the facts, without costs, and the motion granted.

The record supports an order of special findings enabling the child to petition CIS for special immigrant juvenile status (*see* 8 USC § 1101 [a] [27] [J] [Immigration and Nationality Act]; 8 CFR 204.11 [c], [d]; *Matter of Marisol N.H.*, 115 AD3d 185, 188-189 [2d Dept 2014]). The evidence establishes that the child was unmarried and under the age of 21 at the time of the special findings hearing and order (*see* 8 CFR 204.11 [c]). The Family Court's appointment of a guardian (petitioner) rendered the child dependent on a juvenile court (*see id.*; *Matter of Antowa McD.*, 50 AD3d 507 [1st Dept 2008]).

The evidence that the child had had no contact with his parents, and received no support from them, since at least September 2014 established that reunification with the parents was not viable due to neglect or abandonment (*see* 8 USC § 1101 [a] [27] [J]; Family Ct Act § 1012 [f] [ii]; Social Services Law § 384-b [5] [a]; *Matter of Akasha J.G. [Vincent G.]*, 149 AD3d 734 [2d Dept 2017]). The parents' consent to the appointment of a guardian and waiver of service also demonstrate an intent to relinquish their parental rights.

In determining whether reunification was viable, the Family Court should not have refused to consider evidence of circumstances that occurred after the child's 18th, but before his 21st, birthday (*see* Family Ct Act § 661 [a]; 8 CFR 204.11 [c] [1]; *Matter of Goran S.*, 152 AD3d 698, 700 [2d Dept 2017]; *Matter of Sing W.C. [Sing Y.C.—Wai M.C.]*, 83 AD3d 84, 90-91 [2d Dept 2011]).

The record demonstrates that it is not in the best interests of the child to return to Albania (*see* 8 USC § 1101 [a] [27] [J]; 8 CFR 204.11 [c]). The evidence shows that the child suffered political persecution in Albania that his parents were unable to prevent (*see Matter of Juan R.E.M. [Juan R.E.]*, 154 AD3d 725, 727 [2d Dept 2017]), that he had had no recent contact with his parents and was not sure if they would accept him if he returned (*see Matter of Alamgir A.*, 81 AD3d 937, 940 [2d Dept 2011]), and that he was doing well in petitioner's care (*see Matter of Marcelina M.-G. v Israel S.*, 112 AD3d 100, 114-115 [2d Dept 2013]). Concur—Friedman, J.P., Kapnick, Kern, Singh, González, JJ.

47.   A natural mother may petition for the custody of her child where the father is deceased.

☐ **In the Matter of Marisela Castellanos, Appellant,**

<table>
<tr><td>v
Luis A. Recarte, Respondent.</td></tr>
</table>

142 A.D. 3d 552 (2nd Dep't August 10, 2016)

Bruno J. Bembi, Hempstead, NY, for appellant.

Appeal by the mother from an order of the Family Court, Nassau County (Danielle M. Peterson, J.), dated October 1, 2015. The order, without a hearing, dismissed the mother's petition for custody of the subject children and, in effect, for an order making special findings so as to enable the subject children to petition the United States Citizenship and Immigration Services for special immigrant juvenile status pursuant to 8 USC § 1101 (a) (27) (J).

Ordered that the order is reversed, on the law, without costs or disbursements, the petition is reinstated, and the matter is remitted to the Family Court, Nassau County, for a hearing and a new determination thereafter of the petition for custody of the subject children and, in effect, for an order making special findings so as to enable the subject children to petition the United States Citizenship and Immigration Services for special immigrant juvenile status pursuant to 8 USC § 1101 (a) (27) (J).

On or about August 28, 2015, the mother filed a petition pursuant to Family Court Act article 6 seeking sole custody of her two children, who were then ages 15 and 12. In her verified petition, she stated that the father died in 2004, she and the children moved from Honduras to the United States in 2014, and the children were pursuing special immigrant juvenile status (hereinafter SIJS) as a means to obtain lawful permanent residency status in the United States (*see generally* 8 USC § 1101 [a] [27] [J]; *Matter of Marisol N.H.*, 115 AD3d 185, 188-191 [2014]). Her petition was unopposed. When the mother appeared with counsel, the Family Court dismissed her custody petition on the sole ground that it was unnecessary since she already had custody by operation of law.

The mother appeals, arguing, among other things, that the Family Court erred in dismissing her custody petition, and that an order of custody will enable the children to seek SIJS so that they are not "deported to a violent and chaotic country where they have neither mother nor father."

SIJS is a form of immigration relief that affords undocumented children a pathway to lawful permanent residency and citizenship (*see Matter of Marisol N.H.*, 115 AD3d at 188; *Matter of Marcelina M.-G. v Israel S.*, 112 AD3d 100, 106-107 [2013]). Pursuant to 8 USC § 1101 (a) (27) (J) (as amended by the William Wilberforce Trafficking Victims Protection Reauthorization Act of 2008, Pub L 110-457, 122 US Stat 5044) and 8 CFR 204.11, a "special immigrant" is a resident alien who, inter alia, is under 21 years of age, is unmarried, and has been legally committed to, or placed under the custody of, an individual appointed by a state or juvenile court. Additionally, for a juvenile to qualify for SIJS, a court must find that reunification of the juvenile with one or both of the juvenile's parents is not viable due to parental abuse, neglect, abandonment, or a similar basis found under state law (*see* 8 USC § 1101 [a] [27] [J] [i]; *Matter of Marisol N.H.*, 115 AD3d at 188; *Matter of Maria P.E.A. v Sergio A.G.G.*, 111 AD3d 619, 620 [2013]), and that it would not be in the juvenile's best interests to be returned to his or her native country or country of last habitual residence (*see* 8 USC § 1101 [a] [27] [J] [ii]; 8 CFR 204.11 [c] [6]; *Matter of Maria P.E.A. v Sergio A.G.G.*, 111 AD3d at 620; *Matter of Trudy-Ann W. v Joan W.*, 73 AD3d 793, 795 [2010]). "Only once a state juvenile court has issued this factual predicate order may the child, or someone acting on his or her behalf, petition the United States Citizenship and Immigration Services [hereinafter USCIS] for SIJS" (*Matter of Marisol N.H.*, 115 AD3d at 188-189, citing 8 CFR 204.11 [d]; *see Matter of Hei Ting C.*, 109

AD3d 100, 104-105 [2013]). Ultimately, the determination of whether to grant SIJS to a particular juvenile rests with USCIS and its parent agency, the Department of Homeland Security. Thus, when making the requisite SIJS findings, the state or juvenile court is not actually "rendering an immigration determination" (*Matter of Marcelina M.-G. v Israel S.*, 112 AD3d at 109; *see Matter of Marisol N.H.*, 115 AD3d at 188-189; *H.S.P. v J.K.*, 223 NJ 196, 212, 121 A3d 849, 859 [2015]).

In New York, a child's parent or guardian may request that the Family Court issue an order making special findings so that the child may petition USCIS for SIJS (*see Matter of Hei Ting C.*, 109 AD3d at 104). This relief may be sought in the context of a Family Court Act article 6 custody proceeding (*see e.g. Matter of Ramirez v Palacios*, 136 AD3d 666[2016]; *Matter of Tommy E.H. [Silvia C.]*, 134 AD3d 840, 841-842 [2015]), or a Family Court Act article 6 guardianship proceeding (*see e.g. Matter of Anibal H. [Maria G.G.H.]*, 138 AD3d 841 [2016]; *Matter of Cecilia M.P.S. v Santos H.B.*, 116 AD3d 960, 961 [2014]).

Here, although the mother was presumptively entitled to custody of the children as their surviving parent (*see* Domestic Relations Law § 81; *Baker v Bronx Lebanon Hosp. Ctr.*, 53 AD3d 21, 25 [2008]; *Matter of Pernice v Cote*, 116 AD2d 945, 946 [1986]; Alan D. Scheinkman, Practice Commentaries, McKinney's Cons Laws of NY, Book 14, Domestic Relations Law § 81; *cf. Matter of Pettaway v Savage*, 87 AD3d 796 [2011]), "[a] natural parent has standing to seek legal custody of his or her child" (*Matter of Sanchez v Bonilla*, 115 AD3d 868, 869 [2014]; *see* Domestic Relations Law § 70 [a]; Family Ct Act § 511; *Debra H. v Janice R.*, 14 NY3d 576 [2010]), and "[u]nopposed petitions for custody brought by a natural parent have been granted" for SIJS purposes (*Matter of Marisol N.H.*, 115 AD3d at 190, citing *Matter of Maria P.E.A. v Sergio A.G.G.*, 111 AD3d 619 [2013]).

Accordingly, the Family Court should not have dismissed the custody petition without conducting a hearing and considering the children's best interests. Instead, the court should have proceeded to conduct a hearing on the petition, which sought a custody order as well as an order making the requisite declaration and special findings so as to enable the children to petition for SIJS (*see Matter of Cecilia M.P.S. v Santos H.B.*, 116 AD3d at 961; *Matter of Marisol N.H.*, 115 AD3d at 188, 190-192; *cf. Matter of Maria P.E.A. v Sergio A.G.G.*, 111 AD3d at 619-620). Mastro, J.P., Austin, Sgroi and Maltese, JJ., concur.

48. A mother may petition for the custody of her child without establishing paternity.

☐ **In the Matter of Any Mileybi Galeano Jimenez, Appellant,**

v

Gregorio Barrera Perez, Respondent.

---

144 A.D. 3d 1036 (2nd Dep't November 23, 2016)

Bruno J. Bembi, Hempstead, NY, for appellant.

Ronna L. DeLoe, New Rochelle, NY, attorney for the child.

Appeal by the mother from an order of the Family Court, Nassau County (Robin M. Kent, J.), dated April 27, 2016. The order, without a hearing, dismissed her custody petition.

Ordered that the order is reversed, on the law, without costs or disbursements, the petition is reinstated, and the matter is remitted to the Family Court, Nassau County, for a hearing and a new determination thereafter of the petition for custody of the subject child and, if warranted, an order, inter alia, making specific findings so as to enable the subject child to petition the United States Citizenship and Immigration Services for special immigrant juvenile status pursuant to 8 USC § 1101 (a) (27) (J).

In April 2016, the mother filed a petition pursuant to Family Court Act article 6 for sole custody of the subject child for the purpose of obtaining an order, inter alia, making specific findings so as to enable the child to petition the United States Citizenship and Immigration Services for special immigrant juvenile status (hereinafter SIJS) pursuant to 8 USC § 1101 (a) (27) (J). In an order dated April 27, 2016, the Family Court dismissed the petition, without a hearing, on the ground that the alleged father's paternity had not been established.

The Family Court erred in dismissing the petition in which the mother sought to be awarded sole custody of the subject child. A natural parent may seek legal custody of his or her child (*see* Domestic Relations Law § 70 [a]; Family Ct Act § 511; *Matter of Sanchez v Bonilla*, 115 AD3d 868 [2014]; SCPA 1703), irrespective of whether the natural parent is presumptively entitled to custody of the child (*see Matter of Castellanos v Recarte*, 142 AD3d 552, 554 [2016]). Thus, the mere fact that paternity has not been established for the putative father does not preclude the mother's custody petition or the issuance of an order, inter alia, making specific findings so as to enable the subject child to petition the United States Citizenship and Immigration Services for SIJS pursuant to 8 USC § 1101 (a) (27) (J) (*see Matter of Haide L.G.M. v Santo D.S.M.*, 130 AD3d 734 [2015]; *Matter of Miguel C.-N. [Hosman C.-N.—Cruz Ermelinda C.-N.]*, 119 AD3d 562 [2014]; *Matter of Diaz v Munoz*, 118 AD3d 989 [2014]).

Accordingly, since the Family Court dismissed the custody petition without conducting a hearing or considering the child's best interests, the matter must be remitted to the Family Court, Nassau County, for a hearing and a new determination thereafter of the petition for custody of the subject child and, if warranted, an order, inter alia, making specific findings so as to enable the subject child to petition the United States Citizenship and Immigration Services for SIJS pursuant to 8 USC § 1101 (a) (27) (J) (*see Matter of Castellanos v Recarte*, 142 AD3d at 554-555; *Matter of Juana A.C.S. v Dagoberto D., 114 AD3d 689* [2014]). Balkin, J.P., Dickerson, Hinds-Radix and Brathwaite Nelson, JJ., concur.

49. Neglect (via physical abuse) can be established where both the child and the parent engage in physical contact.

> ☐ **In the Matter of Ena S.Y. Martha R.Y., Appellant; Antonio S., Respondent.**

140 A.D. 3d 778 (2d Dep't June 1, 2016)

Bruno J. Bembi, Hempstead, NY, for appellant.

John M. Zenir, Westbury, NY, attorney for the child.

Appeal from an order of the Family Court, Nassau County (Robin M. Kent, J.), dated July 1, 2015. The order, insofar as appealed from, after a hearing, denied that branch of the mother's motion for the issuance of an order, inter alia, making specific findings so as to enable the subject child, Ena S.Y., to petition the United States Citizenship and Immigration Services for special immigrant juvenile status pursuant to 8 USC § 1101 (a) (27) (J) which sought a finding that reunification of the child, Ena S.Y., with one of her parents is not viable due to parental abuse, neglect, or abandonment.

Ordered that the order is reversed insofar as appealed from, on the law and the facts, without costs or disbursements, that branch of the mother's motion which sought a finding that reunification of the child, Ena S.Y., with one of her parents is not viable due to parental neglect is granted, and it is found that reunification of the child, Ena S.Y., with one of her parents is not viable due to parental neglect.

In April 2015, the mother filed a petition pursuant to Family Court Act article 6 to be appointed guardian of her daughter, Ena S.Y. (hereinafter the child), and moved for the issuance of an order declaring that the child is dependent on the Family Court and making specific findings that she was unmarried and under 21 years of age, that reunification with her father was not viable due to parental abandonment, abuse, or neglect, and that it would not be in her best interests to be returned to Honduras, her previous country of nationality and last habitual residence, so as to enable her to petition the United States Citizenship and Immigration Services for special immigrant juvenile status (hereinafter SIJS) pursuant to 8 USC § 1101 (a) (27) (J). The Family Court granted the guardianship petition and thereafter held a hearing on the mother's motion for the issuance of an order making the requisite declaration and specific findings so as to enable the child to petition for SIJS.

Pursuant to 8 USC § 1101 (a) (27) (J) (as amended by the William Wilberforce Trafficking Victims Protection Reauthorization Act of 2008, Pub L 110-457, 122 US Stat 5044) and 8 CFR 204.11, a "special immigrant" is a resident alien who, inter alia, is under 21 years of age, is unmarried, and has been legally committed to, or placed under the custody of, an individual appointed by a state or juvenile court. Additionally, for a juvenile to qualify for SIJS, a court must find that reunification of the juvenile with one or both of the juvenile's parents is not viable due to parental abuse, neglect, abandonment, or a similar basis found under state law (*see* 8 USC § 1101 [a] [27] [J] [i]; *Matter of Maria P.E.A. v Sergio A.G.G.*, 111 AD3d 619, 620 [2013]; *Matter of Trudy-Ann W. v Joan W.*, 73 AD3d 793, 795 [2010]), and that it would not be in the juvenile's best interests to be returned to his or her native country or country of last habitual residence (*see* 8 USC § 1101 [a] [27] [J] [ii]; 8 CFR 204.11 [c] [6]; *Matter of Maria P.E.A. v Sergio A.G.G.*, 111 AD3d at 620; *Matter of Trudy-Ann W. v Joan W.*, 73 AD3d at 795).

Here, following the hearing, the Family Court found that the child was under 21 years of age, unmarried, and dependent on the Family Court, and that it would not be in her best interests to return to Honduras. However, the court denied the motion on the ground that the mother failed to establish that reunification of the child with her father is not viable due to parental abuse, neglect, or abandonment. We disagree.

At the hearing, the mother testified that when she and the father were living together with the child, the father would physically mistreat her in the presence of the children. The mother further testified that she and the father separated on or about December 31, 2014, when the father came home drunk, kicked and hit her, and engaged in a physical altercation with the child. The father admitted that on the night in question, he and the mother and the child "pushed each other" and he "had been drinking."

To establish neglect, the petitioner must establish, by a preponderance of the evidence, that the child's physical, mental, or emotional condition has been impaired or is in imminent danger of becoming impaired, and that the actual or threatened harm to the child is due to the failure of the parent or caretaker to exercise a minimum degree of care in providing the child with proper supervision or guardianship (*see* Family Ct Act § 1012 [f] [i] [B]; *Nicholson v Scoppetta*, 3 NY3d 357, 368 [2004]). Acts of domestic violence in the presence of children may establish neglect (*see Matter of Joshua V. [Rahsaan J.]*, 137 AD3d 1153, 1153-1154 [2016]). Further, "[n]eglect may be established by even a single incident of excessive corporal punishment" (*Matter of Joseph O'D. [Denise O'D.]*, 102 AD3d 874, 875 [2013]).

Here, the father's conduct constituted neglect, which established that his reunification with the child is not viable. Accordingly, that branch of the mother's motion which sought a finding that reunification of the child with one of her parents is not viable due to paternal neglect should have been granted.

The mother's remaining contentions need not be addressed in light of our determination. Leventhal, J.P., Chambers, Hinds-Radix and Connolly, JJ., concur.

50.   A hearing is required on a guardianship petition.

See, Matter of Francisco M-G-, below.

51.   Inappropriate remarks by a Judge indicating he is predisposed to deny SIJ motions should result in the case being transferred to another Judge.

See, Matter of Francisco M-G-, below.

52.   Guardianship can be granted to an uncle even though the child visits regularly with his mother who is financially unable to support him and does not function as his caretaker.

100 A.D. 3d 900 (2d Dep't Nov 21, 2012)

In the Matter of Francisco M.-G., Appellant, **v** **Marcelina M.-G., Appellant, et al., Respondent. Jason J. M.-G., Nonparty Appellant.**

Stephen Kolnik, Yonkers, N.Y., for petitioner-appellant.

Helene Migdon Greenberg, Elmsford, N.Y., for respondent-appellant.

Paul Hastings LLP, New York, N.Y. (Kevin Broughel of counsel), for nonparty-appellant.

In a proceeding pursuant to Family Court Act article 6 for the appointment of the petitioner, Francisco M.-G., as the guardian of Jason J. M.-G., a person under 21 years of age, the petitioner appeals, and Jason J. M.-G. and Marcelina M.-G. each separately appeal, from an order of the Family Court, Westchester County (Klein, J.), entered November 4, 2011, which, without a hearing, denied the motion of Jason J. M.-G. for the issuance of an order declaring that he is dependent on the Family Court and making specific findings that he is unmarried and under 21 years of age, that reunification with one or both of his parents is not viable due to parental abuse, neglect, or abandonment, and that it would not be in his best interest to be returned to his previous country of nationality or last habitual residence, so as to enable him to petition the United States Citizenship and Immigration Services for special immigrant juvenile status pursuant to 8 USC § 1101 (a) (27) (J), and, sua sponte, dismissed the petition for the appointment of the petitioner as the guardian of Jason J. M.-G.

Ordered that the appeal by Marcelina M.-G. is dismissed, without costs or disbursements, as she is not aggrieved by the order appealed from (*see* CPLR 5511); and it is further,

Ordered that the order is reversed on the appeals by the petitioner and Jason J. M.-G., on the law, without costs or disbursements, the guardianship petition is reinstated, and the matter is remitted to the Family Court, Westchester County, for a hearing before a different Judge and new determination thereafter on the petition for the appointment of the petitioner as the guardian of Jason J. M.-G., and, thereafter, if warranted, a hearing and a new determination on the motion for the issuance of an order making the requisite declaration and specific findings.

Jason J. M.-G. is a native of Honduras, is under 21 years of age, and is unmarried. He and his older sister entered the United States in 2008 and, since that time, he has been living with his uncle, Francisco M.-G. Although Jason visits regularly with his mother, who is also in the United States, she allegedly is unable to financially support him, and does not function as his caretaker. Jason has never known his father, who abandoned him at birth.

On December 17, 2009, Francisco filed a petition, seeking to be appointed Jason's guardian. In conjunction with the petition, Jason moved for the issuance of an order making the requisite declaration and specific findings to enable him to apply to the United States Citizenship and Immigration Services for special immigrant juvenile status pursuant to 8 USC § 1101 (a) (27) (J). The petition and motion were unopposed. The Family Court, sua sponte, dismissed the petition without conducting a hearing, and thereafter denied the motion without conducting a hearing.

The Family Court erred in dismissing the guardianship petition without conducting a hearing. When considering guardianship appointments, the infant's best interest is paramount (*see* SCPA 1707 [1]; *Matter of Stuart*, 280 NY 245, 250 [1939]; *Matter of Ashley W. [Verdele F.]*, 85 AD3d 807 [2011]; *Matter of Trudy-Ann W. v Joan W.*, 73 AD3d 793, 794 [2010]). The fact that the mother lives in the United States and maintains contact with Jason is not an automatic bar to the granting of Francisco's petition, as it has been alleged that the mother voluntarily relinquished control of Jason, does not support him financially, and has, at certain times, shown little concern for his safety and well-being (*see Matter of Garrett D. v Kevin L.*, 56 AD3d 1183 [2008]; *Matter of Dellolio v Tracy*, 35 AD3d 737 [2006]; *Matter of Vincent A.B. v Karen T.*, 30 AD3d 1100, 1101 [2006]; *Matter of Ruggieri v Bryan*, 23 AD3d 991, 992 [2005]).

Accordingly, the matter must be remitted to the Family Court, Westchester County, for a hearing and new determination on the guardianship petition. A hearing on Jason's motion for an order of special findings, as required by Federal law, should be held thereafter, if warranted, as Jason may be able to satisfy the prerequisites for obtaining such an order based on the new determination regarding guardianship (*see* 8 USC § 1101 [a] [27] [J] [i]; *Matter of Ashley W. [Verdele F.]*, 85 AD3d 807 [2011]; *Matter of Jisun L. v Young Sun P.*, 75 AD3d 510, 512 [2010]; *Matter of Trudy-Ann W. v Joan W.*, 73 AD3d at 795). In light of certain remarks made by the Family Court Judge, indicating that he was predisposed to deny motions, such as Jason's, for an order making such special findings, we deem it appropriate that the matter be heard and determined by a different Judge. Skelos, J.P., Dickerson, Hall and Roman, JJ., concur.

53. A Petitioner is aggrieved for the purposes of filing an appeal where a Referee signs an order of special findings but refuses to make a finding of abandonment.

See Claudio, below.

54. In Claudio, the AFC took a position contrary to the child receiving SIJ status (see Rules of the Chief Judge section 7.2(d))

> ☐ **In the Matter of Claudio D.A.I. Segundo A., Appellant; Maria D.I.L., Respondent.**

225 A.D. 3d 868 (2d Dep't Mar. 13, 2024)

Montenza Law Firm, P.C., New York, NY (Athena Matos of counsel), for appellant.

Wendy Pelle-Beer, Fresh Meadows, NY, attorney for the child.

In a guardianship proceeding pursuant to Family Court Act article 6, the petitioner appeals from an order of the Family Court, Queens County (Juanita E. Wing, Ct. Atty. Ref.), dated April 5, 2023. The order, insofar as appealed from, after a hearing, in effect, denied that branch of the petitioner's motion which was for a specific finding that the reunification of the subject child with the mother is not viable due to abuse, neglect, and/or abandonment, so as to enable the subject child to petition the United States Citizenship and Immigration Services for special immigrant juvenile status pursuant to 8 USC § 1101 (a) (27) (J).

Ordered that the order is modified, on the law, on the facts, and in the exercise of discretion, (1) by deleting from the sixth paragraph thereof the phrase beginning with the words "after assisting the child" and ending with the words "life in this country," and substituting therefor the phrase "and due to the Mother's abandonment of the child," and (2) by deleting from the seventh paragraph thereof the phrase "with the assistance of his parents"; as so modified, the order is affirmed insofar as appealed from, without costs or disbursements.

In 2021, the petitioner commenced this proceeding pursuant to Family Court Act article 6 to be appointed as guardian of the subject child for the purpose of obtaining an order declaring that the child is dependent on the Family Court and making specific findings so as to enable the child to petition the United States Citizenship and Immigration Services for special immigrant juvenile status (hereinafter SIJS) pursuant to 8 USC § 1101 (a) (27) (J). Subsequently, the petitioner moved for the issuance of an order making the requisite declaration and specific findings so as to enable the child to petition for SIJS.

In an order dated April 5, 2023, made after a hearing, the Family Court, among other things, in effect, denied that branch of the petitioner's motion which was for a specific finding that the reunification of the child with the mother is not viable due to abuse, neglect, and/or abandonment. The petitioner appeals.

Here, the Family Court did not grant all of the relief sought in the petitioner's motion, which included a specific finding that reunification of the child with the mother "is not viable due to abuse, neglect and/or abandonment under New York law, as defined by Social Services Law, Section 384 .☐☐ and Family Court Act § 1012 (f), within the meaning of .☐☐ 8 USC § 1101 (a) (27) (J)." In other words, the petitioner's appeal does not relate solely to the language used in the order appealed from. Therefore, contrary to the contention of the child, the petitioner is aggrieved by the order (*see Mixon v TBV, Inc.*, 76 AD3d 144, 156-157 [2010]; *cf. Matter of Josue M.A.P. [Coreas Mancia—Perez Lue]*, 143 AD3d 827, 828 [2016]).

In making specific factual findings, the Family Court "is not rendering an immigration determination"; rather, "the final decision regarding [SIJS] rests with the federal government, and, as shown, the child must apply to that authority" (*Matter of Marcelina M.-G. v Israel S.*, 112 AD3d 100, 109 [2013] [internal quotation marks omitted]).

In reviewing a court's determination of a motion for specific findings, "[t]his Court's power to review the evidence is as broad as that of the hearing court, and where .☐☐ the record is sufficiently complete to make our own factual determinations, we may do so" (*Matter of Fifo v Fifo*, 127 AD3d 748, 751 [2015] [internal quotation marks omitted]; *see Matter of Briceyda M.A.X. [Hugo R.A.O.]*, 190 AD3d 752, 753-754 [2021]). Here, based upon our independent factual review, the record supports a finding that reunification of the child with his mother is not a viable option due to parental abandonment (*see Matter of Joel A.A.R. [Sara I.R.T.—Eddy A.A.G.]*, 216 AD3d 1167, 1170 [2023]; *Matter of Jose E.S.G. [Mejia—Salguero]*, 193 AD3d 856, 858 [2021]; *Matter of Mohamed B.*, 83 AD3d 829, 832 [2011]).

Accordingly, the order should be modified as indicated herein. Duffy, J.P., Wooten, Ford and Taylor, JJ., concur.

55. It is possible the Second Department will not see a minor to be aggrieved for the purpose of filing an appeal where a special findings order contains a finding that reunification with one or both parents is not possible even though CIS rejects the I-360 application claiming the language in the order is general in nature and lacks specifics.

> ☐ **In the Matter of Josue M.A.P., Appellant. Jose Dimas Coreas Mancia, Petitioner; Araceli Carolina Perez Lue et al., Respondents.**

143 A.D. 3d 827 (2nd Dep't October 12, 2016)

Peter K. Nardone, Mount Kisco, NY (Myriam Jaidi of counsel), for appellant.

Appeal by the child, Josue M.A.P., from an order of the Family Court, Westchester County (Michelle I. Schauer, J.), entered August 11, 2015. The order, insofar as appealed from, without a hearing, granted that branch of the petitioner's motion which was for a specific finding that reunification of the subject child with one or both of his parents was not viable due to parental neglect or abandonment.

Ordered that the appeal is dismissed, without costs or disbursements, as the appellant is not aggrieved by the portion of the order appealed from (*see* CPLR 5511; *Mixon v TBV, Inc.*, 76 AD3d 144, 156 [2010]).

In January 2015, the petitioner commenced this proceeding pursuant to Family Court Act article 6 to be appointed guardian of Josue M.A.P. (hereinafter the child), for the purpose of obtaining an order declaring that the child is dependent on the Family Court and making special findings so as to enable him to petition the United States Citizenship and Immigration Services for special immigrant juvenile status (hereinafter SIJS) pursuant to 8 USC § 1101 (a) (27) (J) (*see generally Matter of Blanca C.S.C. [Norma C.]*, 141 AD3d 580[2016]; *Matter of Maria P.E.A. v Sergio A.G.G.*, 111 AD3d 619, 620 [2013]; *Matter of Trudy-Ann W. v Joan W.*, 73 AD3d 793, 795 [2010]). Thereafter, the petitioner moved for the issuance of an order making the requisite declaration and specific findings so as to enable the child to petition for SIJS (*see Matter of Blanca C.S.C. [Norma C.]*, 141 AD3d at 580). In an "order for special findings" entered August 11, 2015, the Family Court granted the motion and set forth the requisite findings.

The child, who is now 20 years old, appeals. His sole challenge relates to that branch of the petitioner's motion which sought a finding that reunification of the child with one or both of his parents was not viable due to parental neglect or abandonment. He argues that certain language in the order appealed from renders the order "useless for the purpose of seeking [SIJS]," and that the Family Court essentially failed to find that reunification with one or both of his parents was not viable due to neglect or abandonment. However, contrary to his contentions, the order specifically states that "reunification with one or both of his parents is not viable due to abandonment, abuse, and/or neglect." Thus, the child is not aggrieved and the appeal must be dismissed (*see Matter of Charle C.E. [Chiedu E.]*, 129 AD3d 721, 721-722 [2015]; *Mixon v TBV, Inc.*, 76 AD3d 144, 156 [2010]; *cf. Matter of Jeison P.-C. [Conception P.]*, 132 AD3d 876, 877 [2015]; *Matter of Marvin E.M. de P. [Milagro C.C.—Mario Enrique M.G.]*, 121 AD3d 892, 892 [2014]). Rivera, J.P., Leventhal, Maltese and Barros, JJ., concur.

56. The record must contain evidence that reunification with at least 1 parent is not possible.

☐ In the Matter of Marvin E.M. De P. Milagro C.C., Appellant; Mario Enrique M.G. et al., Respondents.

121 A.D. 3d 892 (2nd Dep't October 15, 2014)

Bruno Joseph Bembi, Hempstead, N.Y., for appellant.

Cheryl L. Kreger, Jericho, N.Y., attorney for the child.

In a guardianship proceeding pursuant to Family Court Act article 6, the petitioner appeals from an order of the Family Court, Nassau County (Stack, J.H.O.), dated November 26, 2013, which, upon the granting of the petition in an order dated June 11, 2013, and after a hearing, denied her motion for the issuance of an order making special findings so as to enable the subject child to petition the United States Citizenship and Immigration Services for special immigrant juvenile status pursuant to 8 USC § 1101 (a) (27) (J).

Ordered that the order dated November 26, 2013, is affirmed, without costs or disbursements.

In March 2013, the petitioner filed a petition pursuant to Family Court Act article 6 to be appointed guardian of her nephew, Marvin E. M. de P. (hereinafter the child), for the purpose of obtaining an order declaring that the child is dependent on the Family Court and making specific findings that he is unmarried and under 21 years of age, that reunification with his parents is not viable due to abandonment, neglect, or abuse, and that it would not be in his best interests to be returned to El Salvador, his previous country of nationality and last habitual residence, so as to enable him to petition the United States Citizenship and Immigration Services for special immigrant juvenile status (hereinafter SIJS) pursuant to 8 USC § 1101 (a) (27) (J). Thereafter, the petitioner moved for the issuance of an order making the requisite declaration and specific findings to enable the child to petition for SIJS. After a hearing, the

Family Court determined that the child was under 21 years of age, unmarried, dependent on the Family Court, and that it would not be in his best interests to return to El Salvador. However, the court denied the petitioner's motion on the ground that she failed to show that reunification of the child with his parents was not viable.

Pursuant to 8 USC § 1101 (a) (27) (J) (as amended by the William Wilberforce Trafficking Victims Protection Reauthorization Act of 2008, Pub L 110-457, 122 US Stat 5044) and 8 CFR 204.11, a special immigrant is a resident alien who is, inter alia, under 21 years of age, unmarried, and dependent upon a juvenile court or legally committed to an individual appointed by a state or juvenile court. The appointment of a guardian constitutes the necessary declaration of dependency on a juvenile court for special immigrant juvenile status purposes (*see Matter of Trudy-Ann W. v Joan W.*, 73 AD3d 793, 795 [2010]; *Matter of Antowa McD.*, 50 AD3d 507 [2008]). Additionally, for a juvenile to qualify for special immigrant juvenile status, a court must find that reunification of the juvenile with one or both of the juvenile's parents is not viable due to parental abuse, neglect, abandonment, or similar parental conduct defined under State law, and that it would not be in the juvenile's best interest to be returned to his or her native country or country of last habitual residence (*see Matter of Trudy-Ann W. v Joan W.*, 73 AD3d at 795).

Upon our independent factual review, we find that, contrary to the petitioner's contention, the record supports the Family Court's determination as to reunification (*see Matter of Mira v Hernandez*, 118 AD3d 1008 [2014]; *Matter of Maria S.Z. v Maria M.A.*, 115 AD3d 970 [2014]; *Matter of Nirmal S. v Rajinder K.*, 101 AD3d 1130 [2012]).

The petitioner's remaining contentions either are without merit or are not properly before this Court. Skelos, J.P., Leventhal, Hinds-Radix and Maltese, JJ., concur.

57.   Once a finding of neglect against a particular parent is made, it necessarily follows that reunification with the parent is not viable.

> ☐ **In the Matter of Eddy A.P.C., Appellant; Maria G.C.S. et al., Respondents. (Proceeding No. 1.) In the Matter of Cleidy F.P.C., Appellant; Maria G.C.S. et al., Respondents. (Proceeding No. 2.)**

226 A.D. 3d 1005 (2nd Dep't April 24, 2024)

Jones Day, New York, NY (Jennifer Del Medico, Jack L. Millman, and Graziella Pastor of counsel), for appellants.

In related proceedings pursuant to Family Court Act article 6, the subject children appeal from an order of the Family Court, Kings County (Lisa Aschkenasy, Ct. Atty. Ref.), dated June 28, 2023. The order, after a hearing, denied the subject children's motion for the issuance of an order, inter alia, making specific findings so as to enable them to petition the United States Citizenship and Immigration Services for special immigrant juvenile status pursuant to 8 USC § 1101 (a) (27) (J).

Ordered that the order is reversed, on the facts, without costs or disbursements, the subject children's motion for the issuance of an order, inter alia, making specific findings so as to enable them to petition the United States Citizenship and Immigration Services for special immigrant juvenile status pursuant to 8 USC § 1101 (a) (27) (J) is granted, and it is found that reunification of the subject children with their mother is not viable due to parental abandonment and neglect and that it would not be in the best interests of the subject children to return to Guatemala, their previous country of nationality and last habitual residence.

In March 2023, the subject children, Eddy A.P.C. and Cleidy F.P.C., who arrived in the United States from Guatemala in 2019, filed separate petitions pursuant to Family Court Act article 6 seeking to have their father appointed as their guardian. Thereafter, the children moved for the issuance of an order declaring that they were dependent on the Family Court and making specific findings that they are unmarried and under 21 years of age, that reunification with their mother was not viable due to parental neglect, and that it would not be in their best interests to be returned to Guatemala, their previous country of nationality and last habitual residence, so as to enable them to petition the United States Citizenship and Immigration Services for special immigrant juvenile status (hereinafter SIJS) pursuant to 8 USC § 1101 (a) (27) (J). The court appointed the father as guardian of the children. However, in an order dated June 28, 2023, the court, after a hearing, found neglect on the part of the mother, but denied the children's motion on the ground that they failed to establish that reunification with their mother was not viable. The children appeal.

" 'Pursuant to 8 USC § 1101 (a) (27) (J) (as amended by the William Wilberforce Trafficking Victims Protection Reauthorization Act of 2008, Pub L 110-457, 122 US Stat 5044) and 8 CFR 204.11, a 'special immigrant' is a resident alien who is, inter alia, under 21 years of age, unmarried, and dependent upon a juvenile court or legally committed to an individual appointed by a state or juvenile court' " (*Matter of Briceyda M.A.X. [Hugo R.A.O.]*, 190 AD3d 752, 753 [2021], quoting *Matter of Trudy-Ann W. v Joan W.*, 73 AD3d 793, 795 [2010]). "Additionally, for a juvenile to qualify for special immigrant juvenile status, a court must find that reunification of the juvenile with one or both of the juvenile's parents is not viable due to parental abuse, neglect, abandonment, or a similar basis found under State law, and that it would not be in the juvenile's best interest to be returned to his or her native country or country of last habitual residence" (*Matter of Briceyda M.A.X. [Hugo R.A.O.]*,

190 AD3d at 753, quoting *Matter of Maria P.E.A. v Sergio A.G.G.*, 111 AD3d 619, 620 [2013]; *see* 8 USC § 1101 [a] [27] [J]; 8 CFR 204.11 [c]).

" 'While the credibility assessment of a hearing court is accorded considerable deference on appeal, where, as here, the Family Court's credibility determination is not supported by the record, this Court is free to make its own credibility assessments and overturn the determination of the hearing court' " (*Matter of Norma U. v Herman T.R.F.*, 169 AD3d 1055, 1056-1057 [2019], quoting *Matter of Dennis X.G.D.V.*, 158 AD3d 712, 714 [2018]). Here, the petitions were granted prior to the children's 21st birthdays (*see Matter of Juan R.E.M. [Juan R.E.]*, 154 AD3d 725 [2017]), the children are unmarried, and since the Family Court appointed the father as the children's guardian, the children are dependent on a juvenile court within the meaning of 8 USC § 1101 (a) (27) (J) (i) (*see Matter of Jose E.S.G. [Mejia—Salguero]*, 193 AD3d 856 [2021]; *Matter of Grechel L.J.*, 167 AD3d 1011, 1013 [2018]). Based upon our independent review, the record supports a finding that reunification of the children with their mother is not viable due to the mother's abandonment of the children. The record reflects that the mother provided little to no emotional support to the children while in Guatemala before the mother abandoned the children entirely by moving to the United States and after the children arrived in the United States, the mother continued to neglect the children (*see Matter of Rina M.G.C. [Oscar L.G.—Ana M.C.H.]*, 169 AD3d 1031, 1033 [2019]; *Matter of Enis A.C.M. [Blanca E.M.—Carlos V.C.P.]*, 152 AD3d 690 [2017]). The record further reflects that the mother failed to protect the children from gang violence in Guatemala and did not provide emotional support with regard to the threat of gang violence (*see Matter of Victor R.C.O. [Canales]*, 172 AD3d 1071 [2019]). Further, the record supports a finding that it would not be in the best interests of the children to return to Guatemala, their previous country of nationality and country of last habitual residence (*see Matter of Briceyda M.A.X.*

[Hugo R.A.O.], 190 AD3d at 754; *Matter of Keilyn GG. [Marlene HH.]*, 159 AD3d 1295, 1297 [2018]).

Accordingly, the Family Court should have granted the children's motions for the issuance of an order, inter alia, making the requisite declaration and specific findings so as to enable them to petition for SIJS. Duffy, J.P., Miller, Voutsinas and Love, JJ., concur.

58.   Neglect can be found where a parent inflicts excessive corporal punishment and requires the child to work at age 12 instead of attending school on a regular basis.

☐ **In the Matter of Palwinder K., Appellant,**
v
Kuldeep K. et al., Respondents.

148 A.D. 3d 1149 (2nd Dep't March 29, 2017)

Genet Getachew, Brooklyn, NY, for appellant.

Kelli M. O'Brien, Goshen, NY, attorney for the child.

Appeal by the petitioner from an order of the Family Court, Queens County (Marilyn J. Moriber, Ct. Atty. Ref.), dated January 8, 2016. The order, after a hearing, denied the petitioner's motion for the issuance of an order making specific findings so as to enable the subject child, Lovepreet S., to petition the United States Citizenship and Immigration Services for special immigrant juvenile status pursuant to 8 USC § 1101 (a) (27) (J).

Ordered that the order is reversed, on the facts, without costs or disbursements, the petitioner's motion for the issuance of an order making specific findings so as to enable the subject child to petition the United States Citizenship and Immigration Services for special immigrant juvenile status pursuant to 8 USC § 1101 (a) (27) (J) is granted, and it is found that reunification of the subject child with one or both of his parents is not viable due to parental neglect, and that it would not be in his best interests to return to India, his previous country of nationality and last habitual residence.

In February 2015, the petitioner filed a petition pursuant to Family Court Act article 6 to be appointed the guardian of Lovepreet S. (hereinafter the child), who was born in India. The petitioner subsequently moved for the issuance of an order making the findings necessary for the child to petition the United States Citizenship and Immigration Services for special immigrant juvenile status (hereinafter SIJS) pursuant to 8 USC § 1101 (a) (27) (J). The petitioner's motion sought specific findings that the child was under 21 years of age and unmarried, that he was dependent upon the Family Court, that reunification with one or both of his parents was not viable due to parental abuse, neglect, or abandonment, and that it would not be in his best interests to be returned to India. At the conclusion of a hearing, the Family Court granted the guardianship petition. However, the court denied the petitioner's motion on the ground that she failed to establish that reunification of the child with one or both of his parents was not viable due to parental abuse, neglect, or abandonment.

Pursuant to 8 USC § 1101 (a) (27) (J) (as amended by the William Wilberforce Trafficking Victims Protection Reauthorization Act of 2008, Pub L 110-457, 122 US Stat 5044) and 8 CFR 204.11, a "special immigrant" is a resident alien who, inter alia, is under 21 years of age, is unmarried, and has been legally committed to, or placed under the custody of, an individual appointed by a state or juvenile court. Additionally, for a juvenile to qualify for special immigrant juvenile status, a court must find that reunification of the juvenile with one or both of the juvenile's parents is not viable due to parental abuse, neglect, abandonment, or a similar basis found under state law (*see* 8 USC § 1101 [a] [27] [J] [i]; *Matter of Wilson A.T.Z. [Jose M.T.G.—Manuela Z.M.]*, 147 AD3d 962 [2d Dept 2017]; *Matter of Maria P.E.A. v Sergio A.G.G.*, 111 AD3d 619, 620 [2013]; *Matter of Trudy-Ann W. v Joan W.*, 73 AD3d 793, 795 [2010]), and that it would not be in the juvenile's best interests to be returned to his or her native country or country of last habitual residence (*see* 8 USC § 1101 [a] [27] [J] [ii]; 8 CFR 204.11 [c] [6]; *Matter of Maria P.E.A. v Sergio A.G.G.*, 111 AD3d at 620; *Matter of Trudy-Ann W. v Joan W.*, 73 AD3d at 795).

Based upon our independent factual review, we conclude that the record supports a finding that reunification of the child with one or both of his parents is not a viable option based upon parental neglect, which includes the infliction of excessive corporal punishment and requiring the child to begin working at the age of 12 instead of attending school on a regular basis (*see Matter of Ena S.Y. [Martha R.Y.—Antonio S.]*, 140 AD3d 778, 780 [2016]; *Matter of Mohamed B.*, 83 AD3d 829, 832 [2011]; *Matter of Alamgir A.*, 81 AD3d 937, 938-939 [2011]). The record further supports a finding that it would not be in the best interests of the child to return to India (*see Matter of Varinder S. v Satwinder S.*, 147 AD3d 854[2d Dept 2017]; *Matter of Marcelina M.-G. v Israel S.*, 112 AD3d 100, 114-115 [2013]; *Matter of Trudy-Ann W. v Joan W.*, 73 AD3d at 796).

Accordingly, the Family Court should have granted the petitioner's motion for the issuance of an order making the requisite findings so as to enable the child to petition for SIJS. Since the record is sufficient for this Court to make its own findings of fact and conclusions of law, we find that reunification of the child with one or both of his parents is not viable due to parental neglect, and that it would not be in his best interests to return to India, his previous country of nationality and habitual residence (*see Matter of Varinder S. v Satwinder S.*,

<u>147 AD3d 854</u>). Eng, P.J., Hall, Roman and Hinds-Radix, JJ., concur.

☐ **In the Matter of Gurwinder S., Appellant.**

155 A.D. 3d 959 (2nd Dep't November 22, 2017)

Jill M. Zuccardy, New York, NY, for appellant.

Appeal by the child from an order of the Family Court, Queens County (Julie Stanton, Ct. Atty. Ref.), dated September 29, 2016. The order, after a hearing, denied the child's motion for the issuance of an order, inter alia, making specific findings so as to enable him to petition the United States Citizenship and Immigration Services for special immigrant juvenile status pursuant to 8 USC § 1101 (a) (27) (J).

Ordered that the order is reversed, on the facts, without costs or disbursements, the child's motion for the issuance of an order, inter alia, making specific findings so as to enable him to petition the United States Citizenship and Immigration Services for special immigrant juvenile status pursuant to 8 USC § 1101 (a) (27) (J) is granted, and it is found that reunification of the child with his father is not viable due to parental neglect, and that it would not be in the child's best interests to return to India, his previous country of nationality and last habitual residence.

In December 2015, Baldev S. (hereinafter the petitioner) filed a petition pursuant to Family Court Act article 6 to be appointed as guardian for the subject child for the purpose of obtaining an order declaring that the child is dependent on the Family Court and making specific findings that he is unmarried and under 21 years of age, that reunification with one or both of his parents is not viable due to parental abuse, neglect, or abandonment, and that it would not be in his best interests to be returned to India, his previous country of nationality and country of last habitual residence, so as to enable the child to petition the United States Citizenship and Immigration Services for special immigrant juvenile status (hereinafter SIJS) pursuant to 8 USC § 1101 (a) (27) (J). Thereafter, the child moved for the issuance of an order making the requisite declaration and specific findings so as to enable him to petition for SIJS. In an order dated September 29, 2016, the Family Court denied the child's motion on the ground that he failed to establish that reunification of the child with one or both of his parents was not viable due to parental abuse, neglect, or abandonment, and that it would not be in the child's best interests to return to India. The child appeals.

Pursuant to 8 USC § 1101 (a) (27) (J) (as amended by the William Wilberforce Trafficking Victims Protection Reauthorization Act of 2008, Pub L 110-457, 122 US Stat 5044) and 8 CFR 204.11, a special immigrant is a resident alien who, inter alia, is under 21 years of age, unmarried, and dependent upon a juvenile court or legally committed to an individual appointed by a state or juvenile court. Additionally, for a juvenile to qualify for SIJS, a court must find that reunification of the juvenile with one or both of the juvenile's parents is not viable due to parental abuse, neglect, abandonment, or a similar basis found under state law (*see* 8 USC § 1101 [a] [27] [J] [i]; *Matter of Maria P.E.A. v Sergio A.G.G.*, 111 AD3d 619, 620 [2013]; *Matter of Trudy-Ann W. v Joan W.*, 73 AD3d 793, 795 [2010]), and that it would not be in the juvenile's best interests to be returned to his or her previous country of nationality or country of last habitual residence (*see* 8 USC § 1101 [a] [27] [J] [ii]; 8 CFR 204.11 [c] [6]; *Matter of Maria P.E.A. v Sergio A.G.G.*, 111 AD3d at 620; *Matter of Trudy-Ann W. v Joan W.*, 73 AD3d at 795).

Based upon our independent factual review, we find that reunification of the child with his father is not a viable option due to parental neglect, which includes the infliction of excessive corporal punishment and requiring the child to begin working at the age of 15 instead of attending school on a regular basis (*see Matter of Palwinder K. v Kuldeep K.*, 148 AD3d 1149, 1151 [2017]; *Matter of Kamaljit S.*, 114 AD3d 949 [2014]). The record also supports a finding that it would not be in the child's best interests to be returned to India (*see Matter of Palwinder K. v Kuldeep K.*, 148 AD3d at 1151; *Matter of Varinder S. v Satwinder S.*, 147 AD3d 854, 856 [2017]).

Accordingly, the Family Court should have granted the child's motion for the issuance of an order, inter alia, making the requisite specific findings so as to enable him to petition for SIJS. Since the record is sufficient for this Court to make its own findings of fact and conclusions of law, we find that reunification of the child with his father is not viable due to parental neglect, and that it would not be in his best interests to return to India, his previous country of nationality and last habitual residence. Chambers, J.P., Cohen, Barros and Christopher, JJ., concur.

59.   On appeal, the Appellate Department power to review the evidence is as broad as that of the hearing court.

> **In the Matter of Kamaljit S., Appellant. Gardeep S., Respondent,**
> **v**
> **Jasvinder K. et al., Respondents.**

114 A.D.3d 949 (2d Dep't Feb. 26. 2014)

Joseph H. Nivin, Jamaica, N.Y., for appellant.

In a proceeding pursuant to Family Court Act article 6 for the appointment of Gardeep S. as guardian of the child Kamaljit S., Kamaljit S. appeals from an order of the Family Court, Queens County (Pach, J.H.O), dated March 12, 2013, which, upon the granting of the guardian petition in an order dated February 5, 2013, and after a hearing, denied his motion for the issuance of an order making special findings so as to enable him to petition the United States Citizenship and Immigration Services for special immigrant juvenile status pursuant to 8 USC § 1101 (a) (27) (J).

Ordered that the order is reversed, on the facts, without costs or disbursements, the motion is granted, it is declared that Kamaljit S. is dependent on the Family Court, and it is found that he is unmarried and under 21 years of age, that reunification with one or both of his parents is not viable due to parental neglect, and that it would not be in the best interests of Kamaljit S. to return to India, his previous country of nationality and last habitual residence.

In this proceeding in which Gardeep S. was appointed the guardian of Kamaljit S., Kamaljit moved for the issuance of an order making specific findings that would allow him to apply to the United States Citizenship and Immigration Services for special immigrant juvenile status (hereinafter SIJS). After a hearing, the Family Court determined that Kamaljit was under 21 years of age, unmarried, and dependent on the Family Court. However, the court denied Kamaljit's motion on the ground that Kamaljit failed to show that reunification with one or both of his parents was not viable and that it was not in his best interests to return to his country of origin, India.

Pursuant to 8 USC § 1101 (a) (27) (J) (as amended by the William Wilberforce Trafficking Victims Protection Reauthorization Act of 2008, Pub L 110-457, 122 US Stat 5044) and 8 CFR 204.11, a "special immigrant" is a resident alien who is, inter alia, under 21 years of age, unmarried, and "declared dependent on a juvenile court located in the United States or whom such a court has legally committed to, or placed under the custody of, an agency or department of a State, or an individual or entity appointed by a State or juvenile court located in the United States" (8 USC § 1101 [a] [27] [J] [i]). For the juvenile to qualify for SIJS status, it must also be determined that reunification with "1 or both" of the juvenile's parents is not viable due to parental abuse, neglect, abandonment, or a similar basis found under State law (*id.*), and that it would not be in the juvenile's best interest to be returned to his or her native country or country of last habitual residence (*see* 8 USC § 1101 [a] [27] [J] [ii]).

This Court's power to review the evidence is as broad as that of the hearing court, and where, as here, the record is sufficiently complete to make our own factual determinations, we may do so (*see Matter of Jisun L. v Young Sun P.*, 75 AD3d 510, 511-512 [2010]; *Matter of Trudy-Ann W. v Joan W.*, 73 AD3d 793, 795 [2010]). Based upon our independent factual review, we find that the record supports Kamaljit's contentions that reunification with his mother was not viable due to parental neglect, and that it would not be in Kamaljit's best interests to be returned to India (*see Matter of Marcelina M.-G. v Israel S.*, 112 AD3d 100, 115 [2013]; *Matter of Mohamed B.*, 83 AD3d 829, 832 [2011]). Accordingly, the Family Court should have granted Kamaljit's motion. Mastro, J.P., Chambers, Lott and Miller, JJ., concur.

60. It is appropriate to grant a motion for special findings where the record establishes that the child was abandoned by his parents and it was not in his best interests to return to India.

> ☐ **In the Matter of Varinder S., Petitioner,**
> **v**
> **Satwinder S. et al., Respondents. Lovepreet S., Nonparty Appellant.**

147 A.D. 3d 854 (2ⁿᵈ Dep't February 8, 2017)

Kelli M. O'Brien, Goshen, NY, for nonparty appellant.

Appeal by the nonparty child from an order of the Family Court, Orange County (Christine P. Krahulik, J.), dated February 23, 2016. The order, after a hearing, denied the child's motion for the issuance of an order, inter alia, making specific findings so as to enable him to petition the United States Citizenship and Immigration Services for special immigrant juvenile status pursuant to 8 USC § 1101 (a) (27) (J).

Ordered that the order is reversed, on the law and the facts, without costs or disbursements, the child's motion for the issuance of an order, inter alia, making specific findings so as to enable him to petition the United States Citizenship and Immigration Services for special immigrant juvenile status pursuant to 8 USC § 1101 (a) (27) (J) is granted, and it is found that reunification of the subject child with one or both of his parents is not viable due to parental abandonment, and that it would not be in his best interests to return to India, his previous country of nationality and last habitual residence.

In March 2015, Varinder S. (hereinafter the petitioner) filed a petition pursuant to Family Court Act article 6 to be appointed guardian of Lovepreet S. (hereinafter the child), for the purpose of obtaining an order declaring that the child is dependent on the Family Court and making specific findings that he is unmarried and under 21 years of age, that reunification with one or both of his parents is not viable due to parental abandonment, and that it would not be in his best interests to be returned to India, his previous country of nationality and country of last habitual residence, so as to enable the child to petition the United States Citizenship and Immigration Services for special immigrant juvenile status (hereinafter SIJS) pursuant to 8 USC § 1101 (a) (27) (J). Thereafter, the child moved for the issuance of an order making the requisite declaration and specific findings so as to enable him to petition for SIJS. In an order dated February 23, 2016, made after a hearing, the Family Court denied the motion, finding that the child failed to establish that reunification with one or both of his parents was not viable due to parental abandonment and that it would be contrary to his best interests to be returned to India.

Pursuant to 8 USC § 1101 (a) (27) (J) (as amended by the William Wilberforce Trafficking Victims Protection Reauthorization Act of 2008, Pub L 110-457, 122 US Stat 5044) and 8 CFR 204.11, a special immigrant is a resident alien who, inter alia, is under 21 years of age, unmarried, and dependent upon a juvenile court or legally committed to an individual appointed by a state or juvenile court. Additionally, for a juvenile to qualify for SIJS, a court must find that reunification of the juvenile with one or both of the juvenile's parents is not viable due to parental abuse, neglect, abandonment, or a similar basis found under state law (*see* 8 USC § 1101 [a] [27] [J] [i]; *Matter of Maria P.E.A. v Sergio A.G.G.*, 111 AD3d 619, 620 [2013]; *Matter of Trudy-Ann W. v Joan W.*, 73 AD3d 793, 795 [2010]), and that it would not be in the juvenile's best interests to be returned to his or her previous country of nationality or country of last habitual residence (*see* 8 USC § 1101 [a] [27] [J] [ii]; 8 CFR 204.11 [c] [6]; *Matter of Maria P.E.A. v Sergio A.G.G.*, 111 AD3d at 620; *Matter of Trudy-Ann W. v Joan W.*, 73 AD3d at 795).

Based upon our independent factual review, we find that reunification of the child with one or both of his parents is not a viable option due to parental abandonment (*see Matter of Anibal H. [Maria G.G.H.]*, 138 AD3d 841, 843 [2016]), and that it would not be in his best interests to return to India (*see Matter of Miguel C.-N. [Hosman C.-N.—Cruz Ermelinda C.-N.]*, 119 AD3d 562, 563 [2014]).

Accordingly, the Family Court should have granted the child's motion for the issuance of an order, inter alia, making the requisite specific findings so as to enable him to petition for SIJS. Since the record is sufficient for this Court to make its own findings of fact and conclusions of law, we find that reunification of the child with one or both of his parents is not viable due to parental abandonment, and that it would not be in his best interests to return to India, his previous country of nationality and last habitual residence (*see Matter of Carlos*

<u>A.M. v Maria T.M.</u>, 141 AD3d 526, 528-529 [2016]). Leventhal, J.P., Roman, Sgroi and Connolly, JJ., concur.

61. In what was apparently a contested hearing, where the Family Court's credibility determination is not supported by the record, the Appellate Department is free to make its own credibility determination.

> ☐ **In the Matter of Briceyda M.A.X., Appellant. Hugo R.A.O., Respondent. Maria H.X.C., Nonparty Respondent. (Proceeding No. 1.) In the Matter of Ingrid C.A.X., Appellant. Hugo R.A.O., Respondent. Maria H.X.C., Nonparty Respondent. (Proceeding No. 2.) In the Matter of Dulce P.A.X., Appellant. Hugo R.A.O., Respondent. Maria H.X.C., Nonparty Respondent. (Proceeding No. 3.)**

190 A.D. 3d 752 (2nd Dep't January 13, 2021)

Davis Polk & Wardwell LLP, New York, NY (Hannah B. Gerstenblatt and Corey M. Meyer of counsel), for appellants.

Larry S. Bachner, Jamaica, NY, for respondent-respondent.

Simpson Thacher & Bartlett LLP, New York, NY (Brooke E. Cucinella and Alison M. Sher of counsel), for nonparty respondent.

In guardianship proceedings pursuant to Family Court Act article 6, the subject children appeal from an order of the Family Court, Queens County (Lauren Norton Lerner, Ct. Atty. Ref.), dated November 17, 2020. The order, after a hearing, denied the subject children's motions for the issuance of orders, inter alia, making specific findings so as to enable them to petition the United States Citizen and Immigration Services for special immigrant juvenile status pursuant to 8 USC § 1101 (a) (27) (J).

Ordered that the order is reversed, on the facts, without costs or disbursements, the subject children's motions for the issuance of orders, inter alia, making specific findings so as to enable them to petition the United States Citizen and Immigration Services for special immigrant juvenile status pursuant to 8 USC § 1101 (a) (27) (J) are granted, and it is found that reunification of the subject children with their father is not viable due to parental abandonment and neglect and that it would not be in the best interests of the subject children to return to Guatemala, their previous country of nationality and last habitual residence.

On April 11, 2018, the three subject children, Briceyda M.A.X., Ingrid C.A.X., and Dulce P.A.X., filed separate petitions pursuant to Family Court Act article 6 to have their mother appointed as their guardian. On July 18, 2018, the children separately moved for the issuance of orders declaring that they were dependent on the Family Court and making specific findings that they are unmarried and under 21 years of age, that reunification with their father was not viable due to parental abandonment and neglect, and that it would not be in their best interests to be returned to Guatemala, their previous country of nationality and last habitual residence, so as to enable them to petition the United States Citizens and Immigration Services for special immigrant juvenile status (hereinafter SIJS) pursuant to 8 USC § 1101 (a) (27) (J). The father, who was living in New Jersey, opposed the mother being appointed as guardian for the children and opposed the children's motions for special findings. The Family Court appointed the mother as guardian of the children. However, after a hearing, in an order dated November 17, 2020, the court denied the children's motions. The children appeal.

"Pursuant to 8 USC § 1101 (a) (27) (J) (as amended by the William Wilberforce Trafficking Victims Protection Reauthorization Act of 2008, Pub L 110-457, 122 US Stat 5044) and 8 CFR 204.11, a 'special immigrant' is a resident alien who is, inter alia, under 21 years of age, unmarried, and dependent upon a juvenile court or legally committed to an individual appointed by a state or juvenile court" (*Matter of Trudy-Ann W. v Joan W.*, 73 AD3d 793, 795 [2010]). "Additionally, for a juvenile to qualify for special immigrant juvenile status, a court must find that reunification of the juvenile with one or both of the juvenile's parents is not viable due to parental abuse, neglect, abandonment, or a similar basis found under State law, and that it would not be in the juvenile's best interest to be returned to his or her native country or country of last habitual residence" (*Matter of Maria P.E.A. v Sergio A.G.G.*, 111 AD3d 619, 620 [2013] [citations omitted]; *see* 8 USC § 1101 [a] [27] [J]; 8 CFR 204.11 [c] [6]).

" 'While the credibility assessment of a hearing court is accorded considerable deference on appeal, where, as here, the Family Court's credibility determination is not supported by the record, this Court is free to make its own credibility assessments and overturn the determination of the hearing court' " (*Matter of Norma U. v Herman T.R.F.*, 169 AD3d 1055, 1056-1057 [2019], quoting *Matter of Dennis X.G.D.V.*, 158 AD3d 712, 714 [2018]). Here, based upon our independent factual review, the record supports a finding that reunification of the children with their father is not viable due to the father's abandonment of the children Briceyda M.A.X. and Dulce P.A.X., and educational neglect of the child Ingrid C.A.X. (*see Matter of Victor R.C.O. [Canales]*, 172 AD3d 1071, 1072 [2019]; *Matter of Rina M.G.C. [Oscar L.G.—Ana M.C.H.]*, 169 AD3d 1031, 1033 [2019]; *Matter of Dennis X.G.D.V.*, 158 AD3d at 714-715; *Matter of Enis A.C.M. [Blanca E.M.—Carlos V.C.P.]*, 152 AD3d 690, 692 [2017]; *Matter of Diaz v Munoz*, 118 AD3d 989, 991 [2014]). Further, the record supports a finding that it would not be in the best interests of the children to return to Guatemala, their previous country of nationality or country of last habitual residence (*see Matter of Keilyn GG. [Marlene HH.]*,

<u>159 AD3d 1295</u>, 1297 [2018]; *Matter of Diaz v Munoz*, 118 AD3d at 991; <u>*Matter of Marcelina M.-G. v Israel S.*, 112 AD3d 100</u>, 109 [2013]).

Accordingly, the Family Court should have granted the children's motions for the issuance of orders, inter alia, making the requisite declaration and specific findings so as to enable them to petition for SIJS.

The father's contention that the Family Court should not have appointed the mother as guardian of the children is not properly before us. Mastro, A.P.J., Hinds-Radix, Brathwaite Nelson and Iannacci, JJ., concur.

62. A motion for special findings can include a detailed affidavit from the child to establish her father's neglect.

In the Matter of Maria P.E.A., Petitioner,

v

Sergio A.G.G., Respondent. Brenda E.G.E., Nonparty Appellant.

---

111 A.D. 3d 619 (2nd Dep't November 6, 2013)

— McDermott Will & Emery LLP, New York, N.Y. (Andrew B. Kratenstein and Andrea M. Algrett of counsel), for nonparty appellant.

In a child custody proceeding pursuant to Family Court Act article 6, the subject child, Brenda E.G.E., appeals from an order of the Family Court, Westchester County (Klein, J.), dated December 12, 2011, which, without a hearing, in effect, denied her motion for the issuance of an order, inter alia, making special findings so as to enable her to petition the United States Citizenship and Immigration Services for special immigrant juvenile status pursuant to 8 USC § 1101 (a) (27) (J).

Ordered that the order is reversed, on the law and the facts, without costs or disbursements, the motion is granted, it is declared that Brenda E.G.E. has been legally committed to, or placed under the custody of, an individual appointed by a State or juvenile court, and it is found that she is unmarried and under 21 years of age, that reunification with one or both of her parents is not viable due to parental neglect and abandonment, and that it would not be in the best interest of Brenda E.G.E. to return to El Salvador, her previous country of nationality or last habitual residence.

Brenda E.G.E., a native of El Salvador, is 16 years old and unmarried. Her father, whose whereabouts are unknown, abandoned her when she was six years old. Leaving Brenda in the care of her maternal grandmother, Brenda's mother left El Salvador for the United States when Brenda was 12 years old, but continued to support Brenda financially. Brenda joined her mother in the United States in 2009. At that point, Brenda's grandmother's health had deteriorated significantly, and her neighborhood in El Salvador had become increasingly unsafe due to gang violence.

In 2010, Brenda's mother petitioned the Family Court for sole custody of Brenda. At the custody hearing, the mother testified regarding Brenda's father's abandonment and neglect of Brenda. The Family Court granted Brenda's mother's unopposed petition.

Thereafter, Brenda moved for the issuance of an order making special findings that would allow her to apply to the United States Citizenship and Immigration Services for special immigrant juvenile status—a gateway to lawful permanent residency in the United States. The motion was unopposed. Nevertheless, without a hearing, the Family Court denied the motion. It reasoned that Brenda was not entitled to such an order because her mother was available to care for her and had not abandoned her.

Pursuant to 8 USC § 1101 (a) (27) (J) (as amended by the William Wilberforce Trafficking Victims Protection Reauthorization Act of 2008, Pub L 110-457, 122 US Stat 5044) and 8 CFR 204.11, a "special immigrant" is a resident alien who, inter alia, is under 21 years of age, is unmarried, and has been legally committed to, or placed under the custody of, an individual appointed by a State or juvenile court. Additionally, for a juvenile to qualify for special immigrant juvenile status, a court must find that reunification of the juvenile with one or both of the juvenile's parents is not viable due to parental abuse, neglect, abandonment, or a similar basis found under State law (*see* 8 USC § 1101 [a] [27] [J] [i]; *Matter of Mohamed B.*, 83 AD3d 829, 831 [2011]; *Matter of Trudy-Ann W. v Joan W.*, 73 AD3d 793, 795 [2010]), and that it would not be in the juvenile's best interests to be returned to his or her native country or country of last habitual residence (*see* 8 USC § 1101 [a] [27] [J] [ii]; 8 CFR 204.11 [c] [6]; *Matter of Mohamed B.*, 83 AD3d at 831; *Matter of Trudy-Ann W. v Joan W.*, 73 AD3d at 795).

Brenda is under the age of 21 and unmarried. Inasmuch as the Family Court placed Brenda under her mother's custody, Brenda has been "legally committed to, or placed under the custody of . . . an individual or entity appointed by a State or juvenile court" within the meaning of 8 USC § 1101 (a) (27) (J) (i) (*see Matter of Marcelina M.-G. v Israel S.*, 112 AD3d 100, 108-109 [2d Dept 2013]). Based upon our independent factual review, we find that the record, which includes a detailed affidavit from Brenda, fully supports Brenda's contention that, because her father neglected and abandoned her, reunification with her father is not a viable option (*see Matter of Mohamed B.*, 83 AD3d at 832; *Matter of Trudy-Ann W. v Joan W.*, 73 AD3d at 796). Contrary to the Family Court's determination, the fact that Brenda's mother did not also neglect and abandon her does not preclude the issuance of the order requested (*see Matter of Marcelina M.-G. v Israel S.*, 112 AD3d 100, 111 [2d Dept 2013]). Lastly, the record reflects that it would not be in Brenda's best interests to be returned to El Salvador (*see Matter of Mohamed B.*, 83 AD3d at 831-832; *Matter of Alamgir A.*, 81 AD3d 937, 940 [2011]; *Matter of M.C.*, NYLJ, Mar. 4, 2010 at 25, col 3 [Fam Ct, Suffolk County 2010]). Rivera, J.P., Angiolillo, Chambers and Roman, JJ., concur.

63.   A notice of appeal of an order dated May 15, 2020, can be deemed to be a "premature" notice of appeal of an unsatisfactory amended SIJ order dated July 13, 2020.

See Matter of Rosa M.M.—G below.

64.   A finding of abandonment is appropriate where (1) the father never visited the child in Nicaragua, even though he knew where the child lived; (2) the child never met his father; (3) the father never supported the child; (4) the father never sent the child any gifts or cards; and (5) the father's whereabouts were unknown.

See Matter of Rosa M.M.—G below.

65.   It is appropriate to make a finding that it is not in the child's best interests to return to Nicaragua where (1) his mother resides in the United States and the child would be separated from her; (2) the child's mother consistently cared for and supported him; (3) in Nicaragua, there was no one who could care for him or support him; (4) the child's grandparents in Nicaragua were elderly and began to struggle to care for him; and (5) the child was kidnapped by gangs for 8 days in Nicaragua and they threatened him.

194 A.D. 3d 813 (2d Dep't May 12, 2021)

☐ In the Matter of Rosa M.M.-G., Appellant,

| v |
| Dimas A., Respondent. |

Jadeja-Cimone Law, P.C., Hempstead, NY (Alex N. Ortiz Castro of counsel), for appellant.

In a guardianship proceeding pursuant to Family Court Act article 6, the mother appeals from an amended order of the Family Court, Nassau County (Eileen C. Daly-Sapraicone, J.), dated July 13, 2020. The amended order, insofar as appealed from, without a hearing, in effect, denied those branches of the mother's motion which were pursuant to 8 USC § 1101 (a) (27) (J) for specific findings that reunification of the subject child with his birth father is not viable due to parental abandonment, and that it would not be in the subject child's best interests to be returned to Nicaragua, his previous country of nationality and last habitual residence, as there is no one to care for him or protect him in that country, and thereupon, made specific findings that reunification with the father is not viable as there was no male listed on the child's birth certificate, and that it would not be in the best interests of the child to be returned to Nicaragua, his previous country of nationality and last habitual residence, because the mother resides in the United States of America.

Ordered that on the Court's own motion, the notice of appeal from an order dated May 15, 2020, is deemed to be a premature notice of appeal from the amended order dated July 13, 2020 (*see* CPLR 5520 [c]); and it is further,

Ordered that the amended order dated July 13, 2020, is reversed insofar as appealed from, on the law and the facts, without costs or disbursements, those branches of the mother's motion which were pursuant to 8 USC § 1101 (a) (27) (J) for specific findings that reunification of the subject child with his birth father is not viable due to parental abandonment, and that it would not be in the subject child's best interests to be returned to Nicaragua, his previous country of nationality and last habitual residence, as there is no one to care for him or protect him in that country are granted, and it is found that reunification of the subject child with his birth father, Dimas A., is not viable due to parental abandonment, because the birth father abandoned the child by failing to ever provide him with any care or financial support, and that it would not be in the subject child's best interests to be returned to Nicaragua, his previous country of nationality and last habitual residence, as there is no one to care for him or protect him in that country.

The mother commenced this proceeding to be appointed guardian of the subject child and moved for the issuance of an order making specific findings so as to enable the child to petition the United States Citizenship and Immigration Services for special immigrant juvenile status (hereinafter SIJS) pursuant to 8 USC § 1101 (a) (27) (J). The Family Court granted the mother's petition for guardianship and issued an amended order making specific findings, inter alia, that reunification with the father is not viable as there was no male listed on the child's birth certificate, and that it would not be in the best interests of the child to be returned to Nicaragua, his previous country of nationality and last habitual residence, because the mother resides in the United States of America. On appeal, the mother contends that the Family Court erred in failing to make specific findings that reunification with the father was not viable due to parental abandonment, and that it would not be in the best interests of the child to be returned to Nicaragua as there is no one to care for him or protect him in that country.

Pursuant to 8 USC § 1101 (a) (27) (J) (as amended by the William Wilberforce Trafficking Victims Protection Reauthorization Act of 2008, Pub L 110-457, 122 US Stat 5044) and 8 CFR 204.11, a special immigrant juvenile is a resident alien who, among other things, is under 21 years of age, unmarried, and dependent upon a juvenile court or legally committed to an individual appointed by a state or juvenile court. Additionally, for a child to qualify for SIJS, a court must find that reunification of the child with one or both parents is not viable due to parental abuse, neglect, abandonment, or a similar basis found under state law (*see* 8 USC § 1101 [a] [27] [J] [i]; *Matter of Maria P.E.A. v Sergio A.G.G.*, 111 AD3d 619, 620 [2013]; *Matter of Trudy-Ann W. v Joan W.*, 73 AD3d 793, 795 [2010]), and that it would not be in the child's best interests to be returned to his or her previous country of nationality or country of last habitual residence (*see* 8 USC § 1101 [a] [27] [J] [ii]; 8 CFR 204.11 [c] [6]; *Matter of Maria P.E.A. v Sergio A.G.G.*, 111 AD3d at 620; *Matter of Trudy-Ann W. v Joan W.*, 73 AD3d at 795).

The Family Court erred in failing to make the specific finding that reunification with the father is not viable due to abandonment. Based upon our independent factual review, the record supports the requisite finding that reunification with the child's father is not viable due to parental abandonment (*see Matter of Mardin A.M.-I. [Reyna E.M.-I.—Mardin H.]*, 187 AD3d 913 [2020]; *Matter of Rina M.G.C. [Oscar L.G.—Ana M.C.H.]*, 169 AD3d 1031, 1033 [2019]). The record demonstrates that even though the child's father knew where he lived, the father never visited him. The child has never met his father, his father has never supported him and has never sent gifts or cards, and his father's whereabouts are unknown.

Moreover, the record supports a finding that it would not be in the best interests of the child to be returned to Nicaragua, his previous country of nationality and last habitual residence, as there is no one to care for him or protect him in that country (*see Matter of Mardin A.M.-I. [Reyna E.M.-I.—Mardin H.]*, 187 AD3d 913 [2020]; *Matter of Varinder S. v Satwinder S.*, 147 AD3d 854, 856 [2017]). The record reflects that it would not be in the child's best interests to return to Nicaragua as he would be separated from his mother who has consistently cared for and supported him. In Nicaragua, there is no one who can care for him or support him; as previously set forth, his father has abandoned him. The child's maternal grandparents, with whom he lived after his mother left Nicaragua, are elderly and began to struggle to care for him and protect him. Moreover, the child faces harm from gang violence in Nicaragua, having been threatened by gang members and been kidnapped by them once for approximately eight days. Rivera, J.P., Barros, Christopher and Wooten, JJ., concur.

66.   Family Court's focus on circumstances concerning the Subject's overstaying his visa in the United States was unwarranted as having no bearing on the SIJ motion.

See Matter of Mohammed B, below.

67.   Where the child was beaten regularly by his father, both parents neglected him, and neither parent provided him with emotional or financial support when he lived with ther family members, it is appropriate to grant a motion for special findings.

> **In the Matter of Mohamed B., Appellant. Cynthia C., Petitioner, et al., Respondent.**

83 A.D. 3d 829 (2nd Dep't April 12, 2011)

— Lauren Burke, New York, N.Y. (Daniel M. Gonen of counsel), for appellant.

In a guardianship proceeding pursuant to Family Court Act article 6, the subject child, Mohamed B., appeals from an order of the Family Court, Kings County (Sheares, J.), dated March 11, 2010, which, after a hearing, in effect, denied his motion for the issuance of an order declaring that he is dependent on the Family Court and making specific findings that he is unmarried and under 21 years of age, that reunification with one or both of his parents is not viable due to parental abuse, neglect, or abandonment, and that it would not be in his best interest to be returned to his previous country of nationality or last habitual residence, so as to enable him to petition the United States Citizenship and Immigration Services for special immigrant juvenile status pursuant to 8 USC § 1101 (a) (27) (J).

Ordered that the order is reversed, on the law and the facts, without costs or disbursements, the motion is granted, it is declared that Mohamed B. is dependent on the Family Court, and it is found that he is unmarried and under 21 years of age, that reunification with one or both of his parents is not viable due to parental neglect and abandonment, and that it would not be in the best interest of Mohamed B. to return to Sierra Leone, his previous country of nationality or last habitual residence.

Mohamed B., a native of Sierra Leone, is 19 years old and unmarried. Mohamed lived primarily with his grandmother and older brother while growing up in Sierra Leone, and testified that, during the limited time that he lived with his parents, his father beat him regularly and both parents neglected him. He also testified that when he lived with other family members, his parents did not provide him with emotional or financial support. Mohamed's father died in Sierra Leone in 2007, and his mother remains in that country.

In 2006 Mohamed won a scholarship competition sponsored by a Connecticut church, and the church obtained a visa for him for the purpose of visiting the United States. Prior to his scheduled return to Sierra Leone, Mohamed became separated from his hosts while on a trip to Manhattan. Following the separation, he lived with natives of Sierra Leone whom he met in New York City, and eventually enrolled in high school. Since February 2009, he has lived in New York with his former teacher. There is uncontroverted evidence that Mohamed's former teacher has provided him with financial and emotional support and the ability to pursue educational goals.

In February 2009, with Mohamed's consent, Mohamed's former teacher commenced this proceeding, seeking to be appointed as his guardian. Two months later, Mohamed moved for an order making findings that would enable him to apply to the United States Citizenship and Immigration Services (hereinafter the USCIS) for special immigrant juvenile status pursuant to 8 USC § 1101 (a) (27) (J). Both the petition and the motion were unopposed. The Family Court granted the guardianship petition. However, after expressing concern about the circumstances surrounding Mohamed's separation from his hosts while in Manhattan, it denied the motion in an order dated March 11, 2010.

The Family Court improperly denied Mohamed's motion for the issuance of an order declaring that he is dependent on the Family Court and making specific findings that would allow him to apply to the USCIS for special immigrant juvenile status—a gateway to lawful permanent residency in the United States. Pursuant to 8 USC § 1101 (a) (27) (J) (as amended by the William Wilberforce Trafficking Victims Protection Reauthorization Act of 2008, Pub L 110-457, 122 US Stat 5044) and 8 CFR 204.11, a "special immigrant" is a resident alien who is, inter alia, under 21 years of age, unmarried, and dependent upon a juvenile court or legally committed to an individual appointed by a State or juvenile court. Additionally, for a juvenile to qualify for special immigrant juvenile status, a court must find that reunification of the juvenile with one or both of the juvenile's parents is not viable due to parental abuse, neglect, abandonment, or similar parental conduct defined under State law (*see* 8 USC § 1101 [a] [27] [J] [i]; *Matter of Trudy-Ann W. v Joan W.*, 73 AD3d 793, 795 [2010]), and that it would not be in the juvenile's best interest to be returned to his or her native country or country of last habitual residence (*see* 8 USC § 1101

[a] [27] [J] [ii]; 8 CFR 204.11 [c] [6]; *Matter of Trudy-Ann W. v Joan W.*, 73 AD3d at 795).

Initially, we note that the Family Court's focus on the circumstances surrounding Mohamed's separation from his hosts was unwarranted, as those circumstances had no bearing on the issues before it. Moreover, the Family Court's finding that Mohamed's testimony on the subject of his separation was incredible is not supported by the record (*see Matter of Jasmine A.*, 18 AD3d 546, 548 [2005]; *Matter of New York City Dept. of Social Servs. v Carmen J.*, 209 AD2d 525, 527 [1994]).

As earlier noted, Mohamed is under the age of 21 and unmarried. Inasmuch as a guardian has been appointed for him, he is dependent on a juvenile court within the meaning of 8 USC § 1101 (a) (27) (J) (i) (*see Matter of Trudy-Ann W. v Joan W.*, 73 AD3d at 795; *Matter of Antowa McD.*, 50 AD3d 507 [2008]). Based upon our independent factual review, we find that the record fully supports Mohamed's contention that because his mother neglected and abandoned him, reunification with his mother is not a viable option (*see Matter of Alamgir A.*, 81 AD3d 937 [2011]; *Matter of Jisun L. v Young Sun P.*, 75 AD3d 510, 512 [2010]; *Matter of Emma M.*, 74 AD3d 968, 970 [2010]; *Matter of Trudy-Ann W. v Joan W.*, 73 AD3d at 796; *Matter of Antowa McD.*, 50 AD3d at 507). Lastly, the record reflects that it would not be in Mohamed's best interest to be returned to Sierra Leone (*see Matter of Trudy-Ann W. v Joan W.*, 73 AD3d at 796; *Matter of Antowa McD.*, 50 AD3d at 507). Covello, J.P., Eng, Hall and Roman, JJ., concur.

68.   Paternity need not be established in a guardianship petition brought by the child's mother.

☐ In the Matter of Mardin A.M.-I. Reyna E.M.-I., Appellant; Mardin H., Respondent.

---

187 A.D. 3d 913 (2nd Dep't October 14, 2020)

Jessica Lazo, New York, NY, for appellant.

In a guardianship proceeding pursuant to Family Court Act article 6, the mother appeals from (1) an order of the Family Court, Dutchess County (Tracy C. MacKenzie, J.), dated February 25, 2019, and (2) an order of the same court also dated February 25, 2019. The first order, without a hearing, dismissed the petition to appoint the mother as guardian of the child Mardin A.M.-I. The second order, without a hearing, in effect, denied the mother's motion for the issuance of an order, inter alia, making specific findings so as to enable the subject child to petition the United States Citizenship and Immigration Services for special immigrant juvenile status pursuant to 8 USC § 1101 (a) (27) (J).

Ordered that the orders are reversed, on the law and the facts, without costs or disbursements, the petition to appoint the mother as the guardian of the subject child is reinstated and granted, the mother is appointed as the guardian of the subject child, the mother's motion for the issuance of an order, inter alia, making specific findings so as to enable the subject child to petition the United States Citizenship and Immigration Services for special immigrant juvenile status pursuant to 8 USC § 1101 (a) (27) (J) is granted, it is declared that the subject child is dependent on a juvenile court, and it is found that the subject child is unmarried and under 21 years of age, that reunification with his father is not viable due to parental abandonment, and that it would not be in the subject child's best interests to be returned to Guatemala, his previous country of nationality and last habitual residence.

In December 2018, Mardin A.M.-I. (hereinafter the subject child) filed a petition pursuant to Family Court Act article 6 to have his mother appointed as his guardian for the purpose of obtaining an order, inter alia, making specific findings so as to enable him to petition the United States Citizenship and Immigration Services for special immigrant juvenile status (hereinafter SIJS) pursuant to 8 USC § 1101 (a) (27) (J). Thereafter, the mother moved for the issuance of an order making the requisite declaration and specific findings so as to enable the subject child to petition for SIJS. In two orders, both dated February 25, 2019, the Family Court dismissed the guardianship petition and, in effect, denied the mother's motion as premature on the ground that the paternity of the putative father had not been established. The mother appeals from the orders.

The Family Court should not have dismissed the guardianship petition on the ground that paternity had not been established. A natural parent may be appointed guardian of his or her own child (*see* Family Ct Act § 661 [a]; *Matter of Marisol N.H.*, 115 AD3d 185, 190 [2014]), and the mere fact that paternity has not been established for the putative father does not preclude the guardianship petition or the issuance of an order making specific findings enabling the subject child to petition for SIJS (*see Matter of Linares-Mendez v Cazanga-Payes*, 183 AD3d 738, 739 [2020]; *Matter of Olga L.G.M. [Santos T.F.]*, 164 AD3d 1341, 1342 [2018]; *Matter of Jimenez v Perez*, 144 AD3d 1036, 1037 [2016]).

Furthermore, the Family Court should have granted the petition to appoint the mother as guardian for the subject child until he reaches the age of 21, which is in the child's best interests, the paramount concern in a guardianship proceeding (*see* SCPA 1707 [1]; *Matter of Silvia N.P.L. v Estate of Jorge M.N.P.*, 141 AD3d 654, 655 [2016]).

Additionally, the Family Court should have granted the mother's motion for the issuance of an order making the requisite declaration and specific findings so as to enable the subject child to petition the United States Citizenship and Immigration Services for SIJS. Pursuant to 8 USC § 1101 (a) (27) (J) (as amended by William Wilberforce Trafficking Victims Protection Reauthorization Act of 2008, Pub L 110-457, 122 US Stat 5044) and 8 CFR 204.11, a special immigrant juvenile is a resident alien who, among other things, is under 21 years of age, unmarried, and dependent upon a juvenile court or legally committed to an individual appointed by a state or juvenile court. Additionally, for a child to qualify for SIJS, a court must find that reunification of the child with one or both parents is not viable due to parental abuse, neglect, abandonment, or a similar basis found under state law (*see* 8 USC § 1101 [a] [27] [J] [i]; *Matter of Maria P.E.A. v Sergio A.G.G.*, 111 AD3d 619, 620 [2013]; *Matter of Trudy-Ann W. v Joan W.*, 73 AD3d 793, 795 [2010]), and that it would not be in the child's best interests to be returned to his or her previous country of nationality or country of last habitual residence (*see* 8 USC § 1101 [a] [27] [J] [ii]; 8 CFR 204.11 [c] [6]; *Matter of Maria P.E.A. v Sergio A.G.G.*, 111 AD3d at 620; *Matter of Trudy-Ann W. v Joan W.*, 73 AD3d at 795).

Here, the subject child is under the age of 21 and unmarried, and since we have found that the mother should have been appointed as the subject child's guardian, a finding also should have been made that the child is dependent on a juvenile court within the meaning of 8 USC § 1101 (a) (27) (J) (i) (*see Matter of Maura A.R.-R. [Santos F.R.—Fidel R.]*, 114 AD3d 687, 688-689 [2014]; *Matter of Trudy-Ann W. v Joan W.*, 73 AD3d at 795-796). Further, based upon our independent factual review, the record supports a finding that reunification of the subject child with his father is not a viable option due to parental abandonment (*see Matter of Rina M.G.C. [Oscar L.G.—Ana M.C.H.]*, 169 AD3d 1031, 1033 [2019]; *Matter of Enis A.C.M. [Blanca E.M.—Carlos V.C.P.]*, 152 AD3d 690, 692 [2017]; *Matter of Haide L.G.M. v Santo D.S.M.*,

130 AD3d 734, 736 [2015]; *Matter of Diaz v Munoz*, 118 AD3d 989 [2014]). Lastly, the record supports a finding that it would not be in the best interests of the subject child to return to Guatemala, the subject child's previous country of nationality or country of last habitual residence (*see Matter of Varinder S. v Satwinder S.*, 147 AD3d 854, 856 [2017]; *Matter of Luis R. v Maria Elena G.*, 120 AD3d 581, 583 [2014]; *Matter of Alamgir A.*, 81 AD3d 937, 940 [2011]).

Accordingly, the Family Court should have granted the guardianship petition and the mother's motion for the issuance of an order, inter alia, making the requisite declaration and specific findings so as to enable the subject child to petition for SIJS. Mastro, J.P., Miller, Maltese and Wooten, JJ., concur.

69.   It is appropriate to issue an order of special findings where the child's father abandoned her since birth and her mother inflicted excessive corporal punishment and failed to supply her with adequate food and supervision.

See Matter of Trudy-Ann, below.

70.   It is appropriate to find that it is not in the child's best interests to return to Jamaica where she would have no place to live and no means of supporting herself.

> **In the Matter of Trudy-Ann W., Appellant,**
> **v**
> **Joan W. et al., Respondents.**

73 A.D. 3d 793 (2nd Dep't May 4, 2010)

—Milbank, Tweed, Hadley & McCloy, LLP, New York, N.Y. (Robert L. Lindholm, Stacey J. Rappaport, and Thomas H. Santoro of counsel), for appellant.

In a proceeding pursuant to Family Court Act article 6 for the appointment of the maternal aunt of the petitioner, a person under 21 years of age, as her guardian, the petitioner, Trudy-Ann W., appeals from (1) an order of the Family Court, Kings County (Kennedy, J.), dated March 4, 2010, which, after a hearing, denied the petition and dismissed the proceeding, and (2) an order of the same court, also dated March 4, 2010, which, after a hearing, denied her motion for the issuance of an order declaring that she is dependent on the Family Court and making specific findings that she is unmarried and under 21 years of age, that reunification with one or both of her parents is not viable due to parental abuse, neglect, or abandonment, and that it would not be in her best interest to be returned to her previous country of nationality or last habitual residence, so as to enable her to petition the United States Citizenship and Immigration Services for special immigrant juvenile status pursuant to 8 USC § 1101 (a) (27) (J).

Ordered that the orders are reversed, on the law and the facts, without costs or disbursements, the petition and the motion are granted, Alcie S., the maternal aunt of Trudy-Ann W., is appointed as the guardian of Trudy-Ann W., it is declared that Trudy-Ann W. is dependent on the Family Court, and it is found that Trudy-Ann W. is unmarried and under 21 years of age, that reunification with one or both of her parents is not viable due to parental abuse, neglect, and abandonment, and that it would not be in the best interest of Trudy-Ann W. to return to Jamaica, West Indies, her previous country of nationality and last habitual residence.

Trudy-Ann W., a native of Jamaica, West Indies, is 20 years old, unmarried, and has lived in the United States with her maternal aunt, Alcie S., since 2007. Trudy-Ann's father, whose whereabouts are unknown, abandoned her at birth, while her mother, who continues to reside in Jamaica, neglected and abused her by inflicting excessive corporal punishment and failing to supply her with adequate food and supervision. Trudy-Ann left her mother's home at age 16. There is uncontroverted evidence that, since 2007, Alcie S. has provided Trudy-Ann with a loving home, financial and emotional support, and the ability to pursue educational goals.

Previously, Family Court Act § 661 was deemed applicable only to individuals under 18 years of age (*see Matter of Vanessa D.*, 51 AD3d 790 [2008]; *Matter of Luis A.-S.*, 33 AD3d 793 [2006]). Pursuant to a 2008 amendment, however, Family Court Act § 661 (a) now explicitly authorizes the appointment of a guardian for a person "who is less than twenty-one years old who consents to the appointment or continuation of a guardian after the age of eighteen." Accordingly, in January 2010, Trudy-Ann sought the appointment of Alcie S. as her guardian. Both Alcie S. and Trudy-Ann's mother consented to the appointment. In an order dated March 4, 2010, the Family Court nevertheless denied the petition and dismissed the proceeding on the ground that Trudy-Ann had failed to establish a basis for the relief requested. In a separate order, also dated March 4, 2010, the Family Court denied Trudy-Ann's motion for the issuance of an order making a declaration and specific findings that would enable her to apply to the United States Citizenship and Immigration Services (hereinafter USCIS) for special immigrant juvenile status pursuant to 8 USC § 1101 (a) (27) (J). We reverse both orders.

Under the circumstances of this case, we find that the Family Court's determination of the guardianship petition lacked a sound and substantial basis in the record (*see Matter of Gloria S. v Richard B.*, 80 AD2d 72, 76 [1981]; *cf. Matter of Pleasant Edward G.*, 299 AD2d 358, 358-359 [2002]). Since Trudy-Ann is under 21 years of age, she is an infant for purposes of this guardianship proceeding (*see* Family Ct Act § 661 [a]). When considering guardianship appointments, the infant's best interest is paramount (*see* SCPA 1707 [1]; *Matter of Stuart*, 280 NY 245, 250 [1939]; *Matter of Amrhein v Signorelli*, 153 AD2d 28, 31 [1989]; *see also Matter of Tiffany Nicole L.*, 287 AD2d 717, 718 [2001]). The order denying the guardianship petition and dismissing the proceeding, however, is devoid of any references to Trudy-Ann's best interest.

This Court's power to review the evidence is as broad as that of the hearing court, bearing in mind that in a close case, the factfinder had the advantage of seeing and hearing the witnesses (*see Northern Westchester Professional Park Assoc. v Town of Bedford*, 60 NY2d 492, 499 [1983]). Further, where, as here, the "record is sufficiently complete for us to make our own factual determinations" (*Matter of Lillian R.*, 196 AD2d 503, 504 [1993]), we may do so. Based upon our "independent factual review of the complete record" (*Matter of Steward v Steward*, 25 AD3d 714, 715 [2006]; *see Matter of Allen v Black*, 275 AD2d 207, 209 [2000]), which includes, inter alia, two hearing transcripts and an affidavit from Trudy-Ann, it is evident that her best interest would be served by the appointment of Alcie S. as her guardian (*see Matter of Stuart*, 280 NY at 247; *cf. Eschbach v Eschbach*, 56 NY2d 167, 172-173 [1982]). Accordingly, we appoint Alcie S. as the guardian of Trudy-Ann.

The Family Court also improperly denied Trudy-Ann's motion for the issuance of an order making a declaration and specific findings that would allow her to apply to the USCIS for special immigrant juvenile status—a gateway to lawful permanent residency in the United States. Specifically, the Family Court incorrectly found that Trudy-Ann had not established dependency on the Family Court, had not established that she was abused, neglected, or abandoned, and had not established that it would not be in her best interest to be returned to Jamaica. Pursuant to 8 USC § 1101 (a) (27) (J) (as amended by the William Wilberforce Trafficking Victims Protection Reauthorization Act of 2008, Pub L 110-457, 122 US Stat 5044) and 8 CFR 204.11, a "special immigrant" is a resident alien who is, inter alia, under 21 years of age, unmarried, and dependent upon a juvenile court or legally committed to an individual appointed by a state or juvenile court. Additionally, for a juvenile to qualify for special immigrant juvenile status, a court must find that reunification of the juvenile with one or both of the juvenile's parents is not viable due to parental abuse, neglect, abandonment, or similar parental conduct defined under State law (*see* 8 USC § 1101 [a] [27] [J] [i]; *Matter of E.G.*, 24 Misc 3d 1238[A], 2009 NY Slip Op 51797[U] [2009] [Fam Ct, Nassau County 2009]), and that it would not be in the juvenile's best interest to be returned to his or her native country or country of last habitual residence (*see* 8 USC § 1101 [a] [27] [J] [ii]; 8 CFR 204.11 [c] [6]).

The "appointment of a guardian constitutes the necessary declaration of dependency on a juvenile court" for special immigrant juvenile status purposes (*Matter of Antowa McD., 50 AD3d 507* [2008]). Since we have appointed Alcie S. as Trudy-Ann's guardian, Trudy-Ann is dependent on a juvenile court within the meaning of 8 USC § 1101 (a) (27) (J) (i). Based on our factual review, we find that the record fully supports Trudy-Ann's contention that her father abandoned her and her mother abused and neglected her and that, as a result, reunification with either parent is not a viable option (*see Matter of Antowa McD.*, 50 AD3d at 507). Lastly, the record reflects that, in Jamaica, Trudy-Ann would have nowhere to live, and no means of supporting herself. Accordingly, it is clearly in Trudy-Ann's best interest to continue living with her aunt in the United States (*id.*). Mastro, J.P., Miller, Leventhal and Belen, JJ., concur.

71.   Undocumented aliens can be petitioners

See Matter of Alan S.M.C. below.

72.   Following an unfavorable Family Court decision, it is possible to file a motion to reargue, although quite often these are unsuccessful.

> ☐ **In the Matter of Alan S.M.C., Appellant. (Proceeding No. 1.) In the Matter of Diego A.M.C., Appellant. (Proceeding No. 2.)**

160 A.D. 3d 721 (2nd Dep't April 11, 2018)

Make The Road New York, Jackson Heights, NY (Yasmine Farhang, Luis Batista, and Paul, Weiss, Rifkind, Wharton & Garrison LLP [Jacqueline P. Rubin, Ross A. Wilson, Stephen B. Popernik, and Mary C. Spooner], of counsel), for appellants.

In related proceedings pursuant to Family Court Act article 6, the child Alan S.M.C. appeals from an order of the Family Court, Queens County (Robert I. Caloras, J.), dated March 2, 2018, and the child Diego A.M.C. separately appeals from a second order of the same court, also dated March 2, 2018. The orders, insofar as appealed from, upon reargument, adhered to an original determination in an order of the same court dated February 26, 2018, dismissing guardianship petitions, and denied the children's separate motions for the issuance of an order, inter alia, making specific findings so as to enable each of them to petition the United States Citizenship and Immigration Services for special immigrant juvenile status pursuant to 8 USC § 1101 (a) (27) (J).

Ordered that the orders dated March 2, 2018, are reversed insofar as appealed from, on the law and the facts, without costs or disbursements, upon reargument, the determination in the order dated February 26, 2018, dismissing the guardianship petitions, is vacated, the petitions are reinstated and granted, the mother is appointed as the guardian of the children, the motions of the children for the issuance of an order, inter alia, making specific findings so as to enable them to petition the United States Citizenship and Immigration Services for special immigrant juvenile status pursuant to 8 USC § 1101 (a) (27) (J) are granted, it is declared that the children are dependent on a juvenile court, and it is found that the children are unmarried and under 21 years of age, that reunification with their respective fathers is not viable due to parental abandonment, and that it would not be in their best interests to return to Mexico, their previous country of nationality and last habitual residence.

In February 2018, the subject children each filed a petition pursuant to Family Court Act article 6 to appoint the mother as their guardian, for the purpose of obtaining an order, inter alia, making specific findings that they are unmarried and under 21 years of age, that reunification with the father of each child is not viable due to parental abandonment, and that it would not be in their best interests to be returned to Mexico, their previous country of nationality and last habitual residence, so as to enable them to petition the United States Citizenship and Immigration Services for special immigrant juvenile status (hereinafter SIJS) pursuant to 8 USC § 1101 (a) (27) (J). The children also separately moved for the issuance of an order making the requisite declaration and specific findings so as to enable each of them to petition for SIJS. In an order dated February 26, 2018, the Family Court dismissed the guardianship petitions on the ground that the mother "does not have legal status in this country," and thus, did not constitute a New York domiciliary, as required to be appointed guardian.

Thereafter, the children separately moved, among other things, for leave to reargue with respect to the order dated February 26, 2018. In two orders, both dated March 2, 2018 (one as to each child), the Family Court, inter alia, upon reargument, adhered to its original determination in the order dated February 26, 2018, dismissing the petitions, and denied the children's motions for the issuance of an order, inter alia, making specific findings so as to enable them to petition for SIJS. The children appeal from the orders dated March 2, 2018.

Under the circumstances of this case, the Family Court improperly dismissed the guardianship petitions. Contrary to the court's determination, the mother was not required to demonstrate that she has "legal status in this country" or had taken steps to obtain such status to qualify as a guardian. "[D]omicile means living in [a] locality *with intent* to make it a fixed and permanent home" (*Chen v Guo Liang Lu*, 144 AD3d 735, 737 [2016] [internal quotation marks omitted and emphasis added]; *see* SCPA 103 [15]). An individual's lack of lawful status in the United States is "immaterial to the issue of his [or her] domicile and, therefore, his [or her] eligibility to receive letters [of guardianship]" (*Matter of Lafontant*, 161 Misc 2d 840, 841 [Sur Ct, Rockland County 1994]; *see also Plyler v Doe*, 457 US 202, 227 n 22 [1982]; *Jacoubovitch v Jacoubovitch*, 279 App Div 1027 [1952]; *Taubenfeld v Taubenfeld*, 276 App Div 873, 874 [1949]). Here, notwithstanding the mother's immigration status, the record demonstrates her intent to permanently reside in New York State. Thus, the mother cannot be deemed a "non-domiciliary alien" who is ineligible to receive letters of guardianship (SCPA 707 [1] [c]). Further, upon our independent factual review, we find that the best interests of the children would be served by the appointment of the mother as their guardian (*see Matter of Axel S.D.C. v Elena A.C.*, 139 AD3d 1050, 1051 [2016]; *Matter of Maura A.R.-R. [Santos F.R.—Fidel R.]*, 114 AD3d 687, 689 [2014]).

Furthermore, the Family Court should have granted the children's motions for the issuance of an order making the requisite declaration and specific findings so as to enable them to petition for SIJS. Pursuant to 8 USC § 1101 (a) (27) (J) (as amended by the William Wilberforce Trafficking Victims Protection Reauthorization Act of 2008, Pub L 110-457, 122 US Stat 5044) and 8 CFR 204.11, a "special immigrant" is a resident alien who is, inter alia, under 21 years of age, unmarried, and dependent upon a juvenile court or legally committed to an individual appointed by a state or juvenile court. Additionally, for a juvenile to qualify for SIJS, a court must find that reunification of the juvenile with one or both of the juvenile's parents is not viable due to parental abuse, neglect, abandonment, or a similar basis found under state law (*see* 8 USC § 1101 [a] [27] [J] [i]; *Matter of Marvin E.M. de P. [Milagro C.C.—Mario Enrique M.G.]*, 121 AD3d 892, 893 [2014]; *Matter of Maria P.E.A. v Sergio A.G.G.*, 111 AD3d 619, 620 [2013]; *Matter of Trudy-Ann W. v Joan W.*, 73 AD3d 793, 795 [2010]), and that it would not be in the juvenile's best interests to be returned to his or her native country or country of last habitual residence (*see* 8 USC § 1101 [a] [27] [J] [ii]; 8 CFR 204.11 [c] [6]; *Matter of Marvin E.M. de P. [Milagro C.C.—Mario Enrique M.G.]*, 121 AD3d at 893; *Matter of Maria P.E.A. v Sergio A.G.G.*, 111 AD3d at 620; *Matter of Trudy-Ann W. v Joan W.*, 73 AD3d at 795).

Here, the children are under 21 years of age and unmarried, and since we have appointed the mother as the children's guardian, the children are dependent on a juvenile court within the meaning of 8 USC § 1101 (a) (27) (J) (i) (*see Matter of Silvia N.P.L. v Estate of Jorge M.N.P.*, 141 AD3d 656, 657 [2016]; *Matter of Axel S.D.C. v Elena A.C.*, 139 AD3d at 1052). Further, based upon our independent factual review, we conclude that the record supports a finding that reunification of the children with their respective fathers is not a viable option due to parental abandonment (*see Matter of Diaz v Munoz*, 118 AD3d 989, 991 [2014]). The record also supports a finding that it would not be in the best interests of the children to return to Mexico (*see Matter of Palwinder K. v Kuldeep K.*, 148 AD3d 1149, 1151 [2017]; *Matter of Wilson A.T.Z. [Jose M.T.G.—Manuela Z.M.]*, 147 AD3d 962, 964 [2017]).

Accordingly, the Family Court should have granted the guardianship petitions and the children's motions for the issuance of an order making the requisite declaration and specific findings so as to enable them to petition for SIJS. Inasmuch as the record is sufficient for this Court to make its own findings of fact and conclusions of law, we declare that the children are dependent on the Family Court, and we find that the children are unmarried and under 21 years of age, that reunification with one or both of their parents is not viable due to parental abandonment, and that it would not be in their best interests to return to Mexico (*see Matter of Axel S.D.C. v Elena A.C.*, 139 AD3d at 1052). Dillon, J.P., Sgroi, Miller and Brathwaite Nelson, JJ., concur.

73.   The Appellate Department can apply independent factual review of a denied SIJ guardianship petition.

☐ **In the Matter of Axel S.D.C., Appellant,**

v

Elena A.C., et al., Respondents.

139 A.D. 3d 1050 (2d Dep't May 25, 2016)

Lutheran Social Services of New York, New York, NY (Priya Arvind Patel of counsel), for appellant.

Appeals from two orders of the Family Court, Queens County (Julie Stanton, Ct. Atty. Ref.), both dated April 28, 2016. The orders, after a hearing, denied the motion of the subject child for the issuance of an order, inter alia, making special findings so as to enable him to petition the United States Citizenship and Immigration Services for special immigrant juvenile status pursuant to 8 USC § 1101 (a) (27) (J), and dismissed the petition to appoint Daniel J.K. as his guardian.

Ordered that the orders are reversed, on the law and the facts, without costs or disbursements, the petition to appoint Daniel J.K. as the guardian of the subject child is reinstated and granted, Daniel J.K. is appointed as the guardian of the child, the child's motion for the issuance of an order, inter alia, making special findings so as to enable him to petition the United States Citizenship and Immigration Services for special immigrant juvenile status pursuant to 8 USC § 1101 (a) (27) (J) is granted, it is declared that the child is dependent on a juvenile court, and it is found that the child is unmarried and under 21 years of age, that reunification with his father is not viable due to parental neglect, and that it would not be in the child's best interests to return to El Salvador, his previous country of nationality and last habitual residence.

In March 2015, the subject child, Axel S.D.C., filed a petition pursuant to Family Court Act article 6 to appoint Daniel J.K. as his guardian, for the purpose of obtaining an order, inter alia, making special findings that he is unmarried and under 21 years of age, that reunification with his father is not viable due to parental neglect, abandonment, or abuse, and that it would not be in his best interests to be returned to El Salvador, his previous country of nationality and last habitual residence, so as to enable him to petition the United States Citizenship and Immigration Services for special immigrant juvenile status (hereinafter SIJS) pursuant to 8 USC § 1101 (a) (27) (J). Thereafter, the child moved for the issuance of an order making the requisite declaration and special findings so as to enable him to petition for SIJS. In two orders dated April 28, 2016, the Family Court denied the child's motion and dismissed the guardianship petition.

Under the circumstances of this case, the Family Court improperly dismissed the guardianship petition. Since the child is under 21 years of age, he is an infant for purposes of this guardianship proceeding (*see* Family Ct Act § 661 [a]; *Matter of Trudy-Ann W. v Joan W.*, 73 AD3d 793, 794 [2010]). When considering guardianship appointments, the infant's best interests are paramount (*see* SCPA 1707 [1]; *Matter of Alamgir A.*, 81 AD3d 937, 938 [2011]; *Matter of*

Stuart, 280 NY 245, 250 [1939]). Based upon our independent factual review, we find that the child's best interests would be served by the appointment of Daniel J.K. as his guardian (*see Matter of Marisol N.H.*, 115 AD3d 185, 191 [2014]; *Matter of Maura A.R.-R. [Santos F.R.—Fidel R.]*, 114 AD3d 687, 689 [2014]; *Matter of Alamgir A.*, 81 AD3d at 938; *Matter of Trudy-Ann W. v Joan W.*, 73 AD3d at 794).

Further, the Family Court should have granted the child's motion for the issuance of an order making the requisite declaration and special findings so as to enable him to petition for SIJS. Pursuant to 8 USC § 1101 (a) (27) (J) (as amended by the William Wilberforce Trafficking Victims Protection Reauthorization Act of 2008, Pub L 110-457, 122 US Stat 5044) and 8 CFR 204.11, a "special immigrant" is an undocumented resident who, inter alia, is under 21 years of age, unmarried, and dependent upon a juvenile court or legally committed to an individual appointed by a state or juvenile court. "Additionally, for a juvenile to qualify for special immigrant juvenile status, a court must find that reunification of the juvenile with one or both of the juvenile's parents is not viable due to parental abuse, neglect, abandonment, or similar parental conduct defined under State law, and that it would not be in the juvenile's best interest to be returned to his or her native country or country of last habitual residence" (*Matter of Trudy-Ann W. v Joan W.*, 73 AD3d at 795 [citations omitted]).

Here, the child is under the age of 21 and unmarried, and since we have appointed Daniel J.K. as the child's guardian, the child is dependent on a juvenile court within the meaning of 8 USC § 1101 (a) (27) (J) (i) (*see Matter of Maura A.R.-R. [Santos F.R.—Fidel R.]*, 114 AD3d at 689; *Matter of Trudy-Ann W. v Joan W.*, 73 AD3d at 796). We further find that the record fully supports the child's contention that his reunification with the father is not a viable option due to parental neglect (*see Matter of Tommy E.H. [Silvia C.]*, 134 AD3d

840 [2015]; *see also Matter of Kayla F. [Kevin F.]*, 130 AD3d 724, 725-726 [2015]). Lastly, the record reflects that it would not be in the child's best interests to be returned to El Salvador.

Accordingly, the Family Court should have granted the guardianship petition and the child's motion for the issuance of an order making the requisite declaration and special findings so as to enable him to petition for SIJS. Inasmuch as the record is sufficient for this Court to make its own findings of fact and conclusions of law, we grant the child's motion, declare that the child is dependent on the Family Court, and find that the child is unmarried and under 21 years of age, that reunification with his father is not viable due to parental neglect, and that it would not be in his best interests to return to El Salvador. Rivera, J.P., Cohen, Maltese and LaSalle, JJ., concur.

74. Where the record establishes that the father abandoned the minor then it follows that reunification with the father is no viable because of abandonment.

☐ **In the Matter of Alejandro V.P., Appellant,**

v

Floyland V.D. et al., Respondents.

150 A.D. 3d 741 (2d Dep't May 3, 2017)

Scott Coomes, Hempstead, NY, for appellant.

Appeal by the child from an order of the Family Court, Nassau County (Ellen R. Greenberg, J.), dated January 19, 2017. The order, after a hearing, denied the child's motion for the issuance of an order, inter alia, making specific findings so as to enable him to petition the United States Citizenship and

Immigration Services for special immigrant juvenile status pursuant to 8 USC § 1101 (a) (27) (J).

Ordered that the order is reversed, on the law and the facts, without costs or disbursements, the child's motion for the issuance of an order, inter alia, making specific findings so as to enable him to petition the United States Citizenship and Immigration Services for special immigrant juvenile status pursuant to 8 USC § 1101 (a) (27) (J) is granted, and it is found that reunification of the child with his father is not viable due to parental abandonment, and that it would not be in the child's best interests to return to Guatemala, his previous country of nationality and last habitual residence.

In September 2016, the child filed a petition pursuant to Family Court Act article 6 for Isael E. G. P. (hereinafter the guardian) to be appointed his guardian, for the purpose of obtaining an order declaring that he is dependent on the Family Court and making specific findings that he is unmarried and under 21 years of age, that reunification with one or both of his parents is not viable due to parental abandonment, neglect, or abuse, and that it would not be in his best interests to be returned to Guatemala, his previous country of nationality and country of last habitual residence, so as to enable the child to petition the United States Citizenship and Immigration Services for special immigrant juvenile status (hereinafter SIJS) pursuant to 8 USC § 1101 (a) (27) (J). Thereafter, the child moved for the issuance of an order making the requisite declaration and specific findings so as to enable him to petition for SIJS. In an order dated January 5, 2017, the Family Court granted the guardianship petition. In an order dated January 19, 2017, the Family Court denied the child's motion on the ground that he failed to establish that reunification of the child with one or both of his parents was not viable due to parental abuse, neglect, or abandonment, and that it would not be in the child's best interests to return to Guatemala.

Pursuant to 8 USC § 1101 (a) (27) (J) (as amended by the William Wilberforce Trafficking Victims Protection Reauthorization Act of 2008, Pub L 110-457, 122 US Stat 5044) and 8 CFR 204.11, a special immigrant is a resident alien who, inter alia, is under 21 years of age, unmarried, and dependent upon a juvenile court or legally committed to an individual appointed by a state or juvenile court. Additionally, for a juvenile to qualify for SIJS, a court must find that reunification of the juvenile with one or both of the juvenile's parents is not viable due to parental abuse, neglect, abandonment, or a similar basis found under state law (*see* 8 USC § 1101 [a] [27] [J] [i]; *Matter of Maria P.E.A. v Sergio A.G.G.*, 111 AD3d 619, 620 [2013]; *Matter of Trudy-Ann W. v Joan W.*, 73 AD3d 793, 795 [2010]), and that it would not be in the juvenile's best interests to be returned to his or her previous country of nationality or country of last habitual residence (*see* 8 USC § 1101 [a] [27] [J] [ii]; 8 CFR 204.11 [c] [6]; *Matter of Maria P.E.A. v Sergio A.G.G.*, 111 AD3d at 620; *Matter of Trudy-Ann W. v Joan W.*, 73 AD3d at 795).

Based upon our independent factual review, we find that reunification of the child with his father is not a viable option due to parental abandonment (*see Matter of Varinder S. v Satwinder S.*, 147 AD3d 854 [2017]; *Matter of Anibal H. [Maria G.G.H.]*, 138 AD3d 841, 843 [2016]), and that it would not be in his best interests to return to Guatemala (*see Matter of Carlos A.M. v Maria T.M.*, 141 AD3d 526 [2016]).

Accordingly, the Family Court should have granted the child's motion for the issuance of an order, inter alia, making the requisite specific findings so as to enable him to petition for SIJS. Since the record is sufficient for this Court to make its own findings of fact and conclusions of law, we find that reunification of the child with his father is not viable due to parental abandonment, and that it would not be in his best interests to return to Guatemala, his previous country of nationality and last habitual residence. Eng, P.J., Rivera, Balkin and Barros, JJ., concur.

75.   It was error to deny an SIJ guardianship petition where the child's father physically and emotionally mistreated the child, prevented him from going to school for more than one year, and the child's mother failed to protect him from such mistreatment, and there was no viable caregiver in his native Guatemala.

> ☐ **In the Matter of Jose F.M.P., Appellant. Francisco D.M.G. et al., Respondents.**

204 A.D.3d 801 (2d Dep't April 13, 2022)

The Door's Legal Services Center, New York, NY (Svitlana Kobtseva of counsel), for appellant.

In a guardianship proceeding pursuant to Family Court Act article 6, Jose F.M.P., a child, appeals from an order of the Family Court, Nassau County (Eileen C. Daly-Sapraicone, J.), dated September 20, 2021. The order, insofar as appealed from, after a hearing, in effect, denied those branches of the child's motion which were pursuant to 8 USC § 1101 (a) (27) (J) for specific findings that reunification of the child with his father is not viable due to parental neglect, and that it would not be in the child's best interests to be returned to Guatemala, his country of nationality, as he does not have a viable caregiver in that country.

Ordered that the order is reversed insofar as appealed from, on the law and the facts, without costs or disbursements, and those branches of the child's motion which were pursuant to 8 USC § 1101 (a) (27) (J) for specific findings that reunification of the child with his father is not viable due to parental neglect, and that it would not be in the child's best interests to be returned to

Guatemala, his country of nationality, as he has no viable caregiver in that country, are granted, and it is found that reunification of the child with his father is not viable due to parental neglect, and that it would not be in the child's best interests to be returned to Guatemala, his country of nationality and last habitual residence, as he has no viable caregiver in that country.

In March 2021, Jose F.M.P., then 17 years old (hereinafter the child), commenced this proceeding to have his sister appointed his guardian. The child thereafter moved for the issuance of an order making specific findings so as to enable him to petition the United States Citizenship and Immigration Services for special immigrant juvenile status (hereinafter SIJS) pursuant to 8 USC § 1101 (a) (27) (J). As is relevant to this appeal, in an order dated September 20, 2021, the Family Court, after a hearing, in effect, denied those branches of the child's motion which were for specific findings, inter alia, that reunification with his father is not viable due to parental neglect, and that it would not be in the best interests of the child to be returned Guatemala, his country of nationality and last habitual residence, because he would have no viable caregiver.

Pursuant to 8 USC § 1101 (a) (27) (J) (as amended by the William Wilberforce Trafficking Victims Protection Reauthorization Act of 2008, Pub L 110-457, 122 US Stat 5044) and 8 CFR 204.11, a special immigrant juvenile is a resident alien who, among other things, is under 21 years of age, unmarried, and dependent upon a juvenile court or legally committed to an individual appointed by a state or juvenile court. Additionally, for a child to qualify for SIJS, a court must find that reunification of the child with one or both parents is not viable due to parental abuse, neglect, abandonment, or a similar basis found under state law (see 8 USC § 1101 [a] [27] [J] [i]; *Matter of Rosa M.M.-G. v Dimas A.*, 194 AD3d 813 [2021]), and that it would not be in the child's best interests to be returned to his or her country of nationality or country of last habitual residence (see 8 USC § 1101 [a] [27] [J] [ii]; 8 CFR 204.11 [c] [6]).

The Family Court should have granted that branch of the child's motion which was for a specific finding that reunification with his father is not viable due to parental neglect. Based upon our independent factual review, the record demonstrates that the child's father physically and emotionally mistreated the child, and prevented him from attending school for more than one year and on other occasions without a reasonable justification, and that the child's mother failed to protect him from such mistreatment. Thus, the record supports the requisite finding that reunification with the child's father is not viable due to parental neglect (*see Matter of Victor R.C.O. [Canales]*, 172 AD3d 1071, 1072 [2019]; *Matter of Axel S.D.C. v Elena A.C.*, 139 AD3d 1050, 1052 [2016]).

The record also supports a finding that it would not be in the best interests of the child to be returned to Guatemala, his country of nationality and last habitual residence, as he would have no viable caregiver in that country (*see Matter of Norma U. v Herman T.R.F.*, 169 AD3d 1055, 1057 [2019]).

Accordingly, we reverse the order insofar as appealed from and grant those branches of the child's motion which were pursuant to 8 USC § 1101 (a) (27) (J) for specific findings that reunification of the child with his father is not viable due to parental neglect and that it is not in the best interests of the child to be returned to Guatamala. Dillon, J.P., Duffy, Maltese and Genovesi, JJ., concur.

76. It is necessary to present evidence that the child's reunification with one parent is not viable for reasons of abuse, neglect, abandonment, or a similar basis under state law.

> ☐ **In the Matter of Dimas A., Appellant,**
> **v**
> **Esmirna E.L. et al., Respondents.**

142 A.D.3d 1164 (2d Dep't Sept 28, 2016)

Cohen & Tucker, New York, NY (Stanley Cohen and Elyssa N. Williams, pro hac vice, of counsel), for appellant.

Osato Eugene Uzamere, Jamaica, NY, attorney for the child.

Appeals by the petitioner from two orders of the Family Court, Queens County (Julie Stanton, Ct. Atty. Ref.), both dated August 13, 2015. The first order, upon the filing of a petition pursuant to Family Court Act article 6 to appoint the petitioner as the subject child's guardian, and after a hearing, denied the petitioner's motion for the issuance of an order, inter alia, making specific findings so as to enable the child to petition the United States Citizenship and Immigration Services for special immigrant juvenile status pursuant to 8 USC § 1101 (a) (27) (J). The second order dismissed the guardianship petition.

Ordered that the orders are affirmed, without costs or disbursements.

In June 2014, the petitioner commenced this proceeding pursuant to Family Court Act article 6 to be appointed guardian of Lilibeth M.A. (hereinafter the child). The purpose for seeking guardianship was to obtain an order declaring that the child is dependent on the Family Court and making specific findings that she is unmarried and under 21 years of age, that reunification with one or both of her parents is not viable due to parental neglect, and that it would not be in her best interests to be returned to Guatemala, her previous country of nationality and last habitual residence, so as to enable her to petition the United States Citizenship and Immigration Services for special immigrant juvenile status (hereinafter SIJS) pursuant to 8 USC § 1101 (a) (27) (J). Thereafter, the petitioner moved for the issuance of an order making the requisite declaration and specific findings so as to enable the child to petition for SIJS. In two orders dated August 13, 2015, the Family Court denied the motion and dismissed the guardianship petition, respectively.

Pursuant to 8 USC § 1101 (a) (27) (J) (as amended by the William Wilberforce Trafficking Victims Protection Reauthorization Act of 2008, Pub L 110-457, 122 US Stat 5044) and 8 CFR 204.11, a special immigrant is a resident alien who, inter alia, is under 21 years of age, unmarried, and dependent upon a juvenile court or legally committed to an individual appointed by a state or juvenile court. Additionally, for a juvenile to qualify for SIJS, a court must find that reunification of the juvenile with one or both of the juvenile's parents is not viable due to parental abuse, neglect, abandonment, or a similar basis found under state law (*see* 8 USC § 1101 [a] [27] [J] [i]; *Matter of Maria P.E.A. v Sergio A.G.G.*, 111 AD3d 619, 620 [2013]; *Matter of Trudy-Ann W. v Joan W.*, 73 AD3d 793, 795 [2010]), and that it would not be in the juvenile's best interests to be returned to his or her native country or country of last habitual residence (*see* 8 USC § 1101 [a] [27] [J] [ii]; 8 CFR 204.11 [c] [6]; *Matter of Maria P.E.A. v Sergio A.G.G.*, 111 AD3d at 620; *Matter of Trudy-Ann W. v Joan W.*, 73 AD3d at 795).

Upon our independent factual review, we find that, contrary to the petitioner's contention, the record does not support a determination that the child's reunification with one or both of her parents was not viable due to parental neglect (*see Matter of Miguel A.G.G. [Milton N.G.G.]*, 127 AD3d 858, 859 [2015]; *Matter of Nirmal S. v Rajinder K.*, 101 AD3d 1130 [2012]).

The petitioner's remaining contentions either are without merit or need not be addressed in light of our determination.

Accordingly, the Family Court properly denied the petitioner's motion for the issuance of an order, inter alia, making specific findings so as to enable the child to petition for SIJS, and dismissed the guardianship petition. Dillon, J.P., Cohen, Miller and Brathwaite Nelson, JJ., concur.

77 A guardianship petition cannot be granted after the child turns 21.

144 A.D. 3d 909 (2d Dep't Nov 16, 2016)

> ☐ **In the Matter of Lourdes B.V.I., Appellant,**
> **v**
> **Jose R.D.L.C.Q. et al., Respondents.**

Laura Demastus, Hempstead, NY, for appellant.

Ronna L. DeLoe, New Rochelle, NY, attorney for the child.

Appeals by the petitioner from two orders of the Family Court, Queens County (Margaret M. Mulrooney, Ct. Atty. Ref.), both dated December 18, 2015. The first order, upon a petition to appoint the petitioner as guardian of the subject child, after a hearing, denied the petitioner's motion for the issuance of an order, inter alia, making specific findings so as to enable the child to petition the United States Citizenship and Immigration Services for special immigrant juvenile status pursuant to 8 USC § 1101 (a) (27) (J). The second order dismissed the guardianship petition.

Ordered that the appeals are dismissed as academic, without costs or disbursements.

In March 2015, the petitioner commenced this proceeding pursuant to Family Court Act article 6 to be appointed as guardian for Raul W.D.L.C.-O. (hereinafter the child), for the purpose of obtaining an order declaring that the child is dependent on the Family Court and making specific findings that he is unmarried and under 21 years of age, that reunification with one or both of his parents is not viable due to parental neglect or abandonment, and that it would not be in his best interests to be returned to Ecuador, his previous country of nationality and last habitual residence, so as to enable him to petition the United States Citizenship and Immigration Services for special immigrant juvenile status (hereinafter SIJS) pursuant to 8 USC § 1101 (a) (27) (J). Thereafter, the petitioner moved for the issuance of an order making the requisite declaration and specific findings so as to enable the child to petition for SIJS. In two orders, both dated December 18, 2015, the Family Court denied the motion and dismissed the guardianship petition, respectively. On December 21, 2015, the child turned 21 years old.

"Generally, courts are precluded 'from considering questions which, although once live, have become moot by passage of time or change in circumstances'" (*Matter of Brianna L. [Marie A.]*, 103 AD3d 181, 185 [2012], quoting *Matter of Hearst Corp. v Clyne*, 50 NY2d 707, 714 [1980]; *see Matter of Olga L.M.A. v Ronald A.B.M.*, 135 AD3d 741 [2016]).

Where, as here, a child who consented to the appointment of a guardian after his or her 18th birthday turns 21, the term of appointment of the guardian "*expires on [the child's] twenty-first birthday*, or after such other shorter period as the court establishes upon good cause shown" (SCPA 1707 [2] [emphasis added]). Consequently, once the child turns 21, the court "is divested of subject matter jurisdiction, [and] cannot exercise such jurisdiction by virtue of an order nunc pro tunc" (*Matter of Maria C.R. v Rafael G.*, 142 AD3d 165, 170 [2016]; *see Davis v State of New York*, 22 AD2d 733 [1964]). Thus, the guardianship petition cannot be granted at this juncture.

Furthermore, since "guardianship status, which the Family Court can only grant to individuals under the [age of] 21, is a condition precedent to a declaration allowing a child to seek SIJS," the subject motion for the issuance of an order declaring that the child is dependent on the Family Court and making the requisite specific findings so as to enable him to petition for SIJS has also been rendered academic (*Matter of Maria C.R. v Rafael G.*, 142 AD3d at 174). Leventhal, J.P., Miller, LaSalle and Brathwaite Nelson, JJ., concur.

78. A party is not aggrieved for the purposes of an appeal where the petition and motion for special findings were granted and the appeal "relates solely to certain language in the orders."

☐ In the Matter of Lourdes B.V.I., Appellant,
v
Maria D.C.S. et al., Respondents.

---

147 A.D. 3d 948 (2d Dep't Feb 15, 2017)

Bruno J. Bembi, Hempstead, NY, for appellant.

Tammi D. Pere, West Hempstead, NY, attorney for the child.

Appeals by the petitioner from two orders of the Family Court, Queens County (Juanita E. Wing, Ct. Atty. Ref.), both dated April 12, 2016. The first order granted the petition to appoint the petitioner as guardian of the subject child. The second order, after a hearing, granted the petitioner's motion for the issuance of an order, inter alia, making specific findings so as to enable the child to petition the United States Citizenship and Immigration Services for special immigrant juvenile status pursuant to 8 USC § 1101 (a) (27) (J).

Ordered that the appeals are dismissed, without costs or disbursements, as the appellant is not aggrieved by the orders appealed from (*see* CPLR 5511; *Mixon v TBV, Inc.*, 76 AD3d 144 [2010]).

In March 2016, the petitioner commenced this proceeding pursuant to Family Court Act article 6 to be appointed guardian of Tania C.Z.C. (hereinafter the child), for the purpose of obtaining an order declaring that the child is dependent on the Family Court and making special findings so as to enable her to petition the United States Citizenship and Immigration Services for special immigrant juvenile status (hereinafter SIJS) pursuant to 8 USC § 1101 (a) (27) (J) (*see generally Matter of Blanca C.S.C. [Norma C.]*, 141 AD3d 580[2016]; *Matter of Trudy-Ann W. v Joan W.*, 73 AD3d 793 [2010]). Thereafter, the petitioner moved for the issuance of an order making the requisite declaration and specific findings so as to enable the child to petition for SIJS. In the two orders appealed from, the Family Court granted the guardianship petition and the petitioner's motion, respectively.

The petitioner's challenge on appeal relates solely to certain language in the orders. Since the orders granted the subject petition and motion, the petitioner is not aggrieved and the appeals must be dismissed (*see Matter of Saul E.B.M.*, 145 AD3d 1009 [2016]; *Matter of Josue M.A.P. [Coreas Mancia—Perez Lue]*, 143 AD3d 827 [2016]). Balkin, J.P., Austin, Sgroi and LaSalle, JJ., concur.

79. There must be evidence to support a conclusion that the child's reunification with one parent is not viable due to one of the statutory grounds.

☐ In the Matter of Glenda Yaneth Del Cid Martinez, Appellant,
v
Jesus Martinez, Respondent.

144 A.D. 3d 905 (2d Dep't Nov 16, 2016)

Bruno J. Bembi, Hempstead, NY, for appellant.

Lisa Siano, Merrick, NY, attorney for the child.

Appeal by the mother from an order of the Family Court, Nassau County (Edmund M. Dane, J.), dated March 14, 2016. The order, after a hearing, denied the mother's motion for the issuance of an order, inter alia, making specific findings so as to enable the subject child to petition the United States Citizenship and Immigration Services for special immigrant juvenile status pursuant to 8 USC § 1101 (a) (27) (J).

Ordered that the order is affirmed, without costs or disbursements.

In September 2013, the mother filed a petition pursuant to Family Court Act article 6 seeking sole custody of the subject child for the purpose of obtaining an order, inter alia, making specific findings that the child is unmarried and under 21 years of age, that reunification with his father is not viable due to parental neglect or abandonment, and that it would not be in his best interests to be returned to Honduras, his country of nationality, so as to enable him to petition the United States Citizenship and Immigration Services for special immigrant juvenile status (hereinafter SIJS) pursuant to 8 USC § 1101 (a) (27) (J). The mother moved for the issuance of an order making the requisite declaration and specific findings to enable the child to petition for SIJS. In an order dated March 14, 2016, made after a hearing, the Family Court denied the motion.

Pursuant to 8 USC § 1101 (a) (27) (J) (as amended by the William Wilberforce Trafficking Victims Protection Reauthorization Act of 2008, Pub L 110-457, 122 US Stat 5044) and 8 CFR 204.11, a special immigrant is a resident alien who, inter alia, is under 21 years of age, unmarried, and dependent upon a juvenile court or legally committed to an individual appointed by a state or juvenile court. Additionally, for a juvenile to qualify for SIJS, a court must find that reunification of the juvenile with one or both of the juvenile's parents is not viable due to parental abuse, neglect, abandonment, or a similar basis found under state law (*see* 8 USC § 1101 [a] [27] [J] [i]; *Matter of Maria P.E.A. v Sergio A.G.G.*, 111 AD3d 619, 620 [2013]; *Matter of Trudy-Ann W. v Joan W.*,

73 AD3d 793, 795 [2010]), and that it would not be in the juvenile's best interests to be returned to his or her native country or country of last habitual residence (*see* 8 USC § 1101 [a] [27] [J] [ii]; 8 CFR 204.11 [c] [6]; *Matter of Maria P.E.A. v Sergio A.G.G.*, 111 AD3d at 620; *Matter of Trudy-Ann W. v Joan W.*, 73 AD3d at 795).

Contrary to the mother's contention, the record does not support a determination that the child's reunification with his father is not viable due to parental neglect or abandonment (*see Matter of Leslie J.D. [Maria A.A.G.— Sylvia D.], 140 AD3d 1162* [2016]; *Matter of Miguel A.G.G. [Milton N.G.G.], 127 AD3d 858*, 859 [2015]; *Matter of Marvin E.M. de P. [Milagro C.C.—Mario Enrique M.G.], 121 AD3d 892* [2014]).

The mother's remaining contentions are without merit.

Accordingly, the Family Court properly denied the mother's motion for the issuance of an order, inter alia, making specific findings so as to enable the child to petition for SIJS. Dillon, J.P., Dickerson, Hinds-Radix and Maltese, JJ., concur.

80.   Where the mother received financial assistance for the child's benefit but failed to provide for him, the record established that the child's "physical, mental, or emotional condition . . . had been impaired or was in imminent danger of becoming impaired" under Family Court Act 1012[f][i][A] to support a motion for special findings.

Matter of Wilson A.T.Z., 147 A.D. 3d 962 (2d Dep't Feb 15, 2007)

81. It is possible for the "nonparty child" to file an appeal with the Second Department

Matter of Wilson A.T.Z., 147 A.D. 3d 962 (2d Dep't Feb 15, 2007)

82. It was appropriate to make a finding of neglect under Family Court Act 1012[f][i][A] where the mother received money for the child's benefit and failed to support him.

> ☐ **In the Matter of Wilson A.T.Z., Nonparty Appellant. Jose M.T.G., Petitioner; Manuela Z.M., Respondent.**

146 A.D. 3d 962 (2d Dep't Feb 15, 2017)

Marisa Prestianni, Jamaica, NY, for nonparty-appellant.

Appeal by the nonparty child from an order of the Family Court, Queens County (Nicolette M. Pach, J.H.O.), dated March 1, 2016. The order, after a hearing, in effect, denied the petitioner's motion for the issuance of an order, inter alia, making specific findings so as to enable the child to petition the United States Citizenship and Immigration Services for special immigrant juvenile status pursuant to 8 USC § 1101 (a) (27) (J).

Ordered that the order is reversed, on the facts, without costs or disbursements, the petitioner's motion for the issuance of an order, inter alia, making specific findings so as to enable the nonparty child to petition the United States Citizenship and Immigration Services for special immigrant juvenile status pursuant to 8 USC § 1101 (a) (27) (J) is granted, it is declared that the child is dependent on the Family Court, and it is found that he is unmarried and under 21 years of age, that reunification with one of his parents is not viable due to parental neglect, and that it would not be in his best interests to return to Ecuador, his previous country of nationality and last habitual residence.

In September 2014, the petitioner filed a petition pursuant to Family Court Act article 6 to be appointed the guardian of his son, the nonparty child, Wilson A.T.Z. (hereinafter the child), for the purpose of obtaining an order declaring that the child is dependent on the Family Court and making specific findings that he is unmarried and under 21 years of age, that reunification with one or both of his parents is not viable due to abandonment or neglect, and that it would not be in his best interests to be returned to Ecuador, his previous country of nationality and last habitual residence, so as to enable him to petition the United States Citizenship and Immigration Services for special immigrant juvenile status (hereinafter SIJS) pursuant to 8 USC § 1101 (a) (27) (J). Thereafter, the petitioner moved for the issuance of an order making the requisite declaration and specific findings so as to enable the child to petition for SIJS. Following a hearing, the Family Court, inter alia, determined that the child was under 21 years of age, unmarried, and dependent on the Family Court, and that it would not be in his best interests to be returned to Ecuador. However, the court, in effect, denied the motion on the ground that the petitioner failed to establish that reunification of the child with one or both of his parents was not viable due to parental abuse, neglect, abandonment, or similar circumstances. The child appeals. We reverse.

Pursuant to 8 USC § 1101 (a) (27) (J) (as amended by the William Wilberforce Trafficking Victims Protection Reauthorization Act of 2008, Pub L 110-457, 122 US Stat 5044) and 8 CFR 204.11, a "special immigrant" is a resident alien who, inter alia, is under 21 years of age, is unmarried, and has been legally committed to, or placed under the custody of, an individual appointed by a state or juvenile court. Additionally, for a juvenile to qualify for SIJS, a court must find that reunification of the juvenile with one or both of the juvenile's parents is not viable due to parental abuse, neglect, abandonment, or a similar basis found under state law (*see* 8 USC § 1101 [a] [27] [J] [i]; *Matter of Marvin E.M. de P. [Milagro C.C.—Mario Enrique M.G.]*, 121 AD3d 892, 893 [2014]; *Matter of Maria P.E.A. v Sergio A.G.G.*, 111 AD3d 619, 620 [2013]; *Matter of Trudy-Ann W. v Joan W.*, 73 AD3d 793, 795 [2010]), and that it would not be in the juvenile's best interests to be returned to his or her native country or country of last habitual residence (*see* 8 USC § 1101 [a] [27] [J] [ii]; 8 CFR 204.11 [c] [6]; *Matter of Marvin E.M. de P. [Milagro C.C.—Mario Enrique M.G.]*, 121 AD3d at 893; *Matter of Maria P.E.A. v Sergio A.G.G.*, 111 AD3d at 620; *Matter of Trudy-Ann W. v Joan W.*, 73 AD3d at 795).

Based upon our independent factual review, we find that the record fully supports the petitioner's contention that, because the child's mother neglected him, reunification with the mother is not a viable option (*see Matter of Gabriela Y.U.M. [Palacios]*, 119 AD3d 581, 583 [2014]; *Matter of Miguel C.-N. [Hosman C.-N.—Cruz Ermelinda C.-N.]*, 119 AD3d 562, 564 [2014]; *Matter of Maria P.E.A. v Sergio A.G.G.*, 111 AD3d at 620). Contrary to the Family Court's determination, the record demonstrated that the physical, mental, or emotional condition of the child had been impaired or was in imminent danger of becoming impaired as a result of the failure of the mother to exercise a minimum degree of care "in supplying the child with adequate food, clothing, shelter or education . □□ though financially able to do so or offered financial or other reasonable means to do so" (Family Ct Act § 1012 [f] [i] [A]). Indeed, the petitioner's testimony at the hearing demonstrated that although the mother received financial assistance to provide for the child's clothing and education, the mother failed to use such assistance for the child's benefit. The child's testimony corroborated the petitioner's testimony in this respect.

Accordingly, the Family Court should have granted the petitioner's motion for the issuance of an order making the requisite declaration and specific findings so as to enable the child to petition for SIJS. Inasmuch as the record is sufficient for this Court to make its own findings of fact and conclusions of law, the petitioner's motion is granted, we declare that the child is dependent on the Family Court, and we find that the child is unmarried and under 21 years of age, that reunification with one of his parents is not viable due to parental neglect, and that it would not be in his best interests to return to Ecuador (*see Matter of*

Anibal H. [Maria G.G.H.], 138 AD3d 841, 843 [2016]; *Matter of Tommy E.H. [Silvia C.]*, 134 AD3d 840, 842 [2015]). Rivera, J.P., Cohen, Miller and Brathwaite Nelson, JJ., concur.

83. A parent can sign a waiver of service of process which, regardless of how inartful its language, allows for the case to proceed where "no substantial right of a party was prejudiced by the unartful language".

> ☐ **In the Matter of Juan Armando Paca Secaira, Appellant,**
> **v**
> **Miryam Marlene Caluna, Respondent.**

159 A.D. 3d 826 (2d Dep't Mar 14, 2018)

Bruno J. Bembi, Hempstead, NY, for appellant.

Appeal from an order of the Family Court, Queens County (Craig Ramseur, Ct. Atty. Ref.), dated July 19, 2017. The order, without a hearing, dismissed the father's custody petition.

Ordered that the order is reversed, on the law, without costs or disbursements, the petition is reinstated, and the matter is remitted to the Family Court, Queens County, for further proceedings on the petition consistent herewith, before a different Court Attorney Referee.

In March 2017, the father filed a petition pursuant to Family Court Act article 6 for sole custody of the subject child for the purpose of obtaining an order, inter alia, making specific findings so as to enable the child to petition the United States Citizenship and Immigration Services for special immigrant juvenile status (hereinafter SIJS) pursuant to 8 USC § 1101 (a) (27) (J). In April 2017, the mother executed a document consenting, inter alia, to "waive the issuance of service of process in this matter," to the issuance of a finding that she abandoned the child, and to the appointment of the father as the child's guardian. After the presiding Court Attorney Referee (hereinafter the Referee) advised the father that the waiver form was "not correct because the case that's before the court is not a guardianship case," the mother executed a new document consenting, among other things, to waive service of process and to the issuance of "Letters of Custody." The Referee found that the new waiver form was inadequate because, inter alia, there was no statutory reference to "Letters of Custody." In an order dated July 19, 2017, the Family Court dismissed the custody petition on the ground that the mother had not been timely served with the petition. The father appeals from that order.

Under the circumstances of this case, the Family Court erred in dismissing the petition based on the father's failure to timely serve the mother with the petition. The mother consented, inter alia, to "waive the issuance of service of process in this matter," and since no substantial right of a party was prejudiced by the unartful language in the second waiver form, which referred to custody, the court should have disregarded any mistake and conducted a hearing on the petition (*see* CPLR 2001; *Matter of Ramirez v Palacios*, 136 AD3d 666, 667-668 [2016]; *Matter of Gomez v Sibrian*, 133 AD3d 658, 659 [2015]).

Accordingly, we remit the matter to the Family Court, Queens County, for a hearing and a new determination thereafter of the custody petition and, if warranted, an order, inter alia, making specific findings so as to enable the child to petition for SIJS pursuant to 8 USC § 1101 (a) (27) (J). In light of certain remarks made by the Referee, we deem it appropriate that the hearing be held before a different Court Attorney Referee (*see Matter of Hannah B. [Theresa B.]*, 108 AD3d 528, 531 [2013]). Scheinkman, P.J., Leventhal, Miller and Brathwaite Nelson, JJ., concur.

84.   When CIS revokes the approval of an I-360 based upon alleged deficiencies in the special findings order, the Family Court can amend the order.

See Matter of Santos D. Interiano Argueta, below.

85. For purposes of an appeal, the petitioning parent is an aggrieved party when a Family Court Judge denies a motion to amend a special findings order.

See Matter of Santos D. Interiano Argueta, below.

86. It is appropriate to find that it is not in the child's best interests to return to El Salvador where the mother is unable to protect the child from harm by gang members who made threats against him.

☐ **In the Matter of Santos D. Interiano Argueta, Appellant,**
v
Reina E. Alvarenga Santos, Respondent.

166 A.D. 3d 608 (2d Dep't Nov 7, 2018)

Bruno J. Bembi, Hempstead, NY, for appellant.

Amoachi & Johnson, PLLC, Bayshore, NY (Ala Amoachi of counsel), attorney for the child.

In a proceeding pursuant to Family Court Act article 6, the father appeals from an order of the Family Court, Nassau County (Eileen C. Daly-Sapraicone, J.), dated February 26, 2018. The order denied the motion of the subject child and the father to amend a prior special findings order of the same court (Merik R. Aaron, J.) dated February 22, 2016.

Ordered that the order dated February 26, 2018, is modified, on the facts, by deleting the provision thereof denying the motion to amend the special findings order dated February 22, 2016, and substituting therefor a provision granting the

motion to the extent of (1) deleting from the second paragraph thereof the words
" 'to make judicial determinations about the custody and care of juveniles' within
the meaning of Section 101 (a) (27) (J) of the Immigration and Nationality Act
('INA'), 8 U.S.C. § 1101 (a) (27) (J), and 8 C.F.R. § 204.11 (a)," and substituting
therefor the words "to determine proceedings for the custody of minors
(*see* Family Ct Act § 651 [a])"; (2) deleting from the fourth paragraph thereof
the words "or a similar basis found under state law under INA § 101 (a) (27) (J),
8 U.S.C. § 1101 (A) (27) (J)"; (3) adding to the fourth paragraph thereof, after
the words "neglected him for 4 years," the words "(*see* Family Ct Act § 1012 [f]
[i] [A])"; and (4) deleting from the fifth paragraph thereof the words "within the
meaning of Section 101 (a) (27) (J) of the Immigration and Nationality Act, 8
U.S.C. § 1101 (a) (27) (J), and 8 C.F.R. § 204.11 (d) (2) (iii)," and substituting
therefor the words "because the mother is unable to protect the child from harm
by gang members in El Salvador, who had made threats of violence against him
(*see Matter of Juan R.E.M. [Juan R.E.]*, 154 AD3d 725, 726-727)," and
otherwise denying the motion; as so modified, the order dated February 26,
2016, is affirmed, without costs or disbursements.

In June 2016, the father filed a petition pursuant to Family Court Act article
6 for custody of the subject child for the purpose of obtaining an order, inter
alia, making specific findings so as to enable the child to petition the United
States Citizenship and Immigration Services (hereinafter USCIS) for special
immigrant juvenile status (hereinafter SIJS) pursuant to the Immigration and
Nationality Act (8 USC § 1101 [a] [27] [J]). The child moved for the issuance of
an order making the requisite declaration and specific findings so as to enable
him to petition for SIJS. In an order dated February 22, 2016, the Family Court
granted the child's motion.

Thereafter, the child submitted an I-360 petition for SIJS to USCIS.
Although the I-360 petition was initially approved, USCIS thereafter advised

the child of its intention to "revoke the approval" based upon certain deficiencies in the special findings order. The child then moved to amend the special findings order to address the deficiencies, and the father joined in the motion. In an order dated February 26, 2018, the Family Court denied the motion to amend the special findings order. The father appeals from the order dated February 26, 2018.

Initially, since the father joined in the child's motion to amend the special findings order, the father is aggrieved by the order denying that motion (*see Matter of Moriches Inlet Estates Prop. Owners Assn. v Town of Brookhaven*, 2 AD3d 641, 642 [2003]; *Ciraolo v Melville Ct. Assoc.*, 221 AD2d 582, 582 [1995]).

Under the circumstances presented, we deem it appropriate to amend the special findings order to clarify that the basis for the Family Court's exercise of jurisdiction over this custody proceeding is under New York State law pursuant to Family Court Act § 651 (a). We also deem it appropriate to amend the special findings order to specify that it would not be in the best interests of the child to be returned to El Salvador because the mother is unable to protect the child from harm by gang members in El Salvador, who have made threats of violence against him (*see Matter of Juan R.E.M. [Juan R.E.]*, 154 AD3d at 727). Since the special findings order set forth the basis for its finding that reunification of the child with the mother was not viable on the ground of parental neglect, stating that the mother "failed to financially provide for the child's basic[ ] needs and educationally neglected him for 4 years," we do not deem it necessary to amend that finding, except to clarify that the basis for that finding was under New York State law (*see* Family Ct Act § 1012 [f] [i] [A]). Leventhal, J.P., Chambers, Sgroi and Connolly, JJ., concur.

87. A child is not "dependent upon a juvenile court within the meaning of 8 U.S.C. 1101(a)(27)(J)(i), by virtue of his placement in the custody of the

Commissioner of Social Services". Barros, J., dissenting.

    See Matter of Keanu S., below

88. If a motion for special findings is denied by the Family Court, it is possible to file a motion to renew (albeit within the statutorily permitted time period)

In the Matter of Keanu S., Appellant.

167 A.D. 3d 27 (2d Dep't Oct 17, 2018)

Matter of K.S., 56 Misc 3d 938, affirmed.

APPEARANCES OF COUNSEL

The Legal Aid Society, New York City (*Tamara A. Steckler* and *Marcia Egger* of counsel), for appellant.

OPINION OF THE COURT

Rivera, J.P.

On the instant appeal, this Court is presented with the issue of whether the Family Court properly denied the renewed motion of Keanu S. (hereinafter the child) for the issuance of an order declaring that he is dependent on the Family Court and making specific findings so as to enable him to petition the United States Citizenship and Immigration Services for special immigrant juvenile status pursuant to 8 USC § 1101 (a) (27) (J). Specifically, the Family Court rejected the child's contention that he was dependent upon a juvenile court, within the meaning of 8 USC § 1101 (a) (27) (J) (i), by virtue of his placement in the custody of the Commissioner of Social Services of the City of New York following his adjudication as a juvenile delinquent. For the reasons that follow, we agree with the Family Court's determination and conclude that such a placement does not satisfy the requirement of dependency under the statute.

I. The Juvenile Delinquency Acts

On April 22, 2015, the child, while a high school student, punched another student in the face, causing serious injuries, which included two jaw fractures. For these acts, on July 28, 2015, the presentment agency filed a juvenile delinquency petition, charging the child with committing acts which, if committed by an adult, would constitute the crimes of assault in the second and third degrees. In an order of disposition dated November 2, 2015, the Family Court adjudicated the child a juvenile delinquent and placed him on probation for a period of 12 months.

On January 29, 2016, while under probation supervision, the child and three others punched and kicked another victim, causing serious injuries to the victim, including a laceration on his forehead, and took that victim's jacket, which contained his cell phone. The child was charged, inter alia, with committing acts, which if committed by an adult, would constitute the crimes of assault in the second degree and robbery in the second degree.

On May 19, 2016, the Department of Probation filed a petition alleging that based on the incident on January 29, 2016, and his failure to attend school regularly, the child willfully violated the terms of his probation.

In June 2016, the Family Court remanded the child to the Administration for Children's Services of the City of New York for detention pending further proceedings.

In an order dated July 13, 2016, the Family Court vacated the order of disposition dated November 2, 2015, and placed the child in the custody of the Commissioner of Social Services of the City of New York for a period of 12 months in "non-secure placement."

II. Motion for Order of Specific Findings

On March 10, 2017, the child moved for the issuance of an order making the requisite declaration and specific findings so as to enable him to petition for special immigrant juvenile status (hereinafter SIJS) pursuant to 8 USC § 1101 (a) (27) (J).

In a supporting affidavit, the child averred that he was born in Jamaica in May 2000. The child stated that he was 16 years old and unmarried. The child indicated that he lived with his father in Jamaica after the mother "left the home when I was a baby," and was raised by his aunts and his father. According to the child, the father was murdered when the child was 11 years old. The child stated that "[t]he people that cause[d] my father's death also threatened to hurt me." The child came to the United States when he was 12 years old. In addition, he stated that he had no contact with the mother since she left the family and he did not know where she lived.

The child indicated that, at the time of his motion, he lived in a facility run by Sheltering Arms Child and Family Services, "an organization contracted to provide services by the New York City Administration for Children's Services," due to his adjudication as a juvenile delinquent. Further, he stated that his placement was to continue until December 2, 2017. The child contended that "[t]he only family that has taken care of me lives in the United States," and that he believed he would be "in danger" if he returned to Jamaica.

In a supporting affirmation, the Attorney for the Child argued that the dependency requirement of 8 USC § 1101 (a) (27) (J) (i) should be deemed satisfied by the child's placement in the custody of the Commissioner of Social Services of the City of New York.

In an order dated March 20, 2017, the Family Court denied the motion, with leave to renew, upon the submission of additional papers. Thereafter, the child made a renewed motion.

III. The Order Appealed from

In an order dated June 7, 2017, the Family Court denied the child's renewed motion, stating, in pertinent part:

"This court declines to adopt [the child's] position, and finds that a placement in a juvenile delinquency matter does not satisfy the dependency requirement necessary for an SIJS finding .□□ .

"First, there exists no appellate authority in this State to support a finding that a juvenile delinquency proceeding constitutes a dependency upon the Family Court for [specific] findings in an SIJS matter. Second, such determination would circumvent the legislative intent behind the SIJS statute, and would not further the underlying policies or legislative intent of the SIJS statute. Expanding SIJS to include juvenile delinquency matters would put this court in the untenable position of rewarding immigrant children for committing acts, which if done by an adult, would constitute a crime under the Penal Law—a reward not available to a law abiding immigrant child, and an intent this court is not willing to ascribe to Congress.

"Significantly, under the Illegal Immigration Reform and Immigrant Responsibility Act an adult who is not a U.S. citizen and pleads guilty to certain criminal offenses may be subject to mandatory deportation. Moreover, Criminal Procedure Law § 220.50 (7) mandates that a court advise a noncitizen defendant of the deportation consequences of his or her plea to a felony offense. It is inconceivable that Congress would seek to deport an adult criminal, yet give special immigrant status to a juvenile delinquent. This court finds that to grant [the child's] request, simply because he is under this court's placement order, would disparage the very laudable intent of 8 USC § 1101 (a) (27) (J). Clearly, the facts and circumstances of [the child's] history do not fit within the legislative scheme of the SIJS statute, which is concerned with providing special protection to immigrant children who have experienced maltreatment in their families. [The child's] placement in a non-secure facility stemmed from his admission to an assault in the second degree. Granting an SIJS finding to [the child] is not only contrary to the intent of the SIJS statute, but also does not promote the legislative intent behind article 3 of the Family Court Act which did not envision respondents deriving a benefit from their bad acts. For these reasons, this court declines to expand the definition of dependency upon the court for an SIJS finding to include juvenile delinquency placements" (56 Misc 3d 938, 942-943 [Fam Ct, Queens County 2017] [citations omitted]).

IV. Legal Analysis

The legislative history of SIJS was set forth by this Court in *Matter of Hei Ting C.* (109 AD3d 100, 102-103 [2013]). Briefly, in 1990, Congress created SIJS to address the issue of undocumented and unaccompanied children (*see id.* at 102). "As originally enacted, this legislation defined an eligible immigrant as being one who has been declared dependent on a juvenile court located in the United States and has been deemed eligible by that court for long-term foster care" (*id.* at 102-103 [internal quotation marks omitted]). The legislation also required a determination by the court that it would not be in the immigrant's best interests to return to his or her native country (*see id.* at 103). In 1997, Congress added the further requirement that the juvenile court find the child dependent upon the court "due to abuse, neglect, or abandonment," which limited the beneficiaries of the provision "to those juveniles for whom it was created" (*id.* [internal quotation marks omitted]).

In 2008, Congress again amended the SIJS provisions by removing the requirement that the child be deemed eligible for long-term foster care due to abuse, neglect, or abandonment, and replacing it with a requirement that the juvenile court find that "reunification with 1 or both of the immigrant's parents is not viable due to abuse, neglect, abandonment, or a similar basis found under State law" (*id.* [internal quotation marks omitted]). Following the 2008 amendments, the United States Department of Homeland Security issued a memorandum explaining, inter alia, that the new language added to the definition of "Special Immigrant Juvenile" meant that "a petition filed by an alien on whose behalf a juvenile court appointed a guardian may now be eligible" (*id.*, citing Memorandum by Donald Neufeld and Pearl Chang, *Trafficking Victims Protection Reauthorization Act of 2008: Special Immigrant Juvenile Status Provisions* [Mar. 24, 2009]).

Accordingly, pursuant to 8 USC § 1101 (a) (27) (J), as amended by the William Wilberforce Trafficking Victims Protection Reauthorization Act of 2008 (Pub L 110-457, 122 US Stat 5044), and 8 CFR 204.11, a "special immigrant" is a resident alien who, inter alia, is under 21 years of age, is unmarried, and has been legally committed to, or placed under the custody of, an individual appointed by a state or juvenile court. Additionally, for a juvenile to qualify for SIJS, a court must find that reunification of the juvenile with one or both of the juvenile's parents is not viable due to parental abuse, neglect, abandonment, or a similar basis found under state law (*see* 8 USC § 1101 [a] [27] [J] [i]; *Matter of Castellanos v Recarte*, 142 AD3d 552, 553 [2016]; *Matter of Marisol N.H.*, 115 AD3d 185, 188 [2014]; *Matter of Maria P.E.A. v Sergio A.G.G.*, 111 AD3d 619, 620 [2013]), and that it would not be in the juvenile's best interests to be returned to his or her native country or country of last habitual residence (*see* 8 USC § 1101 [a] [27] [J] [ii]; 8 CFR 204.11 [c] [6]; *Matter of Maria P.E.A. v Sergio A.G.G.*, 111 AD3d at 620; *Matter of Trudy-Ann W. v Joan W.*, 73 AD3d 793, 795 [2010]).

On this appeal, the child urges this Court to find that he has been legally committed to, or placed under the custody of, an individual appointed by a state or juvenile court for SIJS purposes by virtue of his juvenile delinquency adjudication. This Court declines to do so. We agree with the Family Court that the dependency requirement has not been satisfied herein.

The SIJS scheme has laudable purposes, worthy goals, and lofty ideals. This immigration relief affords a pathway to lawful permanent residency and citizenship to undocumented children (*see Matter of Castellanos v Recarte*, 142 AD3d at 553). It is an important piece of legislation that advances much-needed support and special protections to vulnerable persons. However, this reform has requirements that cannot be obviated or circumvented.

"[T]he impetus behind the enactment of the SIJS scheme is to protect a child who is abused, abandoned, or neglected and to provide him or her with an expedited immigration process" (*Matter of Hei Ting C.*, 109 AD3d at 106). As previously observed by this Court, intended beneficiaries of the SIJS provisions are " 'those juveniles for whom it was created, namely abandoned, neglected, or abused children' " (*Matter of Marcelina M.-G. v Israel S., 112 AD3d 100*, 108 [2013], quoting HR Rep 105-405, 105th Cong, 1st Sess at 130, reprinted in 1997 US Code Cong & Admin News at 2941, 2954; *see Matter of Fifo v Fifo, 127 AD3d 748*, 750-751 [2015]; *Matter of Hei Ting C.*, 109 AD3d at 103). Applications for SIJS specific findings have generally been granted where dependency upon the court was established by way of guardianship, adoption, or custody (*see Matter of Hei Ting C.*, 109 AD3d at 106). In addition, this Court has recognized that, under proper circumstances, a child involved in a family offense proceeding involving allegations of abuse or neglect may properly be the subject of such a determination as an intended beneficiary of the SIJS provisions (*see Matter of Fifo v Fifo*, 127 AD3d at 751).

We hold that the child herein is *not* an intended beneficiary of the SIJS provisions. He was not placed in the custody of the Commissioner of Social Services due to his status as an abused, neglected, or abandoned child. Instead, he was placed in the custody of the Commissioner of Social Services after committing acts which, if committed by an adult, would have constituted serious crimes. His violent acts and misconduct have resulted in painful and terrible consequences to his victims. In fact, even while under probation, his encounters with the law persisted. In effect, the child attempts to utilize his wrongdoings and the resultant juvenile delinquency adjudication as a conduit or a vehicle to meet the dependency requirement for SIJS. Such a determination is in conflict with the primary intent of Congress in enacting the SIJS scheme, namely, to protect abused, neglected, and abandoned immigrant children. We cannot fathom that Congress envisioned, intended, or proposed that a child could satisfy this requirement by committing acts which, if committed by adults, would constitute crimes, so as to warrant a court's involvement or the legal commitment to an individual appointed by a state or juvenile court. To hold otherwise would mean that similarly situated children who do not resort to committing such acts, but rather, abide by rules, would not meet the dependency requirement for the issuance of an order making specific findings that would allow them to apply to the United States Citizenship and Immigration Services for SIJS.

Turning to the contentions of our dissenting colleague, we respectfully disagree that the dependency requirement was satisfied and take this opportunity to clarify certain points asserted in the dissenting opinion.

First, contrary to the dissent's assertion, we do not rely upon "dicta" adopted from *Matter of Hei Ting C.* (109 AD3d 100 [2013]) in support of our holding herein. *Matter of Hei Ting C.*, wherein this Court discussed at length the dependency requirement of 8 USC § 1101 (a) (27) (J) (i), is binding authority and precedent. We rely upon the disposition and instruction delineated in that case, as we must as a court of precedent (*see generally People v Garvin*, 30 NY3d 174, 185 [2017] [under the doctrine of stare decisis, "common-law decisions should stand as precedents for guidance in cases arising in the future and that a rule of law once decided by a court, will generally be followed in subsequent cases presenting the same legal problem"] [internal quotation marks omitted]).

Second, to the extent that the dissent discusses opinions from lower courts (*see e.g. Matter of Jose H.*, 54 Misc 3d 324 [Sup Ct, Nassau County 2016]; *Matter of Mario S.*, 38 Misc 3d 444 [Fam Ct, Queens County 2012]), as well as cases rendered by Minnesota and California courts (*see e.g. In re Guardianship of Guaman*, 879 NW2d 668 [Minn Ct App 2016]; *In re Israel O.*, 233 Cal App 4th 279, 182 Cal Rptr 3d 548 [Ct App 2015]; *Leslie H. v Superior Ct.*, 224 Cal App 4th 340, 168 Cal Rptr 3d 729 [Ct App 2014]), which may hold otherwise, we decline to adopt the holdings in those cases.

Third, certain provisions of the Family Court Act addressing dispositional orders in juvenile delinquency proceedings (*see e.g.* Family Ct Act §§ 352.1, 352.2), which are referred to by the dissent, are not relevant to the issue at hand, which involves SIJS. On a similar note, contrary to the dissent's suggestion, the placement of a child in the "custody" of the Commissioner of Social Services in a juvenile delinquency proceeding is not the same as a "custody" determination in the context of a child custody proceeding pursuant to Family Court Act article 6.

Fourth, we have not engaged in any "strained" analysis, as posited by the dissent. "In interpreting a statute, 'our primary consideration is to discern and give effect to the Legislature's intention'" (*People v Silburn*, 31 NY3d 144, 155 [2018], quoting *Matter of Albany Law School v New York State Off. of Mental Retardation & Dev. Disabilities*, 19 NY3d 106, 120 [2012]). That is exactly what we have done here.

This Court has previously affirmed orders denying motions for specific findings so as to enable children to petition for SIJS where one of the requirements has not been established (*see e.g. Matter of Goran S.*, 152 AD3d 698 [2017]; *Matter of Amsi H.D.O. [Maria L.R.—Cesiah O.D.]*, 152 AD3d 524 [2017]; *Matter of Oscar J.L.J. [Segundo R.L.T.]*, 151 AD3d 969 [2017]; *Matter of Christian P.S.-A. [Humberto R.S.-B.—Laura S.A.-C.]*, 148 AD3d 1032 [2017]; *Matter of Hei Ting C.*, 109 AD3d at 102). Where, as here, the dependency requirement, which is a prerequisite for the issuance of an order making a declaration and specific findings so as to enable a child to petition for SIJS is lacking, a denial is similarly warranted.

The child's remaining contentions either are without merit or need not be reached in light of our determination.

Accordingly, we agree with the Family Court's determination to deny the child's renewed motion, and the order is affirmed.

Roman and LaSalle, JJ., concur. Ordered that the order is affirmed, without costs or disbursements.

Barros, J., dissents, and votes to reverse the order, on the law, and grant the child's renewed motion for the issuance of an order declaring that the child is dependent on the Family Court and making specific findings so as to enable the child to petition the United States Citizenship and Immigration Services for special immigrant juvenile status pursuant to 8 USC § 1101 (a) (27) (J), with the following memorandum: The majority's conclusion that an abused, neglected, or abandoned child who is placed in the custody of the Commissioner of Social Services by a juvenile court due to a juvenile delinquency adjudication is not a dependent child within the meaning of 8 USC § 1101 (a) (27) (J) (i) is not supported by the plain language and intent of the statute, and disregards federal immigration policy as reflected in the United States Citizenship and Immigration Services manual, and state policy as reflected in the Family Court Act.

Notably, two thoroughly written and well-reasoned opinions from this state analyzing the federal statute, 8 USC § 1101 (a) (27) (J), and the Family Court Act on this issue have concluded that children who are given custodial placements as a result of juvenile delinquency proceedings meet the dependency requirement of 8 USC § 1101 (a) (27) (J) (*see Matter of Jose H.*, 54 Misc 3d 324 [Sup Ct, Nassau County 2016]; *Matter of Mario S.*, 38 Misc 3d 444 [Fam Ct, Queens County 2012]). Appellate courts in other states have, likewise, recognized that the federal statute expressly contemplates that children who are placed in the custody of a state agency or department as a result of juvenile delinquency proceedings meet the dependency requirement (*see In re Guardianship of Guaman*, 879 NW2d 668, 672 [Minn Ct App 2016] ["The relevant federal statute expressly contemplates the entry of such findings when an immigrant has been declared dependent on a juvenile court (as in child-protection proceedings), has been placed in the custody of a state agency or department (*as in juvenile-delinquency proceedings*), or has been placed in the custody of an individual or entity by a state or juvenile court (as in guardianship proceedings)" (emphasis added; internal quotation marks and brackets omitted)]; *In re Israel O.*, 233 Cal App 4th 279, 282-283, 182 Cal Rptr 3d 548, 549-550 [Ct App 2015]; *Leslie H. v Superior Ct.*, 224 Cal App 4th 340, 168 Cal Rptr 3d 729 [Ct App 2014]; *In re K. O.-T.*, 2017 WL 6032588, 2017 Md App LEXIS 1206 [Md Ct Spec App, Dec. 6, 2017, No. 2047]). While these authorities do not constitute binding precedent, they are certainly persuasive. For the reasons that follow, I would reverse the order appealed from, and grant the child's renewed motion for an order declaring that the child is dependent on the Family Court and making specific findings so as to enable the child to petition the United States Citizenship and Immigration Services (hereinafter USCIS) for special immigrant juvenile status (hereinafter SIJS) pursuant to 8 USC § 1101 (a) (27) (J).

I. Plain Meaning

"The text of a statute is the clearest indicator of legislative intent" (*Matter of Avella v City of New York*, 29 NY3d 425, 434 [2017] [internal quotation marks omitted]). Where the statutory language is unambiguous, we are bound to give effect to its plain meaning, and we may not resort to extrinsic evidence to discover legislative intent (*see Makinen v City of New York*, 30 NY3d 81, 85 [2017]). The same principles of statutory construction apply to interpreting federal legislation enacted by Congress (*see Ingalls Shipbuilding, Inc. v Director, Office of Workers' Compensation Programs*, 519 US 248, 255 [1997]; *United States v Ron Pair Enterprises, Inc.*, 489 US 235, 240-241 [1989]; *Caminetti v United States*, 242 US 470, 485 [1917]).

A child establishes that he or she is dependent upon the juvenile court under 8 USC § 1101 (a) (27) (J) when he or she "has been declared dependent on a juvenile court" or when such juvenile court "has legally committed to, or placed [such child] under the custody of, an agency or department of a State, or an individual or entity appointed by a State or juvenile court" (8 USC § 1101 [a] [27] [J] [i]).

Here, the recognized "juvenile court" in New York State is the Family Court (*see Matter of Hei Ting C.*, 109 AD3d 100, 105 [2013]). Thus, in determining whether the child meets the dependency requirement of the statute, we must inquire whether the child has been "declared" dependent upon the Family Court, or whether the Family Court has legally committed or placed the child under the custody of an agency or department of a state, or an individual or entity appointed by a state or the Family Court (*see* 8 USC § 1101 [a] [27] [J]). In *Matter of Hei Ting C.*, this Court held that "[a] child becomes dependent upon a juvenile court when the court accepts jurisdiction over the custody of that child" (109 AD3d at 106). Thus, here, the child became dependent upon the Family Court when the court accepted jurisdiction over his custody, and placed him with the Commissioner of Social Services.

The statute, on its face, does not exempt children whose juvenile court custodial placements are the result of juvenile delinquency adjudications. The majority's holding improperly engrafts an exception into the statute "under the guise of creative interpretation or construction not consistent with the plain and ordinary usage and meaning of the statutory language" (*id.* at 107; *see Bender v Jamaica Hosp.*, 40 NY2d 560 [1976]; McKinney's Cons Laws of NY, Book 1, Statutes § 76, Comment ["The function of the courts is to enforce statutes, not to usurp the power of legislation, and to interpret a statute where there is no need for interpretation, to conjecture about or to add to or to subtract from words having a definite meaning, or to engraft exceptions where none exist are trespasses by a court upon the legislative domain"]).

II. Federal Immigration Policy

My colleagues in the majority disregard the plain meaning of the statute because they cannot "fathom that Congress envisioned, intended, or proposed that a child could satisfy this [dependency] requirement by committing acts which, if committed by adults, would constitute crimes, so as to warrant a court's involvement or the legal commitment to an individual appointed by a state or juvenile court." However, the majority's speculation as to congressional intent finds no support in the legislative history, or the publications of the federal agency charged with interpreting and implementing the statute.

The ultimate determination of whether to grant SIJS to a particular juvenile rests with USCIS and its parent agency, the Department of Homeland Security (*see Matter of Nelson A.G.-L. [Maria Y.G.S.]*, 157 AD3d 789 [2018]). USCIS publishes an online manual setting forth its immigration polices (*see* USCIS Policy Manual, available at www.uscis.gov/policymanual/HTML/PolicyManual.html [last accessed Oct. 15, 2018], cached at http://www.nycourts.gov/reporter/webdocs/Homepage-Policy-Manual-USCIS.pdf). Under volume 7, part F, chapter 7, entitled "Special

Immigrant Juveniles," the manual provides that "[f]indings of juvenile delinquency are not considered criminal convictions for purposes of immigration law"; however, such findings may be "part of a discretionary analysis" in which USCIS will consider such findings on a "case-by-case basis based on the totality of the evidence to determine whether a favorable exercise of discretion is warranted" (*see* USCIS Policy Manual, ch 7, available at www.uscis.gov/policymanual/HTML/PolicyManual-Volume7-PartF-Chapter7.html [last accessed Oct. 15, 2018], cached at http://www.nycourts.gov/reporter/webdocs/Special-Immigrant-Juveniles-Chapter-7-Part-F-Volume-7-Policy-Manual.pdf).

Notably, the manual recognizes that state courts meeting the definition of a "qualifying juvenile court proceeding" include "delinquency courts" (*see* USCIS Policy Manual, ch 3, available at www.uscis.gov/policymanual/HTML/PolicyManual-Volume6-PartJ-Chapter3.html#S-A [last accessed Oct. 15, 2018], cached at http://www.nycourts.gov/reporter/webdocs/Documentation-and-Evidence-Chapter3-Part-J-Volume-6-Policy-Manual-U.pdf). If, as asserted by the majority, Congress intended to exclude children adjudicated juvenile delinquents from obtaining SIJS, then it would defy logic for USCIS to include "delinquency courts" in the class of state courts that meet the definition of a qualifying juvenile court proceeding, and for USCIS to consider juvenile delinquency findings in making its ultimate determination on a child's SIJS application.

"[T]he impetus behind the enactment of the SIJS scheme is to protect a child who is abused, abandoned, or neglected and to provide him or her with an expedited immigration process" (*Matter of Hei Ting C.*, 109 AD3d at 106).

"The requirement that a child be dependent upon the juvenile court or, alternatively, committed to the custody of an individual appointed by a state or juvenile court, ensures that the process is not employed inappropriately by children who have sufficient family support and stability to pursue permanent residency in the United States through other .☐☐ procedures" (*id.*).

Thus, the SIJS scheme is not undermined by granting specific findings orders to abused, neglected, or abandoned children over whose custody the Family Court has accepted jurisdiction, regardless of whether such jurisdiction was acquired in a juvenile delinquency proceeding or some other Family Court proceeding.

While the majority opinion is concerned about rewarding the child's misconduct by granting him a specific findings order, it overlooks, or disregards, that a specific findings order is not an award of SIJS. The Family Court does not make an immigration determination when it makes the requisite specific findings. Those findings merely allow the eligible child to apply to USCIS for an immigration determination. While the nature and seriousness of a child's misconduct may be a concern to USCIS for the purpose of making its ultimate determination on the SIJS application, it has no bearing on our determination, as the state court, on the child's eligibility to apply.

The majority's conclusion that the granting of a specific findings order to a child adjudicated a juvenile delinquent would deprive a "similarly situated" rule-abiding child of such order is unfounded, since there is no limit to the number of specific findings orders that may be issued by the Family Court.

III. Equating Juvenile Delinquency with Criminal Conviction

Federal law does not treat children adjudicated as juvenile delinquents as criminal convicts, even for purposes of immigration (*see* USCIS Policy Manual, ch 7, available at www.uscis.gov/policymanual/HTML/PolicyManual-Volume7-PartF-Chapter7.html [last accessed Oct. 15, 2018], cached at http://www.nycourts.gov/reporter/webdocs/Special-Immigrant-Juveniles-

Chapter-7-Part-F-Volume-7-Policy-Manual.pdf). Moreover, it is a well-established state policy that we do not equate children adjudicated as juvenile delinquents with adults convicted of crimes. The basis of a delinquency finding is not the commission of a criminal act, but rather the commission of an act "that would [be] a crime if committed by an adult" (Family Ct Act § 301.2 [1]; *see Matter of Jose H.*, 54 Misc 3d at 332). The use of the phrase "that would [be] a crime if committed by an adult" is not mere semantics, but reflects a strong policy "to protect young persons who have violated the criminal statutes of this State from acquiring the stigma that accompanies a criminal conviction" (*People v Gray*, 84 NY2d 709, 713 [1995]) and "ensure[s] that a juvenile delinquency adjudication is not treated as a crime" (*Green v Montgomery*, 95 NY2d 693, 697 [2001]).

Despite this well-established policy in both federal and state law to not equate children adjudicated as juvenile delinquents with adults convicted of crimes, the Family Court nonetheless stated that "[i]t is inconceivable that Congress would seek to deport an adult criminal, yet give special immigrant status to a juvenile delinquent" (56 Misc 3d 938, 942 [Fam Ct, Queens County 2017]). In determining whether, as a matter of statutory construction, the child meets the dependency requirement of the SIJS statute, the majority gives significant weight to the seriousness of the child's misconduct and the "painful and terrible consequences to his victims." Such considerations play no role in our determination whether to grant a specific findings order, but may play a role in the ultimate determination by USCIS to grant SIJS (*see Matter of Nelson A.G.-L. [Maria Y.G.S.]*, 157 AD3d at 790; *Matter of Enis A.C.M. [Blanca E.M.—Carlos V.C.P.]*, 152 AD3d 690, 692 [2017]). The majority has, in effect, created an immigration consequence to the juvenile delinquency adjudications of abused, neglected, or abandoned children.

Even more troubling, the Court's holding not only bars the child from obtaining a specific findings order, but is so broad that it would preclude neglected, abused, or abandoned children who have committed much less serious misconduct, including graffiti (*see Matter of Oscar G.*, 83 AD3d 468 [2011]), or marijuana possession (*see Matter of Michael I.*, 309 AD2d 598 [2003] [possession of marijuana cigar]), from obtaining a specific findings order. Children who are abused, neglected, or abandoned are presumed to not have sufficient familial support or stability (*see Matter of Hei Ting C.*, 109 AD3d at 106), and, as a result, may become the subject of Family Court proceedings by reason of their misconduct. The misconduct of these children does not make them any less vulnerable than other abused, neglected, or abandoned children over whom the Family Court exercises jurisdiction for custody. The child's misconduct provides the occasion for the Family Court to intervene and protect the child, as well as the public. It is not, however, an occasion for the Family Court to impose an immigration consequence upon them.

IV. "Custody" in Juvenile Delinquency Proceedings

Contrary to the majority's strained analysis, the placement of a child in the custody of the Commissioner of Social Services as a result of a juvenile delinquency adjudication is considered to be a custody determination under the Family Court Act.

"The overriding intent of the juvenile delinquency article is to empower [the] Family Court to intervene and positively impact the lives of troubled young people while protecting the public" (*Matter of Robert J.*, 2 NY3d 339, 346 [2004]). In the disposition phase of juvenile delinquency proceedings, the Family Court's placement options, as well as the factors that the court must consider in making an appropriate disposition, illustrate how children given placement as a result of a juvenile delinquency adjudication are dependent on the Family Court in the same way as children given placement as a result of other Family Court proceedings.

Upon adjudicating a child a juvenile delinquent, the Family Court must enter a dispositional order setting forth whether the juvenile requires "supervision, treatment or confinement" (Family Ct Act § 352.1). "In determining an appropriate order the court shall consider the needs and best interests of the respondent as well as the need for protection of the community" (Family Ct Act § 352.2 [2] [a]). Family Court Act § 352.2 supplies the Family Court with "a broad array of .□□ options," including placement of the child in his or her own home, in foster care, or in a juvenile facility (*see Matter of Jose H.*, 54 Misc 3d at 333). The law generally requires that the court impose the least restrictive placement consistent with the best interests of the child and the safety and needs of the community (*see* Family Ct Act § 352.2 [2]; *Matter of Jose H.*, 54 Misc 3d at 333).

Significantly, in making a dispositional order, the Family Court must consider circumstances impacting the child's living situation, including whether the juvenile's parents abused, neglected, or subjected the child to other "aggravating circumstances" as defined in Family Court Act § 301.2 (*see* Family Ct Act § 352.2 [2] [c]). Thus, in the dispositional phase, the Family Court is charged with looking not only at what the child has done, i.e., the conduct that would be a crime if committed by an adult, but also what has been done to the child, i.e., evidence of neglect, abuse, or abandonment.

Therefore, the Family Court is authorized to, and often does, make custody determinations in the dispositional phase of juvenile delinquency proceedings. When the Family Court has exercised its jurisdiction and made such placements, as here, the child is considered to be "dependent" on the Family Court for the purpose of SIJS (*see Matter of Hei Ting C.*, 109 AD3d at 106).

The case relied upon by the majority as binding precedent, *Matter of Hei Ting C.*, does not support its holding, and is factually inapposite. There, parents were disputing their respective financial obligations toward their children. There was no issue of guardianship or custody over the children (*see id.* at 107), and "no need for intervention by the Family Court to ensure that the [children] were placed in a safe and appropriate custody, guardianship, or foster care situation" (*id.* at 106). In contrast, here, the Family Court committed the child's custody to the Commissioner of Social Services. In so doing, the Family Court necessarily determined that the child required intervention to ensure, inter alia, that the child was placed in a safe and appropriate situation.

V. Independent Factual Review

Based upon our independent factual review, I would conclude that the child meets all of the remaining requirements for a specific findings order. Reunification of the child with one or two parents is not viable because the father was murdered in Jamaica, and the mother abandoned him. The record establishes that, given the circumstances involving the murder of the child's father in Jamaica, the child's lack of familial support in Jamaica, and the child's familial support in this country, it would not be in the child's best interests to be returned to Jamaica. It is undisputed that the child was under 21 years old and unmarried at the time of his renewed motion. Since the child meets all of the requirements for a specific findings order, I vote to reverse the order appealed from, and grant the renewed motion (*see e.g. Matter of Nelson A.G.-L. [Maria Y.G.S.]*, 157 AD3d at 790-791; *Matter of Enis A.C.M. [Blanca E.M.—Carlos V.C.P.]*, 152 AD3d at 692), and thus, leave the ultimate determination of whether the child should be granted SIJS to the appropriate federal agency, USCIS.

VI. Summary

The order appealed from should be reversed. The plain language of the federal statute (8 USC § 1101 [a] [27] [J]), in conjunction with this state's Family Court Act, establishes that the child meets the dependency requirement. Exercising our independent factual review power, I would grant the child's renewed motion for a specific findings order.

89 A motion for leave to renew a denied motion for special findings may be filed in the Family Court and may be granted where the child's affidavit asserts "that her relationship with the parents had changed after the time of the hearing".

☐ In the Matter of Leslie J.D. Maria A.A.G., Appellant; Silvia D. et al., Respondents.

167 A.D. 3d 1004 (2d Dep't Dec. 26, 2018)

Bruno J. Bembi, Hempstead, NY, for appellant.

In a proceeding pursuant to Family Court Act article 6, the petitioner appeals from an order of the Family Court, Nassau County (Tammy S. Robbins, J.), dated March 2, 2018. The order denied the petitioner's motion, in effect, for leave to renew her prior motion for the issuance of an order, inter alia, making specific findings so as to enable the subject child, Leslie J. D., to petition the United States Citizenship and Immigration Services for special immigrant juvenile status pursuant to 8 USC § 1101 (a) (27) (J), which had been denied in an order of the same court (Elaine Jackson Stack, J.H.O.) dated April 1, 2015.

Ordered that the order dated March 2, 2018, is affirmed, without costs or disbursements.

In July 2014, the petitioner commenced this proceeding pursuant to Family Court Act article 6 to be appointed guardian of Leslie J.D. (hereinafter the child), for the purpose of obtaining an order declaring that the child is dependent on the Family Court and making specific findings so as to enable the child to petition for special immigrant juvenile status (hereinafer SIJS) pursuant to 8 USC § 1101 (a) (27) (J). Although the Family Court awarded guardianship of the child to the petitioner, in an order dated April 1, 2015 (hereinafter the April 2015 order), the court, after a hearing, denied the petitioner's motion for the issuance of an order, inter alia, making specific findings so as to enable the child to petition for SIJS. In a decision and order dated February 17, 2016, this Court affirmed the April 2015 order (*see Matter of Leslie J.D. [Maria A.A.G.—Sylvia D.], 136 AD3d 902*, 904 [2016]).

Prior to the issuance of this Court's decision and order affirming the April 2015 order, the petitioner moved in the Family Court, in effect, for leave to renew her prior motion for the issuance of an order, inter alia, making specific findings so as to enable the child to petition for SIJS. In an order dated November 12, 2015, the Family Court denied that motion. This Court affirmed that determination (*see Matter of Leslie J.D. [Maria A.A.G.—Sylvia D.], 140 AD3d 1162*, 1164 [2016]).

In January 2018, the petitioner again moved, in effect, for leave to renew her prior motion for the issuance of an order, inter alia, making specific findings so as to enable the child to petition for SIJS. The petitioner included an affidavit from the child in her motion papers. In an order dated March 2, 2018, the Family Court denied that motion. The petitioner appeals.

A motion for leave to renew "shall be based upon new facts not offered on the prior motion that would change the prior determination" (CPLR 2221 [e] [2]) and "shall contain reasonable justification for the failure to present such facts on the prior motion" (CPLR 2221 [e] [3]). Here, the child's affidavit in support of the motion did not address why the petitioner previously failed to submit the purported new facts asserted in the affidavit, which existed and were known by the child at the time of the original motion (*see* CPLR 2221 [e] [3]).

Since the child's affidavit also did not indicate that her testimony in the initial hearing was mistaken, assert that her relationship with the parents had changed after the time of the hearing, or otherwise explain inconsistencies between her prior testimony and the affidavit, the petitioner failed to show how such facts would change the prior determination (*see*CPLR 2221 [e] [2]; *Matter of Leslie J.D. [Maria A.A.G.—Sylvia D.]*, 140 AD3d at 1164).

Accordingly, we agree with the Family Court's determination denying the petitioner's motion, in effect, for leave to renew her prior motion.

The petitioner's remaining contention is raised for the first time on appeal and is not properly before this Court. Leventhal, J.P., Austin, Duffy and Iannacci, JJ., concur.

90. A motion to renew the denial of a special findings motion must include new facts to "support a determination that reunification of the child with one or both parents is not viable" due to one of the statutory grounds.

☐ **In the Matter of Leslie J.D. Maria A.A.G., Appellant; Sylvia D. et al., Respondents.**

140 A.D. 3d 1162 (2d Dep't June 29, 2016)

Bruno J. Bembi, Hempstead, NY, for appellant.

Appeal from an order of the Family Court, Nassau County (Thomas Rademaker, J.), dated November 12, 2015. The order denied the petitioner's motion, in effect, for leave to renew her prior motion for the issuance of an order, inter alia, making specific findings so as to enable the subject child, Leslie J.D., to petition the United States Citizenship and Immigration Services for special immigrant juvenile status pursuant to 8 USC § 1101 (a) (27) (J).

Ordered that the order is affirmed, without costs or disbursements.

In July 2014, the petitioner commenced this proceeding pursuant to Family Court Act article 6 to be appointed guardian of Leslie J.D. (hereinafter the child), for the purpose of obtaining an order declaring that the child is dependent on the Family Court and making specific findings that she is unmarried and under 21 years of age, that reunification with one or both of her parents is not viable due to parental abandonment, and that it would not be in her best interests to be returned to Belize, her previous country of nationality and last habitual residence, so as to enable her to petition the United States Citizenship and Immigration Services for special immigrant juvenile status (hereinafter SIJS) pursuant to 8 USC § 1101 (a) (27) (J). Thereafter, the petitioner moved for the issuance of an order making the requisite declaration and specific findings so as to enable the child to petition for SIJS. In an order dated April 1, 2015, made after a hearing, the Family Court determined, inter alia, that the child was under 21 years of age, unmarried, and dependent on the Family Court, and that it would not be in her best interests to be returned to Belize. However, the court denied the petitioner's motion on the ground that reunification of the child "with one or both of her parents is a viable option."

While the petitioner's appeal from the order dated April 1, 2015, was pending, the petitioner moved, in effect, for leave to renew her prior motion for the issuance of an order, inter alia, making specific findings so as to enable the child to petition for SIJS. In an order dated November 12, 2015, the Family Court denied that motion.

Thereafter, in a decision and order dated February 17, 2016, this Court affirmed the order dated April 1, 2015, determining that, although the Family Court erred with respect to its interpretation of the element of "reunification," upon this Court's independent factual review, the record did not support a determination that the child's reunification with one or both of her parents was not viable due to abandonment (*see Matter of Leslie J.D. [Maria A.A.G.—Sylvia D.]*, 136 AD3d 902, 904 [2016]).

Pursuant to 8 USC § 1101 (a) (27) (J) (as amended by the William Wilberforce Trafficking Victims Protection Reauthorization Act of 2008, Pub L 110-457, 122 US Stat 5044) and 8 CFR 204.11, a "special immigrant" is a resident alien who, inter alia, is under 21 years of age, is unmarried, and has been legally committed to, or placed under the custody of, an individual appointed by a state or juvenile court. Additionally, for a juvenile to qualify for SIJS, a court must find that reunification of the juvenile with one or both of the juvenile's parents is not viable due to parental abuse, neglect, abandonment, or a similar basis found under State law (*see* 8 USC § 1101 [a] [27] [J] [i]; *Matter of Maria P.E.A. v Sergio A.G.G.*, 111 AD3d 619, 620 [2013]; *Matter of Trudy-Ann W. v Joan W.*, 73 AD3d 793, 795 [2010]), and that it would not be in the juvenile's best interests to be returned to his or her native country or country of last habitual residence (*see* 8 USC § 1101 [a] [27] [J] [ii]; 8 CFR 204.11 [c] [6]; *Matter of Maria P.E.A. v Sergio A.G.G.*, 111 AD3d at 620; *Matter of Trudy-Ann W. v Joan W.*, 73 AD3d at 795).

Here, the record before the Family Court on the petitioner's motion, in effect, for leave to renew, does not support a determination that reunification of the child with one or both of her parents is not viable due to parental abandonment (*see Matter of Miguel A.G.G. [Milton N.G.G.]*, 127 AD3d 858, 859 [2015]; *Matter of Maria S.Z. v Maria M.A.*, 115 AD3d 970, 971 [2014]). The new facts offered on the subject motion would not change the prior determination (*see* CPLR 2221 [e] [2]).

Accordingly, the Family Court properly denied the petitioner's motion, in effect, for leave to renew her prior motion for the issuance of an order, inter alia, making specific findings so as to enable the child to petition for SIJS. Dillon,

J.P., Dickerson, Cohen and Duffy, JJ., concur.

91. "The law does not require a finding that reunification with neither of the child's parents is viable".

> ☐ **In the Matter of Leslie J.D. Maria A.A.G., Appellant; Sylvia D. et al., Respondents.**

136 A.D. 3d 902 (2d Dep't Feb 17, 2016)

Bruno Joseph Bembi, Hempstead, NY, for appellant.

Appeal from an order of the Family Court, Nassau County (Elaine Jackson Stack, J.H.O.), dated April 1, 2015. The order, after a hearing, denied the petitioner's motion for the issuance of an order, inter alia, making special findings so as to enable the subject child to petition the United States Citizenship and Immigration Services for special immigrant juvenile status pursuant to 8 USC § 1101 (a) (27) (J).

Ordered that the order is affirmed, without costs or disbursements.

In July 2014, the petitioner commenced this proceeding pursuant to Family Court Act article 6 to be appointed guardian of Leslie J.D. (hereinafter the child). The purpose in seeking guardianship of the child was to obtain an order declaring that the child was dependent on the Family Court with specific findings that she is unmarried and under 21 years of age, that reunification with one or both of her parents was not viable due to abandonment, and that it would not be in her best interests to be returned to Belize, her previous country of nationality and last habitual residence, so as to enable the child to petition the United States Citizenship and Immigration Services for special immigrant juvenile status (hereinafter SIJS) pursuant to 8 USC § 1101 (a) (27) (J). Thereafter, the petitioner moved for the issuance of an order making the requisite declaration and specific findings to enable the child to petition for SIJS. In an order dated December 1, 2014, the Family Court granted the guardianship petition. In the order appealed from, the Family Court found, after a hearing, that the child was under 21 years of age, unmarried, dependent on the Family Court, and that it would not be in her best interests to return to Belize, but that reunification of the child "with one or both of her parents is a viable option."

Pursuant to 8 USC § 1101 (a) (27) (J) (as amended by the William Wilberforce Trafficking Victims Protection Reauthorization Act of 2008, Pub L 110-457, 122 US Stat 5044) and 8 CFR 204.11, a special immigrant is a resident alien who is, inter alia, under 21 years of age, unmarried, and dependent upon a juvenile court or legally committed to an individual appointed by a state or juvenile court. The appointment of a guardian constitutes the necessary declaration of dependency on a juvenile court for SIJS purposes (*see Matter of Marvin E.M. de P. [Milagro C.C.—Mario Enrique M.G.]*, 121 AD3d 892, 892-893 [2014]; *Matter of Trudy-Ann W. v Joan W.*, 73 AD3d 793, 795 [2010]). Additionally, for a juvenile to qualify for SIJS, a court must find that reunification of the juvenile with one or both of the juvenile's parents is not viable due to parental abuse, neglect, abandonment, or similar parental conduct defined under state law, and that it would not be in the juvenile's best interests to be returned to his or her native country or country of last habitual residence (*see Matter of Mira v Hernandez*, 118 AD3d 1008, 1009 [2014]; *Matter of Trudy-Ann W. v Joan W.*, 73 AD3d at 795).

The Family Court erred with respect to the element of "reunification." The law does not require a finding that reunification with neither of the child's parents is viable, but that reunification with one or both of the child's parents is not viable due to abuse, neglect, abandonment, or a similar basis found under State law (*see* 8 USC § 1101 [a] [27] [J] [i]; *Matter of Haide L.G.M. v Santo D.S.M.*, 130 AD3d 734, 736 [2015]).

Nevertheless, upon our independent factual review, we find that, contrary to the petitioner's contention, the record does not support a determination that the child's reunification with one or both of her parents was not viable due to abandonment (*see Matter of Miguel A.G.G. [Milton N.G.G.]*, 127 AD3d 858, 859 [2015]; *Matter of Mira v Hernandez*, 118 AD3d at 1009; *Matter of Maria S.Z. v Maria M.A.*, 115 AD3d 970, 971 [2014]).

The petitioner's remaining contentions are without merit. Dillon, J.P., Dickerson, Cohen and Duffy, JJ., concur.

[Once Leslie turned 18, she was able to file a new guardanship petition and motion for special findings that were granted].

92. It is error for the Family Court to make a decision without an "assessment of the credibility of witnesses " and without examining "the facts of the case within the context of the required best interests analysis".

See Matter of Grechel, below

93.   Parental neglect is established where "the father inflicted excessive corporal punishment on the child" where "the father often struck her with his belt 'with all his force,' leaving her with 'really painful red marks'" and "the father kicked the mother, in the presence of the child, 'so hard that [the mother] was left with a limp and a bunch of bruises'"

See Matter of Grechel, below

94.   The "child's physical, mental, or emotional condition was impaired or in imminent danger of becoming impaired as the result of the father's misuse of alcoholic beverages" where "the father regularly drank alcoholic beverages to the point that he became 'very angry and aggressive,' that the father beat her and the mother when he returned to the house drunk, and that when the father drank she and her siblings 'tried to hide from him because we were so scared'" as per Family Court Act 1012[f][i][B].

   See Matter of Grechel, below

95.   It would not be in the child's best interests to return to Nicaragua where the child "was harassed by gang members in Nicaragua who threatened to hurt her and" told her to watch herself, "that she was afraid to go to the police 'because the gang members had friends in the police,' that she told her mother about the gang members, but her mother was unable to protect her, and that she ws afraid that, if returned to Nicaragua, the gang members ' will carry out the threats they made to me'".

☐ In the Matter of Grechel L.J., Appellant.

167 A.D. 3d 1011 (2d Dep't Dec. 26, 2018)

   The Legal Aid Society, New York, NY (Adriene Holder and Elizabeth Rieser-Murphy of counsel), for appellant.

   In a guardianship proceeding pursuant to Family Court Act article 6, the child appeals from two orders of the Family Court, Queens County (Margaret M. Mulrooney, Ct. Atty. Ref.), both dated December 13, 2018. The first order, after a hearing, dismissed the child's petition to appoint Cristina I.Q.-E. as guardian of the child. The second order denied the child's motion for the issuance of an order, inter alia, making specific findings so as to enable her to petition the United States Citizen and Immigration Services for special immigrant juvenile status pursuant to 8 USC § 1101 (a) (27) (J).

Ordered that the orders are reversed, on the law and the facts, without costs or disbursements, the petition to appoint Cristina I.Q.-E. as guardian of the child is reinstated and granted, Cristina I.Q.-E. is appointed as the guardian of the child, the child's motion for the issuance of an order, inter alia, making specific findings so as to enable her to petition the United States Citizen and Immigration Services for special immigrant juvenile status pursuant to 8 USC § 1101 (a) (27) (J) is granted, it is declared that the child is dependent on a juvenile court, and it is found that the child is unmarried and under 21 years of age, that reunification with her father is not viable due to parental neglect, and that it would not be in the child's best interests to be returned to Nicaragua, her previous country of nationality and last habitual residence.

In June 2018, Grechel L.J. (hereinafter the child) filed a petition pursuant to Family Court Act article 6 to appoint Cristina I.Q.-E. (hereinafter the proposed guardian) as her guardian for the purpose of obtaining an order declaring that the child is dependent on the Family Court and making specific findings so as to enable her to petition the United States Citizenship and Immigration Services for special immigrant juvenile status (hereinafter SIJS) pursuant to 8 USC § 1101 (a) (27) (J). Thereafter, the child moved for the issuance of an order, inter alia, making the requisite declaration and specific findings so as to enable her to petition for SIJS. In two orders, both dated December 13, 2018, the Family Court dismissed the petition and denied the child's motion. The child appeals.

"When considering guardianship appointments, the infant's best interests are paramount" (*Matter of Axel S.D.C. v Elena A.C.*, 139 AD3d 1050, 1051 [2016]; *see Matter of Alamgir A.*, 81 AD3d 937, 938 [2011]). Here, the Family

Court erred in determining that the proposed guardian should not be appointed (*see generally* Family Ct Act § 355.5 [7] [d] [ii]; Social Services Law § 371 [7]), as it failed to base its decision on any assessment of the credibility of the witnesses at the hearing, and failed to examine the facts of the case within the context of the required best interests analysis (*see* Family Ct Act § 661). Upon our independent factual review of the record, it is in the child's best interests to appoint the proposed guardian. Accordingly, we find that the guardianship petition should have been granted.

Furthermore, the Family Court should have granted the child's motion for the issuance of an order, inter alia, making the requisite declaration and specific findings so as to enable her to petition for SIJS. Pursuant to 8 USC § 1101 (a) (27) (J) (as amended by the William Wilberforce Trafficking Victims Protection Reauthorization Act of 2008, Pub L 110-457, 122 US Stat 5044) and 8 CFR 204.11, a special immigrant juvenile is a resident alien who, inter alia, is under 21 years of age, unmarried, and dependent upon a juvenile court or legally committed to an individual appointed by a state or juvenile court. Additionally, for a child to qualify for SIJS, a court must find that reunification of the child with one or both parents is not viable due to parental abuse, neglect, abandonment, or a similar basis found under state law (*see* 8 USC § 1101 [a] [27] [J] [i]; *Matter of Maria P.E.A. v Sergio A.G.G.*, 111 AD3d 619, 620 [2013]; *Matter of Trudy-Ann W. v Joan W.*, 73 AD3d 793, 795 [2010]), and that it would not be in the child's best interests to be returned to his or her previous country of nationality or country of last habitual residence (*see* 8 USC § 1101 [a] [27] [J] [ii]; 8 CFR 204.11 [c] [6]; *Matter of Maria P.E.A. v Sergio A.G.G.*, 111 AD3d at 620; *Matter of Trudy-Ann W. v Joan W.*, 73 AD3d at 795).

Here, the child is under the age of 21 and unmarried, and since we have found that the proposed guardian should have been appointed as the child's guardian, a finding also should have been made that the child is dependent on a juvenile court within the meaning of 8 USC § 1101 (a) (27) (J) (i) (*see Matter of Maura A.R.-R. [Santos F.R.—Fidel R.]*, 114 AD3d 687, 689 [2014]; *Matter of Trudy-Ann W. v Joan W.*, 73 AD3d at 796). Further, based upon our independent factual review, the record supports a finding that reunification of the child with her father is not a viable option due to parental neglect (*see Matter of Axel S.D.C. v Elena A.C.*, 139 AD3d at 1052). The record demonstrates that the father inflicted excessive corporal punishment on the child, as the child stated in an affidavit in support of her motion that the father often struck her with his belt "with all of his force," leaving her with "really painful red marks on [her] skin," and that the father kicked the mother, in the presence of the child, "so hard that [the mother] was left with a limp and a bunch of bruises" (*see Matter of Gurwinder S.*, 155 AD3d 959, 961 [2017]; *Matter of Ena S.Y. [Martha R.Y.—Antonio S.]*, 140 AD3d 778, 780 [2016]). The record also reflects that the child's physical, mental, or emotional condition was impaired or in imminent danger of becoming impaired as a result of the father's misuse of alcoholic beverages, as the child averred that the father regularly drank alcoholic beverages to the point that he became "very angry and aggressive," that the father beat her and the mother when he returned to the house drunk, and that when the father drank she and her siblings "tried to hide from him because we were so scared" (*see* Family Ct Act § 1012 [f] [i] [B]). Lastly, the record supports a finding that it would not be in the best interests of the child to return to Nicaragua, the child's previous country of nationality or country of last habitual residence. The child averred that she was harassed by gang members in Nicaragua, who threatened to hurt her and "told me to watch myself," that she was afraid to go to the police "because the gang members had friends in the police," that she told her mother about the gang members, but her mother was unable to protect her, and that she was afraid that, if she returned to Nicaragua, the gang members "will carry out the threats they made to me" (*see Matter of Argueta v Santos*, 166 AD3d 608 [2018]).

Accordingly, the Family Court should have granted the guardianship petition and the child's motion for the issuance of an order, inter alia, making the requisite declaration and specific findings so as to enable her to petition for SIJS. Dillon, J.P., Duffy, Connolly and Christopher, JJ., concur.

96. It was error to fail to find a presumption of neglect where the child's father, when living with the child in the United States, "would 'drink every day'" causing him "to become 'aggressive,' '[h]e hit doors, walls, and started to yell at all times of the night,' and that the child became 'scared of [the father]'" and that the "father '[drank] to the point that he could not walk,'" and where the child believed she could not live with him in El Salvador "due to his excessive drinking."

See Matter of Agustin E., below.

97. It was error for the Family Court Judge not to decide that it was not in the child's best interests to return to El Salvador "where gang members had threatened the father in the presence of the child, made the father 'complete tasks and favors for them,' and murdered the child's cousin."

In the Matter of Agustin E., Appellant,
v
Luis A.E.S. et al., Respondents.

---

168 A.D.3d 840 (2d Dep't Jan 16, 2019)

Alexandra Mayen Rivera, Huntington, NY, for appellant.

In a guardianship proceeding pursuant to Family Court Act article 6, the petitioner appeals from an order of the Family Court, Nassau County (Eileen C. Daly-Sapraicone, J.), dated May 21, 2018. The order, after a hearing, denied the petitioner's motion for the issuance of an order, inter alia, making specific findings so as to enable the subject child to petition the United States Citizenship and Immigration Services for special immigrant juvenile status pursuant to 8 USC § 1101 (a) (27) (J).

Ordered that the order is reversed, on the facts, without costs or disbursements, the petitioner's motion for the issuance of an order, inter alia, making specific findings so as to enable the subject child to petition the United States Citizenship and Immigration Services for special immigrant juvenile status pursuant to 8 USC § 1101 (a) (27) (J) is granted, and it is found that reunification of the subject child with her father is not viable due to parental neglect and that it would not be in the best interests of the child to be returned to El Salvador, her previous country of nationality and last habitual residence.

In September 2017, the subject child's uncle, Agustin E. (hereinafter the petitioner), commenced this proceeding pursuant to Family Court Act article 6 to be appointed as guardian of the child, for the purpose of obtaining an order declaring that the child is dependent on the Family Court and making specific findings that she is unmarried and under 21 years of age, that reunification with one or both of her parents is not viable due to parental neglect and abandonment, and that it would not be in her best interests to be returned to El Salvador, her previous country of nationality and last habitual residence, so as to enable the child to petition the United States Citizenship and Immigration Services for special immigrant juvenile status (hereinafter SIJS) pursuant to 8 USC § 1101 (a) (27) (J). Thereafter, the petitioner moved for the issuance of an order making the requisite declaration and specific findings so as to enable the child to petition for SIJS. In an order dated April 27, 2018, the Family Court granted the petition to appoint the petitioner as guardian for the child. In an order dated May 21, 2018, made after a hearing, the court denied the petitioner's motion on the ground that he failed to establish that reunification of the child with one or both of her parents was not viable due to parental neglect or abandonment. The petitioner appeals.

"Pursuant to 8 USC § 1101 (a) (27) (J) (as amended by the William Wilberforce Trafficking Victims Protection Reauthorization Act of 2008, Pub L

110-457, 122 US Stat 5044) and 8 CFR 204.11, a 'special immigrant' is a resident alien who is, inter alia, under 21 years of age, unmarried, and dependent upon a juvenile court or legally committed to an individual appointed by a state or juvenile court" (*Matter of Trudy-Ann W. v Joan W.*, 73 AD3d 793, 795 [2010]; *see Matter of Gurwinder S.*, 155 AD3d 959 [2017]; *Matter of Maria P.E.A. v Sergio A.G.G.*, 111 AD3d 619, 620 [2013]). "Additionally, for a juvenile to qualify for special immigrant juvenile status, a court must find that reunification of the juvenile with one or both of the juvenile's parents is not viable due to parental abuse, neglect, abandonment, or similar parental conduct defined under State law, and that it would not be in the juvenile's best interest to be returned to his or her native country or country of last habitual residence" (*Matter of Marvin E.M. de P. [Milagro C.C.—Mario Enrique M.G.]*, 121 AD3d 892, 893 [2014]; *see Matter of Maria P.E.A. v Sergio A.G.G.*, 111 AD3d at 620; *Matter of Trudy-Ann W. v Joan W.*, 73 AD3d at 795).

Based upon our independent factual review, reunification of the child with her father is not viable due to parental neglect (*see Matter of Axel S.D.C. v Elena A.C.*, 139 AD3d 1050, 1052 [2016]). The petitioner testified that after the father came to the United States with the child, they lived in the petitioner's home, during which time the father would "drink every day," and that the father eventually returned to El Salvador on his own. The petitioner stated in his affidavit in support of his motion that the father's drinking caused him to become "aggressive," "[h]e hit doors, walls, and started to yell at all times of the night," and that the child became "scared of [the father]." Further, the child stated in her affidavit that the father "[drank] to the point that he could not walk," and testified in court that she did not believe she could live with the father if she returned to El Salvador due to his excessive drinking. Thus, the record demonstrates that the father repeatedly misused alcoholic beverages to the extent of producing a state of intoxication or a "substantial manifestation of irrationality," triggering a presumption that the child was neglected by the father

(Family Ct Act § 1046 [a] [iii]; *see Matter of Vita C. [Oksana C.]*, 138 AD3d 739, 740 [2016]). Since the presumption of neglect was not rebutted, the Family Court should have found that reunification of the child with the father was not viable due to parental neglect. The record also supports a finding that it would not be in the child's best interests to be returned to El Salvador, where gang members had threatened the father in the presence of the child, made the father "complete tasks and favors for them," and murdered the child's cousin (*see Matter of Juan R.E.M. [Juan R.E.]*, 154 AD3d 725, 727 [2017]; *Matter of Fatima J.A.J. [Ana A.J.S.—Carlos E.A.F.]*, 137 AD3d 912, 914 [2016]).

Accordingly, the Family Court should have granted the petitioner's motion for the issuance of an order, inter alia, making specific findings so as to enable the child to petition for SIJS. Since the record is sufficient for this Court to make its own findings of fact and conclusions of law, we find that reunification of the child with her father is not viable due to parental neglect, and that it would not be in the child's best interests to be returned to El Salvador, her previous country of nationality and last habitual residence. Mastro, J.P., Austin, Roman and Brathwaite Nelson, JJ., concur.

98. The appellate court is free to make its own credibility determination where the Family Court's determination is not supported by the record.

See Matter of Lucas, below.

99. A finding of neglect by the father is appropriate where the father physically mistreated the mother "in the presence of the child by hitting her with objects such as a book or shoes" causing bruises and, "when the child attempted to defend the mother the father would hit the child", and the father yelled at and punched the child, and the "mother indicated that she had to send the child to live" with a grandparent in El Salvador "because she was afraid of what the father would do to the child," and the father "provided no financial support for the child since she was ten years old."

See Matter of Lucas, below.

100. The Family Court erred in failing to find it was not in the minor's best interests to return to El Salvador where, following the minor's refusal to join a gang, they threatened and assaulted him "multiple times" and hurt him badly, leaving him on the street "and would have killed him on one occasion if not for a police patrol 'coming by that moment'" and "that he was afraid to go outside after the incident when he was almost killed" and the child testified "'if I go back [to El Salvador] they will kill me".

☐ In the Matter of Lucas F.V., Appellant; Jose N.F., Respondent.

---

169 A.D. 3d 802 (2d Dep't Feb 13, 2019)

Binder & Schwartz LLP, New York, NY (Neil S. Binder and Tessa B. Harvey of counsel), for appellant.

In a guardianship proceeding pursuant to Family Court Act article 6, the subject child appeals from an order of the Family Court, Nassau County (Eileen C. Daly-Sapraicone, J.), dated March 15, 2018. The order, after a hearing, denied the child's motion for the issuance of an order, inter alia, making specific findings so as to enable him to petition the United States Citizen and Immigration Services for special immigrant juvenile status pursuant to 8 USC § 1101 (a) (27) (J).

Ordered that the order is reversed, on the facts, without costs or disbursements, the child's motion for the issuance of an order, inter alia, making specific findings so as to enable him to petition the United States Citizenship and Immigration Services for special immigrant juvenile status pursuant to 8 USC § 1101 (a) (27) (J) is granted, and it is found that reunification of the subject child with his father is not viable due to parental neglect and that it would not be in the child's best interests to return to El Salvador, his previous country of nationality and last habitual residence.

In December 2017, Lucas F.V. (hereinafter the child) filed a petition in the Family Court, Nassau County, pursuant to Family Court Act article 6 to have his mother appointed as his guardian for the purpose of obtaining an order declaring that the child is dependent on the Family Court and making specific findings so as to enable him to petition the United States Citizenship and Immigration Services for special immigrant juvenile status (hereinafter SIJS) pursuant to 8 USC § 1101 (a) (27) (J). In an order dated March 12, 2018, the Family Court granted the guardianship petition appointing the mother as the child's guardian. Thereafter, the child moved for the issuance of an order, inter alia, making the requisite declaration and specific findings so as to enable him to petition for SIJS. In an order dated March 15, 2018 (hereinafter the March 2018 order), made after a hearing, the Family Court found that the child was under 21 years of age, unmarried, and dependent on the court, but denied the motion on the ground that the child failed to establish that his reunification with the father was not viable due to parental abandonment, neglect, or abuse, and that it would not be in the child's best interests to return to El Salvador, his previous country of nationality and last habitual residence. The child appeals from the March 2018 order.

Pursuant to 8 USC § 1101 (a) (27) (J) (as amended by the William Wilberforce Trafficking Victims Protection Reauthorization Act of 2008, Pub L 110-457, 122 US Stat 5044) and 8 CFR 204.11, a special immigrant juvenile is a resident alien who, inter alia, is under 21 years of age, unmarried, and dependent upon a juvenile court or legally committed to an individual appointed by a state or juvenile court. Additionally, for a child to qualify for SIJS, a court must find that reunification of the child with one or both parents is not viable due to parental abuse, neglect, abandonment, or a similar basis found under state law (see 8 USC § 1101 [a] [27] [J] [i]; _Matter of Maria P.E.A. v Sergio A.G.G.,_ 111 AD3d 619, 620 [2013]; _Matter of Trudy-Ann W. v Joan W.,_ 73 AD3d 793, 795 [2010]), and that it would not be in the child's best interests to be returned to his or her previous country of nationality or country of last habitual residence (*see* 8 USC § 1101 [a] [27] [J] [ii]; 8 CFR 204.11 [c] [6]; *Matter of Maria P.E.A. v Sergio A.G.G.*, 111 AD3d at 620; *Matter of Trudy-Ann W. v Joan W.*, 73 AD3d at 795).

"While the credibility assessment of a hearing court is accorded considerable deference on appeal, where, as here, the Family Court's credibility determination is not supported by the record, this Court is free to make its own credibility assessments and overturn the determination of the hearing court" (*Matter of Dennis X.G.D.V.*, 158 AD3d 712, 714 [2018] [citations omitted]). Based upon our independent factual review, the record supports a finding that reunification of the child with the father is not a viable option due to parental neglect (*see Matter of Ena S.Y. [Martha R.Y.—Antonio S.]*, 140 AD3d 778, 780 [2016]). The record demonstrates that when the child lived with the mother and the father in El Salvador, the father would physically mistreat the mother in the presence of the child by hitting her with objects such as a book and shoes, causing her bruising, and that, when the child attempted to defend the mother, the father would hit the child. The child also averred in his affidavit that "[w]hen [the father] would get angry, which was often, he became very violent toward me, yelling at me and punching me," and the mother indicated that she had to send the child to live with his maternal grandmother in El Salvador because she was afraid of what the father would do to the child. The record also demonstrates that the father had provided no financial support for the child since the child was 10 years old. Thus, the father's conduct, including acts of domestic violence perpetrated in the presence of the child, constituted neglect (*see Matter of Malachi M. [Mark M.]*, 164 AD3d 794, 795 [2018]; *Matter of Melady S. [Elio S.]*, 144 AD3d 926, 927-928 [2016]), which established that the child's reunification with the father is not viable (*see Matter of Ena S.Y. [Martha R.Y.—Antonio S.]*, 140 AD3d at 780).

The record also does not support the Family Court's determination that the child failed to show that it would not be in his best interests to return to El Salvador. The child testified that gang members in El Salvador tried to recruit him, but he refused to join, that after his refusal to join, the gang members threatened and assaulted him multiple times, "hurt me[ ] very bad," "left me on the streets after they beat me up," and would have killed him on one occasion if not for a police patrol "coming by that moment," that he was afraid to go outside after the incident when he was almost killed, and that "if I go back [to El Salvador] they will kill me" (*see Matter of Argueta v Santos*, 166 AD3d 608 [2018]; *Matter of A.M.G. v Gladis A.G.*, 162 AD3d 768 [2018]). The mother's testimony at the hearing supported the child's testimony.

Accordingly, the Family Court should have granted the child's motion for the issuance of an order, inter alia, making the requisite specific findings so as to enable him to petition for SIJS. Inasmuch as the record is sufficient for this Court to make its own findings of fact and conclusions of law, we find that reunification of the child with his father is not viable due to parental neglect, and that it would not be in the child's best interests to return to El Salvador. Dillon, J.P., Austin, Miller and Duffy, JJ., concur.

101. In a custody proceeding, "Where the father listed the mother's address as 'unknown' on the petition and testified at a hearing that he had no information about the mother's whereaouts. Since the parties had separated 13 or 14 years earlier, the process server's three attempts to serve process at an address in Honduras, without attesting to any efforts to verify that this was the mother's address, did not constitute due diligence."

☐ **In the Matter of Marvin Golman Gutierrez Ferrera, Appellant,**
v
Glenda A. Benitez Serrano, Respondent.

189. A.D.3d 1230 (2d Dep't Dec. 16, 2020)

Bruno Joseph Bembi, Hempstead, NY, for appellant.

In a proceeding pursuant to Family Court Act article 6, the father appeals from (1) an order of the Family Court, Nassau County (Sharon N. Clarke, Ct. Atty. Ref.), dated February 14, 2020, and (2) an order of the same court also dated February 14, 2020. The first order, after a hearing, dismissed the petition without prejudice. The second order denied the father's motion for the issuance of an order, inter alia, making specific findings so as to enable the subject child to petition the United States Citizenship and Immigration Services for special immigrant juvenile status pursuant to 8 USC § 1101 (a) (27) (J).

Ordered that the orders are affirmed, without costs or disbursements.

The father filed a petition for custody of the subject child for the purpose of obtaining an order, inter alia, making specific findings so as to enable the child to petition the United States Citizenship and Immigration Services for special immigrant juvenile status (hereinafter SIJS) pursuant to 8 USC § 1101 (a) (27) (J). Thereafter, the father moved for the issuance of an order making the requisite declaration and specific findings so as to enable the child to petition for SIJS.

Along with the petition, the father submitted affidavits of service attesting that, after three unsuccessful attempts to serve the mother at a residence in Honduras, the "affix and mail" method of service was utilized (*see* CPLR 308 [4]). However, since the process server had not attested to any efforts he had made to verify that the address at which service was attempted was, in fact, the mother's residence, the Family Court twice adjourned the matter to allow the father time to verify the mother's address. As of the final adjourned date, the father had not submitted any further information or an updated affidavit of service. The court therefore dismissed the petition without prejudice. The court further denied the father's motion for the issuance of an order, inter alia, making the requested specific findings so as to enable the child to petition for SIJS.

If service cannot be effected, with due diligence, pursuant to CPLR 308 (1) or (2), a party may serve process by affixing the summons and petition to the door of the recipient's "actual place of business, dwelling place or usual place of abode," and by mailing them either to the last known residence or actual place of business (CPLR 308 [4]; *see also* Domestic Relations Law § 75-g; CPLR 313). "The due diligence requirement of CPLR 308 (4) must be strictly observed, given the reduced likelihood that a summons served pursuant to that section will be received" (*Gurevitch v Goodman*, 269 AD2d 355, 355 [2000]; *see McSorley v Spear*, 50 AD3d 652, 653 [2008]).

Here, where the father listed the mother's address as "unknown" on the petition and testified at a hearing that he had no information about the mother's whereabouts since the parties had separated 13 or 14 years earlier, the process server's three attempts to serve process at an address in Honduras, without attesting to any efforts to verify that this was the mother's address, did not constitute due diligence (*see Holbeck v Sosa-Berrios*, 161 AD3d 957, 958 [2018]; *McSorley v Spear*, 50 AD3d at 653). Accordingly, we agree with the Family Court's determination dismissing the petition without prejudice.

Furthermore, we agree with the Family Court's determination denying the father's motion for the issuance of an order, inter alia, making specific findings so as to enable the child to petition for SIJS, since, in light of the dismissal of the custody petition, it could not be shown that the child was dependent upon the Family Court (*see* 8 USC § 1101 [a] [27] [J] [i]; 8 CFR 204.11; *Matter of Hei Ting C.*, 109 AD3d 100, 104 [2013]). Chambers, J.P., LaSalle, Iannacci and Christopher, JJ., concur.

102. Under the Uniform Child Custody Jurisdiction and Enforcement Act (D.R.L sec 75 et seq), a child needs 6 months in New York before filing custody petition.

☐ **In the Matter of Aida T.M., Appellant,**

v

Manuel R.T.M., Respondent.

197 A.D. 3d 596 (2d Dep't Aug 17, 2021)

Max Pierre Dubuche, Astoria, NY, for appellant.

In a guardianship proceeding pursuant to Family Court Act article 6, the mother appeals from an order of the Family Court, Queens County (Margaret M. Mulrooney, Ct. Atty. Ref.), dated July 15, 2021. The order, after a hearing, dismissed the petition for lack of subject matter jurisdiction.

Ordered that the order is affirmed, without costs or disbursements.

The parties are the parents of three children, the eldest of whom (hereinafter the child) is the subject of this proceeding. The child was born in Ecuador in August 2000 and will shortly turn 21 years of age. In 2003, the mother relocated to the United States and left the child in the care of his maternal grandparents in Ecuador. In or around April 2021, the child entered the United States without documentation and, since that time, has been residing with his mother in New York. Thereafter, the mother commenced this proceeding to be appointed guardian of the child and also moved for the issuance of an order making specific findings so as to enable the child to petition the United States Citizenship and Immigration Services for special immigrant juvenile status pursuant to 8 USC § 1101 (a) (27) (J). The child executed an affidavit consenting to the mother's petition. In addition, the father executed an affidavit waiving service of process and his appearance at the hearing, and consenting to the mother's petition. In an order dated July 15, 2021, the Family Court, after a hearing, dismissed the mother's petition for guardianship on the ground of lack of subject matter jurisdiction.

Pursuant to the Uniform Child Custody Jurisdiction and Enforcement Act (Domestic Relations Law § 75 *et seq.* [hereinafter UCCJEA]), a New York court has jurisdiction to make an initial child custody determination if New York is the "home state of the child on the date of the commencement of the proceeding, or was the home state of the child within six months before the commencement of the proceeding and the child is absent from this state but a parent or person acting as a parent continues to live in this state" (*id.* § 76 [1] [a]). A child's home state is defined, in pertinent part, as "the state in which a child lived with a parent or a person acting as a parent for at least six consecutive months immediately before the commencement of a child custody proceeding" (*id.* § 75-a [7]). A New York court may also exercise jurisdiction if "a court of another state does not have jurisdiction under paragraph (a) of this subdivision, or a court of the home state of the child has declined to exercise jurisdiction on the ground that this state is the more appropriate forum .□□ , and .□□ the child and the child's parents, or the child and at least one parent or a person acting as a parent, have a significant connection with this state other than mere physical presence; and .□□ substantial evidence is available in this state concerning the child's care, protection, training, and personal relationships" (*id.* § 76 [1] [b] [i], [ii]). Finally, a New York court may exercise jurisdiction where a court having jurisdiction has declined to exercise it on the ground that a court of this state is the more appropriate forum (*see id.* § 76 [1] [c]), or where no other court of any other state would have jurisdiction under the aforesaid provisions (*see id.* § 76 [1] [d]). As relevant here, an initial custody determination includes an initial custody determination made in a guardianship proceeding (*see id.* § 75-a [3], [4]). In applying the UCCJEA, "[a] court of this state shall treat a foreign country as if it were a state of the United States" (*id.* § 75-d [1]).

Here, the mother concedes that New York does not qualify as the child's home state since the child has not been residing in the state for at least six consecutive months immediately before the commencement of this proceeding (*see id.* § 75-a [7]). Moreover, the mother's contention that the Family Court should have exercised jurisdiction pursuant to Domestic Relations Law § 76 (1) (b) was not raised before the Family Court and is unpreserved for appellate review (*see Matter of Adonnis M. [Kenyetta M.]*, 194 AD3d 1048, 1052 [2021]).

The mother's remaining contentions either are without merit, are improperly raised for the first time on appeal, or need not be reached in light of our determination.

Accordingly, the Family Court properly dismissed the petition for lack of subject matter jurisdiction. Dillon, J.P., Wooten, Zayas and Genovesi, JJ., concur.

103. If a child is married, the New York Family Court will dismiss an SIJ guardianship petition Although the definition of a special immigrant juvenile in 8 U.S.C. 1101(a)(27)(J) does not use the word "child".

☐ **In the Matter of Elena G.R., Appellant,**

v

Oscar D.V.H., Respondent.

---

212 A.D.3d 628 (2d Dep't Jan 11, 2023)

Bruno Joseph Bembi, Hempstead, NY, for appellant.

In a guardianship proceeding pursuant to Family Court Act article 6, the petitioner appeals from an order of the Family Court, Nassau County (Darlene D. Harris, J.), dated June 3, 2022. The order, insofar as appealed from, dismissed the petition to appoint the petitioner as the guardian of the subject child, and denied the petitioner's motion for the issuance of an order making specific findings so as to enable the child to petition the United States Citizenship and Immigration Services for special immigrant juvenile status pursuant to 8 USC § 1101 (a) (27) (J).

Ordered that the order is affirmed insofar as appealed from, without costs or disbursements.

In July 2021, the petitioner commenced this proceeding pursuant to Family Court Act article 6 to be appointed guardian of the subject child for the purpose of obtaining an order making specific findings so as to enable her to petition the United States Citizenship and Immigration Services for special immigrant juvenile status (hereinafter SIJS) pursuant to 8 USC § 1101 (a) (27) (J). Thereafter, the petitioner moved for the issuance of an order making the requisite specific findings so as to enable the child to petition for SIJS. By order dated June 3, 2022, the Family Court, inter alia, dismissed the guardianship petition and denied the petitioner's motion. The court determined that the child was married and therefore did not qualify for SIJS.

Pursuant to 8 USC § 1101 (a) (27) (J) (as amended by the William Wilberforce Trafficking Victims Protection Reauthorization Act of 2008, Pub L 110-457, 122 US Stat 5044) and 8 CFR 204.11, a special immigrant juvenile is a resident alien who, among other things, is under 21 years of age, unmarried, and dependent upon a juvenile court or legally committed to an individual appointed by a state or juvenile court. Additionally, for a juvenile to qualify for SIJS, a court must find that reunification of the juvenile with one or both of the juvenile's parents is not viable due to parental abuse, neglect, abandonment, or a similar basis found under state law (see 8 USC § 1101 [a] [27] [J] [i]; *Matter of Maria P.E.A. v Sergio A.G.G.*, 111 AD3d 619, 620 [2013]; *Matter of Trudy-Ann W. v Joan W.*, 73 AD3d 793, 795 [2010]), and that it would not be in the juvenile's best interests to be returned to his or her native country or country of last habitual residence (*see* 8 USC § 1101 [a] [27] [J] [ii]; *Matter of Trudy-Ann W. v Joan W.*, 73 AD3d at 795).

Here, although the child is under 21 years of age, she was married on December 4, 2021, and therefore, did not meet the criteria for SIJS (*see* 8 CFR 204.11 [b] [2]; *Matter of Marisol N.H.*, 115 AD3d 185, 189 [2014]). Accordingly, the Family Court properly denied the petitioner's motion for the issuance of an order making specific findings so as to enable the child to petition for SIJS, and dismissed the guardianship petition (*see Matter of Dimas A. v Esmirna E.L.*, 142 AD3d 1164, 1165 [2016]). Barros, J.P., Brathwaite Nelson, Ford and Warhit, JJ., concur.

104. Although a child was born in Canada, it may be possible to show that his country of nationality is Peru.

See Matter of Jelitza Benavides, below.

105. The Petitioner must submit enough evidence to establish abandonment.

2024 N.Y. Slip Op 03176 (2d Dep't June 12, 2024)
Decided on June 12, 2024 SUPREME COURT OF THE STATE OF NEW YORK Appellate Division, Second Judicial Department
MARK C. DILLON, J.P.
BETSY BARROS
DEBORAH A. DOWLING
LILLIAN WAN, JJ.

2023-04080
(Docket No. V-10786-22)
228 A.D.3d 756 (2d Dep't June 12, 2024)

In the Matter of Jelitza Benavides Fernandez, petitioner- appellant,

v

Jose Antonio Baca Otero, respondent; Jayce T. B. B. (Anonymous), nonparty-appellant.

Bruno J. Bembi, Hempstead, NY, for petitioner-appellant.

Paul D. Stone, Tarrytown, NY, for nonparty-appellant.

DECISION & ORDER

In a proceeding pursuant to Family Court Act article 6, the mother and the subject child separately appeal from an order of the Family Court, Westchester County (Michelle I. Schauer, J.), dated April 24, 2023. The order, after a hearing, denied the mother's motion for the issuance of an order, inter alia, making specific findings so as to enable the subject child to petition the United States Citizenship and Immigration Services for special immigrant juvenile status pursuant to 8 USC § 1101(a)(27)(J).

ORDERED that the order is affirmed, without costs or disbursements.

In December 2022, the mother commenced this proceeding pursuant to Family Court Act article 6, seeking sole custody of the subject child. Thereafter, the mother moved for the issuance of an order, inter alia, making specific findings so as to enable the child to petition the United States Citizenship and Immigration Services for special immigrant juvenile status (hereinafter SIJS) pursuant to 8 USC § 1101(a)(27)(J). After a hearing, in an order dated March 16, 2023, the Family Court awarded the mother sole custody of the child, and in an order dated April 24, 2023, the court denied the mother's motion for the issuance of an order, inter alia, making specific findings so as to enable the child to petition for SIJS. The mother and the child separately appeal from the order dated April 24, 2023.

Contrary to the conclusion of the Family Court, the mother established that Peru, not Canada, was the child's previous country of nationality or the country of last habitual residence where the child's birth was registered (*see Matter of Briceyda M.A.X. [Hugo R.A.O.]*, 190 AD3d 752, 754). It is undisputed that the child is under the age of 21 years, unmarried, and legally committed to an individual appointed by the court. However, under the circumstances of this case, the mother failed to submit sufficient evidence that the father abandoned the child. Accordingly, the court properly denied the mother's motion for the issuance of an order, inter alia, making specific findings so as to enable the child to petition for SIJS.

DILLON, J.P., BARROS, DOWLING and WAN, JJ., concur.

ENTER:

Darrell M. Joseph

Clerk of the Court

106. It can be established that reunification with the child's parents is not viable where neither parent contributed to the financial support of the child since the child arrived in the United States.

See Matter of Eriseldo, below

107. It can be established that it is not in his best interests to return to Albania where he had "been the target of several assaults because of his family's political affiliation, and the parents were unable to protect him" and he was "doing well" in the Petitioner's care.

> ☐ **In the Matter of Eriseldo C., a Child Alleged to be Neglected. Rezart V., Appellant,**
>
> **v**
>
> **Dashmir C. et al., Respondents.**

217 A.D. 3d 512 (2d Dep't June 13, 2013)

Turturro Law, P.C., Brooklyn (Natraj S. Bhushan of counsel), for appellant.

Order, Family Court, Bronx County (Aija M. Tingling, J.), entered on or about May 20, 2021, which denied petitioner and the subject child's motion for an order of special findings enabling the child to petition for Special Immigrant Juvenile Status, unanimously reversed, on the law and the facts, without costs, and the motion granted nunc pro tunc.

The evidence shows that the subject child was unmarried, under the age of 21, and dependent on a juvenile court at the time of the special findings order (*see generally* 8 USC § 1101 [a] [27] [J]; 8 CFR 204.11; *Matter of Carlos A.M. v Maria T.M., 141 AD3d 526* [2d Dept 2016]).

Exercising our power to review the record and make our own factual determination (*see Matter of Luis R. v Maria Elena G., 120 AD3d 581*, 581-583 [2d Dept 2014]), we find that the record further supports a finding that reunification with the child's parents is not viable within the meaning of Family Ct Act § 1012 (f) (i) (A) and (B) and Social Services Law § 384-b (5) (a). The hearing testimony established that the child's parents have not contributed to his financial support or maintained contact with him since he came to the United States (*see Matter of Sara D. v Lassina D., 206 AD3d 553*, 553-554 [1st Dept 2022]; *Matter of Khan v Shahida Z., 184 AD3d 506*, 506-507 [1st Dept 2020]).

We also find that it would not be in the child's best interests to return to Albania. In addition to his testimony regarding parental abandonment, the child testified that he had been the target of several assaults because of his family's political affiliation, and the parents were unable to protect him (*see Matter of Juan R.E.M. [Juan R.E.]*, 154 AD3d 725, 727 [2d Dept 2017]). The child presented evidence that he is doing well in petitioner's care (*see Khan v Shahida Z.*, 184 AD3d at 507). Concur—Kern, J.P., Kennedy, Scarpulla, Pitt-Burke, Higgitt, JJ.

The decision and order of this Court entered herein on December 29, 2022 (211 AD3d 651 [2022]) is hereby recalled and vacated (*see* 2023 NY Slip Op 68622[U] [2023] [decided simultaneously herewith]).

☐ **In the Matter of Eriseldo C., an Infant. Reszart V., Appellant,**
v
Dashmir C. et al., Respondents.

[Recalled and vacated, see 2023 NY Slip Op 03209.]

211 A.D. 3d 651 (2d Dep't Dec. 29, 2022)

Turturro Law, P.C., Brooklyn (Natraj S. Bhushan of counsel), for appellant.

Order, Family Court, Bronx County (Aija M. Tingling, J.), entered on or about May 20, 2021, which denied petitioner and the subject child's motion for an order of special findings enabling the child to petition for Special Immigrant Juvenile Status, unanimously reversed, on the law and the facts, without costs, and the motion granted.

The evidence shows that the subject child was unmarried, under the age of 21, and dependent on a juvenile court at the time of the special findings order (*see generally* 8 USC § 1101 [a] [27] [J]; 8 CFR 204.11; *Matter of Carlos A.M. v Maria T.M.*, 141 AD3d 526 [2d Dept 2016]).

Exercising our power to review the record and make our own factual determination (*see Matter of Luis R. v Maria Elena G.*, 120 AD3d 581, 581-583 [2d Dept 2014]), we find that the record further supports a finding that reunification with the child's parents is not viable within the meaning of Family Court Act § 1012 (f) (i) (A)-(B) and Social Services Law § 384-b (5) (a). The hearing testimony established that the child's parents have not contributed to his financial support or maintained contact with him since he came to the United States (*see Matter of Sara D. v Lassina D.*, 206 AD3d 553, 553-554 [1st Dept 2022]; *Matter of Khan v Shahida Z.*, 184 AD3d 506, 506-507 [1st Dept 2020]).

We also find that it would not be in the child's best interests to return to Albania. In addition to his testimony regarding parental abandonment, the child testified that he had been the target of several assaults because of his family's political affiliation, and the parents were unable to protect him (*see Matter of Juan R.E.M. [Juan R.E.]*, 154 AD3d 725, 727 [2d Dept 2017]). The child presented evidence that he is doing well in petitioner's care (*see Khan v Shahida Z.*, 184 AD3d at 507). Concur—Kern, J.P., Kennedy, Scarpulla, Pitt-Burke, Higgitt, JJ.

108.   The Family court can vacate an SIJ guardianship order following the Subject's 21st birthday.

> ☐ **In the Matter of Rosa M.G.G., Appellant,**
> **v**
> **Jose M.Y. et al., Respondents.**

217 A.D. 3d 863 (2d Dep't June 21, 2023)

Bruno J. Bembi, Hempstead, NY, for appellant.

In a guardianship proceeding pursuant to Family Court Act article 6, the petitioner appeals from an order of the Family Court, Nassau County (Sharon N. Clarke, Ct. Atty. Ref.), dated October 5, 2022. The order vacated an order of the same court dated September 9, 2022, granting the petitioner temporary guardianship of the subject child, and dismissed the proceeding for lack of subject matter jurisdiction.

Ordered that the order is affirmed, without costs or disbursements.

In May 2022, the petitioner commenced this proceeding pursuant to Family Court Act article 6 to be appointed guardian of the subject child, her cousin, so as to enable the child to petition the United States Citizenship and Immigration Services for special immigrant juvenile status (hereinafter SIJS) pursuant to 8 USC § 1101 (a) (27) (J). Thereafter, the petitioner moved for the issuance of an order making specific findings so as to enable the child to obtain SIJS. After a hearing, the Family Court issued two orders, both dated September 9, 2022. The first order granted the petitioner temporary guardianship of the child and was to expire on March 8, 2023, after the subject child's 21st birthday. The second order granted the petitioner's motion for the issuance of an order making specific findings so as to enable the child to obtain SIJS. Subsequently, in an order dated October 5, 2022, the Family Court vacated the order granting the petitioner temporary guardianship of the child and dismissed the proceeding for lack of subject matter jurisdiction. The petitioner appeals from the order dated October 5, 2022.

Contrary to the petitioner's contention, the Family Court properly dismissed the proceeding for lack of subject matter jurisdiction (*see Matter of Michael R.C.S. [Tito S.—Julio C.A.]*, 147 AD3d 767 [2017]; *Matter of Maria C.R. v Rafael G.*, 142 AD3d 165, 170 [2016]). Connolly, J.P., Brathwaite Nelson, Chambers and Voutsinas, JJ., concur.

109. Where mother sent child to live with father in the USA, who "quickly abandoned" her, leaving her with her aunt, and the record contains a statement from the mother stating she was unable to give the child the "love and attention she needs", the record "clearly established" that it was in the child's best interests to remain living with her aunt.

See Matter of Antowa McD, below

110. The "Family Court's appointment of a guardian constitutes the necessary declaration of dependency on a juvenile court" for SIJ purposes.

> **In the Matter of Antowa McD., an Infant, Appellant. Deonne Andrea W., Petitioner,**
>
> **v**
>
> **Wayne McD. et al., Respondents.**

50 A.D. 3d 507 (2d Dep't April 24, 2008)

McDermott Will & Emery LLP, New York (Andrew B. Kratenstein of counsel), for appellant.

Christa Stewart, New York (Jason A. Cade of counsel), for Amici Curiae.

Order, Family Court, Bronx County (Alma Cordova, J.), entered on or about January 26, 2007, which, insofar as appealed from, denied appellant child's motion for findings that would enable her to petition the United States Citizenship and Immigration Services for special immigrant juvenile status pursuant to 8 USC § 1101 (a) (27) (J), unanimously reversed, on the law and the facts, without costs, the motion granted, and the matter remanded to Family Court to issue an order making the requested findings.

Appellant was sent by her mother from her native Jamaica to live with her father in the United States at the age of four in 2003, but was quickly abandoned by her father, who left her with her aunt. Upon her mother refusing to take her back, she has continued to reside with the aunt. Although Family Court issued letters of guardianship to the aunt, it refused to make the factual findings that would enable appellant to apply for special immigrant juvenile status, i.e., that she was eligible for long-term foster care due to abuse, neglect or abandonment, and that it would not be in her best interests to be returned to Jamaica. This was error given a record that clearly establishes parental abandonment, contains a statement from the mother that she is unable "to give [appellant] the love and attention she needs," and clearly establishes that it is appellant's best interests to continue living in her aunt's loving and nurturing home. Family Court's appointment of a guardian constitutes the necessary declaration of dependency on a juvenile court (*Matter of Menjivar*, 29 Immigr L & Pro Rptr B2-37 [1994], construing, inter alia, 8 CFR 204.11 [a]). Concur—Lippman, P.J., Friedman, Sweeny and Moskowitz, JJ.

111. It is appropriate to find abandonment and neglect where the child's parents lived in Bangladesh, "his parents inflicted excessive corporal punishment and failed to provide him with adequate supervision" and failed to communicate with him for more than seven years.

See Matter of Alamgir, below.

112. It is not impermissible forum shopping for a minor, who moved from Florida to New York and resided in New York more than 6 months, to see guardianship in the New York Courts.

See Matter of Alamgir, below.

113. A petitioner in an SIJ guardianship proceeding need not show "extraordinary circumstances" to obtain guardianship.

See Matter of Alamgir, below.

114. It is not in a minor's best interest to return to Bangladesh where he "would have no where to live, and no means of supporting himself."

In the Matter of Alamgir A., Appellant.

81 A.D. 3d 937 (2d Dep't Feb 22, 2011)

Milbank, Tweed, Hadley & McCloy LLP, New York, N.Y. (Eric I. Weiss and Stacey Rappaport of counsel), for appellant.

In a guardianship proceeding pursuant to Family Court Act article 6, the subject child, Alamgir A., appeals from an order of the Family Court, Queens County (McGrady, Ct. Atty. Ref.), dated March 8, 2010, which, after a hearing, denied his motion for an order making findings that he is dependent on the Family Court, that he is unmarried and under 21 years of age, that reunification with one or both of his parents is not viable due to parental abuse, neglect, or abandonment, and that it would not be in his best interest to be returned to his previous country of nationality or last habitual residence, so as to enable him to petition the United States Citizenship and Immigration Services for special immigrant juvenile status pursuant to 8 USC § 1101 (a) (27) (J), and denied the petition of Mohammed Uddin for appointment as the guardian of the subject child.

Ordered that the order is reversed, on the law and the facts, without costs or disbursements, the motion and the petition are granted, it is found that Alamgir A. is dependent on the Family Court, and it is found that Alamgir A. is unmarried and under 21 years of age, that reunification with one or both of his parents is not viable due to parental neglect and abandonment, and that it would not be in the best interest of Alamgir A. to return to Bangladesh, his previous country of nationality or last habitual residence, and the matter is remitted to the

Family Court, Queens County, for the entry of an appropriate order appointing Mohammed Uddin as the guardian of the subject child.

Alamgir A., a native of Bangladesh, is 20 years old, unmarried, and has lived in the United States with nonrelatives since age 12. He states in an affidavit that when he was in Bangladesh, his parents inflicted excessive corporal punishment upon him and failed to provide him with adequate supervision. Alamgir's parents remain in Bangladesh, and have not communicated with Alamgir in more than seven years.

Alamgir moved from Florida to New York in December 2008, and has lived in Queens with Mohammed Uddin and Uddin's family since March 2009. There is uncontroverted evidence that, since 2009, Uddin has provided Alamgir with a loving home, financial and emotional support, and the ability to pursue educational goals.

Uddin filed a petition dated July 15, 2009, seeking appointment as Alamgir's guardian. Alamgir submitted an affidavit consenting to the appointment and asking for the same relief. Several months later, Alamgir moved for an order making findings that would enable him to apply to the United States Citizenship and Immigration Services (hereinafter the USCIS) for special immigrant juvenile status pursuant to 8 USC § 1101 (a) (27) (J). Both the petition and the motion were unopposed.

In an order dated March 8, 2010, the Family Court denied the motion and the petition, opining that Florida was the proper venue for any guardianship issues, and that Uddin and Alamgir had engaged in forum shopping. It further stated, without analysis, that Uddin had failed to demonstrate extraordinary circumstances justifying a guardianship appointment. We reverse.

Turning to the merits, when considering guardianship appointments, the infant's best interest is paramount (*see* SCPA 1707 [1]; *Matter of Stuart*, 280 NY 245, 250 [1939]; *Matter of Trudy-Ann W. v Joan W.*, 73 AD3d 793, 794 [2010]; *Matter of Amrhein v Signorelli*, 153 AD2d 28, 31 [1989]). The order appealed from, however, is devoid of any references to Alamgir's best interest.

"This Court's power to review the evidence is as broad as that of the hearing court, bearing in mind that in a close case, the factfinder had the advantage of seeing and hearing the witnesses. Further, where, as here, the record is sufficiently complete for us to make our own factual determinations, we may do so" (*Matter of Trudy-Ann W. v Joan W.*, 73 AD3d at 795 [internal quotation marks and citations omitted]). Based upon our "independent factual review of the complete record" (*Matter of Steward v Steward*, 25 AD3d 714, 715 [2006]; *see Matter of Allen v Black*, 275 AD2d 207, 209 [2000]), which includes, inter alia, two hearing transcripts and an affidavit from Alamgir, it is evident that Alamgir's best interest would be served by the appointment of Uddin as his guardian (*see Matter of Stuart*, 280 NY at 250; *Matter of Trudy-Ann W. v Joan W.*, 73 AD3d at 795; *cf. Eschbach v Eschbach*, 56 NY2d 167, 172-173 [1982]). Accordingly, Mohammed Uddin should be appointed as Alamgir's guardian.

The Family Court also improperly denied Alamgir's motion for an order making findings that would allow him to apply to the USCIS for special immigrant juvenile status—a gateway to lawful permanent residency in the United States. Pursuant to 8 USC § 1101 (a) (27) (J) (as amended by the William Wilberforce Trafficking Victims Protection Reauthorization Act of 2008, Pub L 110-457, 122 US Stat 5044) and 8 CFR 204.11, a "special immigrant" is a resident alien who is, inter alia, under 21 years of age, unmarried, and dependent upon a juvenile court or legally committed to an individual appointed by a state or juvenile court. Additionally, for a juvenile to qualify for special immigrant juvenile status, a court must find that reunification of the juvenile with one or both of the juvenile's parents is not viable due to parental abuse, neglect, abandonment, or similar parental conduct defined under state law (*see* 8 USC § 1101 [a] [27] [J] [i]; *Matter of Trudy-Ann W. v Joan W.*, 73 AD3d at 795), and that it would not be in the juvenile's best interest to be returned to his or her native country or country of last habitual residence (*see* 8 USC § 1101 [a] [27] [J] [ii]; 8 CFR 204.11 [c] [6]; *Matter of Trudy-Ann W. v Joan W.*, 73 AD3d at 795).

As earlier noted, Alamgir is under the age of 21 and unmarried. "The appointment of a guardian constitutes the necessary declaration of dependency on a juvenile court for special immigrant juvenile status purposes" (*Matter of Trudy-Ann W. v Joan W.*, 73 AD3d at 795 [internal quotation marks omitted]; *see Matter of Antowa McD.*, 50 AD3d 507 [2008]). Since we have appointed Uddin as Alamgir's guardian, Alamgir is dependent on a juvenile court within the meaning of 8 USC § 1101 (a) (27) (J) (i). Based on our factual review, we find that the record fully supports Alamgir's contention that his parents neglected and then abandoned him, and that, as a result, reunification with either parent is not a viable option (*see Matter of Trudy-Ann W. v Joan W.*, 73 AD3d at 796; *Matter of Antowa McD.*, 50 AD3d at 507). Lastly, the record reflects that in Bangladesh, Alamgir would have nowhere to live, and no means of supporting himself. Accordingly, it is clearly in Alamgir's best interest to continue living with Uddin in the United States (*see Matter of Trudy-Ann W. v Joan W.*, 73 AD3d at 796; *Matter of Antowa McD.*, 50 AD3d at 507). Dillon, J.P., Dickerson, Hall and Roman, JJ., concur.

115. Once the Family Court appoints a guardian, the minor is dependent on a juvenile court.

In the Matter of Jisun L., Petitioner,
v
Young Sun P. et al., Respondents. Imel P., Nonparty Appellant.

75 A.D. 3d 510 (2d Dep't July 6, 2010)

Lauren A. Burke, New York, N.Y., for nonparty appellant.

In a proceeding pursuant to Family Court Act article 6 for the appointment of the petitioner as guardian of Imel P., a person under 21 years of age, Imel P. appeals from an order of the Family Court, Kings County (Sheares, J.), dated April 6, 2010, which, after a hearing, in effect, denied his motion for the issuance of an order declaring that he is dependent on the Family Court and making specific findings that he is unmarried and under 21 years of age, that reunification with one or both of his parents is not viable due to parental abuse, neglect, or abandonment, and that it would not be in his best interest to be returned to his previous country of nationality or last habitual residence, so as to enable him to petition the United States Citizenship and Immigration Services for special immigrant juvenile status pursuant to 8 USC § 1101 (a) (27) (J).

Ordered that the order is reversed, on the law and the facts, without costs or disbursements, the motion is granted, it is declared that Imel P. is dependent on the Family Court, and it is found that Imel P. is unmarried and under 21 years of age, that reunification with one or both of his parents is not viable due to parental abuse and neglect, and that it would not be in his best interest to be returned to South Korea, his country of nationality and last habitual residence.

The appellant, Imel P. (hereinafter Imel), a native of South Korea, has lived in the United States with his aunt, the petitioner Jisun L., and her husband, since 2008. In November 2009 the petitioner commenced the instant proceeding in the Family Court, Kings County, seeking to be appointed Imel's guardian. In connection with the petition, Imel moved for the issuance of an order declaring that he is dependent on the Family Court and making specific findings that he is unmarried and under 21 years of age, that reunification with one or both of his parents is not viable due to parental abuse, neglect, or abandonment, and that it would not be in his best interest to be returned to his previous country of nationality or last habitual residence, so as to enable him to petition the United States Citizenship and Immigration Services for special immigrant juvenile status pursuant to 8 USC § 1101 (a) (27) (J), "a gateway to lawful permanent residency in the United States" (*Matter of Trudy-Ann W. v Joan W.*, 73 AD3d 793, 795 [2010]). After conducting a hearing at which Imel and the petitioner testified, the Family Court, in effect, denied Imel's motion. Imel appeals, and we reverse.

Pursuant to 8 USC § 1101 (a) (27) (J) (as amended by the Trafficking Victims Protection Reauthorization Act of 2008, Pub L 110-457, 122 US Stat 5044) and 8 CFR 204.11, a "special immigrant" is a resident alien who, inter alia, is under 21 years of age, unmarried, and dependent upon a juvenile court or legally committed to an individual appointed by a State or juvenile court (*see Matter of Trudy-Ann W. v Joan W.*, 73 AD3d 793 [2010]). In addition, for a juvenile to qualify for special immigrant juvenile status, a court must find that the juvenile's reunification with one or both parents is not viable due to parental abuse, neglect, abandonment, or similar parental conduct defined under State law (*see* 8 USC § 1101 [a] [27] [J] [i]; *see also Matter of Trudy-Ann W. v Joan W.*, 73 AD3d 793 [2010]), and that it would not be in the juvenile's best interest to be returned to his or her country of nationality or country of last habitual residence (*see* 8 USC § 1101 [a] [27] [J] [ii]; 8 CFR 204.11 [c] [6]; *see also Matter of Trudy-Ann W. v Joan W.*, 73 AD3d 793 [2010]).

This Court's power to review the evidence is as broad as that of the hearing court (*id.* at 795). Moreover, "where, as here, the record is sufficiently complete to make our own factual determinations . . . we may do so" (*id.* [internal quotation marks and citation omitted]). Here, the record reveals that Imel is under 21 years of age and unmarried. Further, the record reveals that the Family Court appointed the petitioner as Imel's guardian and, as such, Imel is dependent on a juvenile court within the meaning of 8 USC § 1101 (a) (27) (J) (i) (*see Matter of Trudy-Ann W. v Joan W.*, 73 AD3d 793 [2010]; *Matter of Antowa McD.*, 50 AD3d 507 [2008]).

In addition, the record reveals that Imel's parents abused and neglected him and that, as a result, reunification with either parent is not a viable option (*see Matter of Emma M.*, 74 AD3d 968 [2010]; *Matter of Trudy-Ann W. v Joan W.*, 73 AD3d 793 [2010]; *Matter of Antowa McD.*, 50 AD3d at 507). Finally, the record reflects that it is in Imel's best interest to continue living with the petitioner in the United States and, thus, that it would not be in his best interest to be returned to South Korea (*see Matter of Trudy-Ann W. v Joan W.*, 73 AD3d 793 [2010]; *Matter of Antowa McD.*, 50 AD3d at 507).

Accordingly, we make the declaration and special findings as indicated. Dillon, J.P., Dickerson, Lott and Austin, JJ., concur.

116. An order of adoption satisfies the requirement of dependency on the Family Court which can then decide a motion for special findings.

Matter of Emma M.

In the Matter of the Adoption of Emma M., an Infant, Appellant.

74 A.D. 3d 968 (2d Dep't June 8, 2010)

McDermott Will & Emery LLP, New York, N.Y. (Andrew B. Kratenstein of counsel), for appellant.

In an adoption proceeding pursuant to Domestic Relations Law article 7, the petitioner appeals from an order of the Family Court, Kings County (Lynch, J.H.O.), dated May 6, 2009, which, upon renewal and reargument, adhered to an original determination in an order dated February 25, 2009, denying her motion for the issuance of an order declaring that she is dependent on the Family Court and making specific findings that she is unmarried and under 21 years of age, that reunification with one or both of her biological parents is not viable due to parental abuse, neglect, or abandonment, and that it would not be in her best interest to be returned to her previous country of nationality or last habitual residence, so as to enable her to petition the United States Citizenship and Immigration Services for special immigrant juvenile status pursuant to 8 USC § 1101 (a) (27) (J).

Ordered that the order dated May 6, 2009, is reversed, on the law and the facts, without costs or disbursements, upon renewal and reargument, the determination in the order dated February 25, 2009, denying her motion for the issuance of an order declaring that she is dependent on the Family Court and making specific findings that she is unmarried and under 21 years of age, that reunification with one or both of her biological parents is not viable due to parental abuse, neglect, or abandonment, and that it would not be in her best interest to be returned to her previous country of nationality or last habitual residence is vacated, the motion for that relief is granted, it is declared that the petitioner is dependent on the Family Court, and it is found that the petitioner is unmarried and under 21 years of age, that reunification with one or both of her biological parents is not viable due to parental neglect and abandonment and that it would not be in the petitioner's best interest to be returned to Granada, her previous country of nationality and last habitual residence.

Insofar as relevant here, a person may apply to the United States Citizenship and Immigration Services for "special immigrant juvenile status" when (1) he or she is under the age of 21 years and is unmarried, (2) a juvenile court has declared that it is not viable that he or she be reunited with one or both parents due to "abuse, neglect, abandonment, or a similar basis found under State law," and that it would not be in the applicant's best interest to be returned to his or her previous country of nationality or country of last habitual residence, and (3) the applicant has been legally committed to an individual appointed by a juvenile court (8 USC § 1101 [a] [27] [J], as amended by Pub L 110-457, 122 US Stat 5044; *see* 8 CFR 204.11).

The petitioner, a native of Grenada, is unmarried, is under 21 years of age, and has lived in the United States since 2003. Her mother has been deceased for many years. Her father, who continues to reside in Grenada, neglected and largely ignored her throughout her life. Moreover, the petitioner's father consented to her adoption by the Brooklyn couple with whom she now lives. In 2006, when the petitioner was 16 years old, the Family Court approved the adoption. In early 2009, shortly after her 18th birthday, in the context of the adoption proceeding, the petitioner moved the Family Court for the issuance of an order making the declaration and findings necessary to allow her to apply for special immigrant juvenile status. In an order dated February 25, 2009, the Family Court denied the motion, and, in an order dated May 6, 2009, adhered to its original determination upon renewal and reargument. We reverse the order dated May 6, 2009, and, upon renewal and reargument, we grant the motion.

The record before the Family Court on the petitioner's motion for leave to renew and reargue established that she is unmarried and under 21 years of age, and by reason of her adoption, had been legally committed by the Family Court to her adoptive parents, who were appointed by the Family Court when it approved the adoption. Further, the record established that the petitioner's reunification with her parents was not viable in view of her biological mother's death and her biological father's neglect and abandonment of her, culminating in his consent to her adoption. Finally, the evidence established that it would not be in the petitioner's best interest to be returned to Grenada (*cf. Matter of Antowa McD.*, 50 AD3d 507 [2008]). Rivera, J.P., Fisher, Florio and Austin, JJ., concur.

117. "The law does not require a finding that reunification with one or both" parents is viable, but the contrary.

> ☐ **In the Matter of Haide L.G.M., Respondent,**
> **v**
> **Santo D.S.M., Respondent. Cindy X.G.M., Nonparty Appellant.**

130 A.D. 3d 734 (2d Dep't July 8, 2015)

Goodwin Procter LLP, New York, N.Y. (Anne A. Gruner and Amanda Willis Rabbat of counsel), for nonparty appellant

Appeal from an order of the Family Court, Nassau County (Elaine Jackson Stack, J.H.O.), dated October 6, 2014. The order, after a hearing, denied the motion of the subject child for the issuance of an order, inter alia, making special findings so as to enable her to petition the United States Citizenship and Immigration Services for special immigrant juvenile status pursuant to 8 USC § 1101 (a) (27) (J).

Ordered that the order is reversed, on the law and the facts, without costs or disbursements, the motion of the subject child is granted, it is declared that the subject child is dependent on the Family Court, and it is found that she is unmarried and under 21 years of age, that reunification with one or both of her parents is not viable due to parental abuse, neglect, abandonment, or similar parental conduct defined under State law, and that it would not be in her best interests to return to Honduras, her previous country of nationality and last habitual residence.

Cindy X.G.M. (hereinafter the child), a native of Honduras, is 17 years old and unmarried. In February 2014, the child's mother commenced the instant custody proceeding, and the child subsequently moved for the issuance of an order, inter alia, making special findings so as to enable her to petition the United States Citizenship and Immigration Services for special immigrant juvenile status pursuant to 8 USC § 1101 (a) (27) (J). The mother was awarded sole custody of the child. Following a hearing, however, the court denied the child's motion insofar as the child sought a finding that her reunification with one or both of her parents is not viable due to parental abuse, neglect, or abandonment.

Pursuant to 8 USC § 1101 (a) (27) (J) (as amended by the William Wilberforce Trafficking Victims Protection Reauthorization Act of 2008, Pub L 110-457, 122 US Stat 5044) and 8 CFR 204.11, a "special immigrant" is a resident alien who, inter alia, is under 21 years of age, is unmarried, and has been legally committed to, or placed under the custody of, an individual appointed by a state or juvenile court. Additionally, for a juvenile to qualify for special immigrant juvenile status, a court must find that reunification of the juvenile with one or both of the juvenile's parents is not viable due to parental abuse, neglect, abandonment, or a similar basis found under state law (*see* 8 USC § 1101 [a] [27] [J] [i]; *Matter of Marcelina M.-G. v Israel S.*, 112 AD3d 100 [2013]; *Matter of Mohamed B.*, 83 AD3d 829, 831 [2011]; *Matter of Trudy-Ann W. v Joan W.*, 73 AD3d 793, 795 [2010]), and that it would not be in the juvenile's best interests to be returned to his or her native country or country of last habitual residence (*see* 8 USC § 1101 [a] [27] [J] [ii]; 8 CFR 204.11 [c] [6]; *Matter of Mohamed B.*, 83 AD3d at 831; *Matter of Trudy-Ann W. v Joan W.*, 73 AD3d at 795).

Here, the record supports the Family Court's findings that the child is under the age of 21 and unmarried; that the child was "legally committed to, or placed under the custody of an individual or entity appointed by a State or juvenile court" within the meaning of 8 USC § 1101 (a) (27) (J) (i) (*see Matter of Maria P.E.A. v Sergio A.G.G.*, 111 AD3d 619, 620 [2013]); and that it would not be in the child's best interests to be returned to Honduras (*see Matter of Mohamed B.*, 83 AD3d at 831-832).

The court erred, however, with respect to its recital of the element of "reunification." The law does not require a finding that reunification with one or both of her parents *is* viable, but that reunification with one or both of her parents is *not* viable due to abuse, neglect, abandonment, or a similar basis found under State law (*see* 8 USC § 1101 [a] [27] [J] [i]; *Matter of Marcelina M.-G. v Israel S.*, 112 AD3d at 110-113). We have the authority to make that finding, and upon our independent factual review of the record, we find that the child's reunification with her father is not a viable option due to abandonment (*see Matter of Diaz v Munoz*, 118 AD3d 989, 991 [2014]; *Matter of Gabriel H.M. [Juan B.F.]*, 116 AD3d 855, 857 [2014]). Balkin, J.P., Austin, Sgroi and LaSalle, JJ., concur.

118. A record must contain sufficient evidence to establish that the minor's reunification with one or both parents is not viable based upon the statutorily enumerated grounds.

> ☐ **In the Matter of Miguel A. Nieto Mira, Appellant,**
> **v**
> **Sonia E. Hernandez, Respondent.**

118 A.D. 3d 1008 (2d Dep't June 25, 2014)

Bruno Joseph Bembi, Hempstead, N.Y., for appellant.

In a child custody proceeding pursuant to Family Court Act article 6, the father appeals from an order of the Family Court, Nassau County (Phillips, Ct. Atty. Ref.), dated August 21, 2013, which, after a hearing, denied his motion for the issuance of an order, inter alia, making special findings so as to enable the subject child to petition the United States Citizenship and Immigration Services for special immigrant juvenile status pursuant to 8 USC § 1101 (a) (27) (J), and, in effect, dismissed the petition.

Ordered that the order is affirmed, without costs or disbursements.

In June 2013, the father filed a petition pursuant to Family Court Act article 6 for custody of his son (hereinafter the child), who was under 21 years old, for the purpose of obtaining an order declaring that the child has been legally committed to, or placed under the custody of, an individual appointed by a state family or juvenile court, that reunification with one or both of his parents is not viable due to abandonment, neglect, or abuse, and that it would not be in his best interests to be returned to El Salvador, his previous country of nationality and last habitual residence, so as to enable him to petition the United States Citizenship and Immigration Services for special immigrant juvenile status pursuant to 8 USC § 1101 (a) (27) (J). Thereafter, the father moved for the issuance of an order making the requisite declaration and specific findings to enable the child to petition for special immigrant juvenile status. In an order dated August 21, 2013, made after a hearing, the Family Court denied the motion and, in effect, dismissed the custody petition.

Pursuant to 8 USC § 1101 (a) (27) (J) (as amended by the William Wilberforce Trafficking Victims Protection Reauthorization Act of 2008, Pub L 110-457, 122 US Stat 5044) and 8 CFR 204.11, a "special immigrant" is a resident alien who, inter alia, is under 21 years of age, is unmarried, and has been legally committed to, or placed under the custody of, an individual appointed by a State family or juvenile court. Additionally, for a juvenile to qualify for special immigrant juvenile status, a court must find that reunification of the juvenile with one or both of the juvenile's parents is not viable due to parental abuse, neglect, abandonment, or a similar basis found under State law (*see* 8 USC § 1101 [a] [27] [J] [i]; *Matter of Maria P.E.A. v Sergio A.G.G.*, 111 AD3d 619, 620 [2013]; *Matter of Trudy-Ann W. v Joan W.*, 73 AD3d 793, 795 [2010]), and that it would not be in the juvenile's best interests to be returned to his or her native country or country of last habitual residence (*see* 8 USC § 1101 [a] [27] [J] [ii]; 8 CFR 204.11 [c] [6]; *Matter of Maria P.E.A. v Sergio A.G.G.*, 111 AD3d at 620; *Matter of Trudy-Ann W. v Joan W.*, 73 AD3d at 795).

Upon our independent factual review, we find that, contrary to the father's contention, the record does not support a determination that the child's reunification with one or both of his parents was not viable due to parental abuse, neglect, abandonment, or a similar basis found under State law (*see Matter of Maria S.Z. v Maria M.A.*, 115 AD3d 970 [2014]; *Matter of Nirmal S. v Rajinder K.*, 101 AD3d 1130 [2012]).

The father's remaining contentions either need not be addressed in light of our determination, are without merit, or are not properly before this Court. Skelos, J.P., Lott, Roman and LaSalle, JJ., concur.

119. It is only necessary to show that reunification with one parent is not viable for purposes of an SIJ motion.

In the Matter of Karen C., Appellant.

---

111 A.D. 3d 622 (2d Dep't Nov 6, 2013)

—Theo Liebmann, Hempstead, N.Y., for appellant.

Steven Banks, New York, N.Y. (Marcia Egger and Cristina Romero of counsel), for amicus curiae The Legal Aid Society of New York, and Karen

Freedman, New York, N.Y. (Shirim Nothenberg of counsel), for amicus curiae Lawyers for Children, Inc. (one brief filed).

In a proceeding pursuant to Family Court Act article 6 for the appointment of Juan C.G. as coguardian of the child Karen C., Karen C. appeals from an order of the Family Court, Nassau County (Corrigan, J.), dated June 28, 2013, which, upon the granting of the guardianship petition in an order dated June 12, 2013, and after a hearing, denied her motion for the issuance of an order, inter alia, making special findings so as to enable her to petition the United States Citizenship and Immigration Services for special immigrant juvenile status pursuant to 8 USC § 1101 (a) (27) (J).

Ordered that the order is reversed, on the law and the facts, without costs or disbursements, the motion is granted, it is declared that Karen C. is dependent on the Family Court, and it is found that she is unmarried and under 21 years of age, that reunification with one or both of her parents is not viable due to parental abandonment, and that it would not be in the best interests of Karen C. to return to El Salvador, her previous country of nationality and last habitual residence.

Karen C. was born in El Salvador in January 1993. Karen's father abandoned her before she was born, and thereafter did not provide support for her and failed to communicate with her. Karen's mother left El Salvador when the child was approximately one year old, leaving Karen in the care of her maternal grandmother. Since that time, Karen's mother has lived in the United States. In approximately 2007, at the age of 14, Karen came to the United States, where she has lived primarily with her mother, stepfather, and three half-siblings.

In 2013 Karen filed a petition seeking the appointment of her stepfather as her coguardian with her mother. Karen also moved for the issuance of an order making special findings that would allow her to apply to the United States Citizenship and Immigration Services for special immigrant juvenile status (hereinafter SIJS).

In an order dated June 12, 2013, the Family Court granted the guardianship petition. However, the court denied Karen's motion for an order making special findings for the purpose of filing an application for SIJS. The court held that the Karen was not eligible for such an order because she failed to show that reunification with one or both of her parents was not viable and that [*2]it was not in her best interests to return to her country of origin, El Salvador.

Pursuant to 8 USC § 1101 (a) (27) (J) (as amended by the William Wilberforce Trafficking Victims Protection Reauthorization Act of 2008, Pub L 110-457, 122 US Stat 5044) and 8 CFR 204.11, a juvenile "special immigrant" is a resident alien who is, inter alia, under 21 years of age, unmarried, and "declared dependent on a juvenile court located in the United States or whom such a court has legally committed to, or placed under the custody of, an agency or department of a State, or an individual or entity appointed by a State or juvenile court located in the United States" (8 USC § 1101 [a] [27] [J] [i]). For the juvenile to qualify for SIJS, it must also be determined that reunification of the juvenile with "1 or both" of the juvenile's parents is not viable due to parental abuse, neglect, abandonment, or a similar basis found under State law (*see* 8 USC § 1101 [a] [27] [J] [i]; *Matter of Mohamed B.*, 83 AD3d 829, 831 [2011]; *Matter of Trudy-Ann W. v Joan W.*, 73 AD3d 793, 795 [2010]), and that it would not be in the juvenile's best interests to be returned to his or her native country or country of last habitual residence (*see* 8 USC § 1101 [a] [27] [J] [ii]; 8 CFR 204.11 [c] [6]; *Matter of Mohamed B.*, 83 AD3d at 831; *Matter of Trudy-Ann W. v Joan W.*, 73 AD3d at 795).

Here, Karen is under the age of 21 and unmarried. Inasmuch as the Family Court granted the guardianship petition and appointed her stepfather as coguardian, the child is dependent on the Family Court in that she has been "legally committed to, or placed under the custody of . . . an individual or entity appointed by a State or juvenile court located in the United States," within the meaning of 8 USC § 1101 (a) (27) (J) (i).

Based upon our independent factual review, we find that the record, which includes detailed affidavits from Karen and her mother, fully supports the conclusion that because her father abandoned her, reunification with her father is not a viable option (*see Matter of Mohamed B.*, 83 AD3d at 832; *Matter of Alamgir A.*, 81 AD3d 937, 939-940 [2011]; *Matter of Trudy-Ann W. v Joan W.*, 73 AD3d at 796; *see also Matter of Emma M.*, 74 AD3d 968, 970 [2010]). Moreover, the fact that Karen's mother was not shown to have neglected, abused, or abandoned Karen does not preclude the issuance of the order of special findings for the purpose of the SIJS application, in light of the terms of the applicable statute, which provides that a child may qualify for SIJ status where he or she has been neglected, abused or abandoned by "1 or both" parents (8 USC § 1101 [a] [27] [J] [i]; *see Matter of Marcelina M.-G. v Israel S.*, 112 AD3d 100 [2d Dept 2013]). Additionally, the record reflects that it would not be in Karen's best interests to be returned to El Salvador (*see Matter of Mohamed B.*, 83 AD3d at 831-832; *Matter of Alamgir A.*, 81 AD3d at 940; *Matter of Trudy-Ann W. v Joan W.*, 73 AD3d at 796). Accordingly, the Family Court should have granted Karen's motion for the issuance of an order making specific findings so as to enable her to petition for SIJS. Skelos, J.P., Balkin, Lott and Hinds-Radix, JJ., concur.

120. The fact that the minor has an aunt and other family in Honduras does not mean it is not in her best interests to remain with her mother, who was granted custody, and who lived in New York.

☐ In the Matter of Mayra P. Diaz, Petitioner,

v

Rene Munoz, Respondent. Lesby Julissa Munoz Diaz, Nonparty Appellant.

118 A.D. 3d 989 (2d Dep't June 25, 2014)

Janis M. Noto, Bay Shore N.Y., for nonparty appellant.

In a child custody proceeding pursuant to Family Court Act article 6, the subject child, Lesby Julissa Munoz Diaz, appeals from an order of the Family Court, Nassau County (Aaron, J.), dated July 25, 2013, which, after a hearing, denied the motion of the petitioner, her mother, in which she joined, for the issuance of an order making special findings that would enable the subject child, Lesby Julissa Munoz Diaz, to petition the United States Citizenship and Immigration Services for special immigrant juvenile status pursuant to 8 USC § 1101 (a) (27) (J).

Ordered that the order is reversed, on the law and the facts, without costs or disbursements, the motion is granted, it is declared that the subject child, Lesby Julissa Munoz Diaz, is dependent on the Family Court, and it is found that she is unmarried and under 21 years of age, that reunification with one or both of her parents is not viable due to parental abandonment, and that it would not be in her best interests to return to Honduras, her previous country of nationality and last habitual residence.

The subject child was born in Honduras in 1995. At the time of the commencement of the instant proceeding, she was 17 years old and unmarried, and she had been living with her mother in Nassau County since at least February 2012. The child's mother filed a petition for custody, and subsequently moved for the issuance of an order making special findings that would allow the child to apply to the United States Citizenship and Immigration Services for special immigrant juvenile status (hereinafter SIJS) pursuant to 8 USC § 1101

(a) (27) (J). The Family Court set the matters down for separate hearings. Following a hearing on the issue of custody, the court granted the mother's petition and awarded her custody of the child.

At the separate hearing on the motion for a special findings order, it was established that the child previously lived with her aunt and other family members in Honduras, she had never met her father, and she was concerned about gang violence in Honduras. After the hearing, the Family Court denied the motion for an order making special findings. Although the court found that it was in the child's best interests to award custody to the mother on Long Island and that the child's father had abandoned her, it nonetheless made a finding that it was not in the child's best interests to remain in the United States. In reaching this determination, the court found that reunification with one of the child's parents, her mother, was viable. We reverse.

Pursuant to 8 USC § 1101 (a) (27) (J) (as amended by the William Wilberforce Trafficking Victims Protection Reauthorization Act of 2008, Pub L 110-457, 122 US Stat 5044) and 8 CFR 204.11, a juvenile "special immigrant" is a resident alien who is, inter alia, under 21 years of age, unmarried, and "declared dependent on a juvenile court located in the United States or whom such a court has legally committed to, or placed under the custody of, an agency or department of a State, or an individual or entity appointed by a State or juvenile court located in the United States" (8 USC § 1101 [a] [27] [J] [i]). For a juvenile to qualify for SIJS, it must be determined that reunification of the juvenile with "1 or both" of the juvenile's parents is not viable due to parental abuse, neglect, abandonment, or a similar basis found under State law (8 USC § 1101 [a] [27] [J] [i]; *Matter of Marcelina M.-G. v Israel S.*, 112 AD3d 100 [2013]; *Matter of Karen C.*, 111 AD3d 622, 623 [2013]; *Matter of Trudy-Ann W. v Joan W.*, 73 AD3d 793, 795 [2010]), and that it would not be in the juvenile's best interests to be returned to his or her native country or country of last habitual residence (*see* 8 USC § 1101 [a] [27] [J] [ii]; 8 CFR 204.11 [c] [6]; *see Matter of Marcelina M.-G. v Israel S.*, 112 AD3d 100 [2013]; *Matter of Karen C.*, 111 AD3d at 623; *Matter of Trudy-Ann W. v Joan W.*, 73 AD3d at 795).

The statutory definition of SIJS "allow[s] a juvenile court to consider the *nonviability* of family reunification with just one parent, rather than both" (*Matter of Marcelina M.-G.*, 112 AD3d at 112 [emphasis added]). Since the Family Court correctly found that the child was abandoned by her father, the record supports a finding that reunification with one of the child's parents was not viable. Furthermore, contrary to the court's determination, the record established that it would not be in the child's best interests to return to Honduras. Significantly, the court awarded custody to the mother, who lives in Nassau County. Accordingly, the court should have granted the motion for an order making the requisite special findings so as to enable the child to apply for SIJS. Since the record is sufficient for this Court to make its own findings of fact and conclusions of law, the motion is granted, we declare that the child is dependent on the Family Court, and we find that she is unmarried and under 21 years of age, that reunification with one of her parents is not viable due to parental abandonment, and that it would not be in her best interests to return to Honduras (*see Matter of Maura A.R.-R. [Santos F.R.—Fidel R.]*, 114 AD3d 687 [2014]; *Matter of Marcelina M.-G. v Israel S.*, 112 AD3d 100; *Matter of Karen C.*, 111 AD3d 622 [2013]; *Matter of Trudy-Ann W. v Joan W.*, 73 AD3d at 796). Skelos, J.P., Austin, Sgroi and LaSalle, JJ., concur.

121. Children become dependent upon the family court in a family offense proceeding and thus can move for an order of special findings where the family offense proceeding determines the children were neglected by their father based upon his physical, mental, and verbal abuse.

> **☐ In the Matter of Eliverta Fifo, Appellant,**
> **v**
> **Ismail Fifo, Respondent. Joni Fifo et al., Nonparty Appellants.**

127 A.D. 748 (2d Dep't April 1, 2015)

Simpson Thacher & Bartlett LLP, New York, N.Y. (Daniel Y. Shin and Mary Kay Vyskocil of counsel), for petitioner-appellant.

Davis Polk & Wardwell LLP, New York, N.Y. (Andrew Ditchfield, Sharon Katz, and Tina Hwa Joe of counsel), and Sanctuary for Families Center for Battered Women's Legal Services, New York, N.Y. (Jennifer Lissette Anzardo of counsel), for nonparty appellants (one brief filed).

McDermott Will & Emery LLP, New York, N.Y. (Andrew B. Kratenstein of counsel), for amicus curiae Theo Liebmann, Leigh Goodmark, Marjory D. Fields, Legal Aid Society, Safe Passage Project, Door's Legal Services Center, New York Chapter of the American Immigration Lawyers Association, Peter Cicchino Youth Project, Day One, Central American Refugee Center, Legal Services for Children, Volunteers of Legal Service, Kids in Need of Defense, and Safe Center LI.

Appeals from an order of the Family Court, Kings County (Ilana Gruebel, J.), dated July 29, 2013. The order denied the motion of the subject children for the issuance of an order declaring that each of them is dependent on the Family Court and making specific findings that each of them is unmarried and under 21 years of age, that reunification with one or both of their parents is not viable due to parental abuse, neglect, or abandonment, and that it would not be in each of their best interests to be returned to their previous country of nationality or last habitual residence, so as to enable each of them to petition the United States Citizenship and Immigration Services for special immigrant juvenile status pursuant to 8 USC § 1101 (a) (27) (J).

Ordered that the appeal by the mother is dismissed, without costs or disbursements, as she is not aggrieved by the order appealed from (*see* CPLR 5511); and it is further,

Ordered that the order is reversed on the appeal by the subject children, on the law and the facts, without costs or disbursements, and the matter is remitted to the Family Court, Kings County, for the making of specific findings as to whether it would not be in the best interests of each of the children to be returned to Albania, and, thereafter, for a new determination of the children's motion consistent herewith.

Pursuant to 8 USC § 1101 (a) (27) (J) (as amended by the William Wilberforce Trafficking Victims Protection Reauthorization Act of 2008, Pub L 110-457, 122 US Stat 5044) and 8 CFR 204.11, a "special immigrant" is a resident alien who is, inter alia, under 21 years of age, unmarried, and dependent upon a juvenile court or legally committed to an individual appointed by a state or juvenile court (*see Matter of Mohamed B.*, 83 AD3d 829, 831 [2011]). For purposes of qualification for "special immigrant juvenile status" pursuant to 8 USC § 1101 (a) (27) (J), "[a] child becomes dependent upon a juvenile court when the court accepts jurisdiction over the custody of that child, irrespective of whether the child has been placed in foster care or a guardianship situation" (*Matter of Hei Ting C.*, 109 AD3d 100, 106 [2013]). "Additionally, for a juvenile to qualify for special immigrant juvenile status, a court must find that reunification of the juvenile with one or both of the juvenile's parents is not viable due to parental abuse, neglect, abandonment, or similar parental conduct defined under State law, and that it would not be in the juvenile's best interest to be returned to his or her native country or country of last habitual residence" (*Matter of Trudy-Ann W. v Joan W.*, 73 AD3d 793, 795 [2010] [citations omitted]).

In this family offense proceeding, the petitioner, the mother of the subject children (hereinafter the mother), filed a petition seeking an order of protection against the father, alleging that the father had committed certain family offenses against her and the children. The Family Court issued a temporary order of protection directing the father, inter alia, to stay away from the mother and the children. Thereafter, the children moved for the issuance of an order declaring that each of them is dependent on the Family Court, and making specific findings that each of them is unmarried and under 21 years of age, that reunification with their father is not viable due to neglect, and that it would not be in each of their best interests to be returned to Albania, their previous country of nationality and last habitual residence. If the court were to grant their motion, each of the children intended to petition the United States Citizenship and Immigration Services for special immigrant juvenile status (hereinafter SIJS). In the order appealed from, dated July 29, 2013, the Family Court denied the children's motion.

Contrary to the Family Court's determination, in support of their motion, the children established that they were dependent upon a juvenile court. While guardianship, adoption, and custody are not directly or presently at issue in this family offense proceeding (*see generally Matter of Hei Ting C.*, 109 AD3d at 106), under the particular circumstances of this case, the children have become dependent upon the Family Court. The children's mother has filed a family offense petition against the father seeking an order of protection, alleging that the father has assaulted her and the children. In their motion, the children claimed that they have been neglected by the father based on allegations including physical, mental, and verbal abuse. After conducting an investigation, the Administration for Children's Services concluded that certain of these allegations were substantiated. On May 6, 2013, shortly after the children made their motion, the Family Court issued an order of protection, effective for two years, directing the father, inter alia, to stay away from the mother and the children.

While a family offense proceeding, or the mere issuance of an order of protection, will not always give rise to a determination that a child has become dependent upon a juvenile court, based on the particular circumstances of this case, we conclude that such a determination is warranted here. As we have previously observed, the intended beneficiaries of the SIJS provisions of the Immigration and Nationality Act are limited to " 'those juveniles for whom it was created, namely abandoned, neglected, or abused children' " (*Matter of Marcelina M.-G. v Israel S.*, 112 AD3d 100, 108 [2013], quoting HR Rep 105-405, 105th Cong, 1st Sess at 130, reprinted in 1997 US Code Cong & Admin News at 2941, 2954; *see Matter of Hei Ting C.*, 109 AD3d at 103; *Yeboah v United States Dept. of Justice*, 345 F3d 216, 222 [3d Cir 2003]). Thus, while, for example, a child support proceeding will not give rise to a determination that a child has become dependent upon a juvenile court (*see Matter of Hei Ting C.*, 109 AD3d 100 [2013]), under the proper circumstances, a child involved in a family offense proceeding involving allegations of abuse or neglect may properly be the subject of such a determination as an intended beneficiary of the SIJS provisions.

Here, the Family Court did not make specific findings as to whether reunification with one or both of the parents was not viable due to parental abuse, neglect, abandonment, or similar parental conduct defined under State law, and whether it would not be in each of the children's best interests to be returned to Albania (*see Matter of Trudy-Ann W. v Joan W.*, 73 AD3d at 795). Of course, in reviewing motions such as the children's motion here, "[t]his Court's power to review the evidence is as broad as that of the hearing court, and where . □□ the record is sufficiently complete to make our own factual determinations, we may do so" (*Matter of Luis R. v Maria Elena G.*, 120 AD3d

581, 582 [2014]). Upon our independent factual review, we conclude that the record here is sufficient to establish that reunification of the children with the father is not viable. While the Family Court, in the order appealed from, referred to the fact that the children live with the mother, "the fact that a child has one fit parent available to care for him or her 'does not, by itself, preclude the issuance of special findings under the SIJS statute'" (*Matter of Marisol N.H.*, 115 AD3d 185, 190-191 [2014], quoting *Matter of Marcelina M.-G. v Israel S.*, 112 AD3d at 111). "Rather, a child may be eligible for SIJS findings 'where reunification with just one parent is not viable as a result of abuse, neglect, abandonment, or a similar state law basis'" (*Matter of Marisol N.H.*, 115 AD3d at 191, quoting *Matter of Marcelina M.-G. v Israel S.*, 112 AD3d at 110).

However, the record is insufficient for us to make specific findings as to whether it would not be in the best interests of each of the children to be returned to Albania. Accordingly, we reverse the order and remit the matter to the Family Court, Kings County, for the making of specific findings as to whether it would not be in the best interests of each of the children to be returned to Albania, and, thereafter, for a new determination of the children's motion consistent herewith. Balkin, J.P., Dickerson, Sgroi and Cohen, JJ., concur.

122. A child support order does not satisfy the requirement for SIJ status "that a child be 'dependent on a juvenile court'". See Family Court Act sec 413.

| In the Matter of Hei Ting C., Appellant. (Proceeding No. 1.) |
| In the Matter of Wai C., Appellant. (Proceeding No. 2.) |

109 A.D. 100 (2d Dep't July 17, 2013)

APPEARANCES OF COUNSEL

Baker & Hostetler LLP, New York City (*Timothy S. Pfeifer, Seanna R. Brown* and *Jacqlyn R. Rovine* of counsel), for appellants.

OPINION OF THE COURT

Cohen, J.

The assumption of responsibility for serving the best interests of a child by providing protection and guidance to a child appearing before the court goes to the very core of our legal system. Indeed, children have long enjoyed the benefit of their own assigned counsel in custody proceedings. We require our courts to review and approve settlements of infants' claims. We have a long-established juvenile system of justice that is specifically designed to protect and rehabilitate delinquent children. However, it was only fairly recently that some notion of distinguishing the status of children from that of adults was addressed in our immigration laws. Taking effect in 2009, a form of immigration status known as special immigrant juvenile status is now offered to a class of undocumented immigrant children, providing them with a gateway to lawful permanent residency in the United States. Before a child can petition the United States Citizenship and Immigration Services for special immigrant juvenile status, a state court must first acquire jurisdiction and make certain declarations with respect to the child. On this appeal, we are asked to determine whether the Family Court, after issuing a support order in a related child support proceeding, properly denied the petitions of a sister and brother for the issuance of orders declaring each of them to be dependent on the Family Court, and making the specific findings required to enable them to petition the United States Citizenship and Immigration Services for special immigrant juvenile status pursuant to 8 USC § 1101 (a) (27) (J).

Specifically at issue in this case is whether a child becomes dependent on a juvenile court within the meaning of the federal statute when one of the child's parents files a petition for child support upon which the Family Court enters an order of support. Although several decisions of this Court and the Appellate Division, First Department, have addressed the questions of whether a guardianship petition and an adoption proceeding satisfy the dependency prong for special findings relative to special immigrant juvenile status, answering both questions in the affirmative (*see Matter of Ashley W. [Verdele F.]*, 85 AD3d 807 [2011]; *Matter of Mohamed B.*, 83 AD3d 829 [2011]; *Matter of Sing W.C. [Sing Y.C.—Wai M.C.]*, 83 AD3d 84 [2011]; *Matter of Alamgir A.*, 81 AD3d 937 [2011]; *Matter of Jisun L. v Young Sun P.*, 75 AD3d 510 [2010]; *Matter of Emma M.*, 74 AD3d 968 [2010]; *Matter of Trudy-Ann W. v Joan W.*, 73 AD3d 793 [2010]; *Matter of Antowa McD.*, 50 AD3d 507 [2008]), no appellate decisions in this state have addressed the question of whether an order issued by the Family Court that does not award or affect the custody of a child satisfies the dependency prong. For the reasons set forth below, we hold that a child support order does not satisfy the requirement for special immigrant juvenile status that a child be "dependent on a juvenile court" (8 USC § 1101 [a] [27] [J] [i]).

Background

In 1990, Congress created special immigrant juvenile status (hereinafter SIJS) to address the issue of undocumented and unaccompanied children. These children, who lack a lawful immigration status, endure the continual threat of deportation, cannot work legally, and are constantly vulnerable to exploitation. As originally enacted, this legislation defined an eligible immigrant as being one who "has been declared dependent on a juvenile court located in the United States and has been deemed eligible by that court for long-term foster care" (Immigration Act of 1990, Pub L 101-649, tit I, § 153 [a], 104 US Stat 4978, 5005, adding 8 USC § 1101 [a] [27] [J] [i]). It also required a determination by the court that it would not be in the immigrant's best interests to return to his or her native country (*see* Immigration Act of 1990, Pub L 101-649, tit I, § 153 [a], 104 US Stat 4978, 5005-5006, adding 8 USC § 1101 [a] [27] [J] [ii]). In 1997, Congress added the further requirement that the juvenile court find the child dependent upon the court "due to abuse, neglect, or abandonment" (Pub L 105-119, tit I, § 113, 111 US Stat 2440, 2460, amending 8 USC § 1101 [a] [27] [J] [i]) which limited the beneficiaries of the provision "to those juveniles for whom it was created" (143 Cong Rec H10809-01, H10815, H10844 [Nov. 13, 1997]).

In 2008, Congress again amended the SIJS provision. In the "William Wilberforce Trafficking Victims Protection Reauthorization Act of 2008," Congress expanded the definition of who qualified as a "special immigrant juvenile," enabling more children to qualify for the status (Pub L 110-457, 122 US Stat 5044 [Dec. 23, 2008]). The amendments removed the requirement that the immigrant child had to be deemed eligible for long-term foster care due to abuse, neglect, or abandonment, and replaced it with a requirement that the juvenile court find that "reunification with 1 or both of the immigrant's parents is not viable due to abuse, neglect, abandonment, or a similar basis found under State law" (Pub L 110-457, tit II, § 235 [d] [1], 122 US Stat 5079 [Dec. 23, 2008], amending 8 USC § 1101 [a] [27] [J] [i]). The amendments also expanded eligibility to include, in addition to children declared dependent on a juvenile court, those who had been placed in the custody of "an individual or entity appointed by a State or juvenile court" (*id.*). Following the 2008 amendments, the United States Department of Homeland Security issued a memorandum explaining, inter alia, that the new language added to the definition of "Special Immigrant Juvenile" meant that "a petition filed by an alien on whose behalf a juvenile court appointed a guardian may now be eligible" (Memorandum by Donald Neufeld and Pearl Chang, *Trafficking Victims Protection Reauthorization Act of 2008: Special Immigrant Juvenile Status Provisions* [Mar. 24, 2009]).

Pursuant to the 2008 amendments, a "special immigrant" is a resident alien who is under 21 years old, is unmarried, and has been either "declared dependent on a juvenile court" or legally committed to the custody of an individual appointed by a state or juvenile court (*see* 8 USC § 1101 [a] [27] [J] [i]; 8 CFR 204.11). Additionally, for a juvenile to qualify for SIJS, a court must find that reunification of the juvenile with one or both of the juvenile's parents is not viable due to parental "abuse, neglect, abandonment, or a similar basis found under State law," and that it would not be in the juvenile's best interests to be returned to his or her previous country of nationality or country of last habitual residence (8 USC § 1101 [a] [27] [J] [i]). "Under federal law, a person who is granted [SIJS] is able to achieve lawful permanent residency in the United States without first obtaining a visa" (*Matter of Sing W.C. [Sing Y.C.—Wai M.C.]*, 83 AD3d at 86).

The enactment of the SIJS provision demonstrates Congress's intent to provide special protection to children who have experienced maltreatment in their families (*see* Wendi J. Adelson, *The Case of the Eroding Special Immigration Juvenile Status*, 18 J Transnat'l L & Pol'y 65, 67 [Fall 2008]). The provision employs a unique hybrid procedure that directs the collaboration of state and federal systems, "recognizing that juvenile courts have particularized training and expertise in the area of child welfare and abuse," which places them in the best position to make determinations on the best interests of the child and potential for family reunification (David B. Thronson, *Kids Will Be Kids? Reconsidering Conceptions of Children's Rights Underlying Immigration Law*, 63 Ohio St LJ 979, 1005 [2002]). However, it is the federal government that still retains control over the final immigration determination (*see id.* at 1007).

In New York, a child may request that the Family Court, recognized as a juvenile court (*see* 8 CFR 204.11 [a]), issue an order making special findings and a declaration so that he or she may petition the United States Citizenship and Immigration Services for SIJS (*see e.g. Matter of Jisun L. v Young Sun P.*, 75 AD3d 510 [2010]). Specifically, the findings of fact must establish that: (1) the child is under 21 years of age; (2) the child is unmarried; (3) the child is dependent upon a juvenile court or legally committed to an individual appointed by a state or juvenile court; (4) reunification with one or both parents is not viable due to abuse, neglect, abandonment, or a similar basis; and (5) it is not in the child's best interests to be returned to his or her home country (*see* 8 USC § 1101 [a] [27] [J] [ii]; 8 CFR 204.11 [c]). With the declaration and special findings, the eligible child may then seek the consent of the Department of Homeland Security for SIJS (*see* 8 USC § 1101 [a] [27] [J] [iii]).

This case involves Hei Ting C. and Wai C., a sister and brother who were born in Hong Kong. Their parents were divorced in Hong Kong in 2006, and the father and Wai moved to New York in the summer of 2008. Although the father was awarded full custody of the children, Hei Ting remained in Hong Kong with her mother until she finished the school year. Her mother refused to care for her, and Hei Ting alleges that she had to support herself using a credit card provided to her by her father. After completing the school year, Hei Ting relocated to New York to join her father and brother. Hei Ting and Wai currently live in Queens with their father, and both children remain unmarried.

Both Hei Ting and Wai describe their mother as physically and verbally abusive. Although their mother also subsequently relocated to New York, they live exclusively with their father and have little or no contact with her. They have received no emotional or voluntary financial support from their mother.

The father filed a petition pursuant to Family Court Act article 4 in the Family Court, seeking a support order on consent. In December 2011, the Family Court entered the requested support order on consent. Hei Ting and Wai then filed a joint motion, within the support proceeding, for the issuance of special findings necessary for them to obtain SIJS, arguing that the existence of a support order made them dependent upon the Family Court. At the time the motion was filed, they were both under the age of 21 and contended that reunification with their mother was not viable, as she was physically and emotionally abusive toward them. They also argued that it would not be in their best interests to return to Hong Kong, since their father, who is their source of care and support, is in the United States, and their return would remove them from further educational opportunities. There would also be no adults to take care of them in Hong Kong. In two orders dated December 20, 2011, made after a hearing, the Family Court, in effect, converted the motion to separate petitions for the issuance of special findings, and denied the petitions. In two orders dated January 4, 2012, made, in effect, upon reargument, the Family Court adhered to its original determinations. Hei Ting and Wai now appeal.

Analysis

In determining whether a child becomes "dependent on a juvenile court" for SIJS purposes when a child support order is entered, this Court must examine the facts of each particular case.

While the appellants make well-reasoned arguments for allowing orders directing child support payments to satisfy the requirement for SIJS that a child be "dependent on a juvenile court" (8 USC § 1101 [a] [27] [J] [i]), this Court declines to adopt that position. As discussed above, the impetus behind the enactment of the SIJS scheme is to protect a child who is abused, abandoned, or neglected and to provide him or her with an expedited immigration process. The requirement that a child be dependent upon the juvenile court or, alternatively, committed to the custody of an individual appointed by a state or juvenile court, ensures that the process is not employed inappropriately by children who have sufficient family support and stability to pursue permanent residency in the United States through other, albeit more protracted, procedures. In this case, there has been no need for intervention by the Family Court to ensure that the appellants were placed in a safe and appropriate custody, guardianship, or foster care situation, and the appellants have not been committed to the custody of any individual by any court (*cf. Matter of Ashley W. [Verdele F.], 85 AD3d 807* [2011]; *Matter of Mohamed B., 83 AD3d 829* [2011]; *Matter of Sing W.C. [Sing Y.C.—Wai M.C.], 83 AD3d 84*[2011]; *Matter of Alamgir A., 81 AD3d 937* [2011]; *Matter of Jisun L. v Young Sun P., 75 AD3d 510* [2010]; *Matter of Trudy-Ann W. v Joan W., 73 AD3d 793* [2010]).

While the appellants met all of the other requirements for SIJS, the Family Court correctly determined that the dependency requirement had not been satisfied. A child becomes dependent upon a juvenile court when the court accepts jurisdiction over the custody of that child, irrespective of whether the child has been placed in foster care or a guardianship situation (*see In re Menjivar*, File A 70 117 167 [INS Administrative Appeals Unit, Dec. 27, 1994]). The Family Court has only granted applications for SIJS special findings where dependency upon the court was established by way of guardianship, adoption, or custody. The cases cited by the appellants in support of their motion only addressed matters involving guardianship or custody (*see e.g. Matter of Alamgir A.*, 81 AD3d at 938; *Matter of Jisun L. v Young Sun P.*, 75 AD3d at 511; *Matter of Trudy-Ann W. v Joan W.*, 73 AD3d at 794).

The appellants assert that their case is analogous to guardianship cases because, in a child support case, the child is

"dependent upon the Family Court for his [or her] very maintenance and survival . . . [W]here the parent fails to live up to [the duty of financial support], the child is dependent upon the court to intervene and order the absent parent to fulfill [his or] her duty to provide [his or] her child with what [he or] she is able."
They maintain that while they were not themselves litigants in a court proceeding, the fact that they were the subject of a court proceeding determining their future

financial welfare made them dependent upon the juvenile court. However, as the Family Court correctly noted, "[a] child support application does not address custody issues, rather it addresses a parent's failure to pay child support to the custodial parent."

This Court has set the appropriate standards for dependency on the juvenile court in its prior decisions addressing guardianship and adoption proceedings (*see Matter of Ashley W. [Verdele F.]*, 85 AD3d at 809; *Matter of Mohamed B.*, 83 AD3d at 831-832; *Matter of Sing W.C. [Sing Y.C.—Wai M.C.]*, 83 AD3d at 86; *Matter of Alamgir A.*, 81 AD3d at 939-940; *Matter of Jisun L. v Young Sun P.*, 75 AD3d at 511-512; *Matter of Emma M., 74 AD3d 968*, 969-970 [2010]; *Matter of Trudy-Ann W. v Joan W.*, 73 AD3d at 795-796). Proceedings for child support involve litigation between the parents regarding the required financial responsibility each parent has with respect to the child (*see* Family Ct Act § 413 [1] [a]). There are no determinations in a child support proceeding commenced pursuant to Family Court Act § 413 that relate to the actual guardianship and custody of the child.

While the appellants argue that this distinction creates a categorical limitation contrary to congressional intent, this is not the case. Courts are not to legislate under the guise of creative interpretation or construction not consistent with the plain and ordinary usage and meaning of the statutory language (*see Hartford Underwriters Ins. Co. v Union Planters Bank, N.A.*, 530 US 1, 10 [2000]; *Park 'N Fly, Inc. v Dollar Park & Fly, Inc.*, 469 US 189, 194 [1985]). We are constrained to read and give effect to the law as it was written in accordance with the plain meaning of the words used by Congress, not as we may think it should have been written (*see William J. Jenack Estate Appraisers & Auctioneers, Inc. v Rabizadeh, 99 AD3d 270*, 275-276 [2012]; *Puello v Bureau of Citizenship & Immigration Servs.*, 511 F3d 324, 327 [2d Cir 2007]).

Finally, we observe that allowing Family Court proceedings which are not related to custody and guardianship matters to serve as a vehicle for obtaining SIJS special findings would not further the underlying policies behind the SIJS scheme, i.e., to protect abused, neglected, and abandoned immigrant children, and would also risk opening the door to abuse of the SIJS process.

Accordingly, the orders dated January 4, 2012, are affirmed insofar as appealed from. The appeals from the orders dated December 20, 2011, are dismissed, as those orders were superseded by the orders dated January 4, 2012, made, in effect, upon reargument.

Eng, P.J., Dillon and Lott, JJ., concur.

Ordered that the appeals from the orders dated December 20, 2011, are dismissed, without costs or disbursements, as those orders were superseded by the orders dated January 4, 2012, made, in effect, upon reargument; and it is further,

Ordered that the orders dated January 4, 2012, are affirmed insofar as appealed from, without costs or disbursements.

123. A natural parent may petition for custody of her own children.

See Matter of Pineda Sanchez, below.

124. Mother and children were entitled to a hearing on their custody petition and motion of special findings.

115 A.D. 3d 868 (2d Dep't March 19, 2014)

> **In the Matter of Cecilia Maribel Pineda Sanchez, Appellant,**
> **v**
> **Jose Santos Hernandez Bonilla, Respondent.**

—Bruno Joseph Bembi, Hempstead, N.Y., for appellant.

In a child custody proceeding pursuant to Family Court Act article 6, the petitioner appeals from an order of the Family Court, Nassau County (Stack, J.H.O.), dated August 14, 2013, which, without a hearing, dismissed the custody petition.

Ordered that the order is reversed, on the law, without costs or disbursements, the custody petition is reinstated, and the matter is remitted to the Family Court, Nassau County, for a hearing and new determination of the petition thereafter.

The Family Court erred in dismissing the petition in which the mother sought orders of custody for her two teenaged children. A natural parent has standing to seek legal custody of his or her child (*see* Domestic Relations Law § 70 [a]; Family Ct Act § 511; *Debra H. v Janice R.*, 14 NY3d 576 [2010], *cert denied* 562 US —, 131 S Ct 908 [2011]; *Matter of Marcelina M.-G. v Israel S.*, 112 AD3d 100 [2013]; *T.V. v New York State Dept. of Health*, 88 AD3d 290, 301 [2011]). According to the petitioner, the children's father has abandoned the children and, due to their immigration status, they could be returned to El Salvador where they have been subjected to abuse by family members and threats by gang members. The petitioner has alleged that awarding her custody would be in the best interests of the children, since it would enable the children to apply for special immigrant juvenile status (*see Matter of Maria G.G.U. v Pedro H.P.*, 114 AD3d 691 [2014]; *Matter of Marisol N.H.*, 115 AD3d 185 [2d Dept 2014]; *Matter of Maura A.R.-R. [Santos F.R.]*, 114 AD3d 687 [2014]).

Accordingly, since the Family Court dismissed the subject petition without conducting a hearing or considering the best interests of the children, we remit the matter to the Family Court, Nassau County, for a hearing and a new determination of the custody petition thereafter (*see Matter of Maria E.S.G. v*

Jose C.G.L., 114 AD3d 677 [2014]; *Matter of Francisco M.-G. v Marcelina M.-G.*, 100 AD3d 900 [2012]; *Matter of Ashley W. [Verdele F.]*, 85 AD3d 807, 809 [2011]). Mastro, J.P., Dillon, Leventhal and Duffy, JJ., concur.

125. An appellate court can render an independent factual review of the record.

☐ **In the Matter of Tommy E.H. Silvia C., Appellant.**

134 A.D. 3d 840 (2d Dep't. Dec. 19, 2015)

Kohan Law Group, P.C., Manhasset, N.Y. (Michael Kohan of counsel), for appellant.

Lisa Siano, Merrick, N.Y., attorney for the child.

Appeal from an order of the Family Court, Nassau County (Ellen R. Greenberg, J.), dated September 5, 2014. The order, after a hearing, denied the mother's motion for the issuance of an order, inter alia, making special findings so as to enable the subject child, Tommy E.H., to petition the United States Citizenship and Immigration Services for special immigrant juvenile status pursuant to 8 USC § 1101 (a) (27) (J).

Ordered that the order is reversed, on the law and the facts, without costs or disbursements, the mother's motion for the issuance of an order, inter alia, making special findings so as to enable the subject child, Tommy E.H., to petition the United States Citizenship and Immigration Services for special immigrant juvenile status pursuant to 8 USC § 1101 (a) (27) (J) is granted, it is declared that Tommy E.H. has been legally committed to, or placed under the custody of, an individual appointed by a state or juvenile court, and it is found that he is unmarried and under 21 years of age, that reunification with one of his parents is not viable due to parental neglect and abandonment, and that it would not be in his best interests to return to El Salvador, his previous country of nationality and last habitual residence.

In April 2014, the mother filed a petition pursuant to Family Court Act article 6 for sole custody of her child, Tommy E.H. (hereinafter the child), for the purpose of obtaining an order, inter alia, making specific findings that he is unmarried and under 21 years of age, that reunification with one of his parents is not viable due to abandonment, neglect, or abuse, and that it would not be in his best interests to be returned to El Salvador, his previous country of nationality and last habitual residence, so as to enable him to petition the United States Citizenship and Immigration Services for special immigrant juvenile status (hereinafter SIJS) pursuant to 8 USC § 1101 (a) (27) (J). Thereafter, the mother moved for the issuance of an order making the requisite declaration and specific findings so as to enable the child to petition for SIJS. In an order dated June 11, 2014, the Family Court awarded the mother sole custody of the child. In the order appealed from, dated September 5, 2014, the Family Court denied the mother's motion for the issuance of an order, inter alia, making specific findings so as to enable the child to petition for SIJS.

Pursuant to 8 USC § 1101 (a) (27) (J) (as amended by the William Wilberforce Trafficking Victims Protection Reauthorization Act of 2008, Pub L 110-457, 122 US Stat 5044) and 8 CFR 204.11, a "special immigrant" is a resident alien who, inter alia, is under 21 years of age, unmarried, and dependent upon a juvenile court or legally committed to an individual appointed by a state or juvenile court. "Additionally, for a juvenile to qualify for special immigrant juvenile status, a court must find that reunification of the juvenile with one or both of the juvenile's parents is not viable due to parental abuse, neglect, abandonment, or similar parental conduct defined under State law, and that it would not be in the juvenile's best interest to be returned to his or her native country or country of last habitual residence" (*Matter of Trudy-Ann W. v Joan W.*, 73 AD3d 793, 795 [2010] [citations omitted]).

Here, the child is under the age of 21 and unmarried, and has been "legally committed to, or placed under the custody of . ☐☐ an individual . ☐☐ appointed by a State or juvenile court" within the meaning of 8 USC § 1101 (a) (27) (J) (i) (*see Matter of Pineda v Diaz*, 127 AD3d 1203, 1204 [2015]; *Matter of Maria P.E.A. v Sergio A.G.G.*, 111 AD3d 619, 620 [2013]). Further, based upon our independent factual review, we find that the record supports the mother's contentions that the child's reunification with his father was not viable due to neglect and abandonment (*see Matter of Maria P.E.A. v Sergio A.G.G.*, 111 AD3d at 620; *Matter of Mohamed B.*, 83 AD3d 829, 832 [2011]), and that it would not be in the best interests of the child to be returned to El Salvador (*see Matter of Miguel A.G.G. [Milton N.G.G.]*, 127 AD3d 858 [2015]; *Matter of Marisol N.H.*, 115 AD3d 185, 191 [2014]).

Accordingly, the Family Court should have granted the mother's motion for the issuance of an order making the requisite declaration and specific findings so as to enable the child to petition for SIJS. Inasmuch as the record is sufficient for this Court to make its own findings of fact and conclusions of law, the mother's motion is granted, we declare that the child has been legally committed to, or placed under the custody of, an individual appointed by a state or juvenile court, and we find that the child is unmarried and under 21 years of age, that reunification with one of his parents is not viable due to parental abandonment, and that it would not be in his best interests to return to El Salvador (*see Matter of Gomez v Sibrian*, 133 AD3d 658 [2d Dept 2015]; *Matter of Diaz v Munoz*, 118 AD3d 989, 991 [2014]; *Matter of Marcelina M.-G. v Israel S.*, 112 AD3d 100, 115 [2013]; *Matter of Trudy-Ann W. v Joan W.*, 73 AD3d at 795). Balkin, J.P., Hall, Cohen and Hinds-Radix, JJ., concur.

126.   A mother may be appointed guardian of her own children.

See Matter of Maria G.G.U below

127. The Petitioner and Subject in an SIJ guardianship petition have the right to a hearing before a Family Court Judge.

114 A.D.3d 691 (2d Dep't Feb 5, 2014)

In the Matter of Maria G.G.U., Appellant,
v
Pedro H.P., Respondent.

—Bruno Joseph Bembi, Hempstead, N.Y., for appellant.

In three related guardianship proceedings pursuant to Family Court Act article 6, the petitioner appeals from an order of the Family Court, Nassau County (Stack, J.H.O.), dated January 9, 2013, which, without a hearing, denied her applications for the issuance of an order declaring that the subject children, Anibal H., Jose P.H., and Marlene G.H., are dependent on the Family Court and making specific findings that they are unmarried and under 21 years of age, that reunification with one or both of their parents is not viable due to parental abuse, neglect, or abandonment, and that it would not be in their best interests to be returned to their previous country of nationality or last habitual residence, so as to enable them to petition the United States Citizenship and Immigration Services for special immigrant juvenile status pursuant to 8 USC § 1101 (a) (27) (J), and dismissed the guardianship petitions.

Ordered that the order is reversed, on the law, without costs or disbursements, the guardianship petitions are reinstated, and the matters are remitted to the Family Court, Nassau County, for a hearing and new determination of the petitions, and, thereafter, if warranted, a hearing and a new determination of the applications for the issuance of an order making the requisite declaration and special findings.

The Family Court erred in dismissing the petitions in which Maria G.G.U. sought to be appointed as guardian of her natural children. Contrary to the Family Court's determination, the fact that the petitioner is the natural parent of the children does not preclude the court from appointing the petitioner as guardian of the children (*see Matter of Marisol N.H.*, 115 AD3d 185 [2014] [decided herewith] SCPA 1703). Here, the petitioner has alleged that appointing her as guardian would be in the best interests of the children, since it would enable the children to apply for special immigrant juvenile status (hereinafter SIJS) (*see Matter of Marisol N.H.*, 115 AD3d 185 [2014] [decided herewith]). According to the petitioner, the children's father has abandoned the children, and, without SIJS, the children may be returned to El Salvador where gang members have threatened and extorted them and there is no one to support or protect them.

Accordingly, since the Family Court dismissed the guardianship petitions without conducting a hearing or considering the children's best interests, the matter must be remitted to the Family Court, Nassau County, for a hearing and new determination of the guardianship petitions thereafter (*see Matter of Francisco M.-G. v Marcelina M.-G.*, 100 AD3d 900, 901 [2012] *Matter of Ashley W. [Verdele F.]*, 85 AD3d 807, 809 [2011]). A hearing on the applications for an order making the requisite declaration and findings, as required by federal law in support of an application for SIJS, should be held thereafter, if warranted (*see* 8 USC § 1101 [a] [27] [J] [i] *Matter of Francisco M.-G. v Marcelina M.-G.*, 100 AD3d at 901). Mastro, J.P., Rivera, Leventhal and Chambers, JJ., concur.

128. The record must contain enough evidence to prove the required elements of an SIJ claim – in this case, either neglect or abandonment and that it is not in the child's best interests to return to her home country.

See Matter of Tzu Y.W. below

129. The fact that a child enters the United States with an F-1 visa to attend school may indicate the child has not been abandoned.

228 A.D.3d 875 (2d Dep't 6/20/24)

☐ In the Matter of Tzu Y.W. Yating W., Appellant; Chia-Chi W. et al., Respondents.

Kopchian Law, New York, NY (Adam S. Kopchian of counsel), for appellant.

Lulu Wu, Flushing, NY, attorney for the child.

In a proceeding pursuant to Family Court Act article 6, the petitioner appeals from an order of the Family Court, Orange County (Christine P. Krahulik, J.), dated August 4, 2023. The order, insofar as appealed from, after a hearing, denied the petitioner's motion for the issuance of an order, inter alia, making specific findings so as to enable the subject child to petition the United States Citizenship and Immigration Services for special immigrant juvenile status pursuant to 8 USC § 1101 (a) (27) (J).

Ordered that the order is affirmed insofar as appealed from, without costs or disbursements.

In September 2022, the petitioner commenced this proceeding pursuant to Family Court Act article 6 seeking to be appointed guardian of the subject child, her niece, who arrived in the United States from Taiwan in 2018 on an F-1 student visa. The petitioner subsequently moved for the issuance of an order declaring that the child is dependent on the Family Court and making specific findings that she is unmarried and under 21 years of age, that reunification with her parents is not viable due to abuse, neglect, and/or abandonment, and that it would not be in her best interests to be returned to Taiwan, her previous country of nationality and last habitual residence, so as to enable the child to petition the United States Citizen and Immigration Services for special immigrant juvenile status (hereinafter SIJS) pursuant to 8 USC § 1101 (a) (27) (J). In an order dated August 4, 2023, the Family Court, after a hearing, granted the petitioner's guardianship petition but denied her motion for the issuance of an order, inter alia, making the findings required so as to enable the child to petition for SIJS. The petitioner appeals.

" 'Pursuant to 8 USC § 1101 (a) (27) (J) (as amended by the William Wilberforce Trafficking Victims Protection Reauthorization Act of 2008, Pub L 110-147, 122 US Stat 5044) and 8 CFR 204.11, a "special immigrant" is a resident alien who is, inter alia, under 21 years of age, unmarried, and dependent upon a juvenile court or legally committed to an individual appointed by a state or juvenile court' " (*Matter of Briceyda M.A.X. [Hugo R.A.O.]*, 190 AD3d 752, 753 [2021], quoting *Matter of Trudy-Ann W. v Joan W.*, 73 AD3d 793, 795 [2010]). " 'Additionally, for a juvenile to qualify for special immigrant juvenile status, a court must find that reunification of the juvenile with one or both of the juvenile's parents is not viable due to parental abuse, neglect, abandonment, or a similar basis found under State law, and that it would not be in the juvenile's best interest to be returned to his or her native country or country of last habitual residence' " (*Matter of Briceyda M.A.X. [Hugo R.A.O.]*, 190 AD3d at 753, quoting *Matter of Maria P.E.A. v Sergio A.G.G.*, 111 AD3d 619, 620 [2013]).

Here, contrary to the petitioner's contention, the record does not support a finding that the child's reunification with her parents is not viable due to parental abandonment or neglect, or that it would not be in the child's interests to be returned to her previous country of nationality and last habitual residence (*see Matter of Ofelia del C.D.F. v Felicia F.M.*, 167 AD3d 879[2018]; *Matter of*

Karnail S. v Malkit K., 163 AD3d 581 [2018]; *cf. Matter of Eddy A.P.C. [Maria G.C.S.]*, 226 AD3d 1005 [2024]).

Accordingly, the Family Court properly denied the petitioner's motion for the issuance of an order making the requisite declaration and specific findings so as to enable the child to petition for SIJS. Brathwaite Nelson, J.P., Maltese, Voutsinas and Love, JJ., concur.

130. Neither the Petitioner nor the child were aggrieved in an appeal of an order granting SIJ status.

145 A.D.3d 1009 (2d Dep't 12/28/16)

☐ **In the Matter of Saul E.B.M. et al., Appellants.**

Bruno J. Bembi, Hempstead, NY, for appellants.

Appeal from an order of the Family Court, Queens County (Juanita E. Wing, Ct. Atty. Ref.), dated February 8, 2016. The order, after a hearing, granted the child's motion for the issuance of an order, inter alia, making specific findings so as to enable him to petition the United States Citizenship and Immigration Services for special immigrant juvenile status pursuant to 8 USC § 1101 (a) (27) (J).

Ordered that the appeal is dismissed, without costs or disbursements, as the appellants are not aggrieved by the order appealed from (*see* CPLR 5511; *Mixon v TBV, Inc.*, 76 AD3d 144, 156-157 [2010]).

In December 2015, the subject child, Saul E.B.M., commenced this proceeding pursuant to Family Court Act article 6 to have his father appointed as his guardian, for the purpose of obtaining an order declaring that he is dependent on the Family Court and making specific findings that he is unmarried and under 21 years of age, that reunification with his mother is not viable due to parental neglect or abandonment, and that it would not be in his best interests to be returned to El Salvador, his previous country of nationality and last habitual residence, so as to enable him to petition the United States Citizenship and Immigration Services for special immigrant juvenile status (hereinafter SIJS) pursuant to 8 USC § 1101 (a) (27) (J). Thereafter, the child moved for the issuance of an order making the requisite declaration and specific findings so as to enable him to petition for SIJS. In the order appealed from, the Family Court granted the child's motion for the issuance of an order making the requisite declaration and specific findings, inter alia, that reunification with the child's mother is not viable due to parental abandonment and that it would not be in the best interests of the child to be returned to El Salvador.

Since the order appealed from granted the subject motion, the child is not aggrieved (*see Matter of Josue M.A.P. [Coreas Mancia—Perez Lue]*, 143 AD3d 827, 828 [2016]; *see also Mixon v TBV, Inc.*, 76 AD3d 144, 156-157 [2010]). Moreover, the father is not aggrieved by the order (*see Matter of Fifo v Fifo*, 127 AD3d 748, 749 [2015]; *Mixon v TBV, Inc.*, 76 AD3d at 156-157). Accordingly, the appeal must be dismissed. Chambers, J.P., Dickerson, Duffy and Connolly, JJ., concur.

Federal Cases

R.F.M. v. Nielsen, 365 F. Supp. 3d 350 (S.D.N.Y. 2019)(successful class action lawsuit challenging CIS' position that it was legal error for Family Courts to grant guardianship to minors over 18 years of age yet under 21).

Calle v Whitaker, 2019 U.S. Dist. LEXIS 19317 (EDNY 2019)(federal challenge to denial of I-360 dismissed for lack of jurisdiction, relating how the Clerk of the

Queens County Family Court delayed months following the minor's 21st birthday before sending out the guardianship order).

In re 21st Birthday Denials of Special Immigrant Juv. Status Applications by USCIS, 637 F.Supp 3d 23 (EDNY 2022)(federal lawsuit finding jurisdiction to review denials of I-360 applications and requiring CIS to use the actual hour of the minor's birth to determine whether the application was received before or after the 21st birthday, as well as ordering CIS to make possible hand delivery of I-360 applications at a local CIS office).

Calero v INS, 957 F.2d 50 (2d Cir. 1992)(Court of Appeals decision holding there was federal question jurisdiction to consider appointment of a guardian for a minor in deportation proceedings but holding that in this particular case a guardian was unnecessary).

59687398R00208